European Perspectives on Inclusive Education in Canada

Featuring leading voices in the field from across Canada and Europe, this edited collection offers empirical analyses of the historical, social, cultural, and legislative determinants of inclusive education in Canadian schools.

Covering four thematic areas including the structure, culture, and practices of inclusive education, the volume offers comparative insights from a European perspective, engaging critically with widely held views of Canada as a world leader in inclusive education. Providing rich comparisons with educational systems in Germany, Spain, and Finland, chapters explore in-depth the assessment structures and curricula specific to Canada, as well as educational policy, and explore attitudes and practices in relation to diverse student populations, including refugee and indigenous peoples, and students with special educational needs.

This volume will benefit researchers, academics, and educators with an interest in multicultural education, international and comparative education, as well as educational policy more specifically. Those involved with inclusion and special educational needs will also benefit from this volume.

Theodore Michael Christou is a Professor of Education and an Associate Dean of Graduate Studies in the Faculty of Education, Queen's University, Canada.

Robert Kruschel is a University Teacher and Researcher in the Department of Special Education, University of Leipzig, Germany.

Ian Alexander Matheson is an Assistant Professor of Special Education, Queen's University, Canada.

Kerstin Merz-Atalik is a Professor in the Department of Special Education, Ludwigsburg University of Education, Germany.

Routledge Research in International and Comparative Education

This is a series that offers a global platform to engage scholars in continuous academic debate on key challenges and the latest thinking on issues in the fast-growing field of International and Comparative Education.

Titles in the series include:

Interpreting International Education
In Honour of Professor Jeff Thompson
Edited by Mary Hayden

The Evolution of Transnational Education
Pathways, Globalisation and Emerging Trends
Edited by Christopher Hill, Judith Lamie and Tim Gore

Belonging in Changing Educational Spaces
Negotiating Global, Transnational, and Neoliberal Dynamics
Edited by Karen Monkman and Ann Frkovich

A Framework for Critical Transnational Research
Advancing Plurilingual, Intercultural, and Inter-epistemic Collaboration in the Academy
Edited by Manuela Guilherme

European Perspectives on Inclusive Education in Canada
Critical Comparative Insights
Theodore Michael Christou, Robert Kruschel, Ian Alexander Matheson, and Kerstin Merz-Atalik

For more information about this series, please visit: https://www.routledge.com/Routledge-Research-in-International-and-Comparative-Education/book-series/RRICE

European Perspectives on Inclusive Education in Canada

Critical Comparative Insights

Edited by Theodore Michael Christou, Robert Kruschel, Ian Alexander Matheson, and Kerstin Merz-Atalik

Routledge
Taylor & Francis Group
NEW YORK AND LONDON

First published 2022
by Routledge
605 Third Avenue, New York, NY 10158

and by Routledge
4 Park Square, Milton Park, Abingdon, Oxon, OX14 4RN

Routledge is an imprint of the Taylor & Francis Group, an informa business

Library of Congress Cataloging-in-Publication Data
A catalog record for this title has been requested

ISBN: 978-1-032-06263-1 (hbk)
ISBN: 978-1-032-06927-2 (pbk)
ISBN: 978-1-003-20457-2 (ebk)

DOI: 10.4324/9781003204572

Typeset in ITC New Baskerville Std
by KnowledgeWorks Global Ltd.

With and through this conversation, we hope to inspire future scholarship and practice supporting inclusion of diverse learners in schools.

Contents

List of Figures

List of Tables

About the Editors and Authors

Ines Boban is a teacher and scholar with experience in one of the first secondary schools with "integration classes" in Hamburg, Germany. She is an established researcher within the field of Inclusion in relation to human rights and international education. She is based at Martin-Luther-University Halle-Wittenberg in the Department for Inclusive and Special Education.

Anna Bollesen completed the Master of Education (English/Pedagogy) as well as the additional course of study concerning German as a second language in Münster in 2017. She now teaches at a secondary school in Neuss.

Jenn de Lugt is an Associate Professor of Inclusive Education at the University of Regina in Saskatchewan. She is particularly interested in research related to supporting students with emotional and behavioural challenges in inclusive classrooms and is currently investigating ways in which educative mental health programmes in schools can foster open dialogue, reduce stigma, and enhance mental health literacy of children and youth.

Theodore Michael Christou is a Professor of Social Studies and History Education at Queen's University as well as the Associate Dean of Graduate Studies. His research concerns the history and philosophy of education, focusing on curriculum theory and worldviews.

Nastasia Herold studied Romance Philology, specialised on French and Portuguese studies, and is currently a PhD student at Leipzig University (Germany). Her main research is in the fields of Romance and Algonquian studies and in the Digital Humanities. She spent several months in the Atikamekw community of Manawan in the Province of Quebec and does research with the First Nation on their language, history, and culture.

Andreas Hinz is Professor for Inclusive and Special Education at Martin-Luther-University Halle-Wittenberg. He has worked as a teacher and as a member of multiple research groups considering "integrative" school experiments in primary schools in Hamburg, Germany.

Markku Jahnukainen is a Professor of Special Education in the Department of Education at the University of Helsinki, Finland, and an Adjunct Professor at the University of Alberta, Canada. His work is focused on transitions and life-courses of individuals with diverse educational needs, and comparative educational policy related to inclusive and special education.

David Jahr is working at the "Research Institute for Social Cohesion" at the University of Halle-Wittenberg. His research focuses on reconstructive classroom research, including pedagogy and didactics, political education, and service learning.

Britta Klopsch is former teacher and now educational scientist at Karlsruhe Institute for Technology (KIT). She is currently working as an assistant professor. Her research interest is on school development, student's deeper learning, and teacher professionalism.

Annette Korntheuer holds a professorship for Social Work at the Catholic University of Eichstaett-Ingolstadt. She has work experience as a temporary professor for inclusion and disability at the University of Kassel and as educational consultant for the City of Munich. She has been engaged in various comparative projects on refugee integration in Germany and Canada. She is member of the executive board of the German Network for forced migration studies.

Andreas Köpfer is a Professor for Research in Inclusive Education at the University of Education Freiburg, Germany. His research focuses on international comparative perspectives on Inclusive Education, critical spatial theory in education, and reconstructive social research. Recently, he has published the International Handbook of Inclusive Education, co-edited by Justin J. W. Powell and Raphael Zahnd.

Margaret Kress is an Adjunct Professor with the Mi'kmaq Wolastoqey Centre and the Faculty of Education—University of New Brunswick. Her research focuses on transformative philosophies and practices supporting frameworks of inclusion, diversity, and human and sovereign rights.

Robert Kruschel is working in the Institute for Special Needs Education at the University of Leipzig. His work focuses on inclusive school and system development, governance research, and democratic schools and education.

Jeffrey MacCormack is an Associate Professor of Educational Psychology and Inclusion at the University of Lethbridge, Faculty of Education.

As a former classroom teacher, Dr. MacCormack's research on after-school programmes, executive functions, social competence, and play-based learning is also informed by ten years of experience teaching elementary students and many years of teaching post-secondary adult learners.

Kimberly Maich is a Professor at Memorial University of Newfoundland as well as Certified Teacher, Special Education Specialist, Board-Certified Behaviour Analyst (Doctoral), and Registered Psychologist. Before moving to post-secondary settings, she spent most of her career as a resource teacher and clinical coordinator in school settings.

Ian Alexander Matheson is an Assistant Professor of Special Education at Queen's University in the Faculty of Education. His work has primarily focused on supporting students with learning disabilities related to reading and critically examining the identification process to identify ways to better support exceptional learners.

Kerstin Merz-Atalik is a Professor for "Education Considering Disability, Disadvantage and Inclusion" in Special Education at the University of Education Ludwigsburg. Her research focus is on teacher education for inclusion (in a migration society) and inclusive school development. She has participated in many national and international projects focusing these subjects (e.g., TE4i—Teacher Education for Inclusion/ European Agency) and coordinated cooperative projects on the European level (e.g., TdiverS—Teaching diverse learners in (school) subjects/Comenius). Recent publications relate to international comparative aspects of governance in inclusive education reforms.

Alexandra Minuk is a doctoral student at Queen's University in the Faculty of Education. Her research is focused on the inclusion of students with autism spectrum disorder in public education and the factors associated with classroom placement in either inclusive or specialised settings.

Yolanda Muñoz-Martínez is Associate Professor at the Faculty of Education, University of Alcala, Spain. Her work is aimed at the analysis and development of School improvement strategies from an inclusive perspective as well as teacher education to respond to the diversity of all students. She has participated in several research projects and collaborated with different international organisations such as European Agency for Special Needs and Inclusive Education, Iberoamerican States Organization (OEI), etc.

Sharon Penney Sharon Penney is an associate professor at Memorial University in the Faculty of Education, a Registered Psychologist, and a certified teacher.

Ayça Polat is a Professor at Osnabrück University of Applied Sciences in the Faculty of Business Management and Social Sciences. Her main areas of work and research include social inequality and discrimination, and diversity mainstreaming in Social Work, Health, and Education System.

Gordon L. Porter is the Director of Inclusive Education Canada and has been engaged in the disability rights effort focused on creating inclusive schools for more than four decades. He has consulted and conducted training and seminars throughout Canada and in more than 40 other countries. Dr. Porter has worked as a university professor and senior policy advisor to Education Ministries in Canada, Peru, Panama, Colombia, Portugal, Sweden, and the Netherlands. Dr. Porter received the Canadian Education Association's–Whitworth Award for Research in Education. He was instrumental in developing inclusive education policies in Nova Scotia, New Brunswick, and the North West Territories in Canada and for KHDA in Dubai, UAE. He is a member of the Order of Canada, his country's highest honour, as well as the Order of New Brunswick.

Katharina Reschke is an educational psychologist and researcher who is currently working at the Institute for Education Studies at Heidelberg University. Her research covers a broad range of educational research with a focus on motivation as a predictor of school achievement. For example, in a meta-analysis, she found that motivation and intelligence both serve as important predictors for explaining differences in students' school achievement.

Joachim Schroeder is a Professor of Teaching and Didactic Methodology for Learning Impairments, Faculty of Education, Hamburg University. In the field of International and Cross-cultural Special Education, his research focuses on the desired effects and the unintended side effects of the current universalisation of inclusion in education systems in industrialised countries (Finland, Canada, and Japan), transition and emerging countries (Iran and Peru), and countries of the global south (Malawi).

Steve Sider is a Professor in the Faculty of Education and Director of the Centre for Leading Research in Education at Wilfrid Laurier University. His research focuses on the intersection of special education and school leadership in international, comparative contexts.

Cecilia Simón is Associate Professor in the Department of Developmental and Educational Psychology at Autonomous University of Madrid (UAM), Spain. She is co-coordinator of the research team Equity, Diversity, and Inclusive Education (UAM) and a member of Catalyst for Inclusive Education (Inclusion International). Her focus of research includes equity and inclusive education (cultures, policies, and practices); and school, family, and community partnerships.

Anne Sliwka is a Professor of Educational Sciences at the University of Heidelberg/Germany. Her research focuses on school and school system improvement in an internationally comparative perspective. She has been involved in OECD and EU research projects on school improvement and is currently working on teacher professionalism to enable deeper learning.

Jacqueline Specht is a Professor at the University of Western Ontario's Faculty of Education and Director of the Canadian Research Centre on Inclusive Education. Her research focuses on the development of inclusive practice in schools.

Marcel Veber is a Professor for Educational science with a focus on inclusion from a special education perspective at the University in Osnabrueck in Germany. His research focuses on inclusive education in relation to special education as well as gifted education and inclusive teacher training.

Gabrielle Young is an Associate Professor at Memorial University of Newfoundland, where she teaches courses such as the Nature and Characteristics of Learning Disabilities and Inclusive Practices for Students with Learning Disabilities. She continues to investigate the way in which instructional technologies can meet the learning needs of all students.

Scott Anthony Thompson (Full Professor) teaches and researches in inclusive education, educational psychology, and teacher education. He has been involved in two previous large SSHRC multi-year projects: *The Development of Inclusive Educational Practices for Beginning Teachers* (Dr. Jaqueline Specht, PI) and *Disability Policy Alliance: Learning Collaborative and Equity Coalition* (Dr. MaryAnn McColl, PI). Recently, Dr. Thompson has conducted two Arts-Based Educational Research (ABER) projects, which entailed the composing and professional recording of two CDs as knowledge mobilisation "Songs Inspired from Ducks on the Moon" (just released October 2021 during Autism Awareness month) and "Songs of Beginning Teachers" (released in June 2021 at CSSE).

1 Introduction

Inclusion in International "Dialogue"

Theodore Michael Christou, Robert Kruschel, Ian Alexander Matheson, and Kerstin Merz-Atalik

Ensuring equal access to education for all children, regardless of their race, ethnicity, language, ability, gender, and socio-economic background, is currently one of the central educational policy issues across the world. Since the ratification of the United Nations (UN) *Convention on the Rights of Persons with Disabilities*, by 2009 at the latest, inclusion has been central to educational reform and research internationally. The UN Committee on the Rights of Persons with Disabilities calls upon States to "progressively adopt measures" to ensure that individuals with disabilities complete equitable and quality primary and secondary education and have access to affordable and quality tertiary education (2016).

One of the principal challenges faced by educationalists across the world is the unique history of educational institutions and structures. Reforming schools to foster inclusion means adapting and even sometimes changing the *whole grammar* (Tyack & Tobin, 1994) of existing frameworks, conceptual, and contextual to accommodate the heterogeneous needs of learners and address diversity with an inclusion-oriented concept. This is particularly relevant at the current moment in Europe, where the borders of countries and the union itself are being challenged by global forces, including migration, debates about statehood and the integrity of the nation-state, as well as questions regarding inclusive approaches towards social, linguistic, religious, cultural, and ethnic diversity.

Canada is of interest to scholars of inclusive education across Europe because its provincial and territorial control of education mirrors that of many European countries, where regions and provinces also have autonomy over educational policies and practice. Where states are entirely responsible for education, their populations and diversity are of like size to Canadian provinces. Apart from models of *full inclusion* (e.g., the Atlantic province of New Brunswick), the diverse, unique responses to inclusion can be seen as potential inspiring practices across Europe. Rather than ask Canadians to explore inclusion in their own contexts—a framing that might only be of interest to Canadians—this book engages international scholars to consider Canadian education comparatively.

DOI: 10.4324/9781003204572-1

Besides New Brunswick, Canada's two most populous Anglophone provinces, Ontario and Alberta, have distinct policies and statements on equity, which relate directly to demands of the UN *Convention on the Rights of Persons with Disabilities* (United Nations, 2006). Canada also has a long and unique history with core elements of inclusion, including co-operative learning and career counselling. Where Canada is unique, but of interest internationally, in its particular challenges relating to inclusion, its concept of a *migrant society*, and its unique relationship with Indigenous peoples and with linguistic diversity.

Educators in Canada share a common baseline understanding of what *inclusion* means, drawing on a social value that all individuals in a society deserve the opportunity to learn. This is an effect of the long tradition of inclusive policies, which at least some European countries are not sharing. Inclusion is one thing to define, another to operationalise. Upon further consideration, Canadians might identify historically marginalised groups, including individuals with disabilities; Black, Indigenous, and other people of colour (BIPOC); or members of the Lesbian, Gay, Bisexual, Transgender, Queer or Questioning, Two-spirited plus (LGBTQ2+) community, among others. Perhaps their response would highlight that inclusion involves consideration of how our systems exclude these individuals, and how they need to change to provide equal access to all.

Canada has a history of *multiculturalism* and has been studied for decades as a space where schools have been challenged to include immigrant and refugee students, while also accounting for a history of exclusion with respect to Indigenous peoples and racialised students. Canada, which is constantly among the top group of PISA participating countries, has thus been a site of research on inclusion in schools since the mid-1980s, ranking among the leading countries in this respect. Canada's education system is also observing major shifts in the understanding of the past and values for the present and future. Recent and ongoing discoveries of the unmarked graves of Indigenous children on the sites of former Residential Schools have forced a long overdue confrontation with an ugly past with Indigenous peoples. Racial tensions appear to be at all-time highs with increases in anti-Asian hate crimes (e.g., in Canada), and religious tensions are no better with frequent acts of discrimination, including a targeted attack with a vehicle only months ago. Many countries worldwide are also facing challenges with the diversity caused by increased mobility of refugees. Though we have much work to do in support of inclusive education, there have been tremendous efforts towards realising inclusion in many Canadian schools in Canada, and other countries have taken notice.

In this edited collection, *Inclusion in Education: European and Canadian Perspectives of Diverse Learners in School*, contributors from across Europe examine inclusionary educational practices within Canadian educational spaces of teaching and learning. This project permits Canadian scholars, educational practitioners, teacher educators, and students to examine the ways that inclusion is seen, studied, and understood outside of Canada. The rationale for this project is that it creates a space to have critical discussions about a context widely considered as an example of high-quality inclusive practices, without the barrier of language that would normally limit scholarly discussions to remain *within* a language. Further, it addresses an international audience of scholars who have conducted and are involved in research throughout Canada.

Impetus for This Book

The background to this book goes back to a tradition of the German *integration movement* that reaches back to the 1980s. In the early days of integrative schools, the excursions of scientists, educators, and politicians through Europe and the rest of the world to be inspired and irritated by the different ways and understandings of common schooling were an important political argumentation support in the dispute about the establishment of integrative education. This travel trend is sometimes described as a kind of "integration tourism" (Deppe-Wolfinger, 1990, p. 18).

Then as now, such trips also serve as opportunities for reflection to critically observe the establishing structures and practices in one's own country and to receive new impulses for thought. Following this tradition, a group of 5 staff members and 15 students from Martin-Luther-University Halle-Wittenberg, led by David Jahr and Robert Kruschel, travelled to Canada in September 2016 to the multicultural metropolis of Toronto as well as to the rural province of New Brunswick in order to explore school and out-of-school inclusion on site (see Boban et al., 2018). In European discourse, Canada is one of the frequently mentioned pioneers of inclusive education systems, along with northern European countries. For example, the country is often mentioned as a whole and together with other countries as a counter-model to the exclusive school systems of German-speaking countries (e.g., Powell, 2018, p. 129; Tillmann, 2007, p. 4) or references to specific areas of inclusive pedagogy in Canada can be found (e.g., Löser, 2014). For this reason, the country has long been a model for inclusive developments in the discourse around inclusion. With the foundational work published by Porter and Richler (1991) titled *Changing* Canadian *schools: Perspectives on disability and inclusion*, Sander (2003) considered Canada as the "birthplace" (p. 314) of inclusive schools. Hinz (2006) ennobles Canada as the *north star* for inclusion.

It is therefore not surprising that the group from Martin-Luther-University Halle-Wittenberg chose this country as a destination to delve deeper into the question of inclusive system design. In preparation for the excursion, basic principles of inclusion in Canada and Germany were discussed in a seminar and exploratory research projects were designed, which the fellow travellers then pursued on site. The excursion of the German group to Canada focused on the questions of how human rights-based education can be designed, which contradictions are dealt with in which form, and which particularities are visible in the Canadian discourse on inclusion.

The results of the trip can be found in individual publications (see Doleschal & Welslau, 2019; Ingenerf & Zimmermann, 2019; Röder & Schweizer, 2019) and in an anthology (Jahr & Kruschel, 2019). The numerous, inspiring contacts and impressions on site were the trigger for the creation of the anthology. During the field trip, experienced Canadian scientists and practitioners agreed to support the project with their contributions. Researchers in Germany were also won over to contribute their external perspectives and previous experiences on phenomena of inclusion in Canada. The book was thus both a product of an internationally exchanged discussion about inclusion and part of this ongoing mutual understanding about inclusive education.

Aims of This Volume

Following the 2019 book, this anthology maintains the focus on Canada, but contributors speak from a range of educational settings in different countries within Europe. This is the first English anthology to examine Canadian inclusion from international perspectives, concentrating on the European continent, where there is tremendous interest in studying Canadian inclusion (e.g., Hinz, 2006; Jahr & Kruschel, 2019; Köpfer, 2013; Köpfer & Óskarsdóttir, 2019; Sliwka, 2016; Sliwka et al., 2017; Stein, 2011). This book consists of four sections: Authors unpack the context and discourses of inclusion in Canada, identify examples and types of structures upon which the delivery of inclusive education depends, discuss the layered cultures that permeate inclusion in education, and discuss how inclusion is practiced in many forms.

Within these sections, Canadian authors contextualise and unpack themes offered by international colleagues. In response to the identification of factors that influence inclusion in Canadian schools (Merz-Atalik), considering identity and action (Polat), and the acknowledgement of multiple discourses related to inclusion (Schroeder), Specht and Thompson suggest the importance of thinking about intersectionality rather than difference and in focusing our efforts on doing better within our own contexts rather than drawing satisfaction from doing better than others. Sider recognises the importance of examining inclusive education in regions limited by population and resources (Jahnukainen et al.) and questioning the scope of inclusive pedagogy beyond schools (Jahr & Kruschel, 2019), before offering insight about his own experiences with the relationship between visible (e.g., documentation of supports) and invisible (e.g., beliefs about inclusion) structures, and providing direction for further research in inclusive education. In response Herold's chapter focusing on the challenges of changing a culturally insensitive school system to offer a more holistic education model like that of the Atikamekw peoples, de Lugt emphasises both the progress in Canada's educational journey to Reconciliation and the opportunities that lay ahead of us.

A reversal of our structure permits a focus on Indigenous education and its relationship to inclusion in Canada. Margaret Kress, an author from Canada, introduces a discussion of gentle teaching as a means of reframing a colonial, ablest perspective of inclusion. Boban and Hinz respond, drawing on their experiences as researchers visiting schools in Canada. This section is not hagiographic, highlighting many of the limitations of inclusion in a country renowned for its implementation.

From its inception, this project aimed to initiate conversations that have not been possible in the past. We invite you to consider these conversations as ongoing dialogues about the most important issues we are facing regarding inclusion in Canada and beyond. An inclusive approach to inclusive education is respectful of local context even as it is global in its ambitions.

Before we leave you to read this collection, we would like to express our gratitude: First, we thank all the authors who have made this book what it is. Furthermore, we would like to thank Alexandra Minuk, who contributed to this project as a Graduate Research Fellow, contributing a conscientious eye in the final editing of the book. We thank Peter Dines, who contributed to the project as a translator of German texts into English. Finally, we would like to thank Routledge Publishing for their supportive and productive collaboration.

References

Boban, I., Hinz, A., Jahr, D., & Kruschel, R. (2018). Inklusive Schulsysteme in Kanada – Anregungen für den deutschsprachigen Raum. In E. Feyerer, W. Prammer-Semmler, E. Kladnik, M. Leibetseder, & R. Wimberger (Hrsg.). *System, Wandel, Entwicklung: Akteurinnen und Akteure inklusiver Prozesse im Spannungsfeld von Institution, Profession und Person* (pp. 111–116). Klinkhardt

Deppe-Wolfinger, H. (1990). Zur Geschichte integrativer Klassen und Schulen. In H. Deppe-Wolfinger, A. Prengel, & H. Reiser (Hrsg.), *Integrative Pädagogik in der Grundschule* (pp. 11–34). Juventa.

Doleschal, L., & Welslau, A. (2019). Intervention und Prävention von Bullying an kanadischen Schulen – Eine Interviewstudie. *Zeitschrift für Inklusion Online, 1*(14).

Hinz, A. (2006). Kanada – ein 'Nordstern' in Sachen Inklusion. In A. Platte, S. Seitz, & K. Terfloth (Hrsg.), *Inklusive Bildungsprozesse* (pp. 149–158). Klinkhardt.

Ingenerf, J., & Zimmermann, J. (2019). Kooperation für den täglichen Unterricht – Eine exemplarische Analyse zu den Akteurkonstellationen an einer Schule in New Brunswicks. *Zeitschrift für Inklusion Online*, 1.

Jahr, D., & Kruschel, R. (2019). Inklusion in Kanada. *Internationale Perspektiven auf heterogenitätssensible Bildung*. Beltz Juventa.

Köpfer, A. (2013). *Inclusion in Kanada. Analyse inclusiver Unterrichtsprozesse, Unterstützungsstrukturen und Rollen am Beispiel kanadischer Schulen in den Provinzen New Brunswick, Prince Edward Island und Quebec*. Klinkhardt.

Köpfer, A., & Óskarsdóttir, E. (2019). Analysing support in inclusive education systems—A comparison of inclusive school development in Iceland and Canada since the 1980s focusing on policy and in-school support. *International Journal of Inclusive Education, 23*(7–8), 876–890.

Löser, J. M. (2014). Internationale Entwicklungslinien für inklusive Schulen am Beispiel Kanadas. In E.-K. Franz, S. Trumpa, & I. Esslinger-Hinz (Hrsg.), *Inklusion: Eine Herausforderung für die Grundschulpädagogik* (pp. 61–69). Schneider Hohengehren.

Porter, G. L., & Richler, D. (1991). *Changing Canadian schools: Perspectives on disability and inclusion*. Roeher Institute.

Powell, J. J. W. (2018). Chancen und Barrieren inklusiver Bildung im Vergleich: Lernen von Anderen. *Schriftenreihe Eine für Alle—Die inklusive Schule für die Demokratie, 3*, 24.

Röder, M.-S., & Schweizer, I. (2019). Irritierende Beobachtungen auf einer Exkursion in Kanada als Lernanlässe – eine studentische Perspektive. *Zeitschrift für Inklusion Online, 1*(14).

Sander, A. (2003). Von Integrationspädagogik zu Inklusionspädagogik. *Sonderpädagogische Förderung, 4*(48), 313–329.

Sliwka, A. (2016). Wie andere Schulsysteme mit Diversität und Inklusion umgehen: Das Beispiel der Provinz Alberta in Kanada. In C. Fischer (Hrsg.), *Eine für alles? Schule vor Herausforderungen durch demografischen Wandel* (pp. 67–82). Waxmann.

Sliwka, A., Klopsch, B., & Yee, B. (2017). Kanada. In S. Trumpa, D. Wittek, & A. Sliwka (Hrsg.), *Die Bildungssysteme der erfolgreichsten PISA-Länder. China, Finnland, Kanada und Südkorea* (pp. 109–138). Waxmann.

Stein, A. (2011). Das kanadische Inklusionskonzept – sozialhistoriche, menschenrechtliche und behindertenpolitische Zugänge. *Behindertenpädagogik*, 50(2), 142–168.

Tillmann, K.-J. (2007). *Kann man in heterogenen Lerngruppen alle Schülerinnen und Schüler fördern? Der Blick der Bildungsforschung in das Regelschulsystem. Vortrag auf dem Symposion des VdS auf der DIDACTA am 01.03.2007 in Köln*. bildungsserver.berlinbrandenburg.de/fileadmin/bbb/schule/lehrenundlernen/schulanfang/tillmann07heterogenitaetselektionauchGSOR0712301.pdf

Tyack, D., & Tobin, W. (1994). The "grammar" of schooling: Why has it been so hard to change? *American Educational Research Journal, 31*(3), 453–479.

United Nations. (2006). *Conventions on the Rights of Persons with Disabilities*. United Nations.

Part I

Unpacking Inclusion

2 Canada as a "Driving Force" for Inclusion Activists in European Countries?[1]

Comparative Perspectives on Inclusive Education in Europe and Canada

Kerstin Merz-Atalik

Canada as a "Driving Force" for Inclusion!?

Canada has been observed for decades with its long tradition of inclusive school development by researchers in European countries (e.g., in Germany: Hinz, 2006a; Hinz 2006b; Jahr & Kruschel, 2019; Köpfer, 2013; Köpfer & Óskarsdóttir, 2019; Sliwka, 2016; Sliwka et al., 2018; Stein, 2011). It was within the framework of the discourse about the transition from segregated education systems to comprehensive education systems since the 1960s that the interest in the Canadian education system in the central European countries first developed. During the 1980s and 1990s, there was a more one-sided interest of Canadian researchers in the German education system and its structure (Ungerleider, 2013, as cited in Köpfer, 2013). But especially after the Canadian education system was recognised as one of the most successful in the PISA-survey in 2000 (Organisation for Economic Co-operation and Development [OECD]),[2] the interest in the Canadian educational system has grown. One reason was, in contrast to many European and US school systems, the performance of 15-year-olds in Canada showed no significant socio-economic or ethnic disparities (Bussiere et al., 2001, as cited in Sliwka et al., 2018). Another reason that was widely noticed by European educators, politicians, and researchers was that the quota of students in the lowest *competence level I* were very low compared to the majority of European countries (Sliwka et al., 2018). Ever since PISA 2000 twenty years ago, and especially during the debate about inclusive education systems (UNCRPD, 2006),[3] Canada has been continuously used as a best practice example from whom to learn for inclusive education reform (e.g., in Germany: Hinz, 2007; Köpfer, 2013; Köpfer & Óskarsdóttir, 2019; Nier, 2014; Stein, 2011; Zighan, 2014). Canada was even seen as

DOI: 10.4324/9781003204572-3

the "birthplace of inclusion" (Sander, 2001, unpaged), the "north star of inclusion" (Hinz, 2006b, p. 149; Köpfer, 2013, p. 11), or as the "promised land of inclusion" (Köpfer, 2013, p. 39).

The reception of the Canadian inclusion practice has been found increasingly in the European discourse on inclusion (Köpfer, 2013) as an argument that inclusive education is possible in an educational system that also has a high level of educational outcomes. As Köpfer (2013) noted: "Canada, together with the Scandinavian countries,[4] thus confirmed that there is no contradiction between an educational structure based on equal opportunities and inclusion and an efficient one" (p. 36). Quite recently, there have been many publications focussing on the Canadian success story in dealing with the heterogeneity of learners (e.g., Jahr & Kruschel, 2019). Lindmeier (2020), for example, mentions that German education researchers increasingly refer to international scientific discourse. Many researchers, individuals, and delegations involved in educational policy and stakeholders from different agencies from Europe have travelled abroad to visit schools to gain deeper insights into different systems. For example, Boban and Hinz visited New Brunswick in the year 2004, which has been called *the most inclusive structured system worldwide* (UNESCO n.d., as cited in Boban & Hinz, 2019, p. 445) because the province operates without special classes or special schools at all. The authors earlier described some possible promoting factors for inclusive developments based on their personal experiences and observations (from Canada, India, Brazil, and South Africa):

- Thinly populated regions because tendencies towards decentralisation lead to social distance (e.g., mean institutionalisation);
- Few developed special educational structures and specialisation with their corresponding special interests;
- Key figures who, as pioneers, have influenced practice or politics (for instance, Gordon Porter in New Brunswick);
- Scarce available resources (because special institutions cannot be financed);
- Opportunities provided by political upheaval (e.g., the anti-apartheid movement);
- Clear anti-discrimination policy (Boban & Hinz, 2008, p. 325).

Mainly aspects and factors of support structures, resources, and policies for anti-discrimination, diversity-acceptance, and equity-orientation have been found as favourable to inclusive education development.

Nowadays, the recognition of the huge differences between Canadian districts are also noticed in the discourse in Europe (Schroeder, 2019; Schroeder, in this volume). Just like many countries in Europe with a federalist structure, Canada has no single legislative act standardising the model and the implementation of inclusive education for the whole country; each province has its own autonomous educational strategic plan that specifies the requirements for the organisation of inclusive education (Grynova & Kalinichenko, 2018). On the one hand, inclusion seems to be a widely shared value in Canadian society and its education system, but the authors also see differences in the focus points of research and development.

> Canadian scholars focus on [a] child-centered approach underlying the organization of inclusive education considering difference as a resource, not a drawback. This approach leads to defining inclusion as "the possibility of complete significant integration" (Alberta), "the principle and the right to equal access" (British Columbia), "philosophy, vision, and belief" (Quebec), "the mode of thought" (Manitoba), "attitude, value systems" (Nova Scotia), "the unity of ideas and philosophy" (New Brunswick). Inclusive education is viewed as "a way of thinking and action" (Alberta), "the embodiment of opinion" (Nova Scotia). The education system as a system of services is characterized by such verbs as "ensure," "implement," but common concepts defining "inclusion" and "inclusive education" prove the potential identification of these notions.
>
> (Grynova & Kalinichenko, 2018, p. 33)

Today, even in Canada, the development of inclusion is seen through a critical lens. Just to mention one example, Stagg (2019) stated that there is an ongoing pathologising of student groups, for example, through deficit-oriented classifications of being different or *at-risk* in school legislation. She demonstrates this issue with an example from *Ontario's Equity and Inclusive Education Strategy*, which was last modified in 2016.

> Ontarians share a belief in the need to help students learn and to prepare them for their role in society as engaged, productive and responsible citizens. Yet, some groups of students, including recent immigrants, children from low-income families, Aboriginal students, boys and students with special education needs, among others, may be at risk of lower achievement.
>
> (Ontario Ministry of Education, 2016, para. 3, as cited in Stagg, 2019, p. 20)

Stagg (2019) explains that the public education system is, on the one hand, "… able to simultaneously *advocate* for equity and inclusion, while *maintaining* a normative culture that both perpetuates and permits the discrimination of students based on race, gender and sexual diversity, disability, and socio-economic status" (p. 21) as a result of "damage-centered narratives" (p. 22). Stagg (2019) mentions that risk factors are still seen as individual deficits or challenges, and not as an effect of a non-diversity-oriented culture, system, and structure or educational practice. Stagg (2019) explained:

> In other words, students who are repeatedly placed at-risk, due to the competing normative orders existing in their schools, require more than reactive laws and guidelines that reproduce social norms and negative conceptualizations of difference. (p. 24)

Further, Stagg found that the effect is to position students "within narratives of marginalization, risk, and exclusion," narratives that reify damaging social norms and hierarchies (p. 28).

Inclusive Education: A Global Objective Implemented under Various (National) Strategies and Agendas

On the one hand, inclusive education has become a *global objective* (*UN Agenda for Sustainable Development*, 2015; UNCRPD, 2006; UNESCO, 1994) and global agents try to deliver and implement the idea [e.g., UN, UNESCO, European Agency for Special Needs and Inclusive Education (EASNIE), OECD]. To achieve this objective, it is fundamental that the human right to education for all and the vision of a democratic society that values diversity in all its facets (Powell & Merz-Atalik, 2020) are guiding principles in policy and practice. A shared blueprint for inclusive education for all is provided under the sustainable development goal No. 4 in the *2030 Agenda for Sustainable Development* (ASD), adopted by all United Nations Member States (2015): States are expected to ensure inclusive and equitable quality education and promote lifelong learning opportunities for all. The indicator for the monitoring and assessing achievement of the goal is that, by 2030, gender disparities in education are eliminated and equal access to all levels of education and vocational training for the vulnerable, including persons with disabilities, Indigenous peoples, and children in vulnerable situations is ensured (DSG, 4.5). Thus the underlying concept of inclusion behind the ASD is equal access to all levels of education.

On the other hand, Loreman et al. (2014) noted for the international context that there are not only very different but even competing conceptualisations of inclusion. In many countries, the term *inclusion* was already used in the 1990s in connection with the objective of reducing the risks of exclusion and marginalisation for all learners in the general education system (following UNESCO's *Salamanca Statement* in 1994) and was regarded as a guiding idea for a further development of the concept of *mainstreaming* for traditionally segregated learner groups, which was pursued up to that point with a view to extending it to all learners and all areas of school education. In other countries, until today, the concept of inclusive education has only been realised in accordance with the notion of the United Nations *Convention of the Rights of Persons with Disabilities* (UNCRPD, 2006) and is or has been understood as *integrating children and adults with so called Special Needs (SEN) or disabilities into regular education systems.* The concept of inclusion was interpreted by the United Nations from the beginning much more broadly and focused on the general effects of learner diversity in mainstream teaching. UNESCO[5] (2005) stated in their *Guidelines for Inclusion* one year before the UNCRPD (2006) was adopted by the United Nations:

> The UNESCO sees Inclusion as "a dynamic approach of responding positively to pupil diversity and of seeing individual differences not as problems, but as opportunities for enriching learning." Therefore, the move towards inclusion *is not simply a technical or organisational change but also a movement with a clear philosophy* [emphasis added]. In order for inclusion to be implemented effectively, countries need to define a set of inclusive principles together with practical ideas to guide the transition towards policies addressing inclusion in education. (p. 12)

The UNCRPD "... stopped short of a precise definition of inclusion in education. The term therefore remains contentious, lacking a tight conceptual focus, which may have contributed to ambivalence and confused practices" (Slee, 2020, as cited in UNESCO, 2020, p. 12). As a result, the UN Committee for the Rights of Persons with Disabilities published its General Comment No. 4 in 2016 to make sure inclusive education was comprehensively understood:

> States parties must ensure the realization of the right of persons with disabilities to education through an inclusive education system at all levels, including pre-schools, primary, secondary and tertiary education, vocational training and lifelong learning, extracurricular and social activities, and for all students, including persons with disabilities, without discrimination and on equal terms with others. (para. 3)

Some implementation problems have been discussed from the beginning. Slee and Weiner (2001, p. 94), for example, differentiated between two fields of problems in the implementation of inclusive education: If inclusion is seen as a "technical problem," it needs changes of structures, organisation, and practice in the educational sector, while on the other hand, if inclusion is recognised as "cultural politics," the concept of education itself has to be changed and seen in its interdependence with all aspects of relevance in the society. However, the term inclusion or the distinction *inclusive* is very often used to describe the structural aspect of students with and without special needs or *at risk* or any other form of *non-normality* sharing the same educational system. For example, in Germany, policymakers use the terms *inclusion-classroom* or *inclusive school* very often to define a mainstreaming classroom or school unit with students classified as having special educational needs. This does not really tell us about the concept by which inclusion and equity have been implemented in educational practice. The culture by which education is defined and taking place in the individual school or classroom has to be changed, adapted, and continuously developed in relation to diversity demands. Globally, we not only have to change the structures, we also have to change the *grammar of schools* (Tyack & Tobin, 1994). Even in Italy (Brugger, 2016) and "the Nordic European countries, in which relatively advanced inclusive education systems have been established, inclusive education is seen more as a process and goal then considered as an achieved status" (see Barow & Persson, 2011;[6] Biermann & Powell, 2014;[7] Sigurðardótr et al., 2014,[8] as cited in Powell, 2018, p. 5).

Throughout Europe, we find significant differences in the concept, the scope, and the quality of inclusive schooling. As a finding of a Comenius Network project between six European countries,[9] the involved researchers concluded that "despite considerable differences in education systems across Europe, inclusive educational practices are everywhere to be found" (Powell & Merz-Atalik, 2019, p. 323). The project did not necessarily find inclusive values being put in practice in structural inclusive education systems and, even in segregative and highly stratified educational systems, inspiring examples of inclusive practices could be found (Powell & Merz-Atalik, 2019).

Dilemmas and Tensions for Inclusive Education (in European Countries)

Comparing the countries internationally and how they are transforming their education systems related to the goal of being more inclusive, we do find "dilemmas and tensions involved in reaching the ideal of full inclusion. Moving from where we are now to having systems which cater for every learner's needs, including those with severe disabilities, is difficult" (Helen Clark, Foreword, p. v, UNESCO, 2020).

Based on the dimensions of the *Index for Inclusion*, a guide to school development led by inclusive values (Booth & Ainscow, 2016), there are at least three fields where inclusive values have to be put into action:

- *Inclusive cultures* reflect deeply held values and beliefs and relationships. Creating inclusive cultures is about community building and establishing inclusive values.
- *Inclusive policies* (structures) are concerned with how the school or education system is run and plans to develop inclusive education. It is about developing the school for all and organising support for diversity.

- *Inclusive practices* are about what is learned and taught and how it is learned and taught. It is about constructing curricula for all and orchestrating learning for everyone (p. 17).

While the *Index for Inclusion* focuses on the development within an individual school, the dimensions can also be used to critically assess the education systems, their governance, and policy strategies in terms of inclusive education reforms themselves. What are the values and beliefs behind the system? How are these values and beliefs translated into policies and structures? What effect do these cultures, policies, and structures have for everyday practice in the classroom?

Biermann and Powell (2014) mention that, relative to questions of implementation of inclusive education, "a distinction can be made between three institutional dimensions—educational ideals and disability paradigms (cultural-cognitive), forms of organisation and lemmas (normative), and rights related to education (regulative)" (p. 680). Based on these dimensions, the authors compared the education systems of Iceland, Germany, and Sweden with the outcome "that educational ideals, SEN classifications and school structures have a decisive influence on the implementation of the right to inclusive education" (Biermann & Powell, 2014, p. 695). For an institutional transformation towards a fully inclusive education system to be achieved, the reform must take place in all three pillars (cultural-cognitive, normative, and regulative) and the interconnectivity and interdependency between them must be borne in mind (Merz-Atalik & Beck, 2020).

Cultures, Values, and Beliefs in Education (Systems)

Andreas Schleicher[10] describes (in a foreword to a publication about the PISA success stories) that he is aware that many readers of this book will ask themselves to what extent the observable results of the countries studied are "… the result of culture and context and not of politics and practice. But we should ask ourselves more clearly to what extent culture is not only handed down from the past, but also created by what we do today" (Schleicher, 2018, p. 7). His demand is that countries open themselves up to changes in education systems and develop them without blinkers. Considering that the culture of education systems is "handed down from the past" (evolved historically) and, on the other hand, a "result of current activities" (evolving in the present; Schleicher 2018; p.7), we need to reflect on both as relevant initial conditions for reforms.

Biermann and Powell (2014) decided to compare three European education systems: While in Sweden and Iceland, the basic ideal underlying the education system was found to be the guiding principle of *equality* (e.g., through the school legislation) and, in Germany, this principle was characterised as *performance*. The (meritocratic) performance-orientation in

Germany led historically to homogeneity-oriented structures and strictly segregated lower and upper secondary levels (with three main tracks and nine different special education school types). In Sweden and Iceland, the ideal of equality was followed by a transition to a comprehensive one-school-for-all in social policy. The fact that disability and special needs in Germany are even today recognised as *personal deficits* could also be followed back to this meritocratic root, while in the two Nordic countries, they were increasingly realised as *one aspect of diversity in the inter-dependence between the individual and the environment* (related to the bio-psycho-social concept of International Classification of Functioning [ICF] of the World Health Organisation in 2005) (Biermann and Powell 2014). For many years, the educational science discourse in Germany "was dominated by sociological and empirical questions of educational performance (educational participation, educational success) and—associated with this—educational inequality" and the reasons for inequality were mainly discussed on the basis of individual learners' potential (Lindmeier, 2020, p. 31). But since PISA 2000—and probably as a result of the increase in comparative perspectives—there has been a slight "shift in the discourse towards questions of justice and educational theory" (Lindmeier, 2020, p. 31).

According to Huber, Sturm, and Köpfer (2017), in the German-speaking discourse on inclusive education, the line of research on inclusion as cultural policy has so far only been taken up selectively.

In contrast to the Anglo-American area, the focus of inclusion/exclusion here is less on socio-economic disadvantage and more on the school structure or the multi-tracked school system and the selection mechanisms they contain (Hinz & Kruschel, 2012) an investigation which is particularly necessary in German-speaking countries, since vertically structured school systems can reinforce system-immanent exclusion practices. This could be one reason why inclusion-oriented educational researchers and politicians in these countries preferred to look to the Anglo-American countries (e.g., Canada) and the equity-discourse behind inclusive education regarding their own research and lines of argumentation.

Rights Related to (Inclusive) Education and Educational Policies

There are wide differences in the implementation of the right to inclusive education based on legislative requirements using the following criteria, which are contingent upon either a narrower or broader concept of inclusive education:

- *Basic concept:* Inclusion through spatial integration of selected social groups or individuals into the mainstreamed education system (integration) or as a concept for diversity in education and of learning opportunities for all;

- *Learner focus:* On selected groups or individuals (with a supposed deficit or difference) or with an intersectional focus (seeing all groups, which are actually disadvantaged or marginalised in education systems) or addressing all learners in their individuality;
- *Implementation of rights:* For example, as a *human right of each individual* or the *parents' right to choose between different* schooling options;
- *Responsibility for implementation and quality:* Either as a concept to be claimed by individuals (in contrast to segregation as the regular form), or focusing on the obligations of the system to serve all children or inclusion.

In some countries, the right to inclusive education is negotiable and, for example, parents have a right to choose between special and mainstreaming or inclusive schools (in some German states). But in others, it is almost obligatory for a child to be sent to a special school (as there are no resources and structures in the general schools for supporting inclusion) and the majority of students with SEN access their education in separate special schools (e.g., in Baden-Württemberg), even though there has been no compulsory special education schooling since 2015. In other federal states, there are almost equally financed resources in the two different schooling models (this is also the case, for example, in the Netherlands).

In others, there are almost no special education institutions anymore and inclusion in the neighbourhood schools is the only option for students with SEN (e.g., in Italy or in the federal state of Bremen, Germany). In the northern part of Italy, South Tyrol, with a German-speaking majority in the population, special schools were rigorously closed 20 years ago (due to the centralised education legislation of Italy and right to mainstream education in the 1970s). There are only very few special boarding schools today. The Autonomous School Board of the German Schools in South Tyrol, Italy (2015) clearly defines the concept of inclusion and the individual rights of students with SEN in legislation:

Art. 6 (Right to an inclusive education system)

1 All children and pupils with disabilities have the right to attend a kindergarten and a school which must implement the principle of inclusion. In order to achieve this, the state guarantees an education system which is characterised by the following:

  - It considers the diversity and individual differences of all children, pupils and students as normal and as a resource,
  - It ensures the right of everyone to shared and equal education of high quality,
  - It enables everyone to participate fully in life and learning in kindergarten and school,

- It takes into account the diverse needs, learning opportunities, interests and talents of children, pupils and implements specific measures and educational opportunities tailored to the individual,
- It enables the development of knowledge and skills that promote participation in social life in the family, at work and in leisure time, as well as participation in public life,
- It removes barriers to education and training,
- It guarantees to all, on the basis of the individual life plan and the general enrolment rules, freedom of choice in enrolment in kindergartens and schools and participation in any admission procedures.

2 Compulsory schooling and education and the corresponding rights apply equally to children and pupils with disabilities. The state guarantees the necessary support measures (Landesgesetz vom 14. Juli 2015, Nr. 7 Teilhabe und Inklusion von Menschen mit Behinderungen; translated by the author).

This legislation is a commendable example for inclusive values in cultures, structures, and practices. In Belgium, under the 2014 law (M-decree) on measures for students with SEN, only children able to follow common core curriculum have access to mainstream education. The UNESCO considers that this "effectively excludes most of those with intellectual disabilities" (UNESCO, 2020, p. 34) from inclusive education. School legislation is one of the most relevant indicators for inclusion quotas: While in Italy (as noted above), the quota of all students with SEN in special schools is only 0.88%, in Belgium 80.89% of all students with SEN are placed in full day segregated special schools (EASNIE, 2020). This shows the extreme randomness in schooling pupils with SEN in European Countries.

Duration of Comprehensive Education in European Countries

The different opinions about the structures and institutional frameworks for education are reflected, among other things, in the organisational framework and teaching methods of heterogeneous education systems within Europe. Most European countries in 2020 had a comprehensive school system. Primary school level (ISCED[11] 1) typically lasts six years, although its duration can range between four and seven years (EACEA, 2020; European Commission et al., 2020). Lower secondary education (ISCED 2) starts typically between the ages 10 and 13, and upper secondary level (ISCED 3) between ages 14 and 16. But even in some countries with a community or comprehensive school system, segregation into different tracks, school types, and educational curricula starts with the lower or upper secondary level. In some of them, tracking begins earlier than in the majority, in Grade 4 and at the age of 10 (see Table 2.1; Austria, Germany, and Hungary) at the transition from primary to lower secondary schools into different school types related to their academic development. Today, the majority of European countries school students together in mainstreaming schools (except for students with SEN) until Grade 8–10 or the ages of 14–16 (28 out of 39).

Countries with a rather long duration of joint schooling are also among the ones with a rather inclusive education system for learners with Special Educational Needs (SEN) In Italy, all learners attend the same school until their 18th birthday. The primary school lasts five years, followed by the middle school for all for another three years. After Grade 8, pupils are divided into different schools but only based on the subject area of their special competences (with vocational field reference). All students share the same educational institutions and follow the same curriculum in accordance with the same school legislation. And the parents have the free right to choose the school. Italy is an exception as in the majority of the countries in Europe we still find special schools for pupils with SEN or disabilities.

In Canada, the duration of joint schooling in the majority of the provinces and territories lasts from Grades 1–12 (on the Homepage of the Council of Ministries of Education Canada [CMEC], 2022) with one exception: The education system in Québec is segregated at the transition from primary to secondary school with different tracks in Grade 6 (at least for some of the learners).

We can see a tremendous change in the school systems in the European countries towards a more inclusive system in the last century and Canada often served as a model. Besides the clear policy decisions that are relevant for educational reforms and change processes, "... also practical challenges in deciding on the speed of change, whether for richer countries looking to move away from systems which were originally based on segregation, or for poorer countries looking to create an inclusive system from scratch" (UNESCO, 2020, p. v) have to be taken into account.

Curricula for All: Reduced, Adapted, or Common Core?

In comprehensive school systems, students are mainly taught to a common core curriculum at the primary (ISCED 1) and lower secondary level (ISCED 2). The vast majority of the European countries (39 out of 47) have a single structure system with no segregation into academic level groups or school types with corresponding differentiated—even reduced—curricula (red in Figure 2.1; EACEA, 2020). The Netherlands, Belgium, Lithuania, and Luxembourg, and the four German-speaking countries Austria, Germany, Switzerland, and Lichtenstein are the

Table 2.1 Duration of Joint Schooling, up to Age and Grade Level in 2020/2021

Until the age of 10 (Grade 4)	*Until the age of 11 (Grade 5)*	*Until the age of 12 (Grade 6)*	*Until the age of 13 (Grade 7)*	*Until the age of 14 (Grade 8)*	*Until the age of 15 (Grade 9)*	*Until the age of 16 (Grade 10)*
					Bosnia and Herzegovina	
					North Macedonia	
					Ireland	Denmark
				Serbia	France	Estonia
				Switzerland	Croatia	Spain
				Albania	Cyprus	Finland
				Belgium	Romania	Sweden
	Czechia			Bulgaria	Slovenia	England, Northern Ireland, Scotland, and Wales (UK)
Austria[b]	Liechtenstein			Turkey	Montenegro	Iceland
Germany[c]	Lithuania	Luxembourg[a]	Malta	Italy[a]	Portugal	Norway
Hungary[b]	Slovakia	Netherlands[a]	Latvia	Greece	Poland	Northern Macedonia

Source: Data processed by the author based on Eurydice (2020) and EACEA (2020).

Note

[a] Tracks after Grade 8 related to subject, not learning outcome.
[b] Two tracks in lower secondary.
[c] Three or more tracks in lower secondary.

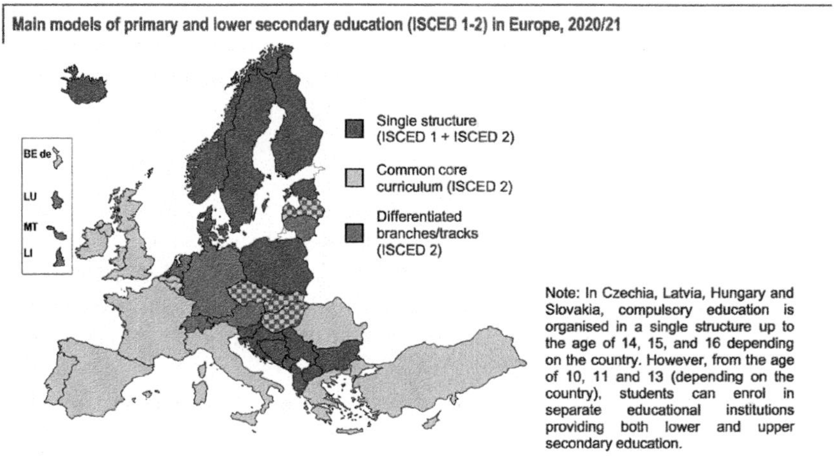

Figure 2.1 Main Models of Primary and Lower Secondary Education (ISCED 1–2) in Europe, 2020/2021.

Source: Eurydice/EACEA (2020, p. 7).

exception, with their *performance level-oriented curricula* in ISCED 2 (blue in Figure 2.1). These structures are rooted in and reflect medieval estate-based societies and have been linked, more or less until today, to prognoses about pupils' future opportunities in the workplace (as blue-collar workers, white-collar workers, or academics). These performance-oriented curricula, which, with their differing curricular levels are connected to different school types, are believed to have a limiting effect on learning opportunities and are reflected in different school leaving certificates.

The different curricular policies influence the way in which education is delivered to students with SEN (Brussino, 2020); they range from individual to group-based adaptations of the common core curriculum to reduced curricula for special groups.

The segregated structure of the systems and the curricula is mirrored in the structure of the teacher training programmes (Merz-Atalik, 2017). This has an impact on the attitudes of society and the protagonists in the education system, like parents, teachers, school administrators, or education policy-makers. For example, the majority of general education teachers are not prepared to teach heterogeneous classrooms and special education teachers are not as competent in subject area methodology. The normative concept of selection and homogenisation of learning groups as a positive prerequisite for performance development of all learners has grown historically over centuries and led to deeply and consistent values and attitudes. The experience in teaching diverse learners is much more pronounced in developed in countries with a tradition of a comprehensive or community school system (especially for regular school teachers). It is therefore hardly surprising that uncertainty often prevails in the debate on inclusion on the part of in-practice teachers in the German-speaking countries (Merz-Atalik, 2017).

Residential and Geographical Disparities

The UNESCO sees some key tenets of inclusion that are ensuring that the diversity of the school-aged population is represented in every classroom and considers, that: "In practice, this goal is undermined by the existence of special schools and by residential and other geographical disparities" (UNESCO, 2020, p. 76).

Besides the difference in the structures of education systems, there are a few more organisational dilemmas for inclusive education, for example, the density and diversity of the population. One research hypothesis has been that, in thinly populated regions (like in New Brunswick in Canada), inclusive education reforms could be more successful because tendencies towards centralisation and institutionalisation of special education services in segregated schools are not in favour as they would lead to social distance (Boban & Hinz, 2008). From the perspective of a German researcher, this connection seems obvious. There is a remarkable difference in the population density between the two countries. At just under 37 million, Canada's population is less than half the size of Germany's, with 83 million, while the country's size (9,984,000 square kilometre) is almost 28 times bigger than Germany (Statista, 2019). So, in Germany, there is an average of 237 people per square kilometre and, in Canada, the population density is four per square kilometre (Statista, 2019). However, the population is spread over a huge area and Canada is the second largest country in the world with almost the size of the whole of Europe.

Evidence from the US shows that levels of inclusion in mainstream schools are higher in rural than in urban settings (Murray, 2018, as cited in Brussino, 2020). This could be an effect of the availability of special education institutions in the immediate environment in urban areas. But on the other hand, in large cities in Germany (e.g., Bremen 82.83%; Hamburg 64.69%; and Berlin 63.49%), the inclusion quota among students with SEN is predominantly higher than in rural areas (e.g., in the state of Bavaria with 26.28%) (Klemm, 2018). This is probably a result of different attitudes towards diversity in rural areas (Brussino, 2020) or the opportunities for an easier transition to these institutions in urban areas (if the community-level policy has an impact on education reform). Another factor could be that there is a stronger involvement of welfare associations and churches in the maintenance of special schools in rural areas. The density of the population, as we can see, has no linear effect on the inclusion quota. So, a country like

Belgium has a very high population density and still the lowest inclusion quota for pupils with SEN in Europe.

Funding of (Inclusive) Education

In many discourses about inclusive education, funding is used as an argument either for or against the development of an inclusive system:

> Increased and improved investment in education is one of the core issues of ET 2020,[12] not only because proper investment in education has positive repercussions on economic growth and employment, but also because of its significant impact on social inclusion.
> (European Commission, 2015, cited in EASNIE, 2016, p. 10)

For example on the one hand, special education teachers in Germany often claim that inclusion is a neo-liberal strategy to reduce the costs for experts and special institutions in the education system. So it is widely recognised, that "despite the fact that the overall costs of inclusive education are difficult to ascertain, there is a general understanding that inclusive education systems cost less to implement and maintain than special education models (Centre for Studies on Inclusive Education, 1997; UNESCO, 2009; Mitchell, 2010; World Health Organization and World Bank, 2011, in UNICEF, 2015; Barrett, 2014)" (EASNIE, 2016, p. 18). In a system like in Germany, where we have almost no two-teacher-systems or multi-professional staff in mainstream schools—neither at the primary nor the secondary level—the implementation of inclusive education (while leaving the special education schools almost untouched) leads to a tremendous rise in additional costs for educational professionals and support assistance in the classrooms. Since the signing of the UNCRPD in Germany (2009), the number of special teachers in almost all of the German states has increased and will increase further in the near future. But if we take the student-teacher ratio in primary schools, for example, into account, we can see that there was a development gap in Germany even before the inclusion reforms.

But additional (special education) teachers in mainstreaming schools do not directly lead to a higher quality in inclusive education if these professional resources are not used within an inclusive framework and if the staff lack training. Finally, "effectiveness in the field of education is an important key. The question is not only about money spent, but also how it is spent and reaching the predetermined goals" (EASNIE, 2016, p. 20). Especially the question of whether *all* schools are financially supported to implement the inclusion reforms must be taken into account. Transferring students from special to (inclusive) mainstream schools "is not automatically a solution unless the requisite human and financial resources exist to provide inclusive education effectively" (UNESCO, 2020, p. 6).

The Role of the Discipline and Profession of Special Education in the Inclusive Education Reform

The first annual conference of special education in the German-speaking countries that took place in Budapest (1994 in Hungary) had the title "Special Education in the Process of European Integration." During the conference, the question arose as to whether there is such a thing as a single concept of European Special Education or many different concepts of special education in Europe. (Bürli, 1994, as cited in Zászkaliczky, 2008). The variety among the different countries has been huge from the very beginning (the end of the 19th century) until today and special education support is offered in various forms of organisation. This variety of forms of special education support "extend along a continuum of segregation (teaching in different buildings), separation (teaching in the same school building but in different rooms) and integration (partly inclusive teaching) towards full inclusion (comprehensive inclusive teaching)" (Powell & Merz-Atalik, 2020). Overcoming the barriers of organisational exclusion is therefore only the first step towards the greatest possible participation in formally organised learning opportunities (Powell & Merz-Atalik, 2020). The "transition from exclusion to inclusion in terms of the placement of learners with SEN is gradual and 'path-dependent' (Blanck et al., 2013; Edelstein, 2016; Powell, 2011, 2016)" (Powell & Merz-Atalik 2020, p. 72) and is very often incremental instead of transformative (Powell & Merz-Atalik, 2020). The existence of "special education support systems [is] increasingly critically understood as part of the problem of producing 'incapacity' (Blanck, 2018; Pfahl, 2011; Tomlinson, 2017)" (Powell & Merz-Atalik, 2020, p. 74). In order to overcome the barriers to implementing inclusive education, it is necessary to overcome the institutionalised as well as the incorporated (through socialisation and professionalisation processes) culture behind a segregated education system.

Conceptualisation, Classification Quota, and Identification of Special Educational Needs

In the vast majority of countries worldwide, under the heading of *special needs* (SEN), groups of students are still placed in categories:

> ... an "all means all" approach to inclusion also means *dropping any stigmatizing labels assigned to children.* Adopting learning approaches on account of such labels limits their potential, ignoring the benefits that varied learning approaches can bring to all children.
>
> (UNESCO, 2020, p. 6)

In some countries, there are up to 13 different categories, such as the US with thirteen detailed clustering and listing of SEN (e.g., Brussino, 2020).

In Europe, only Portugal has recently moved to a non-categorical approach and abandoned any condition-specific labels (Brussino, 2020; UNESCO, 2020). In other countries, the categories mirror the school types in the special education system (e.g., in Germany) and some of the categories are only of relevance during the years spent in the education system (e.g., so-called *special needs in emotional and social development* or *learning*). A survey by the OECD revealed that the way in which SEN is conceptualised and understood shapes policy approaches and practices used to provide education for students with SEN (Brussino, 2020). As UNESCO (2020) recently noted: "Identifying groups makes the disadvantaged ones visible but can reduce children to labels, which can be self-fulfilling. After all, everybody potentially faces barriers to inclusion. Not all children facing inclusion barriers belong to an identifiable or recognised group, while others belong to several" (p. 64). And last but not least, it is a fact, that "students from lower socio-economic backgrounds are more frequently identified with more subjective categories of disability and SEN" (Schifter et al., 2019, as cited in Brussino, 2020, p. 21).

The European Agency highlights "… the fact that countries have different forms of official decision-making, often relating to differing mechanisms for accessing additional resources to meet SEN" (EASNIE, 2020, p. 61), which leads to a variety of classification systems and differing quotas of categorisation. The problem of an allocation of (professional) resources which are regularly not available, or the enabling of learning conditions which are not common in the mainstream education system, has been expressed theoretically under the term *categorisation-resource-dilemma* in German-speaking countries. The dilemma of the need for a categorisation of so-called *special educational needs* was based historically on the segregated system in special education institutions and special school types. Continuing categorisation even in a slightly more inclusive system is mainly caused by political implementation strategies in the inclusive education reforms, which does not sufficiently take into account that an inclusive education reform also covers the need for policy and structural changes (for inclusion as a *technical problem*; Slee & Weiner, 2001). Feuser (2017) describes this dilemma as the implementation of inclusion through integration into a system of segregation. Because special education resources and interventions were not systematically and consistently built up or rather transferred from the special schools to the mainstream schools, this has also legitimised the continuation of a need for reification within inclusive institutions.

EASNIE has collected data from 30 European countries and published cross-country-datasets three times during the last 6 years (data from the year 2014 was published in 2017; data from the year 2016 was published in 2018, and data from the year 2018 was published in 2020). The SEN "identification rates range from 1.02% to 25.12%; the total average for the 31 countries is 4.75%" (EASNIE, 2020, p. 61; see Figure 2.2). The difference in the classification rates is caused by different classifications, different classification systems, and the modes of registration. Iceland (15.34%), Lithuania (13.48%), Slovakia (15.07%), and the UK (Scotland; 25.12%) have been recognised as "outliers" (EASNIE, 2020, p. 61). So, some of the more inclusive education systems in Europe (indicated by a larger quota of all students with SEN in mainstream schools) have

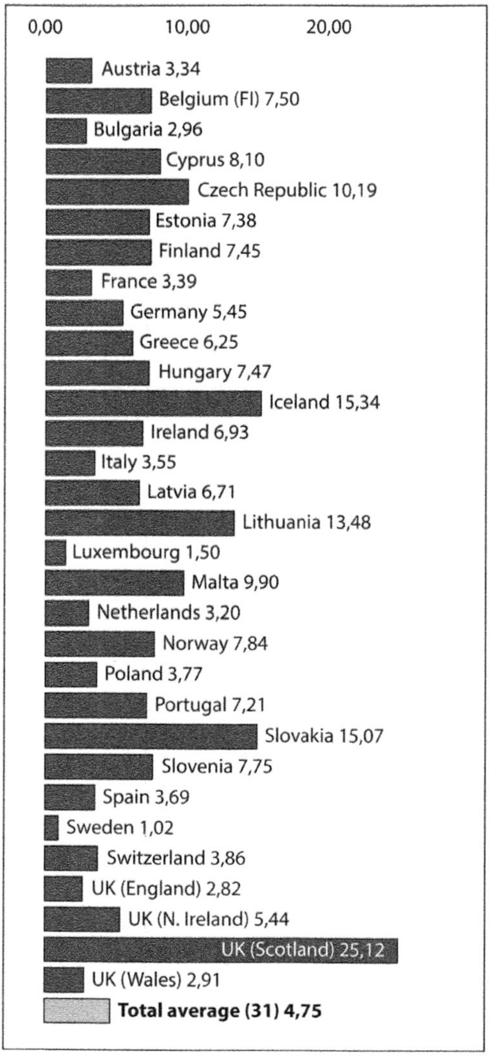

Figure 2.2 Identification Rates. *Note.* Percentage of learners with an official classification of SEN based on the enrolled school population (%) in different school settings, 2018 Dataset[13] (EASNIE, 2020, p. 61).

Source: EASNIE (2020, p. 61).

produced more students classified as having SEN (e.g., Iceland and Scotland) while others with almost no special schools (e.g., Italy) have a quota of classified students comparable to countries with many special schools (e.g., Austria).

Based on the concept of a fully inclusive education system, which caters for all learners and addresses all the needs of all students, we could guess that "the more inclusive the school [system], the less useful categorical data become, as fewer children require identification for support" (UNESCO, 2020, p. 65). Based on this thesis, we could jump to the conclusion that Sweden (1.02% identification rate) and Luxembourg (1.50% identification rate) have the most inclusive education systems in Europe. But on the other hand, we need to connect the identification rates with the quota of students schooled in special schools and classes.

A non-categorical approach would resist aggregating statistics on the number of students with specific conditions or referring to the number of students who received support (UNESCO, 2020). The focus would be on allocating interdisciplinary (professional) resources in the system to allow a diversity-oriented approach to teaching and creating structures in the institutions (the whole-system-approach to inclusive education) with a focus on every individual child and their specific learning capacities and needs (whole-child-approach to education). This is the case, for example, in Finland, where the statistical data identifies the number of students who need an adaptation of the common core curriculum in a percentage instead of counting the numbers based on the traditional SEN classifications. Or, as is the case with migrant children in Canada, where children are not registered on the basis of their ethnic or national migration background and status, but on the multi-lingual approach, which is needed in the schools they attend.

Segregation Quota in Europe

Today, in some countries in Europe, almost all students classified as having SEN are in the mainstreaming schools (e.g., in Italy, Malta, Iceland; see Figure 2.3), while in others, the majority of learners classified as having SEN are schooled in special education systems (special groups or classes in the mainstream schools) and fully segregated special schools (e.g., Belgium, Slovakia, Germany). The special school enrolment rates in Europe range from 0.03% to 6.07%; the total average for the 30 countries is 1.41% (see Figure 2.3).

Despite the ratification of the UNCRPD (since 2006 in all European countries, including the EU itself) "in 'binary' systems such as Belgium, Germany, Austria or Switzerland the spatial separation of regular and special schools is retained" (Powell, 2018, p. 7). The development after the ratification led to an even bigger difference between countries in one region and with the same language (e.g., the German or English-speaking ones).

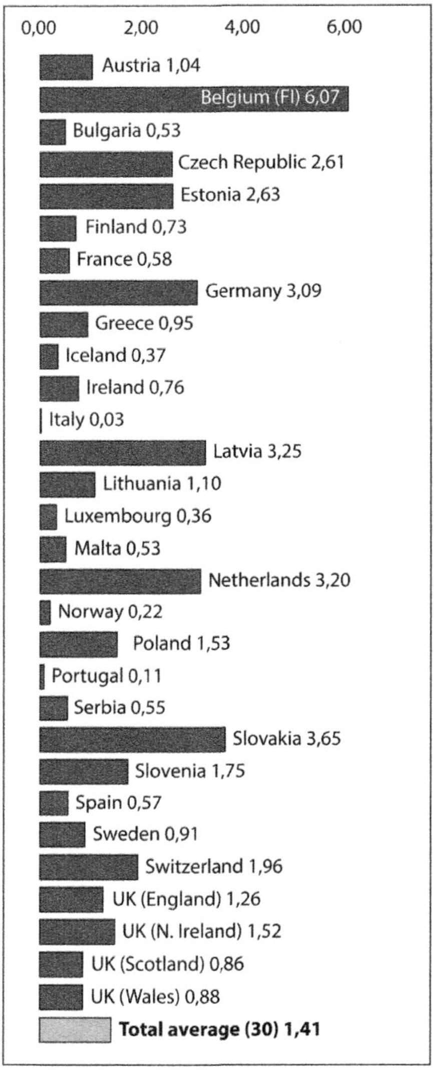

Figure 2.3 Segregation Quotas. *Note.* Percentage of learners who are enrolled in fully separate special schools based on the enrolled school population (%) in different school settings (2018 Dataset) (EASNIE, 2020, p. 76).

Source: EASNIE (2020, p. 76).

Considering the discrepancy between the SEN identification rates, only in a minority of countries of the European Union is the majority of classified students (as SEN) still taught in special schools and/or special classes. Although Sweden (0.91%) and Scotland (0.89%) have a very low and comparable segregation quota, the quotas are very different in their informative value regarding inclusion rates. As "those students in Scotland are a small minority of the more than 20% identified with special education

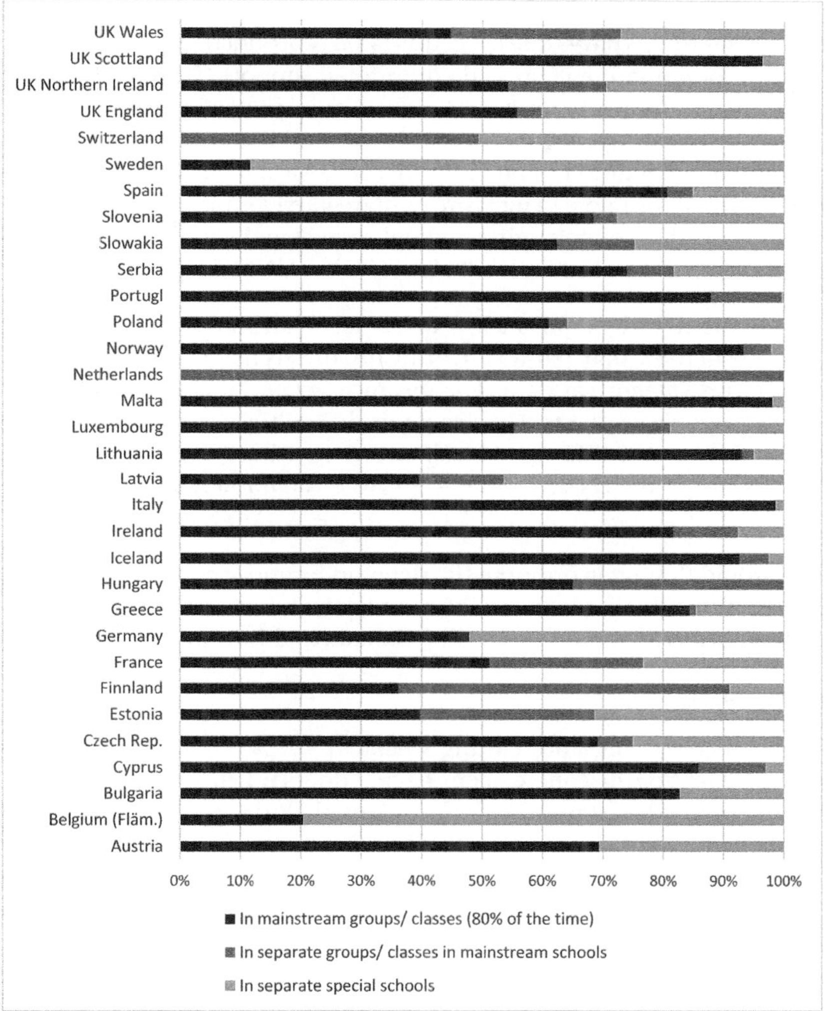

Note. Distribution of all students with SEN in the European countries in different school settings (2018 Dataset). Data processed by the author based on data from EASNIE, 2020.

Figure 2.4 Distribution of All Students with SEN.

needs" (UNESCO, 2020, p. 77; see Figure 2.4). To really get a comprehensive overview, many other factors must be taken into account.

It should be stressed that countries with a strongly developed special school system had greater difficulties implementing the changes required by the inclusive education reform (as mentioned in a presentation by Core Meyer 2011, Head of EASNIE). This is based on the development theory of a *path-dependent* organisational development because any reform starts from the existing institutions and organisations, which are difficult to change due to traditional structures and investments that have been made historically (Blanck et al., 2013). The special schools and classes to this day—due to institutional reproduction—are the main forms of organisation of special educational support (Powell, 2018), not mainly in the Central European German-speaking countries.

The European Agency for Special Needs and Inclusive Education suggested that, in addition to quantitative categorical data on the identification rates and the quota in inclusive or segregated setting, "attendance and learning, feelings of belonging, mutual respect and social esteem should be monitored" (Watkins et al., 2014, as cited in UNESCO, 2020, p. 65).

> Qualitative data on such experiences can capture fine-grained information that paints a drastically different picture than quantitative categorical data. For instance, in an "inclusive classroom" in Canada, students with learning difficulties were made to solve problems on a different blackboard than others, with their backs to the rest of the class (Jordan & McGhie-Richmond, 2014).
>
> (UNESCO, 2020, p. 65)

This would definitely promote the demand for more comparative (qualitative) research based on quality indicators for inclusive education between countries and regions like Canada and Europe.

Conclusion

Forms of borrowing and lending so-called *best practices* in the international education discourse seem to be "doubtful in its usefulness for the national education sector" (Wittek et al., 2018, p. 13). Especially if people only borrow aspects selectively to legitimise their own arguments in the national policy and scientific discourse without acknowledging (sometimes hidden) complex national contexts and frameworks. But an international comparative analysis of determining factors, aspects of governance, and implementation policies can help to gain knowledge about one's own system. This chapter wants to provide some selected insights into the European discourse for Canadian and international scholars and give impulses for international comparative research as far as strengthening the awareness for a globally orientated (research) responsibility for more equity and inclusiveness in education.

Notes

1. With a focus on German-speaking countries.
2. PISA: OECD's Program for International Student Assessment. PISA measures 15-year-olds' ability to use their reading, mathematics, and science knowledge and skills to meet real-life challenges.
3. UN Convention of the Rights of Persons with Disabilities.
4. Especially Finland, because of the comprehensive and inclusive system and the positive results in PISA.
5. United Nations Educational, Scientific and Cultural Organization.

6. Inclusive education in Sweden.
7. Comparison between Germany, Iceland, and Sweden.
8. Inclusive education in Iceland.
9. Research related to "TdiverS—Teaching diverse learners in (school) subjects," Comenius Network (2013–2016; see www.tdivers.eu) between Iceland, Germany, Lithuania, Luxembourg, Sweden, and Spain.
10. Director of the Education and Skills Division of the OECD (2017, in Trumpa et al., 2018).
11. International Standard Classification of Education (ISCED, 2011).
12. European strategic framework for cooperation in education and training (2020).
13. Not all countries provided data.

References

Barrow, T., & Persson, B. (2011). Die Sonderpädagogik in der bildungspolitischen Debatte Schwedens. *Sonderpädagogische Förderung heute, 56*(1), 20–32.

Biermann, J., & Powell, J. W. (2014). Institutionelle Dimensionen inklusiver Schulbildung: Herausforderungen der UN-Behindertenrechtskonvention für Deutschland, Island und Schweden im Vergleich. *Zeitschrift für Erziehungswissenschaften, 17*(4), 679–700.

Blanck, J., Edelstein, B. & Powell, J. (2013). Persistente schulische Segregation oder Wandel zur inklusiven Bildung? Die Bedeutung der UN-Behindertenrechtskonvention für Reformprozesse in den deutschen Bundesländern. *Schweizerische Zeitschrift für Soziologie = Revue Suisse de Sociologie* (2013), 39(5), 267–292.

Boban, I., & Hinz, A. (2008). Inclusive Education-Annährungen an Praxisentwicklungen und Diskurs in verschiedenen Kontexten. In G. Biewer, M. Luciak, & M. Schwinge (Hrsg.), *Begegnung und Differenz: Menschen-Länder-Kulturen. Beiträge zur Heil-und Sonderpädagogik* (pp. 314–329). Klinkhardt.

Boban, I., & Hinz. A. (2019). Menschenrechtbasierte Pädagogik – inklusiv und 'appropriate'? Fragen nach Besuchen in Toronto und New Brunswick. In D. Jahr & R. Kruschel (Hrsg.), *Inklusion in Kanada. Internationale Perspektiven auf heterogenitätssensible Bildung* (pp. 445–448). Beltz Juventa.

Brugger, E. (2016, April). Die Integration von Kindern und Jugendlichen mit einer Behinderung in einem inklusiven Bildungssystem am Beispiel Italien – Südtirol. *Zeitschrift für Inklusion, 1.*

Brussino, O. (2020). *Mapping policy approaches and practices for the inclusion of students with special education needs* (OECD Education Working Paper No. 227). OECD Publishing. https://doi.org/10.1787/600fbad5-en

Bussiere, P., Cartwright, F. Crocker, R., Ma, X., Oderkirk, J., & Zhang, Y. (2001). *Measuring up: The performance of Canada´s youth in reading, mathematics and science OECD PISA Study – First results for Canadians aged 15.* http://www.cmec.ca/docs/pisa20000/CandaReport.EN.pdf

Council of Ministries of Education Canada [CMEC] (2022): Structure of the Education Systems 2016. Chart. https://www.cmec.ca/299/education-in-canada-an-overview/index.html

European Agency for Special Needs and Inclusive Education. (2016). *Financing of inclusive education: Background information report.* https://www.european-agency.org/data/cross-country-reports

European Agency for Special Needs and Inclusive Education. (2020). *European agency statistics on inclusive education: 2018 Dataset cross-country report* [Dataset]. https://www.european-agency.org/data/cross-country-reports

European Commission/EACEA/Eurydice. (2020). *The structure of the European education systems 2020/21: Schematic diagrams.* https://op.europa.eu/en/publication-detail/-/publication/f4784939-1f15-11eb-b57e-01aa75ed71a1/language-en/format-PDF/source-search

Feuser, G. (2017). *Wider die Integration der Inklusion in die Segregation. Zur Grundlegung einer Allgemeinen Pädagogik und entwicklungslogischen Didaktik. Behindertenpädagogik und Integration.* Peter Lang Verlag.

Grynova, M., & Kalinichenko, I. (2018). Trends in inclusive education in the USA and Canada. *Comparative Professional Pedagogy, 8*(2), 28–34.

Hinz, A. (2006a). Kanada – ein 'Nordstern' in Sachen Inklusion. In A. Platte, S. Seitz, & K. Terfloth (Eds.), *Inklusive Bildungsprozesse* (pp. 149–158). Klinkhardt.

Hinz, A. (2006b). A world of difference: Inclusive education in Canada and Germany. *Education Canada, 46*(1), 22–24.

Hinz, A. (2007). Inklusion – Vision und Realität! Herausforderungen in Deutschland und Praxis in Kanada. In D. Katzenbach (Ed.), *Vielfalt braucht Struktur. Heterogenität als Herausforderung für die Unterrichts-und Schulentwicklung* (pp. 81–98). Goethe-Universität.

Hinz, A., & Kruschel, R. (2012). Educational Governance als 'Diagnose-Instrument' für die Analyse eines Projekts zur Etablierung inklusiver Entwicklungen. *Zeitschrift für Inklusion,* (3). https://www.inklusion-online.net/index.php/inklusion-online/article/view/55

Huber, S. G., Sturm, T., & Köpfer, A. (2017). Inklusion und Schulleitung – Schulleitende als Gestaltende inklusiver Schulen in der Schweiz. In B. Lütje-Klose, S. Miller, S. Schwab, & B. Streese (Hg.), *Inklusion: Profile für Schule und Unterricht. Forschungsergebnisse, Konzepte und Beispiele aus Österreich, der Schweiz und Deutschland* (pp. 43–56). Waxmann Verlag.

Jahr, D., & Kruschel, A. (Eds.) (2019). *Inklusion in Kanada. Internationale Perspektiven auf heterogenitätssensible Bildung.* Beltz Juventa.

Jordan, A., & McGhie-Richmond, D. (2014). Identifying effective teaching practices in inclusive classrooms. In C. Forlin and T. Loreman (Eds.), *Measuring inclusive education* (pp. 133–64, Vol. 3). Emerald.

Klemm, K. (2018). *Unterwegs zur inklusiven Schule. Lagebericht 2018 aus bildungsstatistischer Sicht.* Bertelsmann. https://www.bertelsmann-stiftung.de/de/publikationen/publikation/did/unterwegs-zur-inklusiven-schule

Köpfer, A. (2013). *Inclusion in Kanada. Analyse inclusiver Unterrichtsprozesse, Unterstützungsstrukturen und Rollen am Beispiel kanadischer Schulen in den Provinzen New Brunswick, Prince Edward Island und Quebec.* Klinkhardt.

Köpfer, A., & Óskarsdóttir, E. (2019). Analysing support in inclusive education systems—A comparison of inclusive school development in Iceland and Canada since the 1980s focusing on policy and in-school support. *International Journal of Inclusive Education, 23*(7–8), 876–890.

Lindmeier, C. (2020). Bildungsgerechtigkeit und Inklusion – Revisited. In R. Schneider-Reisinger & M. Oberlechner (Hg.), *Diversitätssensible PädagogInnenbildung in Forschung und Praxis. Utopien, Ansprüche und Herausforderungen* (pp. 30–45). Barbara Budrich.

Loreman, T., Forlin, Ch., Chambers, D., Sharma, U., & Deppeler, J. (2014). *Conceptualising and measuring inclusive education* (International Perspectives on Inclusive Education, Vol. 3). Emerald Group Publishing Limited (pp. 3–17). https://doi.org/10.1108/S1479-363620140000003015

Merz-Atalik, K. (2017). Inklusive Lehrerbildung oder Inklusionsorientierung in der Lehrerbildung?! Einblicke in internationale Erfahrungen und Konzepte. In S. Gleiten, G. Geber, A. Grahn, & M. Körniger (Hg.), *Lehrerausbildung für Inklusion Fragen und Konzepte zur Hochschulentwicklung, Beiträge zur Lehrerbildung und Bildungsforschung* (pp. 48–63). Waxmann.

Merz-Atalik, K., & Beck, K. (2020). Governance inklusiver Bildung: Modelle, Strukturen und Netzwerke der inklusiven Bildungsreform im internationalen Vergleich (Südtirol/Italien und Baden-Württemberg/Deutschland). In T. Dietze, G. Dietland, V. Moser, A. Piezunka, L. Röbenack, L. Schäfer, G. Wachtel, & M. Walm (Hrsg.), *Inklusion - Partizipation - Menschenrechte: Transformationen in der Teilhabegesellschaft? 10 Jahre UN-Behindertenrechtskonvention - Eine interdisziplinäre Zwischenbilanz* (pp. 210–218). Klinkhardt.

Nier, A. (2014). *Inklusion in Kanada. Was Deutschland von New Brunswick lernen kann.* GRIN Verlag.

Powell, J. J. W. (2018). Chancen und Barrieren inklusiver Bildung im Vergleich: Lernen von Anderen. *Schriftenreihe Eine für Alle — Die inklusive Schule für die Demokratie, 3,* 1–24.

Powell, J. J. W., & Merz-Atalik, K. (2019). Teaching diverse learners in Europe: Inspiring practices and lessons learned from Germany, Iceland, Lithuania, Luxembourg, Spain and Sweden. In M. Schuelka, C. Johnstone, G.Thomas, & A. J. Artiles (Eds.), *SAGE Handbook of inclusion and diversity in education* (pp. 321–337). Routledge.

Powell, J. J. W., & Merz-Atalik, K. (2020). Die Notwendigkeit inklusiver Bildung für die Erneuerung der Governancekonzepte: Deutschland und Luxemburg im Vergleich. In J. Bude, A. Dlugosch, P. Herzmann, L. Rosen, J. Panagiotopoulou, T. Sturm, & M. Wagner-Willi (Hg.), *Inklusionsforschung im Spannungsfeld von Erziehungswissenschaft und Bildungspolitik* (pp. 71–98). Barbara Budrich.

Sander, A. (2001). Von der integraviten zur inklusiven Bildung – Internationaler Stand und Konsequenzen für die sonderpädagogische Förderung in Deutschland. In A. Hausotter, W. Boppel, & H. Meschenmoser (Hg.), *Perspektiven Sonderpädagogischer Förderung in Deutschland. Dokumentation der Nationalen Fachtagung vom 14–16* (pp. 143–164). European Agency for Development in Special Needs Education.

Schifter, L., et al. (2019). Students from *low-income families and special education.* https://tcf.org/content/report/students-low-income-families-special-education/

Schleicher, A. (2018). Foreword. In A. Sliwka, D. Wittek, & S. Trumpa (Eds.), *Die Bildungssysteme der erfolgreichsten PISA-Länder. China, Finnland, Kanada und Südkorea* (pp.5–7). Waxmann.

Schroeder, J. (2019). Eine `Gewimmel von Diskursen´ zu Inklusion in Kanda. In D. Jahr & A. Kruschel (Eds.). *Inklusion in Kanada. Internationale Perspektiven auf heterogenitätssensible Bildung* (pp. 79–91). Beltz Juventa.

Slee, R. (2020). *Defining the scope of inclusive education.* UNESCO. (Background paper for Global Education Monitoring Report 2020.)

Slee, R., & Weiner, E. (2001). Education reform and reconstruction as a challenge to research genres: Reconsidering school effectiveness research and inclusive schooling, school effectiveness and school improvement. *An International Journal of Research, Policy and Practice, 12*(1), 83–98.

Sliwka, A. (2016). Wie andere Schulsysteme mit Diversität und Inklusion umgehen: Das Beispiel der Provinz Alberta in Kanada. In C. Fischer (Hrsg.), *Eine für alles? Schule vor Herausforderungen durch demografischen Wandel* (pp. 67–82). Waxmann.

Sliwka, A., Klopsch, B., & Yee, B. (2018). Kanada. In S. Trumpa, D. Wittek, & A. Sliwka (Eds.), *Die Bildungssysteme der erfolgreichsten PISA-Länder. China, Finnland, Kanada und Südkorea* (pp. 109–138). Waxmann.

Sliwka, A., Wittek, D., & Trumpa, S. (2018). Die Bildungssysteme der erfolgreichsten PISA-Länder – vier Analogien und ein kritisches Resümee. In S. Trumpa, D. Wittek, & A. Sliwka (Eds.), *Die Bildungssysteme der erfolgreichsten PISA-Länder. China, Finnland, Kanada und Südkorea* (pp. 163–170). Waxmann.

Stagg, J. (2019). Policy or pathologization? *Canadian Journal of Disability Studies, 8*(5), 18–41.

Statista. (2019). Kanada: Gesamtbevölkerung von 2008 bis 2018 (in Millionen Einwohner). https://de.statista.com/statistik/daten/studie/19294/umfrage/gesamtbevoelkerung-in-kanada/

Stein, A. (2011). Das kanadische Inklusionskonzept – sozialhistoriche, menschenrechtliche und behindertenpolitische Zugänge. *Behindertenpädagogik, 2*, 142–168.

Trumpa, S., Wittek, D., & Sliwka, A. (Eds.). (2018). *Die Bildungssysteme der erfolgreichsten PISA-Länder. China, Finnland, Kanada und Südkorea.* Waxmann.

Tyack, D. & Tobin, W. (1994). The "grammar" of schooling: Why has it been so hard to change? *American Educational Research Journal, 31*(3), 453–479.

UNESCO. (1994). *The Salamanca statement and framework for action on special needs education.* https://unesdoc.unesco.org/ark:/48223/pf0000098427

UNESCO. (2005). *Guidelines for inclusion: Ensuring access to education for all.* unesdoc.unesco.org/images/0014/001402/140224e.pdf

UNESCO. (2020). *Global education monitoring report 2020: Inclusion and education: All means all.* https://en.unesco.org/gem-report/report/2020/inclusion

Ungerleider, C. (2003). *Failing our kids: How we are running our public schools.* McClelland & Stewart.

United Nations. (2015). *The sustainable development agenda.* https://www.un.org/sustainabledevelopment/development-agenda/

United Nations. (2006). *Convention on the Rights of Persons with Disabilities.* https://www.un.org/development/desa/disabilities/convention-on-therights-of-persons-with-disabilities.html

Watkins, A., Ebersold, S, & Lénárt, A. (2014). Data collection to inform international policy issues on inclusive education. In C. Forlin & T. Loreman, T. (Eds.), *Measuring inclusive education* (pp. 53–74, Vol. 3). Emerald.

Wittek, D., Trumpa, S., & Sliwka, A. (2018). Die Bildungssysteme der erfolgreichsten PISA-Länder – einleitende und kritische Gedanken. In S. Trumpa, D. Wittek, & A. Sliwka (Eds.). *Die Bildungssysteme der erfolgreichsten PISA-Länder* (pp.11–19). Waxmann.

Zászkaliczky, P. (2008). Heilpädagogik im zusammenwachsenden Europa. In G. Biewer, M. Luciak, & M. Schwinge (Hrsg.), *Begegnung und Differenz: Menschen-Länder-Kulturen. Beiträge zur Heil- und Sonderpädagogik* (pp. 113–129). Klinkhardt.

Zighan, T. (2014). *Kanada – Ein Beispiel für schulische Inklusion. Möglichkeiten und Probleme der Verwirklichung.* Diplomica Verlag.

3 Doing Belonging and Social Coherence

Discourses of Belonging in Canada and Their Influence on Social Cohesion

Ayça Polat

Introduction

> *To those fleeing persecution, terror & war, Canadians will welcome you, regardless of your faith. Diversity is our strength #WelcomeToCanada."*
>
> J. Trudeau on Twitter am 28.01.2017: URL: twitter.com/justintrudeau/status/825438460265762816

Canadian Prime Minister Justin Trudeau sent the Twitter message above in response to former American President Donald Trump's plan to impose an entry ban on people originating from several Muslim-majority countries. The following day, a shooting at a mosque in Québec was carried out, to which Parliament responded: "It was an attack on our most intrinsic and cherished values as Canadians, values of openness, diversity and freedom of religion. Canadians will not be intimidated" (LeBlanc, 2017). On the night of the shooting, Trudeau emphasised on Twitter: "Muslim-Canadians are an important part of our national fabric."[1] Even in the 21st century, statements like this are (still) not self-evident for a head of government of a Western country. In recent years, such a clear positioning on diversity and to the Muslim proportion of the population has been absent in the statements from many Western heads of government up to now.

Statements of this kind and expressions of cohesion all over the country are very significant and encouraging for Canadian Muslims. Experts on right wing extremism regard the increase in attacks on Islamic institutions in Canada, which doubled from 45 to 99 per year between 2012 and 2014, as a result of an Islamophobic election campaign and discourses in society and politics, especially pertaining to Donald Trump's campaign (Michel, 2017).

As the first country with a multicultural policy (*Canadian Multiculturalism Act,* 1985), Canada reflects on an exceptional history in the shaping of coexistence between people of different origins, cultural and

DOI: 10.4324/9781003204572-4

religious beliefs, and orientation. The country's experience and strategies in handling the challenges presented by social diversity can be major impulses for other migration societies.

Using Canada's example, this chapter examines whether an inclusive concept of government, one which emphasises diversity as a country's strength and pursues the promotion of minority rights as a key objective, has a positive impact toward sense of belonging and cohesion in society and, consequently, distils a positive effect on the education process. To do this, Canada's multicultural politics will first be briefly illuminated. Subsequently, theoretical concepts of belonging and cohesion will be presented and an attempt to arrange the Canadian political strategies of *doing belonging* within the theory will be made. In order to compare and assess cohesion in Canadian society, results from representative studies will be used. Finally, the initial assertion that inclusive social politics, which also involve the implementation of affirmative action measures in institutions, is structuring and defining for the creation of education and integration processes, will also be dealt with in detail.

Multiculturalism in Canada

Canada, along with the United States, Australia, and Latin America, belongs to the classic immigration societies. Twenty percent of the Canadian population was not born in the country. The yearly number of immigrants is between 230,000 and 300,000 with Canada receiving 260,000 immigrants in 2014 (Statistics Canada, 2016).[2]

While in the 1960s the descendants of the founding British and French countries still made up around 60% and 30% of the population, respectively, the 2001 census reported that only one third of those surveyed descended solely from British, French, or Canadian families (Statistics Canada, 2003). European immigrants from locations including Germany, Italy, Portugal, and Eastern Europe arrived primarily at the end of the 19th century and accounted for approximately 90% of the immigrants up until 1961. Since the relaxing of previous racialist immigration legislation in 1962 (Bakhov, 2015, p. 11), immigration primarily from Asia and Africa has increased. Between 2012 and 2014, the percentage of immigrants from Asia was approximately 60% and, from Africa, 14% (Statistics Canada, 2016) with the prevailing majority coming from China, India, and the Philippines. Further, countries of origin include Pakistan, Iran, South Korea, United States, Great Britain, Algeria, Nigeria, Egypt, Morocco, and Cameroon (Statistics Canada, 2016).

Because of the highly diverse origins of their immigrants, the last Canadian census reported over 200 ethnicities and languages (Statistics Canada, 2015a). As in many other immigrant countries, social heterogenisation is particularly apparent in large metropolitan areas. The city of Toronto ranks among the most ethnically heterogeneous cities in the world. Over 50% of the inhabitants were not born in Canada (Statistics

Canada, 2016). Besides Toronto, other major cities for immigrants in Canada are Vancouver and Montréal. Proximity to family members and employment opportunities are the main reasons for settling in metropolises. In 2014, over 60% of the immigrants arrived as *economics.* Roughly one quarter came in the context of family reunification, and approximately 12% as refugees (Statistics Canada, 2015b).

In 2017, the country celebrated the 150th anniversary of its confederation. During this time, the pride of many Canadians in their interaction with diversity in Canada was especially apparent. This anniversary offered Canadians—once again—the opportunity to set themselves apart politically from their southern neighbour. The course for today's national identity was set by the current Prime Minister's father, Pierre Trudeau, in the 1970s. To balance the tremendous differences between French and English-speaking Canadians and the separatist efforts of the Province of Québec, multiculturalism was developed.

In 1971, multiculturalism was declared an official government policy under Prime Minister Pierre Trudeau. The *Canadian Multiculturalism Act* (House of Commons Debates, 1971) targeted the adherence and reinforcement of Canada's cultural diversity and treated multiculturality as a special resource of Canadian society. While the advancement of the cultural heritage of ethnic groups was the focus in the initial phase of the multicultural policy, anti-discrimination has moved into the spotlight since the 1980s. Relating thereto are affirmative action programmes in private as well as public institutions with the aim of reducing discriminating structures and the improvement of chances of participation—especially on the employment market. Further, many activities to improve the civic participation of minority groups can be recognised (Schultze & Gerstenkorn, 2015; Winter, 2015).

Challenges of Multiculturalism Policy

Although among those countries worldwide most effectively applying anti-discriminatory measures (Huddleston et al., 2015), multiculturalism in Canada does not remain undisputed. There is criticism that a policy of multiculturalism perpetuates and solidifies processes of *otherings* (Spivak, 1985) and that social and economic inequality as based on categories of difference will not be eliminated. Others see a danger that, through a maximum policy of recognising minority rights, traditional and conservative powers in minority groups will be encouraged and, as a result, could endanger individual rights (Schultze & Gerstenkorn, 2015; Winter, 2015). Despite these dangers, reiterated both politically and socially, multiculturalism is an indispensable component of Canadian society and is fundamentally not challenged across the parties:

> Multiculturalism is enshrined in law and in the constitution; eliminating it would not only be a tedious process. It would also

> be political suicide given the presence of more than 6.2 million foreign-born residents from over 200 countries ... many of whom receive voting rights after 4 years to 6 years of legal residence. In this sense, Canada continues to remain one of the last strongholds for multiculturalism in the world.
>
> (Winter, 2015, p. 651)

Although approval ratings have slightly decreased in recent years, acceptance of official multiculturalism policy, even within the Canadian population, remains high. In a representative study, approximately 84% of those surveyed agreed with the statement that "Canada's multicultural makeup is one of the best things about this country." (Citizenship and Immigration Canada, 2010). In the province of Québec, approval ratings had a greater decrease. In another representative study, 61% of those surveyed indicated that multiculturalism strengthens the national identity (Citizenship and Immigration Canada, 2010). On a political as well as scientific level, the issue of strengthening the sense of belonging of its citizens and immigrants plays a central role in Canadian discourse. This is seen in studies which regularly examine the population's sense of belonging and addresses the factors which are beneficial or rather detrimental (Hou et al., 2016), improving chances that participation at different levels will play a relevant role. What follows is an examination of several studies which give important references to the sense of belonging and social cohesion of Canadians with and without a migrant background.

Belonging and Cohesion in Canadian and German Society

The General Social Survey (GSS) is a preferred database for several analyses. Data for this survey are collected every five years from Canadians, including over 7000 immigrants. The survey includes questions on sense of belonging to Canada as well as to the country of origin (e.g., "What about your sense of belonging to Canada?" and "What about [your sense of belonging] to your country of origin?"). In 2013, the sense of belonging to Canada in nearly every age group of the immigrants' responses was higher than the Canadians' without a migration background (Statistics Canada, 2015c).

Thereby the immigrants who arrived before 2000 showed a higher sense of belonging to Canada (71%) than their country of origin (29%). The difference is lower for immigrants who arrived later (60% to Canada and 44% to country of origin, respectively; Statistics Canada, 2015c). In a similar study by the Expert Council of German Foundations on Integration and Migration (SVR), the number of immigrants who feel they entirely belonged to German society was lower than that of persons without a migrant background (2016):

> Whereas nearly 90 percent of those surveyed from non-EU countries agreed with the question, whether they felt they belonged to

> Germany, around 26 percent of those coming from Turkey disagreed. Regarding immigrants by religious affiliation indicates that Muslims from first generation immigrants feel considerably less belonging as new immigrants from Christian faiths, in the second generation the value increases, but remains lower than the comparison group.
>
> (SVR, 2016a, p. 1)

At the same time, an increase in reservations against Muslims and refugees can be observed in the population in recent years. According to the current Mitte-Studie,[3] approximately 28% of those surveyed with a low level of education and 24% with an average level of education agreed with anti-Muslim statements (Zick et al., 2019). Similar results can be observed with regard to middle income groups (21.6%; Zick et al., 2019).

In a comparative examination of various studies, at present, one cannot rule out a correlation between the increase in social reservations against specific groups of the population and a lower sense of belonging of these groups. This is also valid for the general feeling of recognition and its subsequent life satisfaction. Even though people affected by discrimination do not always make use of advisory and support services, the latest report of the German Federal Anti-Discrimination Agency (ADS) points out that, at 27%, there is a high number of cases of people who feel discriminated against because of their ethnic origin or skin colour (2017).

The high naturalisation rate in Canada also indicates a strong sense of belonging or interest in participation by immigrants (ICC 2015). In 2011, around 86% of those immigrants who had a legal right to nationalisation made use of it (National Household Survey, 2011). High naturalisation rates may certainly be attributed to the fact that Canada accepts dual citizenship.

In international comparative studies, social cohesion, and sense of belonging in Canadian society often rank positively. In the comparative study called *Social Cohesion Radar—Measuring Common Ground*, social cohesion was measured in 34 countries from 2009 to 2012. The basis for analyses was the evaluation of 12 international studies. The authors of the study define social cohesion as:

> the extent of social togetherness in a territorially defined geopolitical entity. … A cohesive society can be characterized by reliable social relations, a positive emotional connectedness of its members to the entity and a pronounced focus on the common good.
>
> (Dragolov et al., 2013, p. 5)

Since it is not possible to go into depth about the findings here, one should bear in mind Canada's high approval ratings with respect to solidarity and helpfulness, social diversity, identity, and perception of fairness in the comparative analyses. In Germany, these values are to some extent considerably lower (Dragolov et al., 2013, p. 33).

Why does Canada receive such high approval ratings from its immigrants? How are the differences to Germany to be explained? This will be addressed in the following section.

Doing Belonging—Is Belonging Doable?

There are a variety of conceptual approaches to the issues of belonging, cohesion, and identification with society, which underlie the studies mentioned above. However, the *subjective reference to collective society* and the associated topic of *recognition and acceptance* play an important role in all the studies.

According to Geisen (2017), the concept of belonging is "applied particularly where subjective references to collective relationships are made and processes of active establishment and (co-)creation of belonging are addressed" (Geisen, 2017, p. 4). Here, he does not mean belonging is a positioning within a collective body "but a result of a continuing process of (re-)positioning, establishing and changing. … thereby issues of socialisation and exclusion take center stage" (Geisen, 2017, p. 4). Belonging, for him, has an ambivalent nature, "because it has the nature of self-obligation; referring to one's own capacity for action, as well as the nature of having obligations externally imposed upon the individual by the social group" (Geisen, 2017, p. 5). The process, which I describe here as *doing belonging,* is a bilateral process which requires continuous development and active maintenance (Geisen, 2017, p. 7). This is not (always) a self-sufficient process. Hegemonic social discourse on minorities, legal regulations, and practices, and also the issues of recognition and inclusion by others—particularly social groups—are crucial to the success of doing belonging. At the subjective level, Mecheril (2003) describes this process as "the management of belonging," which includes individual "strategies of active examination of experiences of belonging and the consequences identified with them" (p. 34), requiring individuals to (re-)position themselves according to changing demand as well as experience. During migration processes and social change, this *management of belonging* can also result in multiple associations or hybrid identities (Hall, 1994, p. 41).

While belonging to one's family of origin may not be formally repealed, the sense of belonging to other collective bodies or even societies may change, culminating in the formal change of citizenship. In his analyses, Berry (2013) identifies that one cannot assume there is a general correlation between multiple associations and social cohesion in a society. This correlation depends much more on the way a society (universally) deals with cultural diversity:

> In societies that promote multiculturalism, these dual identities are secure and compatible, and do not undermine social cohesion. In

> contrast, in societies that are either new to dealing with cultural diversity, or where such diversity is not recognised or accommodated, there is a negative relationship.
>
> (Berry, 2013, p. 673)

In practice, Canadian naturalisation policies reflect this theory. The naturalisation of immigrants plays a relevant role; hence, barriers are removed, immigrants are encouraged to become citizens, and the renunciation of original citizenship is not required. In contrast, alleged loyalty conflicts still play a significant role in the discussion of whether dual citizenship should be allowed in Germany (Kunz, 2017). By implication, the political view on dual citizenship in Germany up to now has perceived even those immigrants who have been living in Germany for several decades could not possibly be loyal to German legislation as long as they were holding citizenship in another country (noticeably, this does not apply to EU citizens). This attitude may be incomprehensible for many immigrants and certainly a relevant factor of influence on the low rates of nationalisation in Germany as well.[4] However, these types of attitudes not only create confusion, but also a lack of trust. Heller (1995, p. 209) observed *familiarity* and *trust* as important requirements for *feeling at home* (as cited in Geisen, 2017, p. 9). Trust is not only relevant on the individual level of social interaction, but also in the way a political system handles its citizens:

> Even in a democracy, feeling at home is based on trust, namely as trust in the constitution and its related political institutions. Freedom to participate and engage in democracy and political action is as much a part of democracy as the negative liberty of non-participation.
>
> (Geisen, 2017, p. 10)

The Canadian concept of *deep diversity* justifies various validity claims of ethno-cultural groups. Yet, it is emphasised "that beside constitutional patriotism, there need to be further elements which create identity as well as a cultural framework which holds society together and guarantees 'unity in diversity'" (Schultze & Gerstenkorn, 2015, p. 162). This does not mean a Canadian national culture in any way, as is often understood in Germany.[5] Much more it applies a policy which appreciates social diversity, linked to the following strategies:

> (i) the maintenance and development of heritage cultures; (ii) intercultural sharing, and the reduction of barriers to full an equitable participation of all Canadians in the life of the larger society; and (iii) the learning of official languages as a basis for such participation.
>
> (Berry, 2013, p. 664)

The term *national identity* needs to be re-interpreted for the Canadian context in the respect that the articles on *nationhood* by Will Kymlicka (2015) are beneficial. He understands *nationhood* not as an (ethnic-) national and conservative understanding of national consciousness, but as a society's self-perception as an inclusive community of solidarity:

> Nationhood works best when it is deep in the background, as a taken for-granted presupposition of social life, such that it can indeed be "invisible." ... for when nationhood is highlighted or primed—when it is taken from the back of people's minds to the front of their minds—there is evidence that it triggers xenophobia.
>
> (Kymlicka, 2015, p. 12)

According to Kymlicka (2015), the attempt to (discursively) establish a new national consciousness and a neo-liberal interpretation of multiculturalism (*Benetton multiculturalism*) misses the goals of an inclusive understanding of multiculturalism:

> the meaning of "equality" was being reduced and reinterpreted in a neoliberal form as essentially equal access to (or perhaps better, equal exposure to) the competitive global marketplace. ... the equal right of all to market themselves and their culture, and to safely consume the cultural products of others, indifferent to issues of disadvantage. In short, inclusion without solidarity.
>
> (Kymlicka, 2015, p. 7)

Kymlicka (2015) has argued that active welfare state politics play a central role in the implementation of a multiculturalism policy which puts equal opportunity, in its original sense, into practice. Furthermore, the question of how immigrants can be encouraged to see themselves as part of a community of solidarity is important:

> A solidarity-promoting multiculturalism would start from the premise that one way to be a proud and loyal Canadian is to be a proud Greek-Canadian or Vietnamese-Canadian, and that the activities of one's group ... are understood as forms of belonging, and of investing in society, not only or primarily in the economic sense, but in a deeper social sense, even (dare I say it?) as a form of nation-building. Indeed, if there is one thing to be said on behalf of Canadian multiculturalism, it is precisely this: multiculturalism in Canada has always been seen, by both immigrants and native-born citizens, as a means of contributing to society, and indeed a form of nation-building.
>
> (Kymlicka, 2015 p. 12)

In 2015, Prime Minister Justin Trudeau told the New York Times Magazine that Canada would possibly become the "first post-national state" (Lawson, 2015) in the world. In his country, there is "no core identity," (Lawson, 2015) a statement which hardly any German Chancellor would allow themselves to say. In this way, he denies the existence of an official Canadian culture. However, in his statement quoted in the introduction of the chapter, he emphasises openness, diversity, and freedom of religion as the innermost and most precious Canadian values and, at the same time, Muslim Canadians as a significant part of the national identity. These ideas are likely reflected in his cabinet, composed of representatives from various minority groups, including politicians who previously arrived in Canada as refugees. Although this reflection of the society should be a matter of course, particularly for government institutions, it is still rare for a country's administrative cabinet to mirror real society.

Racism against the Black and Indigenous populations, which still exists in Canada (however, is not comparable with racism in the United States), should not be ignored. Yet, Trudeau's reactions and statements presented here, which could be supplemented by many more, should not be devalued as purely *symbolic politics*. They are crucial for a society's discourse on issues of belonging and interaction with minorities, and social discourses are "expression and constitutive conditions of society" (Bettinger, 2007, p. 77). Discourse stabilises "the sense of societal order and thus institutionalizes collectively binding knowledge systems" (Bettinger, 2007, p. 77). The sense of societal order that the current Canadian government wants to create and strengthen, especially in interaction with minorities, is of enormous significance for the advancement of an inclusive understanding of solidarity. This is even more imperative in times where nationalistic and right-wing populist politicians propagate views and beliefs which are detrimental to social cohesion and do not ensure the protection of basic rights.

Shaping an inclusive society may not stop at the level of lip service and symbolic gestures, while that alone cannot create trust and social cohesion. Important signs that Canada is serious about implementing equal opportunities in many areas are shown in several studies examining participation chances in different population groups. In the Migrant Integration Policy Index (MIPEX, 2015), in which immigrant and minority policies in over 38 countries are measured based on several indicators, Canadian anti-discrimination policy stands out as being particularly positive (Huddleston et al., 2015). This also applies to employment market policies, which are perceived by comparison as open and flexible:

> Migrant workers and their families have some of the best labour market opportunities in CA, ranked 5th. … CA encourages and supports most newly arrived legal residents to quickly find a job

> matching their skills, making labour market integration a priority from day one in CA. … Permanent residents, reunited family and some temporary residents are given an equal foothold in the CA labour market with equal rights as CA citizens to access jobs, education, training, public services, and benefits.
>
> (Huddleston et al., 2015, p. 30)

This study indicated discriminatory structures on various levels for Germany:

> The gaps in some areas of life—adult and child education, political participation, family reunion—are even larger in DE[6] than in most European countries. DE is one of few countries with a language test abroad, restrictions on dual nationality, limited healthcare entitlements for asylum-seekers and undocumented migrants, and a weak equality body and equality policy. These policies may be disproportionate and ineffective from an integration perspective, with many unintended consequences and negative long-term effects.
>
> (Huddleston et al., 2015, p. 19)

In international comparisons, Canada ranks higher than Germany with respect to participation of immigrant children and, particularly, at-risk populations in education. Fourth place in the MIPEX comparison reflects the results of the most recent PISA study (Huddleston et al., 2015). The authors consider the range of the Canadian education system's specific target-group support, as well as a diversity-aware orientation of teaching content and training especially exemplary (Hudleston et al., 2015). Two very important characteristics of educational policy, which back inclusion and educational justice (e.g., Jungk, 2016).

Canadian PISA results regularly show that neither a high percentage of pupils with migration background nor a low socio-economic status of the family necessarily leads to an educational disadvantage (Organization for Economic Co-operation and Development [OECD], 2016). The OECD comparative studies show that Canada, along with Denmark, Estonia, and Hong Kong belongs to those countries "with a high level of educational equity" (OECD, 2016, p. 4). According to Huddleston et al. (2015): "CA has best practices across the country to address the new needs and opportunities that immigrant students bring to schools. Only pupils in AU and SE benefit from such favourable new opportunities and intercultural education as in CA" (p. 34).[7] The authors see a close correlation between Canada's multiculturalism policy and support measures in the educational system: "Like CA, AU and NZ have developed strong targeted support and diversity policies through their official multiculturalism policies" (Huddleston et al., 2015, p. 34).

While in Germany, education chances for children and youth from socio-economically disadvantaged families and with migration histories have only slightly improved in the 20 years since the "PISA Shock" (Tillmann, 2015, p. 1). The Canadian school system, however, does not abandon children and parents to their *fate*. On the contrary, it attempts to provide a support system which responds to the needs of pupils *and* faculty (Köpfer, 2013):

> The social-economic hierarchization in property, income and prestige as well as ghettoization have been, in any case, up to now subcritical. ... They are intercepted and more than rudimentarily compensated through the Canadian educational system. ... It is highly efficient and open enough to fairly distribute educational chances at secondary and tertiary levels, to a great extent independently from socio-economic status and cultural origin. It leaves scope, however, for multicultural particularities.
>
> (Schultze & Gerstenkorn, 2015, p. 175)

A qualitative analysis of 53 studies indicates for Germany "that the difference in professional skills and educational choices can predominantly, if not fully be explained by social origin: children and youth from migrant families are disadvantaged over their entire educational career up through graduation by their migrant background, but above all by their social origin" (SVR, 2016b, p. 28). From an expert's opinion, comparisons with Canada or Scandinavian countries point out aspects which the German education system could take over or do differently in order to attain more equal opportunity. Whereby it should be noted that there was already recommendation for educational reform in the 1980s, which could have been taken seriously and implemented (Auernheimer, 1981).

Hence, it is certainly not too daring to assume that there is often a lack of staunch political will to effectively implement inclusion processes in the education system, as well as other aspects of German society. Canada's example illustrates that a political system which propagates the belief of diversity as a strength and simultaneously avails the right to elimination of barriers and obstacles can contribute a great deal to social integration and the creation of belonging on various levels of society. As described, the added value of such a political stance appears at various levels of society and for the individual.

Conclusion

Canadian society is interested in the discourse on *shared understandings* and the validity claims of various groups in the country but, more soberly, in comparison to many other societies. This process is perceived as being open and dynamic. Charles Foran of the Institute for Canadian Citizenship once said that the "weak Canadian identity" may be exactly what the world of the 21st century needs because it allows a "healthy flexibility" and a "receptivity to change" (Hasselbach, 2017, p. 3). This *receptivity to change* is certainly an important prerequisite for the success of pluralist social models and for processes of inclusion.

The replication of these kinds of perspectives and beliefs is then particularly crucial when right wing populist and racist ideologists increasingly herald supposed certainties about nations, cultures, religions, or generally differently minded and passionately living persons.

Notes

1. Trudeau, J. [@JustinTrudeau]. (2017, January 29]. *Muslim-Canadians are an important part of our national fabric.* [Tweet]. Twitter. twitter.com/JustinTrudeau/status/825934457471434752
2. In terms of inhabitants, Canada has a higher immigration rate than the United States. In 2013, the immigration rate was 7.3 persons per 1000 inhabitants in Canada and 3.1 persons per 1000 inhabitants in the United States (Statistics Canada, 2016).
3. For the *Mitte-Studie* (*Middle Study*), 1890 persons with German nationality were representatively chosen and surveyed by telephone between September 2018 and February 2019. They were comprised of 986 (52.2%) women and 904 (47.8%) men. The average age was 51.4 years old. Attitudes toward one topic were collected via several statements, including agreement or disagreement with the statement "Muslims should be prohibited from immigrating to Germany."
4. According to the Federal Statistical Office (2017), the fully utilized nationalization rate (i.e., the number of immigrants who filled all requirements for naturalization and became citizens) averaged 2.2% in 2016 in Germany.
5. For example, pushed by former interior minister Thomas de Maizière under the title "Leading culture for Germany. What is that actually? We are not burka" ("Leitkultur für Deutschland. Was ist das eigentlich? Wir sind nicht Burka") in BILD-Zeitung.
6. Abbreviation for Germany.
7. CA = Canada, AU = Australia, NZ = New Zealand, and SE = Sweden.

References

Auernheimer, G. (1981). Über Bildungspolitik in einem Einwanderungsland, das keines sein will. *Demokratische Erziehung, 4*, 245–250.

Bericht der Antidiskriminierungsstelle des Bundes. (2017). *Diskriminierung in Deutschland.* Antidiskriminierungsstelle des Bundes. https://www.antidiskriminierungsstelle.de/SharedDocs/Downloads/DE/publikationen/BT_Bericht/Gemeinsamer_Bericht_dritter_2017.pdf;jsessionid=78B53A8D3310C58149EE53D2A4C06D68.1_cid350?__blob=publicationFile&v=13

Berry, J. (2013). Research on multiculturalism in Canada. *International Journal of Intercultural Relations, 37*(6), 663–675.

Bettinger, F. (2007). Diskurse – Konstitutionsbedingungen des Sozialen. In R. Anhorn, F. Bettinger, & J. Stehr (Eds.), *Foucaults Machtanalytik und Soziale Arbeit* (pp. 75–89). VS.

Bakhov, I. S. (2015). Historical dimension of the formation of multicultural education in Canada. *Pädagogika, 117*(1), 7–15.

Citizenship and Immigration Canada. (2010). *A literature review of public opinion research on Canadian attitudes towards multiculturalism and immigration, 2006–2009.* Government of Canada. http://www.cic.gc.ca/english/resources/research/por-multi-imm/index.asp

Dragolov, G., Ignácz, Z., Lorenz, J., Delhey, J., & Boehnke, K. (2013). *Social cohesion radar measuring common ground. An international comparison of social cohesion methods report.* http://aei.pitt.edu/74134/1/Social_cohesion_radar.pdf

Geisen, T. (2017). Zugehörigkeit im Kontext von Migration. *Migration und Soziale Arbeit, 1*, 4–13.

Government of Canada. (1988). *Canadian Multiculturalism Act 1985.* https://laws-lois.justice.gc.ca/eng/acts/c-18.7/page-1.html

Hall, S. (1994). *Rassismus und kulturelle Identität.* Argument Verlag.

Hasselbach, C. (2017). Einwanderungsparadies Kanada. *Deutsche Welle* (Online). www.dw.com/de/einwandererparadies-kanada/a-37025700

Heller, A. (1995). *Ist die Moderne lebensfähig?* Campus Verlag.

Hou, F., Schellenberg, G., & Berry, J. (2016). *Patterns and determinants of immigrants' sense of belonging to Canada and their source country.* Statistics Canada. www.statcan.gc.ca/pub/11f0019m/11f0019m2016383-eng.htm

House of Commons Debates. (1971, October 8). "Multiculturalism." Canada. Parliament. *Library and Archives Canada, 8545–8548, Appendix, 8580-8585.* 28th Parliament, 3rd Session. https://pier21.ca/research/immigration-history/canadian-multiculturalism-policy-1971

Huddleston, T., Bilgili, Ö., Joki, A.-L., & Vankova, Z. (2015). *Migrant integration policy index 2015.* www.mipex.eu/sites/default/files/downloads/pdf/files/custom/a4/2017.07.27-09.36.58-mipex-2015-custom-book-a4.pdf

Institute for Canadian Citizenship (ICC). (2015). *Ballots of belonging. New citizens on political participation.* www.icc-icc.ca/site/pdfs/BallotsandBelonging FullReportEN.pdf

Jungk, S. (2016). Relatively little is known – Kanadas Bildungserfolg von Zuwandererkindern. *Zeitschrift für Kanada-Studien, 36*(1), 123–138.

Köpfer, A. (2013). *Inklusion in Canada – Analyse inklusiver Unterrichtsprozesse, Unterstützungsstrukturen und Rollen am Beispiel kanadischer Schulen in den Provinzen New Brunswick, Prince Edward Island und Québec.* Klinkhardt Verlag.

Kunz, T. (2017). Vom „ihr "zum „wir"? Das nationale Zugehörigkeitsverständnis als Dreh- und Angelpunkt der gegenwärtigen Entwicklungsphase der Migrationsgesellschaft. *Migration und Soziale Arbeit, 1*, 20–27.

Kymlicka, W. (2015). Solidarity in diverse societies: Beyond neoliberal multiculturalism and welfare chauvinism. *Comparative Migration Studies, 3*(17), 1–19.

Lawson, G. (2015). Trudeau's Canada, again. *New York Times Magazine Online.* http://www.nytimes.com/2015/12/13/magazine/trudeaus-canada-again.html?_r=0

Leblanc, D. (2017). *Quebec City shooting was act of terror against Canada, Trudeau says.* The Globe and Mail. https://beta.theglobeandmail.com/news/news-video/quebec-city-mosque-shooting-terrorism-trudeau/article33826339/?ref=http://www.theglobeandmail.com

Mecheril, P. (2003). *Prekäre Verhältnisse. Über natio-ethno-kulturelle (Mehrfach) Zugehörigkeit.* Waxmann Verlag.
Michel, J. (2017). *Die dunkle Seite Kanadas. Das bunte Kanada Justin Trudeaus ist nur eine Seite des Landes.* www.zeit.de/politik/ausland/2017-02/kanada-anschlag-moschee-quebec-einwanderungspolitik
National Household Survey. (2011). *Obtaining Canadian citizenship.* www12.statcan.gc.ca/nhs-enm/2011/as-sa/99-010-x/99-010-x2011003_1-eng.pdf
Organization for Economic Cooperation and Development. (2016). *PISA 2015 Ergebnisse im Fokus.* www.oecd.org/berlin/themen/pisa-studie/PISA_2015_Zusammenfassung.pdf
Sachverständigenrat Deutscher Stiftungen für Integration und Migration. (2016a). *Integrationsbarometer: Viele Götter, ein Staat: Religiöse Vielfalt und Teilhabe im Einwanderungsland Jahresgutachten 2016 mit Integrationsbarometer.* www.svr-migration.de/wp-content/uploads/2016/04/SVR_JG_2016
Sachverständigenrat Deutscher Stiftungen für Integration und Migration. (2016b). *Doppelt benachteiligt? Kinder und Jugendliche mit Migrationshintergrund im deutschen Bildungssystem.* www.svr-migration.de/publikationen/doppelt-benachteiligt-kinder-und-jugendliche-mit-migrationshintergrund-im-deutschen-bildungssystem
Schultze, R.-O., & Gerstenkorn, N. (2015). Der kanadische Multikulturalismus. Ein Erfolgsmodell sozio-politischer Integration? In K. Sarkowsky, R.-O. Schultze, & S. Schwarze (Eds.), *Migration, regionalization, citizenship, comparing Canada and Europe* (pp. 151–180). Springer.
Spivak, G. C. (1985). Die Rani of Simur: An essay in reading the archives. *History and Theory, 24*(3), 247–272.
Statistics Canada. (2003). *Canada's ethnocultural portrait: The changing mosaic, 2001 census.* www12.statcan.gc.ca/access_acces/archive.action-eng.cfm?/english/census01/products/analytic/companion/etoimm/pdf/96F0030XIE2001008.pdf
Statistics Canada. (2015a). *Linguistic characteristics of Canadians.* www12.statcan.gc.ca/census-recensement/2011/as-sa/98-314-x/98-314-x2011001-eng.cfm#a2
Statistics Canada. (2015b). *Number and percentage distribution of immigrants by region of destination and class, Canada, provinces and territories, 2012 to 2014.* www.statcan.gc.ca/pub/91-209-x/2016001/article/14615/tbl/tbl-02-eng.htm
Statistics Canada. (2015c). *Sense of belonging to Canada, the province of residence and the local community.* www.statcan.gc.ca/pub/89-652-x/89-652-x2015004-eng.htm#a2
Statistics Canada. (2016). *Report on the demographic situation in Canada: Permanent and temporary immigration to Canada from 2012 to 2014.* www.statcan.gc.ca/pub/91-209-x/2016001/article/14615-eng.htm
Tillmann, K. J. (2015). *PISA & Co – eine kritische Bilanz. Bundeszentrale für politische Bildung.* https://www.bpb.de/gesellschaft/bildung/zukunft-bildung/208550/pisa-co-eine-kritische-bilanz?p=0
Winter, E. (2015). Rethinking multiculturalism after its "retreat": Lessons from Canada. *American Behavioral Scientist, 59*(6), 637–657.
Zick, A., Küpper, B., & Berghan, W. (Eds.) (2019). Verlorene Mitte – Feindselige Zustände. Rechtsextreme Einstellungen in Deutschland 2018/19. Verlag Dietz J H.

4 A "Swarm of Discourses"

Inclusion in Canada

Joachim Schroeder

"Inclusion in Canada"—the subtitle of this book—is a kind of *discourse fragment* that can stimulate *discursive critical analysis*. The term *inclusion* refers to a discourse strand that, in the individual contributions of the volume, focuses on a *special discourse* (education), at different *discourse levels* (educational policy, school systems, pedagogical practice) and in a national *discourse space* (Canada).

Discourses are "trans-subjective producers of social reality and socio-cultural patterns of interpretation" (Jäger, 2015, p. 29). As "social stores of knowledge," (Jäger, 2015, p. 26) discourses provide at the same time "guidelines for subject-formation" as well as for the "structuring and shaping of societies" (Jäger, 2015, p. 26). Discourses represent a "reality of their own" (Jäger, 2015, p. 35) because "reality is interpreted according to the discourses by the people possessing knowledge" (Jäger, 2015, p. 36). In modern societies, there is a "swarm of discourses" (Jäger, 2015, p. 92). Nevertheless, it is possible to reconstruct discourse strands as "thematically uniform flows of knowledge through time and space" (Jäger, 2015, p. 81), such as the discursive debate about immigration, gender relations, or ecology (Jäger, 2015, p. 81). Different strands of discourse can be related to each other or even interlinked, and they can be linked together "according to special criteria, for example: discourse strands of exclusion (of immigrants, the disabled, women, young people, the elderly, etc.)" (Jäger, 2015, p. 89). If the spatio-temporal *knowledge flows* are systematised, this is an indication of an overarching discourse system (Foucault, 1974).

In the following sections, I would like to problematise the discursive order hidden in the book subtitle "Inclusion in Canada." For in the discourse space Canada, in the debate about participation in education, the term inclusion is at best *one* discourse-bearing category, which refers above all to *one* discourse group (persons with special needs). In the educational discourse on Indigenous People, at-risk youth, Afro-Canadians, or refugees, on the other hand, there are other categories that determine the respective discourse strand and the related institutionalisation of educational concepts in the school system (see Table 4.1).

DOI: 10.4324/9781003204572-5

Table 4.1 Construction of a "Discourse System" of "Inclusion" for Canada

Discourse group	*Strand of discourse*	*Discourse-bearing category*	*Special discourse (education)*	*Institutionalised discourse (school)*
Persons with Special Needs	Disability	Inclusion	Special Needs Programmes, Inclusive Education	Special Schools/ Classes, Inclusive Schools
At-Risk Youth	Vulnerability	Integration	Alternative Education	Alternative Schools
Indigenous People	Identity	Self-Control	Aboriginal Programmes, First Nations Education	Residential Schools, Survival Schools, First Nations Schools
Afro-Canadians	Racism	Afrocentricity	Afrocentric Education	Black-focused Schools, Afrocentric Schools
Refugees	Immigration	Protection	Refugee Integration Programmes	Reception Centres

The following discourse analysis is based on a stay of several months in Canada (July to October 2016).[1] My perspectives on the cultures, structures, and practices there are explained elsewhere (Schroeder, 2016). This contribution focuses on the discourses. First, I describe the five discourse strands separately. Then, I discuss different inter-relationships between several discourse strands using two examples. Finally, I discuss the overarching discourse system.

Discourse Strands: Separate Analysis

The reflections on the discourse system of exclusion and inclusion in Canada in the field of education should begin with individual discourse strands: in the discourses on *disability* and *vulnerability*, the categories *inclusion* and *integration* are both used. Regarding educational discourses on *ethnic* and *cultural discrimination*, we must distinguish between autochthonous (Indigenous, Afro-Canadians) and allochthonous groups (e.g., refugees). Here, categories such as *self-control*, *Afrocentricity* or *protection* are discourse-bearing.

In the educational policy discourse on disability, the target group is referred to as *students with special needs*, for which there are *special needs programmes*, *special classes*, and occasionally also *special schools*. In Germany, it is often pointed out that Canada had anchored an inclusive school system already by 1982 in its constitution (*Canadian Charter of Rights of Freedoms*; Köpfer, 2012). During the Paralympic Winter Games in Vancouver on March 11, 2010, Canada ratified the UN-CRPD and, since then, the concept of *inclusion* has been a leading category, even though the term *integration* is used just as frequently.

In the province of Québec, *inclusion* refers to the overarching educational policy perspective and *integration* to the organisational process. In the *Guiding Principles* for the promotion of students with handicaps, social maladjustments, or learning disabilities of the Québec School Board Montreal, the text runs as follows:

> Thus, the Board shall endorse the *principle of inclusion* wherein every student is accepted and belongs in the regular classroom. Inclusion involves the students' membership in a general education classroom with chronological age-appropriate classmates, having individualized and relevant learning goals, and being provided with the support necessary to learn. If integration into a regular class is deemed to be inappropriate by the in-school and Student Services Department personnel, in consultation with the student's parents (and the student, if applicable), and any other individuals as deemed appropriate (e.g., external professionals), then an alternative educational setting (e.g., self-contained class, special education school), shall be recommended.
>
> (EMSB, 2000, pp. 4–5)

In the province of Ontario, in the course of restructuring special needs education in 2021, the Toronto District School Board (TDSB) uses a tiered approach to support inclusion:

> Some exceptional students require additional specialized support beyond the resource level. These students access special education programs through an Identification Placement and Review Committee (IPRC) and will be placed in the Home School Program (HSP). HSP is a special education class … in which a student receives support for 50% of the school day. … For students who need a greater degree of academic support than that provided by HSP can be placed in two types of Special Education Classes (SEC): In the Special Education Class Full Time the student is placed for the entire school day, in the Special Education Class with Partial Integration the student is integrated with a regular class for at least one instruction period daily.
>
> (TDSB, 2015, p. 50)

At least in the provinces I visited (British Columbia, Ontario, and Québec), *inclusive education* means that students officially labelled as having a disability are integrated into an interrelated system of mainstream schools, special classes, and special institutions. *Inclusion* is the discourse-supporting category in the field of special education; for example, the special education courses at universities have been mostly renamed "Inclusive Education." However, in the political and educational practice of these provinces, the term plays virtually no role at all.

Alternative Education

So-called *alternative schools,* which are comparable to the German schools of social pedagogy (Schroeder, 2012), are very widespread in Canada. *Alternative schools* are defined as "programs that meet the specific needs of students who may not be able to adapt to the requirements of mainstream schools (for example, timetables, schedules or traditional classrooms)" (McCreary Centre Society, 2008, p. 7).

Currently, this pedagogical field of discourse follows on from *vulnerability,* a term from social inequality research used to describe the social risks of falling into poverty and social exclusion (Castel, 2008, p. 142). In Canada, vulnerable children and adolescents are divided into two groups: *at-risk youth* are affected by serious individual problems (alcohol or drug use, severe mental illness, homelessness, experiences of abuse and discrimination, early pregnancy, crime) and *high-risk youth,* who have also lost contact with their family of origin, their base school, and/or the community (McCreary Centre Society, 2008, p. 8).

Like Germany, social exclusion forces the Canadian school system to take other—*alternative*—paths to ensure school attendance and success for disadvantaged young people. This is where the strengths of the socio-educational alternative schools come into play: small groups, intensive work on relationships, and orientation of the educational content to the requirements of the respective precarious life-situations.

The discourse on vulnerability primarily addresses social groups that are socio-economically deprived. Nevertheless, the category of *poverty* plays only a subordinate role in the Canadian discourse. It would be important to examine in more detail whether this reflects the discourse pattern of "marginal poverty," a perspective of social inequality prevalent in many European industrial societies (Paugam, 2008, p. 165). Compared to so-called developing countries, the proportion of "poor" people in these societies is "marginal" and their visibility in public life is rather low (Paugam, 2008, p. 166). Those affected are stigmatised socially as "welfare cases" and held responsible for their own situation (Paugam, 2008, p. 116). This means that poverty is attributed less to structural social causes than to individualisation (Paugam, 2008, p. 114).

In the alternative schools, too, the educational discourse is predominantly geared towards pupils obtaining a general school leaving certificate. Transitional education (i.e., systematic preparation for the world of work; Thielen, 2011) is neither a practice, a culture, a structure, nor a discourse in the public school system in Canada.

First Nations Education

There is a discursive strand in the educational discourse field relating to schools that leads from the Residential Schools to the Aboriginal programmes or *survival schools* to the current commonly used terms *First Nations* and *Indigenous* education. This discourse strand is above all linked to the term *culture*, and it is about the struggle for *cultural identity*.

Over the course of about a hundred years, nearly 150,000 children—pejoratively referred to as *Indians*—were forced to attend about 130 Residential Schools (boarding schools), where they were often brought up with extreme brutality. Hundreds of children died in the schools from malnutrition, tuberculosis, ill-treatment, and suicide. On the occasion of the opening of the first schools in 1892, an *Indian Act* set as a priority educational goal to "kill the Indian in the child." This story of a *national crime* (Milloy, 1999) and *cultural genocide* (TRC Canada, 2015) explains to a certain extent why some Indigenous people are still distrustful of state educational institutions (Pidgeon et al., 2013).

In the 1970s, the American Indian Liberation Movements emerged throughout North America, fighting for bilingual education (Indigenous languages and English), self-determination with regard to teaching content, and autonomous administration structures (Pidgeon et al., 2013). From the 1980s onwards, the Residential Schools, which were initially run by the church and then by the state, were gradually handed over to the Indigenous peoples. In some states, these *First Nations schools* (sometimes called *Aboriginal programmes*) form legally defined, conceptually differentiated, and relatively autonomous school sub-systems in which a considerable number of the approximately 500,000 school-age First Nations Canadians are taught.

In some Canadian cities (e.g., Winnipeg, Toronto), the concept was mainly oriented towards the US-American survival schools (Biegert, 1979). In 1977, for example, a group of First Nations parents founded a *Native-controlled school* in Toronto because they refused to accept the racist attitudes with which their children were confronted in public schools. They also criticised that their language, their cultural heritage, and their perspectives on history and society were completely lacking in the school curriculum (Berg, 1998; Pellerin, 1982). The school mission statement defines its goal as "to enhance the Indian child's self-concept and sense of pride in himself as an Indian person" (Pellerin, 1982, p. 2). In 1983, the school was renamed from the "Wandering Spirit Survival School" to the "Cultural Survival School" and then in 1989 to the "First Nations School of Toronto," and now it has reclaimed its name as Wandering Spirit School.

Afrocentric Education

The *Afro-Canadians* include groups that were brought to North America by force under colonialism, those who fled or immigrated to Canada from the United States, and those who immigrated from the 1960s onwards, especially from the English-speaking Caribbean (e.g., Jamaica, Trinidad, and Tobago) or from Africa (e.g., Ghana). James (2012) argues that "Canada's historical anti-Black immigration policy was mitigated in large part by the idea, that admitting Blacks meant the nation was just asking for problems (i.e., race riots) that Britain and the U.S. had to bear for having Black residents" (p. 25). The discourse deals above all with racism, the discourse-bearing category is Afrocentricity:

> *Afrocentricity* is a theory that emerged in the early 1980s in the United States within the academic context of African-American studies. In essence, Afrocentricity represents the fact that as human beings, people of African ancestry have the right and responsibility to centre themselves in their own subjective possibilities and potential and through the re-centering process reproduce and refine the best of themselves. The ultimate goal of Afrocentricity is the liberation of African people from the grips of Eurocentrism. The primary and indispensable mechanism to achieve this goal is the fostering of African intellectual agency.
>
> (Dragnea & Erling, 2008, p. 14)

George Dei (1996, 2006) worked out three stable reasoning patterns for the desire of Black youths or their families for Afrocentric schools:

1. Personal and collective experiences of unequal treatment in the public school system due to skin colour;
2. There are no Black teachers in the schools; and
3. Insufficient consideration of the history, cultures, and oppressive experiences of Afro-Canadians in curricula, textbooks, and teaching content.

In the 2009/2010 school year, the first Canadian *Africentric School* opened its doors in Toronto.[2] By 2016/2017, the school had expanded up to Grade 8. The school programme connects three discourse strands: its *mission statement* refers to the Kwanzaa philosophy of Maulana Karenga, who teaches African Studies in Los Angeles (United States). He assumes that there are traditional African values that have survived both violent colonialism and assimilating globalisation and that form an antithesis to Western-style modernity.[3] The *curriculum* takes up the demand, formulated in North America in the 1990s, to replace the "canon of the dead white men" with a curriculum oriented towards diversity (Taylor, 1997, p. 61). In the curriculum, African history is addressed, African literature is read, and the social situation of Afro-Canadians is discussed in class (Banks & Banks, 2006). The *educational philosophy* combines objectives that are critical of racism and strengthen identity (e.g., "Black is beautiful"). The aim is to train a self-confident *Blackness* on the part of Black school children who are marginalised in the public school system, which is characterised as being "white" (Hampton, 2010).

Refugee Education

On average, about 27,000 refugees are admitted per year (Garcea, 2017). *Resettled refugees* are granted Canadian citizenship relatively swiftly within the framework of state programmes, in some cases already upon entry, thus enabling unhindered access to education, work, and health care. *Claimants*, on the other hand, are the small number of refugees who apply for political asylum within Canada and under the "In-Canada Asylum Program," a process which takes on average at least one year (Garcea, 2017).

In the overarching discourse on immigration in Canada, the terms *integration* and *multiculturalism* are closely linked (Taylor, 1997). Integration is a nation-state coded category because the society into which individuals or social groups are to integrate is the society of a nation state.

At the same time, the *Canadian Multiculturalism Act* of 1988 assures ethnic and religious minorities the right to "cultural distinctiveness" (Dib, 2017, p. 100). In Canada's larger cities, the various immigrant groups often live together in "their own" neighbourhoods. This is sometimes criticised as separation and segregation, but it can facilitate the integration process for refugees:

> In fact, organized ethno-religious communities are one reason why refugee reception and integration are more successful in Canada compared to other countries. The Canadian model allows communities to organize since it does not endeavour to forcefully assimilate refugees and immigrants, but rather it recognizes the importance of diversity in social cohesion by constantly building common spaces and venues of voluntary integration. This approach is not about emphasising separateness and divisiveness, but it is about respect of difference and inclusion of all Canadians—from colour and dress to customs and religion.
>
> (Dib, 2017, p. 100)

The *Refugee Protection System* also figures around the term *protection*, a term that is not commonly used in connection with the rest of the *immigration system*. The term *protection* most probably refers discursively to the Geneva Convention on Refugees (UN, 1951), which defines fugitives as particularly vulnerable social groups or places them under special protection. Canada is one of those countries that signed the 1951 Convention and not just the *1967 Protocol on the Status of Refugees*, such as the United States.

For young adults who are no longer required to attend school, access to education and school for refugees is mostly via so-called *reception centres*, which provide language and mathematics courses to ensure the transition to secondary schools or further adult education institutions (Giambrone, 2017). Adolescents under the age of 16 are allowed to attend pre-school, primary, and secondary school anywhere in Canada, even without having completed the naturalisation process, and are integrated as quickly as possible (Giambrone, 2017).

Discourse Strands: A Linked Consideration

Using the example of *disability*, links with other discourse strands (*Indigenous*, *Afrocentricity*) will be discussed. Statistics for the Indigenous schools in Canada show a consistently high proportion of pupils with severe hearing and visual impairments, addictions, physical disabilities, and serious learning and behavioural problems—on average, 30% (Phillips, 2010). These high figures are explained by the living conditions in the reserves (psycho-social consequences of poverty, inadequate medical care, and a lack of prevention, intervention, and rehabilitation services). Therefore, some people claim that Indigenous peoples with disabilities in Canada are "forgotten and ignored" (Phillips, 2010, p. 1).

In British Columbia, a *Special Education Program (SEP)* was introduced in 2003 at First Nation Schools (FNESC, 2016). From that moment in the province, all pupils with a disability were able to receive targeted special educational support in their local schools. Previously, these children had to move to special schools with an attached boarding school far away from home. In most cases, it was no longer possible for students to continue to be taught in their Indigenous language.

So far, there are only a few Indigenous schools with barrier-free school buildings (Schroeder, 2016). In the sometimes very remote *dwarf schools* with sometimes only 15 pupils, *multi-professional* specialist staff for special education, diagnostics, and counselling often cannot be employed for reasons of cost. The very small public schools located in the sparsely populated rural areas of Canada also have this problem because the next larger settlements or small towns are sometimes hundreds of kilometres away. So, it is difficult to take advantage of support programmes if these are not available in the schools themselves or in the communities.

To put it simply, Indigenous children with a disability must choose between two school systems: inclusive public schools, where they generally find a good special educational support infrastructure but where their cultural background or language is hardly considered in the lessons, or bilingual and bicultural Indigenous schools, which can only offer them meagre special educational support.

At the *Africentric School* in Toronto, on the other hand, the introduction of a *special needs programme* was viewed very critically. Many parents were strictly opposed to it because they feared additional stigmatisation of the children and the school:

> A critical challenge for administrators and teachers who wanted to modify, alter, and support the learning experiences for students with exceptionalities was attempting to navigate through the stigma some parents associated with special needs education based on well-founded and historic mistrust of an education system that has over-labeled Black students. ... Special education is extremely political when it comes to Black children. Special education means intelligence; that's what's in the minds of Black people because that's what they have been systematically taught.
>
> (James et al., 2014, p. 46)

The worldwide biologistical concept of the "racism of intelligence" (Bourdieu, 1993, p. 254), which, among other things, postulates that Black people are less intelligent than white people, and therefore could only achieve low school grades, is also partially reified in the discourse of Toronto's urban society. Especially in the media, it is repeatedly claimed that the mainstream schools would transfer their "difficult" Black pupils to the Africentric School and that this would lead to an accumulation of children and adolescents with behavioural problems:

> The media attention that the school has received since even before it was established to present today has been quite negative, biased, limited, disruptive, and damaging. Students interpreted the media attention as leaving the impression that just because it is a group of Black people they think it is going to be horrible .... There is a damaging misconception that the school is filled with a whole bunch of bad kids coming from low socioeconomic statuses and that the school is to just deal with behaviours and fix kids that are rude.
>
> (James et al., 2014, p. 44)

The *Special Needs Program* was finally introduced in 2013, not least to counter the poor image of the school with empirical findings: the proportion of children with special educational needs at the Africentric School in 2014 was no higher than at other schools in Toronto (James et al., 2014, p. 14).

Conclusion: Discursive Patterns in the Discursive Swarm

"Inclusion in Canada" represents a "discursive swarm" (Jäger, 2015, p. 92) with a long historical tradition. In the 19th century, religious minorities, especially Mennonites and Amish, demanded their own schools, which were approved in almost all the provinces (Pellerin, 1982). Only New

Brunswick's school legislation banned separate schools and insisted on the compulsory integration of all children without exception into public schools under state supervision (Pellerin, 1982).

In the schools for cultural and ethnic minorities, this educational tradition of allowing oppressed or marginalised groups to have their own schools (*self-controlled*) continues today: for the First Nations, as a social act of reparation for historically violent assimilation and, for Afro-Canadians, as a public admission that they are particularly hard hit by structural, social, and everyday racism. Canada has traditionally had special schools for children and youth with disabilities or those who have been socially excluded. Many provinces have an approach that keeps two systems open: students with a disability are kept in inclusive settings for as long as possible but without completely abandoning forms of special education. In the case of social disadvantage, on the other hand, priority is given to *alternative schools* for adolescents in Grades 7, 8, and above, which try to ensure that compulsory schooling is provided that takes account of their specific situation along with accompanying social support. Young refugees, on the other hand, are to be placed in public schools as quickly as possible.

Inclusion in Canada stands for a critical examination of the concept of inclusion, which is repeatedly called into question by discriminated, excluded, and marginalised social groups:

> Current definitions and practices of inclusion still leave students on the margins, even when these students are "included." Despite administrators' "very best intentions," "included" students may still underachieve or even drop out; others continue at the bottom of the scale of academic achievement. Minority students, then, should be moved from the margins to the centre; they should not just be grafted onto the existing order. It is insufficient, for example, to include a few sessions dealing with minority themes in a course syllabus and label that action as "inclusive schooling." What we need is a "multi-centric" approach to curricular knowledge. "Centric" locates students within their own cultural frame of reference so that they can connect socially, politically, ideologically, spiritually, and emotionally to the learning process.
>
> (Dei, 1996, p. 177)

Twenty years later, this perspective on inclusion still holds true: in Canada, students are labelled as a matter of course to identify special needs in terms of skin colour, ethnicity, migration experience, or disability. Separate discourse strands are related to each other but are not played off against each other. Historically developed discourse strands are carefully modernised. The self-determination of social groups is a high political and moral value, which also leads to demands for *self-control* on the part of these social groups in the educational system. Inclusion is not idealised one-sidedly as the fairest form of organisation of the school system but is seen—in a pleasantly sober manner—as a strategy of including social groups but which, at the same time, bears the risk of excluding others.

Notes

1. Various institutions have greatly supported my approach to individual strands of discourse: The English School Board Montreal (inclusive education), the Native Indian Teacher Education Program of the University of Vancouver (First Nations education), the McCreary Centre Vancouver (alternative education), the York Centre for Education and Community (YCEC) at York University in Toronto (Afrocentric education), and, at the same university, the Centre for Refugee Studies.
2. The school uses the term *Africentric* instead of *Afrocentric* in its self-designation. I could not get a reason for this.
3. See www.officialkwanzaawebsite.org

References

Banks, J. A., & Banks, C. A. (2006). *Multicultural education: Issues and perspectives.* Wiley & Sons.

Berg, S. (1998). *Wandering spirit survival school. First Nations education and emancipation.* College of Education York University.

Biegert, C. (1979). *Indianerschulen. Als Indianer überleben—von Indianern lernen. Survival schools.* Rowohlt.

Bourdieu, P. (1993). *Soziologische Fragen.* Suhrkamp.

Castel, R. (2008). *Die Metamorphosen der sozialen Frage. Eine Chronik der Lohnarbeit.* UVK.

Dei, G. J. S. (1996). The role of Afrocentricity in the inclusive curriculum in Canadian schools. *Canadian Journal of Education, 21*(2), 170–186.

Dei, G. J. S. (2006). Black-focused schools: A call for re-visioning. *Education Canada, 46*(3), 27–31.

Dib, K. (2017). Refugee integration and Canadian multiculturalism. In A. Korntheuer, P. Pritchard, & D. B. Maehler (Eds.), *Structural context of refugee integration in Canada and Germany* (pp. 99–106). Gesis.

Dragnea, C., & Erling, S. (2008). *The effectiveness of Africentric (Black-focused) schools in closing student success and achievement gaps: A review of the literature.* Toronto District School Board.

English Montreal School Board. (2000). *Policy governing the organizational services for students with handicaps, social maladjustments or learning disabilities.* www.emsb.qc.ca/en/governance_en/pdf/BoardPolicies/StudentServices/Special-Education.pdf

First Nations Education Steering Committee. (2016). *Special education program. Final Report.* www.fnsa.ca/wordpress/wp-content/uploads/2011/05/SEP-Final-Report-2016-2017-Instruction-Booklet-17-08-2016.pdf

Foucault, M. (1974). *Die Ordnung des Diskurses.* Fischer.

Garcea, J. (2017). Canada's refugee protection system. In A. Korntheuer, P. Pritchard, & D. B. Maehler (Eds.), *Structural context of refugee integration in Canada and Germany* (pp. 31–36). Gesis.

Giambrone, A. (2017). The educational system in Canada. In A. Korntheuer, P. Pritchard, & D. B. Maehler (Eds.), *Structural context of refugee integration in Canada and Germany* (pp. 43–48). Gesis.

Hampton, R. E. (2010). Black learners in Canada. *Race and Class, 52*(1), 103–110.

Jäger, S. (2015). *Kritische Diskusanalyse. Eine Einführung* (7th ed.). UNRAST.

James, C. E. (2012). *Life at the intersection. Community, class and schooling.* Fernwood Publishing.

James, C. E., Howard, P., Samaroo, J., Brown, R., & Parekh, G. (2014). *Africentric alternative school research project: Year 3 (2013–2014) report.* www.yumpu.com/en/document/read/54690686/africentric-alternative-school-research-project

Köpfer, A. (2012). Inclusion. In K. Ziemen (Ed.), *Lexikon Inklusion.* Vandenhoeck & Ruprecht.

McCreary Centre Society. (2008). *Making the grade: A review of alternative education programs in British Columbia.* The McCreary Centre Society. http://www.mcs.bc.ca/pdf/AlternateEducationFinal_web.pdf

Milloy, J. (1999). *A national crime: The Canadian government and the residential school system, 1870-1986.* University of Manitoba Press.

Paugam, S. (2008). *Die elementaren Formen der Armut.* Hamburger Edition.

Pellerin, J. (1982). *A case study of three pupils at Wandering Spirit Native Survival School in Toronto.* College of Education University of Saskatchewan.

Phillips, R. (2010). Forgotten and ignored: Special education in First Nations schools in Canada. *Canadian Journal of Educational Administration and Policy, 106,* 1–26.

Pidgeon, M., Munoz, M., Kirkness, V. J., & Archibald, J. (2013). Indian control of Indian education: Reflections and envisioning the next 40 years. *Canadian Journal of Native Education, 36*(1), 5–35.

Schroeder, J. (2012). *Schulen für schwierige Lebenslagen. Studien zu einem Sozialatlas der Bildung.* Waxmann.

Schroeder, J. (2016). Kanada kann auch anders. Vielfältige Schulangebote im "gelobten Land der Inklusion." *Zeitschrift für Inklusion Online, 4*(11). https://www.inklusion-online.net/index.php/inklusion-online/article/view/397

Taylor, C. (1997). *Multikulturalismus und die Politik der Anerkennung.* Fischer.

Thielen, M. (Ed.). (2011). *Pädagogik am Übergang. Arbeitsweltvorbereitung in der allgemeinbildenden Schule.* Klinkhardt.

Toronto District School Board. (2015). *Special education plan 2015.* TDSB. www.docplayer.net/18996635-Special-education-plan-2015.html

Truth and Reconciliation Commission of Canada. (2015). *Honouring the truth, reconciling for the future: summary of the final report of the Truth and Reconciliation Commission of Canada.* Truth and Reconciliation Commission of Canada. www.trc.ca/websites/trcinstitution/File/2015/Findings/Exec_Summary_2015_05_31_web_o.pdf

United Nations. (1951). *Abkommen über die Rechtsstellung der Flüchtlinge.* www.unhcr.org/dach/wp content/uploads/sites/27/2017/03/Genfer_Fluechtlingskonvention_und_New_Yorker_Protokoll.pdf

5 Inclusive Education in Canada

An Overview

Jacqueline Specht and S. Anthony Thompson

Educational policy and funding lies within Canada's ten provincial and three territorial governments, but not solely; Indigenous education is a federal responsibility. As Merz-Atalik (this volume) notes, the Canadian education system has been noted as one of the most successful in the PISA-survey and has had much interest from other countries wishing to determine what we are doing right. While we do some things right and we have the policy in some places, we are not perfect. Things are not as rosy as they may appear once the curtain is lifted, and we see how inclusion is operating at the local levels. In this chapter, we present an overview of the policies and evidence-based practices within inclusive education, paying attention to implementation successes and failures. Next, examples of Canadian provincial/territorial education policy are provided. Then, we consider the supports for the practice of inclusive education. Subsequently, we share data, which gives us pause to question whether inclusive education exists for all students with disabilities in Canada. Finally, through the lens of disability, we will comment on the broader issues of inclusion presented in the chapters by Kerstin Merz-Atalik, Ayca Polat, and Joachim Schröeder. All three chapters provide interesting and thoughtful perspectives on inclusion and ideas that can be used to think about how inclusive education for students operates within Canada compared to countries in Europe.

Policies in Canada

Since the Salamanca Statement (UNESCO, 1994), governments globally have increasingly focused on the development of inclusive education systems. Within Canada, education systems are organised and administered by provinces/territories; no federal educational policy for all students with disabilities exists. All provinces/territories, however, have inclusion within their mandate, which relates to the *Canadian Charter of Rights and Freedoms* (GC, 1982). Section 15 (Equality Rights) addresses the issue of providing education on an equal basis for all

DOI: 10.4324/9781003204572-6

students regardless of difference. The most complex and controversial Charter-based challenges end up before the Supreme Court of Canada. A recent case related to education, equity, and disability was the 2012 decision of *Moore v. British Columbia.* According to the Council of Canadians with Disabilities (2013), the ruling states that when barriers are identified in education for students with disabilities, they must be removed. This ruling confirmed that students with disabilities have a right to receive those necessary accommodations to enable them to access the general education curriculum. The *Charter* has shaped the policies of inclusive education across the country along with similar law that prohibits the discrimination of people with disabilities (e.g., *Canadian Human Rights Act*).

This human rights-based approach to inclusive education is one that permeates the current literature. Perhaps it is an attempt to lessen past exclusionary practices that have existed in education. Educational administrators (i.e., those in power) had the ability to admit, or not, students with disabilities based solely on their own decision (Ellis, 2019). Such policies propagated power and hierarchy rather than equity. Indeed, schooling of people with disabilities in Canada typically has been shown to maintain the power differential between those with and without disabilities and therefore inequality (Parekh & Brown, 2019). A human rights-based approach, however, maintains that schools must focus on barriers that exist to marginalise students because they do not "fit in." What is at stake is to create suitable education for all Canadians (Ainscow, 2020). According to Ainscow, the way to promote equity and inclusion in schools is to: (a) base policies on agreed definitions of inclusion and equity, (b) use evidence-based strategies, (c) use whole school approaches to support teachers in inclusive practice, (d) have the leadership of departments of education promote inclusion and equity for all, and (e) develop policies that draw on the experiences and expertise of all stakeholders in education. With this human rights-based approach to inclusive education in mind, we now turn to the existing state of inclusive education policy in Canada.

As indicated, education in Canada is mandated by various governmental bodies. It should not be surprising then that inclusive education policies and practices differ somewhat across the country. Regardless, all jurisdictions appear to value inclusion as the first choice for students with disabilities, as they all have progressed to become more inclusive over the years (Sokal & Katz, 2015). To begin, the roads to inclusive education in different jurisdictions have been facilitated by reports commissioned by specific provinces or those authored by advocates across Canada over the years. *The MacKay Report* (2006), *Connecting Care and Challenge: Tapping Our Human Potential*, was a call to investigate the ways in which inclusion was practiced in New Brunswick schools.

Although recognised as a province that promoted inclusive education, the government of the day felt a review was necessary. Hall (2015) was commissioned to investigate inclusive education in Nunavut as a result of the auditor general of Canada's concerns about the adequacy of the education of students who were identified with special education needs. The concern was raised because Nunavut's inclusive education documents make no specific mention of such students, rather, inclusive practices and philosophies were articulated (e.g., accepting that students learn at different rates, including all students in regular classrooms, being resourceful to provide supports, and showing respectful pride for Inuit culture). Relating back to Ainscow (2020), Nunavut's approach appears truly inclusive. Potential barriers that may further marginalise children had been considered by looking at education for all, rather than proposing policies and practices that espouse education is somehow different for students who have been identified with a disability. Educators need the pedagogical skills to support all learners; thinking a label is the way to do so may be misguided. In fact, many Canadian policymakers, like those in Nunavut, show a movement away from the medical model. "Prescriptions" to "fix" students do not exist. Again, from a human-rights approach, we must support children's needs, build their strengths within our schools, and continue to create policy that truly respects diversity.

When looking at the realities of inclusive education across Canada, differences exist in policy and on-the-(school)-ground. A province like New Brunswick, for example, mandates that within the public education system, all children attend their neighbourhood school and learn alongside their peers. There are no special schools, classes, or courses (GNB, 2016). In Ontario, however, there is a range of placements available from special schools to education in the neighbourhood schools with same age peers (OME, 2017a). Ontario's approach does not meet Ainscow's framework because segregated placements for students with disabilities still exist, limiting the access to quality education (Parekh & Brown, 2019). Additionally, provincial/territorial documents relating to the education of students with disabilities were created at different times across the country; in truth, these dates vary widely.

The oldest documents appear for Quebec in 1999 and Alberta in 2004. Concerns are raised about the optics of such dated documents given advances in research and practice over the years. Loreman (2018), for example, criticises the Alberta policy. He states that it did "a poor job of supporting inclusion and inclusive practice in schools in 2004, and is all the more tired and outdated in 2018" (para. 2). Most other provinces and territories have updated their education policies and procedures in the last five years (Hutchinson & Specht, 2020). Although these policies and procedures continue to espouse inclusive education as a priority, at the same time, such policies potentially other students identified with special education needs through discussion of different/special approaches to inclusive education as ways to make students fit the norm (Slee, 2013).

Resources to Support Education of Students with Disabilities

Most provincial/territorial ministries of education have resource guides and policy that (ideally) shape the practice of students with disabilities in inclusive settings (e.g., see the *Special Education Policy Manual* produced by the British Columbia Ministry of Education, 2016). Such policies may range from transition planning, quality Individual Education Plan (IEP) development, and effective assessment practices for students with disabilities. Some provincial/territorial ministries also produce resource manuals that assimilate best practices in the area of students with disabilities. For example, in 2019, the Government of Saskatchewan produced *Inclusive Education Modules: A Guide for Classroom Teachers; A Guide for School Based-Leaders; A Guide for Student Support Services Teachers* and in 2013, the Ontario Ministry of Education developed *Learning for All—A Guide to Effective Assessment and Instruction for All Students, Kindergarten to Grade 12.*

Additionally, in Canada, every province/territory has at least one teacher association (also variously named as a federation or union); some jurisdictions have several. Such organisations can impact inclusion as class size and number of students with disabilities is often a negotiated issue between teachers and provincial/territorial governments (Thompson et al., 2015). Generally, teacher federations/associations/unions have suggested that they are in favour of inclusive practice, provided that the resources are in place in classrooms and schools (Thompson et al., 2015).

Sometimes, such teacher associations offer their own resources on a number of topics, such as inclusive education. For example, the Alberta Teachers Association (n.d.) provided a workshop series called *Establishing Inclusive Learning* Environments, which presented different topics within each training segment, such as classroom management and supporting positive behaviours in Alberta schools. The Ontario College of Teachers, who are responsible for the oversight of the professional learning of educators, have promoted the development of resources to support inclusive education (Ontario College of Teachers, n.d.), recently exploring the professional experiences of school principals for inclusive education (Sider et al., 2018). Further, there is an active national, non-government agency (NGO), Inclusive Education Canada (IEC), with its commitment:

> to quality education for all students in inclusive schools and classrooms in Canadian schools. We [IEC] support this by advocating

> for effective policy provision and investment in supports for teachers and students, as well as building capacity in our schools and classrooms to make inclusion both a successful and practical reality. (para. 1 and 2)

IEC endorses and produces resources on inclusive education. So, in sum, to quote Stienstra (2018, p. 1), "disability policy [as with educational policy] in Canada is fragmented across many programs and jurisdictions." At the very heart of this fragmentation is the denial of a human rights-based approach to education as will be highlighted by the examples of inclusive practice across Canada.

Inclusive Education: The State of Practice

Despite the research findings that students with disabilities do better socially and academically in inclusive classrooms (e.g., Waldron & McLeskey, 2010) and the call from ministries of education for more inclusive settings, some students with disabilities continue to be placed in segregated settings (Bennett et al., 2019). The segregation seems to be more pronounced for students with intellectual and developmental disabilities (IDD). Inclusive Education Canada (n.d.) estimates that less than 50% of students with IDD are in inclusive settings across the country. Using Ontario as an example, since September 1998, Ontario law has required the consideration of placement in regular classrooms for students identified with any exceptionality (Regulation 181). In Ontario in 1997 (data collected prior the implementation of Regulation 181), 87.6% of elementary students and 89.2% of secondary students identified with a developmental disability were not in the general education classroom for most of their day. Moving forward to 2017 (latest readily available data; see Bennett et al., 2019), the number of students placed in a general education classroom has changed slightly for elementary (70.9%) but not much for secondary (82.3%). In looking at self-contained segregated classes for students with IDD, there are still a huge number of these compared to self-contained classes for students with other identifications. Some school boards in Ontario still have a large number of self-contained classes for all students identified with special needs. For those school boards who have been decreasing their segregated classes, a disproportionate number still exists for students identified with IDD (Bennett et al., 2019). For example, one board has 51 elementary classes and 74 secondary classes for students with developmental disabilities compared to 21 at elementary and 15 at secondary for all other identified special education needs combined, including gifted.

Even in classrooms that are considered inclusive, students with disabilities may simply be placed in the regular classroom rather than fully participating. As a result, students are not involved with the social or academic work of the class; they are simply taking a seat in the room. Such scenarios are frustrating for many Canadian teachers, students, and families (Reid et al., 2018; Sider et al., in press; Young et al., 2018). The result may be the belief that inclusion does not work, with some heads of teacher associations calling "for changes to inclusion policy for classrooms" (Fraser, 2017). Perhaps policy does need to change but not in ways suggested by such reports. We need not return to less inclusive days; we need policy with legislative backing that does not permit people to be segregated based on a disability. As Valle and Connor (2011) note, it is still a popular belief of educators that students are more or less deserving of an education based on "ability" yet if we substituted other forms of diversity, such views would be unimaginable (e.g., students living in poverty, or girls, etc.).

The question remains as to why some Canadian jurisdictions continue to segregate students and/or place students in inclusive classrooms without the necessary supports. Data show that these practices do not translate into successful lives for adults with disabilities. Alternately, data for inclusive practices with children shows potential to change the trajectory of adult lives. Statistics Canada collects data for adults 15 years of age and over through the Canadian Surveys. Since 1983, Statistics Canada, with the support of Employment and Social Development Canada (ESDC), has conducted seven surveys focused on persons with disabilities: the 1983/1984 Canadian Health and Disability Survey (a supplement of the monthly Labour Force Survey), the 1986 and 1991 Health and Activity Limitation Surveys (HALS), the 2001 and 2006 Participation and Activity Limitation Surveys (PALS), and the 2012 and 2017 Canadian Surveys on Disability (CSD; Furrie, 2018). Data for children under 15 exists in only one data set. The 2001 Participation and Activity Limitation Survey (PALS) is a post-censual survey of adults and children whose everyday activities are limited because of a condition or health problem. A sample of those persons who answered "yes" to the 2001 Census disability filter questions were included in the PALS survey population (Statistics Canada, n.d.).

The data for those over 15 years of age continue to present a somewhat bleak picture for people with disabilities in terms of education, employment, and income. Timmons and Wagner have used the PALS survey to look overall at inclusive environments in Canada. Children who are educated in high inclusive settings are reportedly in better health, enjoy going to school more, progress more quickly in school, and interact more positively with peers compared to students educated in low inclusive settings (Timmons & Wagner, 2008). Given the research that those who are in more inclusive settings are reportedly more successful as adults, we need to change our system to be truly inclusive and not just produce vague policies that enable differential implementation based on the will of the school. There are many places where this is being done well in provincial and territorial jurisdictions in Canada; there need to be more.

Commentary on the Three Papers

We thought an approach to discussing and commenting on the papers in this section would be to look for themes that emerged and caused us to ponder where inclusive education is in Canada based on the ideas raised in the papers.

History/Progress of Inclusion in Canada

As discussed in all chapters, there are many reasons that may explain why Canada has become an inclusive society. From the beginning of the country, we have valued diversity of the settlers. The country was moulded with English and French language, religious, and cultural diversity. The *Canadian Charter of Rights and Freedoms* reaffirmed the right of all Canadians to participate fully in society, including education (Hutchinson & Specht, 2020). Canada is a relatively young country and has formed because of colonisation and immigration. Although the populations of immigrants have changed over the years (Polat, this volume), the diversity has always existed. As immigrants arrived from European countries, diversity was found in language and, as it opened to Asian and African countries, the diversity widened. As a country, we have changed to include difference. With respect to special education, Merz-Atalik notes the density of population as a factor. When looking across the country, one can see that less densely places on our East Coast, for example, have tended to not have separate places for students with disabilities because there was not the population to warrant them. In more densely populated areas like Toronto, Ontario, segregation was easier to accomplish because there were enough students to put in those classrooms. The more densely populated areas also have more bureaucracy. In Ontario, for example, there are 72 school districts (31 English public, 29 English Catholic, 4 French public, and 8 French Catholic) spread across a vast geographic area. In Newfoundland and Labrador, there are two school districts (one French and one English) spread across a vast geographical area. To make changes in the system, there are far less people to discuss it and consensus may be easier to achieve.

As is the case in many colonised countries, we have not embraced the diversity of Indigenous peoples, even as (clearly) Canada is on Indigenous lands. The First Nations, Métis, and Inuit populations have a long history of suffering because of colonisation. They continue to be separate, in the beginning because they were forced and now because of distrust of governments that created the *Indian Act* to keep the "savages" in their place. Among the many atrocities that arose from this act, the

Residential School System is at the fore of discussion currently. The best way to "kill the Indian in the child," was to remove them from their homes and communities and bring them under the rule of governments who stripped them of their languages and culture and replaced it with that of the colonizers (Joseph, 2018).

On June 2, 2008, the Government of Canada began a Truth and Reconciliation Commission (TRC) to speak the truth to the historical and ongoing impacts of colonialism for First Nations persons in Canada. From this process, various calls to action—various paths to reconciliation—were created (TRC: Calls to Action, 2015). Necessarily, there are calls for changes within educational systems. Indeed, at this point in Canadian history, the TRC and its Calls to Action is undoubtedly one of the most significant federal documents that has significance for education. From the TRC (2015), Call to Action 63 states:

> We call upon the Council of Ministers of Education, Canada to maintain an annual commitment to Aboriginal education issues, including: i. Developing and implementing Kindergarten to Grade Twelve curriculum and learning resources on Aboriginal peoples in Canadian history, and the history and legacy of residential schools; ii. Sharing information and best practices on teaching curriculum related to residential schools and Aboriginal history; iii. Building student capacity for intercultural understanding, empathy, and mutual respect; iv. Identifying teacher-training needs relating to the above. (p. 7)

To continue on the path of inclusive education, we suggest the best way to understand it is to pay attention to the TRC Calls to Action and to follow Indigenous ways such as those in afore-mentioned Nunavut policies. Such approaches are human rights-based. Regardless of difference, everyone has a right to an equitable education (Ainscow, 2020). The work that has been accomplished through the TRC acknowledges the harm that has been done by those in power and calls for a solution to be created by those in power together with the community. Inclusive education answers the call to increase understanding, empathy, and mutual respect. Indeed, the TRC's Calls to Action are for all of us to understand difference, not as a threat but as something to celebrate, something from which our communities may learn. As we move to a more accepting culture, all will benefit.

Discourse of Inclusion

Schroeder (this volume) presents the notion of different discourses of inclusion, and these ideas are prevalent in the other two papers. UNESCO (1994) defined inclusion much more broadly than disability.

Schroder invites discussion of the underlying discourses around the inclusion of different marginalised communities. Indeed, there are varying issues related to each discourse and policies in place that discriminate against each group separately and collectively, which are juxtaposed with those meant to stop this discrimination. As Merz-Atalik (this volume) comments, the very nature of identifying and labelling children in the Canadian school system based on deficits can lead to the pathologising of learners rather than respect for their differences and promoting competence. There has been movement away from funding based on labels of disability, but school systems across the country still fund special education differently and earmark pockets of money for special initiatives related to equity across the country. Although the inclusive education movement began for people with disabilities (Hutchinson & Specht, 2020), they now seem left behind in policy and practice. Ontario's *Equity Action Plan* (2017b) discusses that groups of students may be disadvantaged by existing structures, yet no mention is made of beginning to dismantle the special education system that perpetuates these inequities. In Ontario, nearly 42,000 students are not in a regular classroom for most of their day and, as noted previously, many of these students have intellectual disabilities. In spite of research that indicates the regular classroom is as good as or better than a segregated classroom (Hehir et al., 2016), we continue to (re)create two systems of education: regular and special. A recent call for proposals for a book in diversity in Canada omitted the topic of disability. This omission reflects what is often seen in the discourse of diversity. Importantly, we wonder about opening the discussion more to a discourse of intersectionality rather than the discourse of difference. The intersection of ability, race, gender, income, and sexuality produces a picture of inequity. Students in special education programmes are disproportionately male, racialised, and living in poverty (Brown & Parekh, 2013). Further, Indigenous students are designated at higher rates for learning disabilities and behaviour disorders (Lamoureux & Katz, 2020). Inclusive educators need to be aware of the systemic racism inherent in ways of teaching, academic expectations, referral rates for discipline, and segregated programmes (Zinga & Gordon, 2016). The separate special education system perpetuates the inequity by providing those who are already marginalised with a deficient education.

People check more than one box for identity purposes. At times, some identities are more prevalent than others and these need to be dissected and researched, but in a practical sense, we cannot look at people in one way. We are complex beings with multiple identities that create us. We must not confuse inclusion with the discourse of assimilation. Too often, this is the fear and for some of the marginalised groups, a real fear given history of cultural genocide for people Indigenous to the lands of Canada who lost their language and culture. As a people, they do have the underlying discourse of self-control (Schroder, this volume) because others have controlled them for too long with intergenerational harm. In this way, the work of belonging as identified by Polat (this volume) speaks to the need to fit in more than one world in meaningful ways.

Belonging

We think that the underlying issue of belonging as noted by Polat in *doing belonging* is one to consider—how do we create belonging while maintaining identity—not assimilating, but by being allowed to be who you are and what you are and that is accepted and valued. Polat presents research that indicates that social cohesion is more likely in societies that promote multiculturalism and permit dual citizenship (like Canada). It could be that the internal conflict of "who I am" is less when one can say I have many identities and I am not forced to choose one and renounce all others. In this way, the discourse of intersectionality within inclusion created that sense of belonging. King (2003) created a model of making meaning in life comprised of three psychological constructs of our cognition and thoughts; our affect or emotions and feelings; and our behaviour or that way in which we act. These psychological constructs are then played out in our everyday lived experiences allowing us to create meaning in our lives through three strands: *Understanding* (related to thinking), *belonging* (related to our feelings), and *doing* (related to our behaviour). The notion of *doing belonging* presented by Polat is interesting. The idea that we simply cannot feel but must act in order to belong relates well to this model. Teaching diverse learners requires that teachers create environments in which students develop a positive self-concept, a sense of belonging, and the skills and capacities for emotional and intellectual resiliency and achievement (Katz, 2012). When students feel that they have access to the physical space as well as the instructional activities, teachers create that sense of belonging and increase social and academic engagement. When students feel that they are on the periphery, and belonging is blocked because of physical, learning, or cultural barriers, disengagement and often challenging behaviour ensues (Specht & Katz, 2014). School belonging is key in creating mentally healthy children who will develop into mentally healthy adults who create a society where diversity is valued.

Conclusion

Merz-Atalik discusses the tensions of inclusive education in Europe. We daresay they exist in Canada too. All three chapters have identified positive and negative aspects of inclusion in Canada when compared to European countries. We think this book has tremendous value in opening the discussion of inclusion around the world and to learn from each other. It has been interesting to read the view of European researchers on inclusion in Canada. It is certainly true that there are many positives, but when we look deeply, there are many issues that need to be addressed. Perhaps it comes down to not being satisfied with being "better than" but doing better within our own contexts. Better than is a relative term and while high PISA scores may illustrate success in some ways, education should not only create people with knowledge, but citizens who value and respect diversity.

References

Ainscow, M. (2020). Promoting inclusion and equity in education: Lessons from international experiences. *Nordic Journal of Studies in Educational Policy, 6*(1), 7–16.

Alberta Teachers Association. (n.d.). *Establishing inclusive learning environments.* https://www.teachers.ab.ca/For%20Members/Professional%20Development/Workshops/Establishing_inclusive_learning_environment/Pages/EstablishingInclusiveLearningEnvironments.aspx

Bennett, S., Dworet, D. Gallagher, T., & Somma, M. (2019). *Special education in Ontario schools* (8th ed.). Highland Press.

British Columbia Ministry of Education. (2016). *Special education policy manual.* https://www2.gov.bc.ca/assets/gov/education/administration/kindergarten-to-grade-12/inclusive/special_ed_policy_manual.pdf

Brown, R.S., & Parekh, G. (2013). *The intersection of disability, achievement, and equity: A system review of special education in the TDSB.* Toronto District School Board. Intersection of Disability Achievement and Equity.pdf (tdsb.on.ca). https://www.tdsb.on.ca/Portals/research/docs/reports/Intersection%20of%20Disability%20Achievement%20and%20Equity.pdf

Council of Canadians with Disabilities. (2013). *The Moore case: Summary of key points.* http://www.ccdonline.ca/en/humanrights/litigation/Moore-Case-Key-Findings-9Nov2012

Ellis, J. (2019). *A class by themselves? The origins of special education in Toronto and beyond.* University of Toronto Press.

Fraser, E. (2017, November 21). *Teachers call for changes to inclusion policy for classrooms.* Canadian Broadcasting Company (CBC). https://www.cbc.ca/news/canada/new-brunswick/inclusion-policy-new-brunswick-teachers-association-1.4411713

Furrie, A. (2018). *The evolution of disability data in Canada: Keeping in step with a more inclusive Canada.* Statistics Canada. https://www150.statcan.gc.ca/n1/pub/89-654-x/89-654-x2018003-eng.htm

Government of Canada. (1982). *Canadian Charter of Rights and Freedoms.* http://laws-lois.justice.gc.ca/eng/const/page-15.html

Government of New Brunswick. (2016). *10 Year educational plan: Everyone at their best.* http://www2.gnb.ca/content/dam/gnb/Departments/ed/pdf/K12/EveryoneAtTheirBest.pdf

Government of Saskatchewan. (2019). *Inclusive education modules: A guide for classroom teachers: A guide for school based-leaders: A guide for student support services teachers.* Saskatchewan.

Hall, B. (2015). *Reaching and teaching all students – A model to guide the practice of inclusive education in Nunavut: Final report of the external review of inclusive education.* https://www.assembly.nu.ca/reaching-and-teaching-all-students-model-guide-practice-inclusive-education-nunavut-final-report-ext

Hehir, T., Grindal, T., Freeman, B., Lamoreau, R., Borquaye. Y., & Burke, S. (2016). *A summary of the evidence on inclusive education.* https://www.edulinks.org/sites/default/files/media/file/A_Summary_of_the_evidence_on_inclusive_education.pdf

Hutchinson, N., & Specht, J. A. (2020). *Inclusion of learners with exceptionalities in Canadian schools* (6th ed.). Pearson

Inclusive Education Canada. (n.d.). *Our mission.* https://inclusiveeducation.ca/

Joseph, R. P. C. (2018). *21 things you may not know about the Indian Act.* Page Two Books.

Katz, J. (2012). *Teaching to diversity: The three-block model of universal design for learning.* Portage & Main Press.

King, G. (2003). Tying it all together: Frames of reference and meaning in life. In G. A. King, E. G. Brown, & L. K. Smith (Eds.), *Resilience: Learning from the turning points of people with disabilities* (pp. 7–29). Greenwood.

Lamoureux, K., & Katz, J. (2020). Intersectionality, indigeneity, and inclusive education: Reimagining business as usual. *Exceptionality Education International, 30*(2), 12–18.

Loreman, T. (2018). *Disability & inclusive education policy in Alberta: The lowest of priorities.* https://inclusiveeducation.ca/2018/02/02/disability-inclusive-education-policy-in-alberta-the-lowest-of-priorities/

McKay, A. W. (2006). *Connecting care and challenge: Tapping our human potential.* New Brunswick Department of Education. https://www2.gnb.ca/content/dam/gnb/Departments/ed/pdf/K12/mackay/ReportOnInclusiveEducationSummaryDocument.pdf

Ontario College of Teachers. (n.d.). *Ongoing professional learning.* https://www.oct.ca/resources/categories/ongoing-professional-learning

Ontario Ministry of Education. (2013). *Special education: Learning for all – A guide to effective assessment and instruction for all students, kindergarten to grade 12.* http://www.edu.gov.on.ca/eng/general/elemsec/speced/LearningforAll2013.pdf

Ontario Ministry of Education. (2017a). *Special education in Ontario: Kindergarten to grade 12 policy and resource guide.* http://www.edu.gov.on.ca/eng/document/policy/os/onschools_2017e.pdf

Ontario Ministry of Education. (2017b). *Ontario's education equity action plan.* http://www.edu.gov.on.ca/eng/about/education_equity_plan_en.pdf

Parekh, G., & Brown, R. S. (2019). Changing lanes: The relationship between special education placement and students' academic futures. *Educational Policy, 33*(1), 111–35.

Reid, L., Bennett, S., Specht, J., White, R., Somma, M., Li, X., Lattanzio, R., Gavan, K., Kyle, G., Porter, G., & Patel, A. (2018). *If inclusion means everyone, why not me?* https://www.inclusiveeducationresearch.ca/events/inclusive_education_news.html

Sider, S., Maich, K., Morvan, J., Specht, J., & Smith, D. (2018). *Exploring leadership practices through case inquiry: Supporting inclusive schools.* Ontario College of Teachers.

Sider, S., Morvan, J. Maich, K., Specht, J., & McGhie-Richmond, D. (in press). Between, betwixt, and amongst: Intersectionalities where school leadership and inclusive schools meet. In C. McGregor & S. Bedi (Eds.), *Diverse leadership landscapes: Exploring the terrain.* Queen's University Press.

Slee, R. (2013). How do we make inclusive education happen when exclusion is a political predisposition? *International Journal of Inclusive Education, 17*(8), 895–907.

Sokal, L., & Katz, J. (2015). Oh, Canada: Bridges and barriers to inclusion in Canadian schools. *Support for Learning, 30*(1), 42–54.

Specht, J., & Katz, J. (2014). Perspectives on teaching and student diversity. In J. W. Andrews & J. L. Lupart (Eds.), *Diversity education: Understanding and addressing student diversity* (pp. 127–160). Nelson Publishers.

Statistics Canada. (n.d.). *Children with disabilities and their families – Tables – Archived.* https://www150.statcan.gc.ca/n1/en/catalogue/89-586-X

Stienstra, D. (2018). Canadian disability policies in a world of inequalities. *Societies, 8*(2), 36.

Thompson, S. A., Lyons, W., & Timmons, V. (2015). Inclusive education policy: What the leadership of Canadian teacher associations has to say about it. *International Journal of Inclusive Education, 19*(2), 121–140.

Timmons, V. & Wagner, M. (2008). *Inclusive education knowledge exchange initiative: An analysis of the Statistics Canada Participation and Activity Limitation Survey.* Canadian Council on Learning. http://www.ccl-cca.ca/CCL/Research/FundedResearch/201009TimmonsInclusiveEducation.html

Truth and Reconciliation Commission. (2015). *Truth and reconciliation of Canada: Calls to action.* http://trc.ca/assets/pdf/Calls_to_Action_English2.pdf

UNESCO. (1994). *The Salamanca statement and framework for action on special needs education.* UNESCO. https://www.european-agency.org/sites/default/files/salamanca-statement-and-framework.pdf

United Nations Educational, Scientific and Cultural Organization (UNESCO). (1994). *The Salamanca Statement and Framework for Action.* Paper presented at the World Conference on Special Needs Education: Access and Quality, June 7–10, in Salamanca, Spain. United Nations Convention on the Rights of the Child (1989), United Nations Office of the High Commissioner. http://www.ohchr.org/en/professionalinterest/pages/crc.aspx

Valle, J. W., & Connor, D. J. (2011). *Rethinking disability: A disability studies approach to inclusive practices.* McGraw Hill.

Waldron, N. & McLeskey, J. (2010). Inclusive school placements and surplus/deficit in performance for students with intellectual disabilities: Is there a connection? *Life Span and Disability, 13*(1), 29–42.

Young, G., Specht, J., Hunter, F., Terreberry, S., McGhie-Richmond, D., & Hutchinson, N. (2018). "The first day he kicked shoes at me, the last day he brought me a picture of himself": Investigating the practicum experiences of preservice teachers. *Exceptionality Education International, 28*(3), 83–101.

Zinga, D. M., & Gordon, M. K. (2016). "Racism under the radar": Student perceptions of school experiences in a multicultural context. *Race Ethnicity and Education, 19*(5), 1088–1116.

Part II

Structures around Inclusive Education

6 Current Trends in Inclusive and Special Education in Newfoundland and Labrador, Canada, and Finland

Markku Jahnukainen, Kimberly Maich, Sharon Penney, and Gabrielle Young

Introduction

Canada is a vast country bounded on the west and east by the Pacific and Atlantic oceans, to the north by the Arctic Ocean, and to the south and north-western edge, bordering Alaska, by the United States of America. Geopolitically, it is divided into 13 jurisdictions, 10 provinces, and 3 northern territories with vast swaths of rural and northern areas with low population density. Canada has a federal government providing governmental directives in many areas, but not all decision-making happens at the all-encompassing federal level. Since Canadian Confederation in 1867, the provinces and territories have operated from provincial/territorial directives for significant areas like health care and education (rather than national ones), often with little federal direction (Dworet & Bennett, 2002). Therefore, significant diversity is evident across Canada. Even the use and names of Individual Education Plans (IEPs) for students with disabilities vary, for example. In the field of education, this diversity in funding and programming includes the provision of educational programmes through Indigenous and Northern Affairs Canada (Maich et al., 2018). Maich and Sider (2019) summarise these relationships:

> regulations are found at provincial/territorial levels but include multiple informants of policy including international direction, such as the UN Convention on the Rights of Persons with Disabilities (2017) and UNESCO's Salamaca Statement for Framework for Action on Special Needs Education (1994). Provincial education departments (ministries) develop regulations and policies … which [deal] with the identification and placement of SEN. Such provincial regulations are then interpreted and implemented through the local policies and practices for schools organized by boards or districts. (p. 3)

DOI: 10.4324/9781003204572-8

Although jurisdictionally funded and governed platforms like Canada's education system may have many advantages, 13 varied platforms means, at times, vast inconsistencies across the nation such as "including differences in definitions, diagnosis, identification, prevalence, eligibility, placement, services, administration, funding, and teacher training" (Maich et al., 2018, p. 1) and such inconsistencies around inclusion may be intensified in secondary settings (Thompson & Timmons, 2017).

Many Canadian provinces, territories, and/or school boards are using or including elements of *response to intervention*, a model of delivering services that is reflective of the traditional *cascade model*, where most students are in the regular class and learning the regular curriculum (Tier 1), some students require additional supports for some concepts (Tier 2), and a few students receive an alternative curriculum (Tier 3). However, Maich et al. (2018) did find cross-Canada trends towards inclusion of students with disabilities and towards non-categorisation of exceptionality.

Canada, including the province of Newfoundland and Labrador (NL), is at a crossroads between progresses in school-based inclusion that began around the mid-1800s (Dworet & Bennett, 2002) yet with many steps ahead that are mired in complex challenges. While there were early instances of inclusion in NL, it was far more common for students with special education needs to be educated in separate schools. In 1954, Vera Perlin opened her first school for students with cognitive impairments in St. John's, NL with help from donations. The *Canadian Charter of Rights and Freedoms,* 1982 was the impetus for public entry into the school system for students with special education needs also contextualised by international informants to policy. In the 1980s, Canada focused on placement for students with practices like integration or mainstreaming, pushing students with disabilities into school systems (Thompson & Timmons, 2017). By the 1990s, this initial emphasis shifted to calls for one inclusive school system, including the use of meaningful curricula for all students, to cover the range of complex needs in Canadian classrooms (Thompson & Timmons, 2017). This conversation and its practices continue to evolve unevenly across Canada, fraught with complexities and tensions from philosophies to policies to practices, including within its easternmost island province of NL. The NL Premier's Task Force (Government of Newfoundland and Labrador, 2017) reiterated that:

> Every province and territory in Canada embraces the language of inclusive schools. This language extends to the entire school culture and speaks to shared values of diversity and the creation of learning communities that are accepting, welcoming and safe. Within that paradigm, each region has a model outlining the delivery of

> accommodations and supports to students with identified learning needs. Newfoundland and Labrador typifies the national landscape with similar support services, modes of delivery, assessment criteria and categories of support. (p. 6)

Newfoundland and Labrador

Like many areas in Canada, NL has significant spaces and communities that are rural and northern as well as having Indigenous populations. However, as noted above, there is little federal direction with the exception of some federal direction for Indigenous education (Maich & Sider, 2019). Therefore, NL, like each of Canada's 13 jurisdictions, creates provincial policies and equity and inclusion for all community members, as well as those that are specific to school-based practices (Maich & Sider, 2019). In NL's case, the province has moved from a history of a full segregation in the 1980s for students with disabilities to "an internationally embraced model of inclusive education where all children, regardless of religion, culture, gender or ability, can attend the neighbourhood school" (Government of Newfoundland and Labrador, 2017, p. 5). However, policies, practices, and even definitions remain vastly inconsistent across the country and struggles remain in NL's jurisdictional approach to the inclusion of students with disabilities (Maich et al., 2018). Even within NL, inherent and emergent challenges exist around the development of inclusive policies and practices. For example, although the province has over 500,000 residents, almost half of those live in small, rural, and Northern communities (Government of Newfoundland and Labrador, 2017, p. 3), and migration towards city centres is a common phenomenon. The Premier's Task Force (Government of Newfoundland and Labrador, 2017) reports that:

> Between 1996 and 2016, the number of school-aged individuals (5 to 19 years) in the province declined from 125,000 to 80,000, with declines more pronounced in rural areas. Over the next 20 years this number is projected to decline further to 68,000. In rural areas, there are concerns about viability of small schools; availability of programs, particularly at the high school level; extended busing distances; and availability of specialist services. In urban centres, there are increasingly diverse school populations, with higher numbers of immigrants and refugees and a corresponding need for programs and services. (p. 3)

In NL, "inclusive education refers broadly to the climate of social acceptance while special education has traditionally referenced an equitable provision of supports to children with an identified exceptionality"

(Government of NL, 2017, p. 5). More specifically, the Department of Education and Early Childhood Development broadens *inclusion* to a philosophy that incorporates a range of tenets. These goals include:

- The right of all students to attend school with their peers, and to receive appropriate and quality programming;
- A continuum of supports and services in the most appropriate setting (large group, small group, individualised), respecting the dignity of the child;
- A welcoming school culture where all members of the school community feel they belong, realise their potential, and contribute to the life of the school;
- an atmosphere which respects and values the participation of all members of the school community;
- A school community which celebrates diversity; and
- A safe and caring school environment. (NL Department of Education, Definition of Inclusive Schools. (Government of Newfoundland and Labrador, n.d., para. 1)

NL is a province with both urban and rural geographical areas and the Centre for Distance Learning and Innovation (CDLI) offers programming for students from Kindergarten to Grade 12. During the 2016/2017 academic year, CDLI offered 41 different courses to 1233 individual students (Centre for Distance Learning and Innovation, n.d.). The Department of Education and Early Childhood Development moved from a special education to an inclusive education model, phasing in this approach through to 2017. The Newfoundland and Labrador English School District (NLESD) consists of 256 schools, including several alternate sites: hospital schools (i.e., Janeway Children's Health and Rehabilitation Centre, St. John's; Tuckamore Centre, Paradise; Hope Valley Centre, Grand Falls-Windsor; and Western Memorial Hospital, Corner Brook), Newfoundland and Labrador Youth Centre, Horizon Academy, and the Pathfinder Learning Centre (two locations: Corner Brook and Stephenville). These schools provide education for approximately 65,000 students. The NLESD also offers services through the Centre for Distance Learning and Innovation (CDLI; Centre for Distance Learning and Innovation, n.d.).

Hospital schools are also provided to students across the province. The primary purpose is to maintain academic programming for students when they are unable to attend school during periods of hospitalisation, rehabilitation, or treatment (NLESD, n.d.a). Horizon Academy offers services to children from Grade 7 through to the end of secondary studies. This school provides services to students who, for whatever reason, are unable to attend their local school. The school provides services for students with both behavioural and mental health needs. The school generally provides half day services for 50 students split into either morning or afternoon classes. The school is also used to provide services for students who have been hospitalised or incarcerated as they transition back to their home schools (personal communication, C. Stacey, March 17, 2021). The Newfoundland and Labrador Youth Centre in Whitbourne, NL provides schooling for students Grades 7 to the completion of secondary education. The school provides educational services to youth who have been in conflict with the law and placed in secure custody. The Pathfinders Learning Centre has two locations in the western part of the province (Corner Brook and Stephenville). This centre supports and services youth ages 16 and over who want to complete their high school education. The programme offers a general high school diploma and provides self-paced courses for students (NLESD, n.d.c).

Beginning in 1964, NL opened a provincial school for the Deaf. Prior to opening this school, students from NL attended the School for the Deaf in Nova Scotia or the McKay School for the Deaf in Montreal, Québec. When the School for the Deaf opened in 1964, they initially had 54 students and, by 1964, there were 130 students attending the school (Newfoundland and Labrador Association for the Deaf, 1996). In 2010, the school was closed. The report indicated that there were no new enrolments for the fall of 2010 and no new enrolments set for the next five years (CBC, 2010). However, there is still a difference between inclusivity as a societal norm in the province and how to deliver supports for diverse groups of students in inclusive school settings. Since 2006, some identifications of exceptionality in NL publicly funded schools have increased dramatically (e.g., 5896 with specific learning disorder; 1191 with a speech and language disorder) and, overall, the total number of students with exceptionalities increased by 2368 (Government of NL, 2017). Table 6.1 enumerates local students with exceptionalities in the 2016/2017 school year. The total number of students with exceptionalities has increased only slightly between 2006 (20%) and 2017 (22%). More recently, in 2020, NL can be described as having a 26% exceptionality rate where about one in four students are identified. Part of the high percentage is the association of our current exceptionalities with medical diagnoses. A medical diagnosis allows for the school-based identification of an educational exceptionality which leads to access to special education services.

Students, like the above students with such identifications, have undergone comprehensive assessments and are entitled, then, to IEPs and may also utilise multidisciplinary individual support services plans (ISSPs; Government of Newfoundland and Labrador, n.d.b), which includes options such as accommodations, modifications, alternate courses, and resources such as additional support services (e.g., educational assistants) and resources (e.g., assistive technology; Government of Newfoundland and Labrador, n.d.a).

Table 6.1 Number of Students with Exceptionalities (by Type) 2016/2017

Exceptionality	*Number of students per category*
Acquired brain injury	57
Developmental delay	2203
Giftedness	56
Hearing loss	280
Intellectual disability	898
Medical condition	417
Mental illness/mental health	1460
Neurodevelopmental disorder—Autism	1253
Neurodevelopmental disorder—ADHD	2886
Neurodevelopmental disorder—Other	759
Physical disability	194
Specific learning disorder	8901
Speech & language disorder	3408
Vision loss	86
Total exceptionalities (students may have more than one)	22,858
Total students with an exceptionality	14,710

Source: Adapted from Government of Newfoundland and Labrador (2017, p. 8).

Responsive Teaching and Learning Framework

In 2009, NL began its *Inclusive Education Initiative* with the goal of making schools places where all members of the school community feel safe, accepted, and included. A phased-in approach was adopted with new schools joining the initiative each year until 2017, at which time representatives from all public schools received training in inclusive practices, differentiated instruction, and collaborative teaching. Similar to the more commonly known *Response to Intervention* model, within such tiered approaches, an *exceptionality* is an educational determination that may be informed by diagnosis and used to advise teaching and learning and inform the provision of special education services; the purpose of exceptionality and comprehensive assessment is to inform teaching and learning.

Itinerants—school board-level specialists typically with graduate degrees—for inclusive education are responsible for supporting schools as they implement an inclusive education framework. They provide continuous and direct support to all schools through school visits, collaboration with teachers and school teams, and provision of in-service and professional development sessions.

Currently, NL is in the process of phasing in a responsive teaching and learning policy and service delivery model for special education, providing access to special education services based on appropriate data, not solely a medical or psychological diagnosis or identification, including strong evidence that a student's learning needs cannot be met through typical education practices (Government of Newfoundland & Labrador, 2020). Collaborative inquiry is used to inform responsive teaching and learning, whereby educators i) reflect on student progress and teacher practice; ii) develop an improvement plan; iii) implement the plan; and iv) gather and analyse evidence. Within this model, students continue to be supported by IEPs, which provide foundational information and programmes and supports, informed by a variety of data sources but always by assessment and exceptionality. In turn, students deemed exceptional are also supported by a programme planning team, a teaching and learning team, and a service delivery team, as well as a range of itinerant teachers. A responsive teaching and learning focus will guide the future of K-12 education in NL, ensuring that children will receive data-driven, flexible, and appropriate services with clear criteria for such service provision.

Public Perspectives on Inclusion

The most salient media stories reveal five overarching topics when it comes to K-12 inclusive public education (Canadian Broadcasting Corporation [CBC], 2017a, 2017b, 2017c). First and foremost, a generally positive view towards the philosophy of including students with disabilities in the classroom appears to exist; perhaps more so for those who tend to view inclusion as a right and responsibility. Second, that supports and services for students with exceptional learning needs are under-resourced. Third, students who are perceived as having the greatest needs likewise receive the largest share of available resources—including those with major behavioural challenges. Fourth, classroom teachers do not appear to be equipped for the diversity of needs, resources, and technologies that they encounter in inclusive classroom settings—especially so when it comes to students with significant behavioural challenges, who are Deaf and hard of hearing, or with mental health concerns. Fifth, there are challenges with the provision of supports and services based on the diagnosis and/or identification of learning difficulties.

Premier's Task Force

Following comprehensive stakeholder consultation (parents, students, educators, teacher educators, and community groups) and a comprehensive review of the system, the NL provincial government released *The Premier's Task Force on Improving Educational Outcomes* (Government of Newfoundland and Labrador, 2017). Here, the above-noted positive attitude towards the philosophy of inclusive classroom prevailed; however, some advocacy groups were divided on this topic. For example, the Newfoundland and Labrador Association for Community Living (NLACL) strongly supports the concept and the implementation of inclusion (Delaney, 2017), indicating that inclusive education is not just a school responsibility but also a family and community responsibility and a right rather than a theory, fostering a sense of belonging and not a system of segregation for everyone. Students who are educated together, come to appreciate diversity and view, and understand individuals with disabilities as a part of their community (Delaney, 2017).

According to the Government of Newfoundland and Labrador (2017), the provincial inclusion model was phased in beginning in September 2009 without a clear implementation policy. At that point, Newfoundland and Labrador's Department of Education and Early Childhood Education (DEECE) had begun an eight-year phase in of their model of inclusion with a draft format of this policy. The section that addressed inclusion identified nine key areas, which are outlined in Table 6.2.

Media Series

During this same period as the task force (Government of Newfoundland and Labrador 2017), the CBC completed a three-part series interviewing 30 teachers (current, retired elementary teachers, junior high, high school, administrators, instructional resource teachers, and guidance counsellors) on current classroom realities. These 30 educators were from various regions of the province and included individuals from both urban and rural contexts.

Part 1—Inside the Classroom: Inclusive Education

The overarching view from interviewees was that "theoretically inclusion is a wonderful idea" (CBC, 2017a). When they were asked to define inclusion, one participant described it as "all children within the system get the best education so they can be happy working citizens." Participants raised issues around inclusion related to teacher stress, teacher well-being (physical health, mental health), the impact of having diverse classrooms, and feelings of being a failure. They also discussed student stress, trauma/desensitisation, and violence (both those committing such acts and the classroom-wide impact of violent acts). Administrative issues such as class size, numbers of students with IEPs, limited student assistant supports, instructional resource time, and access to guidance services were also noted.

In this episode, teachers suggested that students with significant behavioural difficulties were impacting teacher and student well-being, and that these issues meant time away from curriculum and instruction. The overarching theme was that the limited resources that were available within the schools were being taken up by behavioural needs. Teachers reported feeling deflated because, at the end of the day, they believed that it was impossible to give students what they actually needed

Table 6.2 Components of Inclusion and Accompanying Issues with Implementation

Accessible curriculum	At this point, NL was not using practices like *Universal Design for Learning (UDL), Response to Intervention (RTI),* or *Differentiated Instruction (DI)*; therefore, encouragement was given for future curriculum development to use UDL principles to provide broader curricular accessibility.
Responding to behaviour	Responding to challenging behaviour depleted resources and teachers felt unprepared to deal with behaviour and mental health problems within the classroom.
Proactive special education	There was no formal system of early identification; rather, a system-wide attitude that students should not be identified prior to grade four. Special education remained a reactive approach to students who have fallen behind their peers in academic achievement.
Roles and environments	Confusion regarding roles and instructional environments existed, such as the understanding that all services would be provided within the general education classroom. Instructional resource teachers (IRTs) provided in-class services but struggled with space and guidance counsellors often provided special education services, perhaps without relevant training. Concerns were raised that students with mild difficulties were not being addressed in favour of provided services for more severe disabilities.
Child health services	A lack of collaboration and communication between health and education was evident, with specific issues in communication, transition planning, and speech-language services.
Classroom assistants	Issues such as *student assistants* moving from school to school and a lack of policy for hiring replacements and using substitutes were highlighted, as well as two previous reviews (Government of NL, 2000, 2007) that recommended the introduction of i*nstructional assistants.*
Partial days	Students were routinely sent home for behavioural reasons. Partial day placement was highlighted as becoming problematic and as a pretence of inclusion that leads to school *exclusion.*
Complex needs	Students with complex needs were more likely to be excluded or attend on partial days, especially students with autism spectrum disorder (ASD) and mental health difficulties. Transition planning (e.g., planning for life beyond school) was seldom used.
Systemic issues	Special education services were not well integrated. Often those with special education expertise were not included in the decision-making, policy development, curriculum development. Systems of data collection, internal and external professionals, and internal and externals systems had difficulty communicating.

within the inclusive environment. Teachers and administrators interviewed during this episode reported that students were not getting what they required as resources were often exhausted by problematic behaviours. The participants reported they believed many children within their classrooms did not feel safe, had been traumatised by seeing their teachers as victims of violence, or had been victimised themselves. This episode also indicated that average students and high-achieving students were not obtaining sufficient educational services.

The first episode also raised administrative issues; participants discussed many years of cutbacks that impacted human resources such as guidance counsellors, instructional resources, teachers, *student assistants*, speech/language services, occupational therapy, and psychologists. Participants also suggested that class size has continued to grow, simultaneously increasing teachers' workload.

Part 2—Inside the Classroom: Parent and Student Behaviour

Participants in this second episode discussed both student and parent behaviour, noting that there seemed to be an attitude that swearing is a part of everyday student language coming from homes into the classrooms, with very little (if any) disciplinary consequences (e.g., referral to the principal). They reported, in fact, that when parents are called, teachers could potentially hear the same offensive language. However, participants reported that some calls home resulted in family support while some resulted in parents hanging up on teachers. Teachers reported being threatened by irate parents, and parents getting confrontational during parent-teacher interviews. Participants believed in building relationships with families; however, they reported that many children are "falling between the cracks" (CBC, 2017a).

During this episode, teachers discussed the influence of technology on the children in their classrooms. Teachers discussed early exposure to violent video games and movies, and participants believed this exposure led to increasing mental health difficulties such as anxiety in their students, especially younger students who were not emotionally equipped to handle the content. Participants also reported concerns about unlimited access to technology, citing absences and tiredness following releases of new video games as their students would stay up all night just to finish the newly released game. Participants also reported negative impacts of social media both at school and after school. Teachers reported issues with students such as setting play or romantic dates, settling the score, and buying drugs through social media.

The participants indicated that attending school and completing academic tasks were in competition with sports. They raised issues of pressure placed on them by parents to let their children submit late assignments or write make-up quizzes because of time spent playing hockey or other sports. Several participants raised the issue of the district policy regarding no consequence to students for late assignments and the impact on the teachers who are obligated to always accept late assignments. As well, some of the participants raised the issue regarding student refusal to complete assignments when "they don't want to do what they don't want to do" (CBC, 2017a). They also raised the issue of students whining about assigned work, students putting in very little effort to complete their academic tasks or submitting assignments with nothing completed. Participants reported that all of the above issues led to feelings of inadequacy about their effectiveness as teachers.

The participants also discussed issues surrounding "safe schools" and defined safe schools as "children locked in a classroom for a period of time because of the behaviour of an individual student" (CBC, 2017a). Participants raised issues around increased anxiety from students and students feeling "not safe" at school. The participants discussed that they viewed the bigger issues that were politics and budgets.

Part 3—Inside the Classroom: Math and Full Day Kindergarten

In Part 3, the main theme for this third episode was the impact of the implementation of full day Kindergarten (FDK). The participants reported that FDK was implemented without additional resources, and FDK added significant stressors to an already financially stressed and overburdened school system. The participants noted that they believed the FDK programme resulted in resources designed for specific students being moved into Kindergarten programmes. For example, a Grade four teacher described the loss of instructional resource time (IRT)—additional, specialised teaching units—being transferred into the school's Kindergarten classrooms. Teachers in this episode discussed how FDK caused increased class size, increased supervision duty (200 minutes in a seven-day cycle), and decreased guidance services. The second theme addressed in the episode was difficulties with the province's math curriculum, which participants described as an "inch deep and mile wide" (CBC, 2017a). Related issues raised included new math methods being taught, parents not being able to help, and the impact of literacy or language difficulties on math success. Some students who previously may have excelled at math, for example, are now experiencing difficulty because they are not able to explain their processes.

Parents' Concerns

During the same period as the task force, the CBC interviewed a parent of children with exceptional learning needs (White, 2017). Essentially, the parent suggested that the needs of her children are not being met within the school system. The piece took the reader through a family who experienced difficulty with receiving needed services for their son with a specific learning disorder (SLD). White (2015) had previously interviewed the same family about services and supports for their child and the family reported that "not much had changed" and that they are constantly advocating for their child and the supports required. The parent raised issues related to a two-tier system, families paying out of pocket for tutors, speech services, and other needed services. The parent reported that her child, because he is quiet, often falls through the cracks in the system. The parent reported that because her child is not disruptive, he does not get the attention and services outlined in his IEP. These issues were also raised by teachers and the Premier's Task Force (Government of Newfoundland and Labrador, 2017).

In a separate media piece (Lord, 2019), a parent discussed a lack of resources and specialised services for their child. The school for children who are Deaf and hard of hearing closed in 2010. Children who are Deaf or hard of hearing are now placed within their community school without educators with the necessary skills to communicate with the children. This issue was also raised in the Premier's Task Force (Government of Newfoundland and Labrador, 2017).

An additional media piece addressed the experiences of three families with children with exceptional learning needs and their experiences during the time when schools were shut down during the COVID-19 global pandemic. Mullaley (2020), who interviewed three families, reported that the pandemic has placed additional burdens and stresses on families of children with exceptional learning needs in NL. They reported that, with services stopped during the pandemic, all of the care fell on the parents. While children who are typically developing may have access to Google classroom, this venue was developed for teaching typically developing children and was reported as less helpful for children with disabilities such as cerebral palsy, Down syndrome, ASD, and global developmental delay (Mullaley, 2020). The main message was that the Newfoundland and Labrador English School District (NLESD) cannot deliver remote programmes and provide the necessary supports for these children when other resources are withdrawn, and families are left on their own to provide for all the needs of their children.

The Finland Context

Finland is a rather small European country with around 5.5 million inhabitants and low population density. Finland is part of the European Union but, related to the education policy, every member country follows its own legislation. Finland has ratified the UNESCO's (1994) *Salamanca Statement for Framework for Action on Special Needs Education* as well the United Nation's *Convention on the Rights of Persons with Disabilities*;[1] however, the concept of inclusion is not adopted to legislation, although the direction of support services has been developed step-by-step to that direction during past decades (Jahnukainen & Itkonen, 2021).

Although the history of Finnish *folk education* starts from the late 1800s, it started to develop to more comprehensive direction after Finnish independence from Russian rule in 1917, when the first *Compulsory Education Act* was enacted in 1921. However, it took many decades for every student to be included in the same comprehensive school system. Until the early 1970s, there was a parallel school system with shorter practical and longer academic routes. During the 1970s, comprehensive school (direct translation: *basic school*), lasting nine years, was implemented to the whole country for children beginning at age seven. This was also the start of the expansion of low threshold support services in addition to more traditional full time special education provisions taking place in special schools and self-contained special classes. This model of so-called part time special education provisions within general education schools was introduced. Until the end of the 1980s, this model of support was expanded as the main way of delivering additional support to any students with difficulties in learning. As a last group, students with severe intellectual disabilities joined compulsory education in 1997. Prior to this date, their education was organised by the social welfare services (Jahnukainen & Korhonen, 2003).

The Basic Education Act of 1998 introduced for the first time IEP, which were needed for students in full time special education. The same law also made it officially possible for the instruction of a student considered in need of fulltime special education to be organised based on the IEP in the general education classroom. Even here, *inclusion* is not a term used officially, as Finnish legislation offers placement options "in conjunction of other instruction" (Basic Education Act, 1998). In practice, this means that every child is supposed to enrol in their neighbourhood school. Even though special schools for students exist, the number of special schools as separate institutions has decreased steadily (see Figure 6.1). The special schools serve students with severe disabilities/disorders municipally, regionally, or nationally (e.g., hospital schools and state reform schools).[2]

With the amendment of the *Basic Education Act* in 2010, the special education system was reformulated as a three-tiered system of *Learning and Schooling Support*. Tier 1 (general support) consists of mainly actions made by the regular classroom teacher in terms of differentiation as well as in terms of school-wide efforts to meet the diverse needs of students. This meant transferring more responsibility to classroom teachers as well as the school personnel as a community. Tier 2 (intensified support) consists of remedial support by the class teacher, co-teaching with the special educator, and temporal individual or small group learning with the part time special educator. In practice, this is quite close to the former definition of *part time special education*. Tier 3 (special support) consists of the whole continuum of special education services

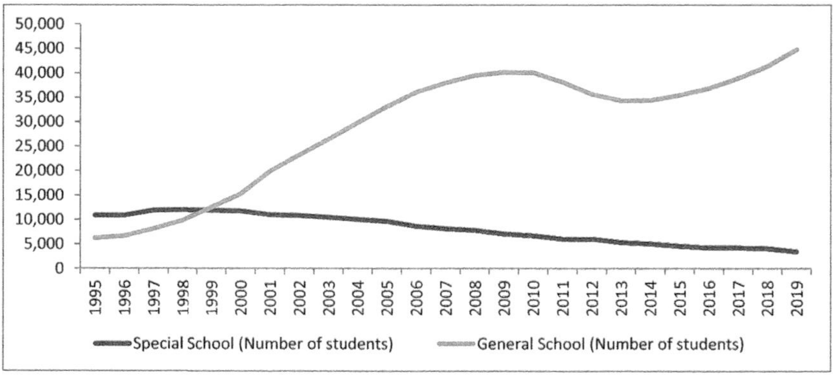

Figure 6.1 Comprehensive School Students Transferred to Full Time Special Education by Grounds for Decision in 2010 (OSF, 2010).

from full time general education to a special school placement and is mostly equivalent with the previous definition of *fulltime special education* (Jahnukainen & Itkonen, 2016).

Due to the *Basic Education Act* reform in 2010, the official statistics related to special education were revised: The gathering of the number of students by disability or learning difficulty was discontinued. From 2011 onwards, the official statistics report only the number of students at the Tier 2 and Tier 3 levels and the placement options of the students at the Tier 3 level, but no information about the reasons for those supports were collected nationwide. Based on the latest available statistics from 2010, the largest disability group (Finnish definition is a *ground for decision*) was students with dysphasia (known also as specific language impairment [SLI]). However, the unspecified group (other reason) was even larger (Table 6.3).

Using the official statistics, it is, however, possible to follow the development of the change of learning environments of students at the Tier 3 level. The decrease of special school provision has been consistent. At the same time, the number of Tier 3 level students in general schools has increased. It is noteworthy that the effect of the funding reform launched in 2010 together with the reform to the tiered system can be seen in the drop of Tier 3 level students in general education schools between the years 2010–2015. Previously, the funding made available through a system of government transfers offered higher funding for Tier 3 students, but after reform, the formula was based on the number of compulsory school-aged students; this is a form of census-based funding (Pulkkinen & Jahnukainen, 2016).

A large-scale national study showed that that the funding reform clearly incentivised municipalities to decrease identification rates for students in special education and to diminish special education

Table 6.3 Comprehensive School Students Transferred to Full Time Special Education by Grounds for Decision in 2010

Ground for decision	*Total (n)*
Severely delayed development	2749
–of whom most severely handicapped	1355
Slightly delayed development	7542
Cerebral dysfunction, physical disability or similar	7344
Emotional disturbance or social maladjustment	5894
Learning difficulties related to autism or Asperger's syndrome	1382
Learning difficulties caused by impaired linguistic development (dysphasia)	9873
Visual impairment	252
Hearing impairment	420
Other reason	11,254
Total	46,710
Share of students in comprehensive school (%)	8.5

Source: Official Statistics of Finland (OSF) (2010).

provision (Pulkkinen et al., 2020). In the longer run, the number of Tier 3 students in general education schools has again started to grow (see Figure 6.1).

Public Discussion in Finland

The discussion about the direction of handling *challenging students* in Finnish compulsory school has been under constant debate since the launch of *Learning and Schooling support schema* (effective from fall 2011 onwards). On the front line have been teachers' voices as well as opinions from the Finnish Teachers' Union. Teacher representatives have been complaining about how the new tiered system and "forced change to inclusion" has increased the number of students in their classrooms and the number of students who are not receiving enough additional supports (Honkasilta et al., 2019). The Finnish Broadcasting Company (YLE) has nurtured critical perspectives on schools by featuring parents' experiences of unsuccessful inclusion/integration (e.g., YLE, 2018b). At the same time, some parents might need to fight for possibilities for their child with disabilities to be able to participate in an inclusive classroom (YLE, 2018a). National research tells us that there are huge differences between municipalities in terms of how the tiered system is implemented (e.g., Pulkkinen & Jahnukainen, 2016). Some municipalities have taken rather progressive steps in placing all students in general education and others have decided to decrease the Tier 3 decisions and replace those with not so demanding Tier 2 decisions (Pulkkinen & Jahnukainen, 2016). This confusing situation was borne because there are no detailed national guidelines in terms of organising the support; the implementation is left for municipalities to be decided. Therefore, in the current Government Programme (2019), it has been stated that the legislation and procedures related to inclusive education should be clarified. The Prime Minister's office and Ministry of Education and Culture has now launched a development programme titled *Right to Learn (2020–2022),* which aims to create a new road map for organising special education. Interestingly, it seems that organising inclusive and special education is going to be one key topic in the field of education policy for the municipal election during the spring of 2021. The leading newspaper in Finland published in February 2021 a rather constructive editorial stating "there will be solutions for the challenge of inclusion" (Helsingin Sanomat, 2021b). This was a comment for the campaign start of the Centre Party of Finland demanding "critical examination of the teaching special students in same groups with the other students" (Helsingin Sanomat, 2021a).

Conclusion

"Despite our best intentions, even well-designed policies can be poorly implemented, constrained by financial resources and the availability of professional competence, and inevitably interpreted in ways that reflect the historical and cultural experiences of specific communities" (Eisenman & Ferretti, 2010, p. 264).

The education of students with additional needs (referred to as disabilities, difficulties, impairments, exceptionalities, etc.) is a highly important topic in education policy globally. Although there might seem to be a shared commitment between different countries and school systems at the ideological level, the local socio-political context as well as historical development will often play a major part in the final decision-making and, in particular, the implementation of certain policies.

In this chapter, we have described the current situation regarding strategies to organise education for students with special educational needs in the province of NL and in the country of Finland. The rationale for this comparison is that both jurisdictions have high general standards of living and a long-lasting commitment to develop the public education system. Our intention has not been to evaluate the policies but rather to investigate the direction in education policies and implementation.

We can summarise that, in a broader picture, the long-standing development has been relatively similar in both jurisdictions: The direction has been from mainly specialised services towards teaching every student in a general classroom. Although the commitment of NL seems to be stronger to implement inclusive environments, it seems that, in both school systems, there exist both inclusive and specialised placement options, at least for some students. Another similarity is that, in both systems, a tiered support model has been used: in Finland, a rather unique model of *Learning and Schooling* support, and in NL, as in other Canadian jurisdictions, a version of the response to interventions adopted based on examples from the United States (e.g., McIntosh et al., 2011).

The most evident difference seems to be in current ways of defining and categorising special educational needs. Finland has abandoned the use of any disability category since 2011; the decisions to offer support in any of the tiers of the Finnish Learning and Schooling support system is based on pedagogical grounds, and those decisions are not directly linked to any medical or psychological diagnosis. In the NL model, the 14 exceptionalities (including giftedness) are based on medical diagnosis. However, based on the older definitions used in Finland, it can be assumed that, in the end, rather similar groups of students are still served in both school systems, although it might be that the used vocabulary is based on different traditions.

The total population served in special education programmes has been growing in many countries over the last decades (e.g., Richardson & Powell, 2011). This seems to be the case in NL as well as in Finland. The share of students with exceptionalities in NL is relatively high compared to many other countries or jurisdictions, but it might be explained by demographics and may be part of the impetus for moving towards a response to intervention model whereby students receive an intervention prior to formal identification. The special education statistics in Finland are challenging to compare to any other school system's because the statistics are based on a K-9 compulsory system rather than K-12 characteristic of many other countries (e.g., Graham & Jahnukainen, 2011). If counting only students at the Tier 3 level, the share of students with significant support needs is 8.5% (OSFL, 2019). However, if the students at the Tier 2 level are also considered, the total share is around 20% (OSFL, 2019, and thus closer to the numbers from NL (Government of Newfoundland and Labrador, 2017).

It is interesting that, considering both school systems, the public discussion has been relatively vivid. The debate about the rights of students with special needs and the teachers attentive to workload concerns seems to be rather universal topics. There seems to be some shared issues to be solved.

Notes

1. UN CRPD was launched in 2006 (UN 2017). Finland was among the first nations to sign it in 2007; however, due to the need to change several other related national laws first, Finland ratified it 10 years later in 2016 (https://www.ykliitto.fi/un-association-of-finland).
2. https://valtionkoulukodit.fi/en/ and https://www.valteri.fi/en/

References

Basic Education Act 628/1998.https://www.finlex.fi/fi/laki/kaannokset/1998/en19980628.pdf

Canadian Broadcasting Company (CBC). (2010, August 2). *Newfoundland school for the deaf set to close.* https://www.cbc.ca/news/canada/newfoundland-labrador/newfoundland-school-for-the-deaf-to-close-1.875906

Canadian Broadcasting Corporation (CBC). (2017a, February 6). *Inside the classroom: Inclusive Education—Part 1* [Video]. YouTube. https://www.youtube.com/watch?v=47PfLkTP80I

Canadian Broadcasting Corporation (CBC). (2017b, February 13). *Inside the classroom: Parent and student behaviour—Part 2* [Video]. YouTube. https://www.youtube.com/watch?v=xuo1U-qnPs4

Canadian Broadcasting Corporation (CBC). (2017c, February 20). *Inside the classroom: Math and full day kindergarten—Part 3* [Video]. YouTube.

Canadian Charter of Rights and Freedoms, s 7, Part 1 of the Constitution Act, 1982, being Schedule B to the Canada Act 1982 (UK), 1982, c 11.

Centre for Distance Learning and Innovation. (n.d.). *About us.* https://www.cdli.ca/about-us.html

Delaney, A. (2017, February 11). "Not just a nice idea": The importance of inclusion in and beyond the classroom. *Canadian Broad Casting Company (CBC)*. https://www.cbc.ca/news/canada/newfoundland-labrador/inclusion-education-importance-1.3977102

Eisenman, L., & R. Ferretti, R. (2010). Changing conceptions of special education. *Exceptional Children, 76*(3), 262–264.

Government of Newfoundland and Labrador. (2000). Supporting learning: Ministerial panel on educational delivery in the classroom. Department of Education and Early Child Development.

Government of Newfoundland and Labrador. (2007). Focusing on students: Report of the ISSP/Pathways Commission. Department of Education and Early Child Development.

Government of Newfoundland and Labrador. (2017). *The Premier's task force on improving educational outcomes. Now is the time.* https://www.gov.nl.ca/education/files/task_force_report.pdf

Government of Newfoundland and Labrador. (2020). *Responsive teaching and learning policy.* https://www.gov.nl.ca/education/files/RTL-Policy.pdf

Government of Newfoundland and Labrador. (n.d.a). Department of Education and Early Childhood Development. https://www.gov.nl.ca/education/k12/inclusion/

Government of Newfoundland and Labrador. (n.d.b). Department of Education and Early Childhood Development. *Services delivery model for students with exceptionalities.* https://www.gov.nl.ca/education/forms/studentsupport/sdmodel/

Graham, L., & Jahnukainen, Markku (2011): Wherefore Art Thou, Inclusion? Analysing the Development of Inclusive Education in New South Wales, Alberta and Finland. Journal of Education Policy 26 (2), 263–288.

Helsingin Sanomat. (2021a). *Keskusta haluaa "tarkastella kriittisesti" erityisoppilaiden opettamista samoissa ryhmissä muiden kanssa.* https://www.hs.fi/politiikka/art-2000007790995.html

Helsingin Sanomat. (2021b). *Koulujen inkluusion ongelmiin löytyy ratkaisuja* https://www.hs.fi/paakirjoitukset/art-2000007800482.html

Honkasilta, J., Ahtiainen, R., Hienonen, N., & Jahnukainen, M. (2019). Inclusive and special education and the question of equality in education: The case of Finland. In. M. Schuelka, C. Johnstone, G. Thomas, & Alfredo Artiles (Eds.), *The SAGE handbook on inclusion and diversity in education* (pp. 481–495). SAGE.

Jahnukainen, M., & Itkonen, T. (2016). Tiered intervention. History and trends in Finland and the United States. *European Journal of Special Needs Education, 31*(1), 140–150.

Jahnukainen, M., & Itkonen, T. (2021). Steps to Inclusion? The role of tiered intervention in Finland and in the United States. In A. Köpfer, J.W. Powell, & R. Zahnd (Eds.), *International handbook of inclusive education. Global, national and local perspectives* (pp. 345–356). Barbara Budrich.

Jahnukainen, M., & Korhonen, A. (2003). Integration of students with severe and profound intellectual disabilities into the comprehensive school system: Teachers' perceptions of the education reform in Finland. *International Journal of Disability, Development and Education, 50*(2), 169–180.

Lord, R. (2019, November 2). *"They are hurting him": Newfoundland family fights for education equality.* Global News. https://globalnews.ca/news/6113747/ewfoundland-human-rights-complaint/

Maich, K., Hill, R., & Somma, M. (2018). Canadian school programs for students with emotional/behavioral disorders: A decade of programs, policy, and practice. *Emotional and Behavioural Difficulties, 23*(4), 441–456.

Maich, K., & Sider, S. (2019). Special education needs and disabilities in secondary education (Canada). *Bloomsbury Education and Childhood Studies.*

McIntosh, K., MacKay, L. D., Andreu, T., Brown, J. A., Mathews, S., Gietz, C., & Bennett, J. L. (2011). Response to intervention in Canada: Definitions, the evidence base, and future directions. *Canadian Journal of School Psychology, 26*(1) 1, 18–43.

Mullaley, R. (2020, April 24). Newfoundland and Labrador children with disabilities are not getting help they need during the pandemic, parents say. *The Telegram.* https://www.saltwire.com/newfoundland-labrador/news/newfoundland-and-labrador-children-with-disabilities-not-getting-help-they-need-during-pandemic-parents-say-442032/

Newfoundland and Labrador Association for the Deaf. (1996). *NLAD history.* http://www.nlad.org/history

Newfoundland and Labrador English School District (NLESD). (n.d.a). *Hospital schools* https://www.nlesd.ca/schools/schoolprofile.jsp?id=270

Newfoundland and Labrador English School District (NLESD). (n.d.b). *Newfoundland and Labrador youth centre.* https://www.nlesd.ca/schools/schoolprofile.jsp?id=575

Newfoundland and Labrador English School District (NLESD). (n.d.c). *Pathfinders learning centre.* https://sites.google.com/a/nlesd.ca/pathfinder/admissions

Official Statistics of Finland (OSF). (2010). *Comprehensive school pupils transferred to special education by ground for decision of acceptance or transfer in 2010.* http://www.stat.fi/til/erop/2010/erop_2010_2011-06-09_tau_004_en.html

Official Statistics of Finland (OSF). (2019). *Comprehensive school pupils having received special support, 1995–2019.* http://www.stat.fi/til/erop/2019/erop_2019_2020-06-05_tau_007_en.html

Pulkkinen, J., & Jahnukainen, M. (2016). Finnish reform of the funding and provision of special education: The views of principals and municipal education administrators. *Educational Review, 68*(2), 171–188.

Pulkkinen, J., Räikkönen, E., Jahnukainen, M., & Pirttimaa, R. (2020). How do educational reforms change the share of students in special education? Trends in special education in Finland. *European Educational Research Journal, 19*(4), 364–384.

Richardson, J., & Powell, J.J.W. (2011). Comparing special education. Origins to contemporary paradoxes. Stanford University Press: Stanford, CA.

Thompson, S., & Timmons, V. (2017). Authentic inclusion in two secondary schools: "It's the full meal deal. It's not just in the class. It's everywhere." *Exceptionality Education International, 27*(1), 62–84.

United Nations (UN). (2017). *Convention on the rights of persons with disabilities (CRPD).* www.un.org/development/desa/disabilities/convention-on-the-rights-of-personswith-disabilities.html

United Nations Educational, Scientific and Cultural Organization (UNESCO). (1994). *Salamanca statement and framework for action on special needs education* http://unesdoc.unesco.org/images/0009/000984/098427eo.pdf.

White, J. (2015, May 25). *Inclusion model can mean extra cost for some parents.* Canadian Broadcasting Company (CBC). [Video]. https://www.cbc.ca/news/canada/newfoundland-labrador/inclusion-model-can-mean-extra-costs-for-some-parents-1.3082487

White, J. (2017, February 8). *"It's a continuing battle": Parents of children with learning disabilities still struggling with inclusion.* Canadian Broadcasting Company (CBC). https://www.cbc.ca/news/canada/newfoundland-labrador/learning-disabilities-inclusive-education-1.3972329

YLE. (2018a). Erityislapsen koulunkäynti on jatkuvaa taistelua – asennekasvatukselle kouluissa huutava tarve [The schooling of a special child is constant fight – There is a gross need for an attitude change at schools]. https://yle.fi/uutiset/3-10154280

YLE. (2018b). Kysely: Kerro, saako lapsesi tarpeeksi tukea koulussa – vai joudutko taistelemaan erityislapsesi puolesta? [A questionnaire: Tell us, does you child receive enough support at school – Or should you fight for your child with special needs?]. https://yle.fi/uutiset/3-10174932

7 Education for Young Refugees

Processes of Inclusion and Exclusion in Munich and Toronto

Annette Korntheuer

Introduction

> We [are] not targeting the refugee students any more than the students from the high poverty neighbourhoods, than the students with special education needs, or with English language development needs. We are just trying to say that there are students with a lot of different needs that you need to be aware of in order to effectively educate them.
>
> (Mr. Mitchell [pseudonym], Secondary School Principal, Toronto)

Young refugees, as the Canadian principal Mr. Mitchell makes clear, are only one group among many whose special needs must be taken into account in educational institutions. Canada and its provinces stand for integrated education systems and for inclusive schooling. In contrast, Germany, and Bavaria in particular, focus on early ability tracking in separate school types (Esser, 2016). This chapter analyses processes of *inclusion* and *exclusion* of young refugees in these two school settings (Korntheuer, 2016, Korntheuer et al., 2018a, 2018b).[1]

The sharp increase in the number of asylum seekers and refugees in Canada and Germany in 2015 and 2016 poses both a major social challenge and the opportunity to effectively meet the needs of newcomers to both countries (Immigration, Refugees and Citizenship Canada [IRCC], 2017; Korntheuer et al., 2020; Sachverständigenrat für Integration und Migration [SVR], 2017). Between 2015 and 2020, 158,480 refugees were brought to Canada under the so-called resettlement scheme (IRCC, 2021). The aim of *resettlement* is the permanent integration of refugees from the often-overburdened neighbouring states of the countries directly affected by armed conflict (Korntheuer et al., 2017). In Germany, on the other hand, the largest numbers of refugees come to the country as asylum seekers. In 2015, more than 890,000 asylum seekers were registered in Germany. In the same year, 476,649 persons applied for asylum and 140,915 were granted the right

DOI: 10.4324/9781003204572-9

to stay (Korntheuer et al., 2017; SVR, 2017). Since 2017, the number of new arrivals in Germany has temporarily fallen sharply, but central challenges remain: to improve access to education for those who are already in the country and to provide effective supports for newcomers in the age of displacement (Castles et al., 2014).

Since 2015, there is a growing body of empiric evidence on specific influencing factors for the educational participation of refugee students (Brenner & Kia-Keating, 2017; Bunar, 2018; Crul et al., 2019 Lechner & Huber, 2015; Maurice & Will 2021; Pastoor, 2017; Pavia Lareiro, 2019; Vanderplaat, 2017; Will et al., 2018). Research on newly arrived migrant students emphasises two main fields of influencing factors: (i) school structural factors, such as integration/transition models, the availability of institutionalised assessment, ability tracking, segregation, available support systems, and school cultures; and (ii) individual factors, such as the socio-economic status of the families, age at arrival, educational attainment in the country of origin or transition countries, and language abilities (Diehl et al., 2016). Both fields are closely interrelated. Refugee students can be shown as a particularly vulnerable group that is frequently affected by exclusion in the education system due to individual and structural factors.

Studies stress that due to the pre-, trans-, and post-forced migration situations, most refugee students have interrupted school careers to some degree (Lechner & Huber, 2015; UNESCO, 2018; Will et al., 2018). Furthermore, the living situation in camps and shelters is frequently criticised as a significant barrier to the successful educational participation of refugee children and youths (Crul et al., 2019; Korntheuer et al., 2017; ; Vey & Gunsch, 2021; Vogel & Stock, 2017). The UNESCO world education report states that regulations around asylum can have a negative impact on the educational access of refugee children and youths (UNESCO, 2018). For Germany's context, this has been broadly discussed (Robert Bosch Expertenkommission, 2015; Schroeder, 2003). Nevertheless, resilience and high educational aspirations are important positive factors in quantitative and qualitative studies (Hynie et al., 2012; Korntheuer et al., 2017; Will et al., 2018; Worbs & Bund, 2016).

In this chapter, the terms *exclusion* and *inclusion* are defined on the basis of system-theoretical considerations. The first step is to examine the basic theoretical context. Due to gaps in knowledge, the study employed a qualitative and explorative research design. Data collection, sampling, and data analysis are clarified in a second step. The presentation of the results focuses on processes of inclusion and exclusion at both locations. References to theories of institutional and structural discrimination become clear in the discussion of the results. Finally, in the conclusion, the question arises as to how both cities could learn from each other in order to enable more inclusive models of schooling young refugees and which further research projects should be pursued.

Theoretical Context: Systems Theory and Institutional Discrimination

Mechanisms of inclusion and exclusion in educational systems are examined in this chapter from a systems-theoretical perspective (Kronauer, 2010; Luhmann, 1997; Stichweh, 2009). If we are to talk about the extent to which people move *within* systems (inclusion) or are *debarred* from systems (exclusion), it becomes necessary to consider the limits of systems and their environment. Systems observe themselves and other systems in order to respond to environmental demands and balance them with the system's own needs. This relation of systems to each other is expressed in the term *system reference*. In accordance with the theory of system references, societal sub-systems can influence each other. It can be assumed, for example, that the educational system is often strongly influenced by other functional systems, for example, by legal regulations (Merkens, 2006).

The theory of institutional discrimination attempts to address the relationship between school as an organisation and its social environment using "system-theoretical means" (Gomolla & Radtke, 2009, p. 12). In their study, Gomolla and Radtke (2009) reveal the mechanisms of institutional discrimination of students with a migration background. The concept of membership plays a central role regarding inclusion or exclusion in the schools. Membership criteria of the school organisation are often constructed as excluding conditions for children with a migration background. The membership role is associated with a number of tasks, expectations of action, and behaviour. In particular, membership criteria such as language and school readiness, age, parental commitment, and cultural connectedness have an impact on students' access to schooling institutions. However, the central point of reference for the interpretation of the criteria lies in the organisation of the school itself, which must remain functional (Gomolla, 2013; Gomolla & Radtke, 2009). A school can both control the size of its classes and influence the homogeneity of their student body through broadening and restricting membership criteria. However, the maintenance of the institution is at the centre of organisational functionality. This can lead to schools specialising in newly arrived migrant children simply because they are threatened with closure. Special provisions in so-called welcome-, integration-, or transition-classes create an institutional space that is ascribed to children with a migration background. In the sense of system theory, mechanisms of complexity reduction, autopoiesis, and system reference become effective (Hasse & Schmidt, 2012).

As *direct mechanisms of institutional discrimination*, Gomolla and Radtke name the location of transition classes at lower secondary schools only. The application of quotas for foreigners, increased referral to non-selective comprehensive schools, and restrictive decision-making practice regarding the transition to academic tracks in secondary schools are also mentioned. *Direct institutional discrimination* is also created through *positive discrimination* with the intention of providing support in parallel and separated support systems, even if this often has negative consequences and side effects. *Indirect institutional discrimination* usually results from the uniform treatment of diverse students. The same rules are applied to children with a migration experience as they do to German first-language speakers, which leads to structural discrimination against one group because the specific learning requirements of second language learners are not taken into account (Feagin & Feagin, 1986; Gomolla & Radtke, 2009).

Using Luhmann's concept of *system levels,* Hormel (2007) proposes the distinction between *interactional, institutional,* and *structural discrimination.* Interactional discrimination refers to direct interactions between individuals and groups as well as to social constructions of self and others. Hormel also understands *institutional* as structures in organisations that lead to the discrimination of certain groups. The level of structural discrimination reveals itself as: "Economic, political and legal discrimination in the immigration society centrally dependent on the institution of citizenship or the associated allocation of different residence permits" (Gomolla & Radtke, 2009, p. 255).

Citizenship and legal status categories create a state-regulated basis for selective access to organisations and functional systems. They play key roles in determining the modes of exclusion and inclusion in law, economics, health care, and, not least, education (Hormel, 2007).

Methodology

Research Design and Leading Questions

Educational structures and educational experience of young refugees were investigated within an explorative, qualitative study. Data were collected through responsive interviews with young refugees ($N = 40$) in Toronto and Munich and as well as through expert interviews ($N = 25$) in both cities (Korntheuer, 2016, 2019; Korntheuer et al., 2018a, 2018b). The data from the expert interviews led to the reconstruction of educational system structures for young refugees on the basis of structural content analysis (Mayring, 2008). The interviews with the young refugees were used to analyse their educational experiences (Korntheuer, 2019). This chapter refers to the results of the structural content analysis of the interviews with experts.

Based on the 25 interviews with experts in Munich and Toronto, educational structures of young refugees were described and their connection to processes of inclusion and exclusion at both research locations was reconstructed. The study is based on the following research questions:

1. What structures operate for young refugees in Munich and Toronto in the areas of informal, non-formal, and formal education?[2]
2. What are the structural resources in terms of support systems and what are structural barriers?
3. Which processes of inclusion and exclusion can be determined?
4. What are the differences and similarities between the structures in Munich and Toronto?

Sample and Access to the Field

For this part of the study, 13 interviews were conducted in Toronto and 12 interviews with experts in Munich. To achieve a high variance in the data, the interview partners were selected taking into account different fields of work and with different functions and professional backgrounds. Within this data pool, a further theoretical sampling could then be carried out. Eight interviews with experts were selected with regard to maximum and minimum contrast between the characteristics of the interview partners and the categories addressed in the interview (Table 7.1). Further interviews from the data pool were included to deepen and contrast the categories. Access to the interview partners was gained through professional networks.

Data Collection and Analysis

The expert interviews were conducted as semi-structured qualitative interviews. In the form of systematic expert interviews, the data collection was primarily oriented towards the generation of information (Kruse, 2015).

The qualitative content analysis according to Mayring (2008) was chosen as the analysis method. This places a theory-based coding scheme at the beginning of the analysis. According to Mayring (2008), its goal is "to filter out and summarise certain topics, contents and aspects from the material" (p. 89). The technical literature, however, criticises this procedure devised by Mayring for not being open enough. Thus, a rigid category system leads to the loss of inadmissible or unfitting aspects (Gläser & Laudel, 2009, p. 199). Reinhoffer (2008) describes a suitable solution for dealing with deductive and inductive processes with respect to the research work described here. He combines both procedures by deriving formal categories from a metatheory, but the differentiation of subcategories is carried out inductively (Reinhoffer, 2008).

Table 7.1 Sample of the Study

	Munich[a] *N* = *12*	*Toronto*[a] *N* = *13*	*Total*[a] *N* = *25*
Professional background			
Teaching	5	4	9
Social work/social pedagogy	4	4	8
Others	3	2	5
Functional role			
Principal/programme director	5	2	7
Settlement worker and social worker	3	4	7
Teacher	2	2	4
Other	2	4	6
Work experience with young refugees			
Less than 5 years	2	3	5
5–10 years	3	1	4
Longer than 10 years	7	2	9
Personal migration or refugee experience	1	7	8
Institution			
School	3	6	9
Community organisation	5	7	12
Other	2	0	2

Note

[a] Values missing in some categories.

Results: Forms and Processes of Inclusion and Exclusion in Toronto and Munich

Inclusion in Specialised Education in Munich versus Inclusive School System in Toronto

The schooling of young refugees in Munich mainly takes place in programmes and courses specially targeting this group. These include language courses, school projects, the state-recognised *SchlaU Schule*,[3] and transition and integration classes at vocational schools.

The needs and life situations of adolescents and young adults are at the centre of the communicative processes and schooling structures of the specialised education courses. Here, both the far-reaching and individualised needs for support and the legal framework of asylum law can be considered and dealt with. Thus, instead of feelings of hopelessness and dependence, those of participation, belonging, and recognition are fostered among young refugees. This emotional stabilisation can also protect children and youth in other ways (e.g., when the fundamental feeling of insecurity and existential fears are triggered by the asylum process). The advantages of specialised courses must nevertheless be weighed against the disadvantages of segregated educational processes.

In Toronto, inclusion mechanisms are encouraged at all levels of formal secondary education. The following quotation from a principal in Toronto describes the orientation towards a diverse and multicultural student body:

> I think that what we trying to do is to establish a culture that shows an understanding that for a variety of reasons students cannot always fulfil the institutional expectation without some flexibility and some support.
>
> (Mr. Mitchell *[pseudonym]*, Principal, secondary school, Toronto)

The membership conditions for participation at the secondary school are very open with regard to age (up to 21 years of age), performance level (including students with special learning needs and limited former schooling), and linguistic and literacy skills (e.g., including students who are illiterate and English Language Learners). These membership criteria represent effective inclusion conditions for young refugees. The regulations of the Ministry of Education also stipulate that students must have access to assessment and support systems (Rutokowsky, 2009).

Secondary schools in Toronto are places that involve community organisations. Inclusion in secondary school means, ideally, not only the possibility of obtaining a schooling certificate, but also, access to important social networks and support in obtaining legal status. Belonging to a community high school, the actors feel responsible for providing holistic support for the young refugees, as the Guidance Department's management makes clear here:

> We are a community high school; rather than just working on education we work on a lot of other aspects too, like health, mental health issues, we've got all kinds of agencies coming in, we've got 37 agencies to help work with the students.
>
> (Jenny *[pseudonym]*, Head of the Guidance Department, Toronto)

Risks of Exclusion through the Inter-Connection between Asylum Processes and Educational Biographies in Munich and Toronto

In both Munich and Toronto, the asylum system and the education system overlap, leading to specific risks of exclusion. In line with Hormel (2007), processes of structural discrimination can be shown for Munich:

- Securing legal status through low-threshold dual vocational training, which can (initially) lead to exclusion from certain segments of the vocational training system and to exclusion from further school-based education.
- Restriction of access to financial supports.

- Asylum-specific work restrictions and short-term residence permits.
- Living situations in initial reception facilities and mass shelters.

Young refugees cannot be considered as a homogeneous group. Some sub-groups are more exposed to risks of exclusion than others. Those who are still in the asylum procedure or whose asylum application has been rejected are particularly affected. Depending on their legal status, they are excluded from important areas of social participation. Accommodation in initial reception facilities and the shelter system for asylum seekers and the residence and housing obligations can be mentioned as forms of physical confinement leading to a high risk of exclusion. In the case of young refugees, processes of exclusion *from* society occur through the denial of rights and restrictive access to institutions as well as exclusion *in* society through partial exclusion from certain areas of education (Kronauer, 2010).

Interviews with experts in Toronto also show that the group of asylum seekers is strongly exposed to risks of exclusion. These result primarily from the asylum process and the limited access to rights and financial resources. The interview partners emphasise the following factors in particular:

- Exclusion from student loans and the imposition of (higher) international tuition fees, which leads to exclusion in the field of post-secondary education.
- Psychosocial burdens due to status uncertainty, resulting in absenteeism and discontinuation of educational processes.
- Difficult economic situation leading to summer jobs and undeclared work instead of summer courses and extracurricular activities.
- Negative housing conditions that leave little room for concentrated learning.
- Getting involved with illegal networks as an environment that leaves no room for educational processes.

The asylum process is accompanied by a psychosocial burden that can lead to the abandonment of educational careers, as described here by a settlement worker at school:[4] "Especially when they go through this immigration hearing period they need, their whole attention is on that more than school" (Ajith *[pseudonym]*, Settlement worker, Toronto).

Indirect Discrimination through Bureaucratic Routines in Toronto and Open Exclusion through Restrictive Membership Criteria and Declaration of "Non-Responsibility" in Munich

The analysis reveals bureaucratic routines in Toronto that act as indirect mechanisms of institutional exclusion in secondary schools. Thus, within secondary school, administrative routines are applied equally to all students without discriminatory intent but carry the risk of exclusion for some. The interviewees from the Newcomer Assessment Centre describe how several documents must be completed for youth to be admitted to a neighbourhood school. This bureaucratic process is often an obstacle for young refugees. One education professional points out that the Newcomer Assessment Centre has many incomplete documents. If teenagers or young adults do not pick them up, it is likely that they have not started attending secondary school in Toronto:

> They can't come to us because they don't have their documents. We can't give out the package. We can assess them, but we can't give out the package. Unless they have that. So, we have those files sitting here, just people waiting to get their documents together.
>
> (Carol [pseudonym], Education Professional at the Newcomer Assessment Centre, Toronto)

In the highly stratified Bavarian school system, on the other hand, the homogenisation of the student body continues to be an important functional feature. Grammar schools (Gymnasien) and mid-range secondary schools (Realschulen) construct their membership criteria regarding the language level in such a way that they largely represent excluding conditions for young refugees. They declare themselves not responsible for this group. In terms of system function, it makes no sense for these school types to offer language support if they have no interest in migrant and refugee students and the complexity and range of their programmes would have to increase significantly (Gomolla & Radtke, 2009). Another clear exclusion criterion is the age on arrival of the young refugees. If, however, young refugees and migrants are of great functional importance for securing the continued existence of the institution, their acceptance is assessed positively by the school administration. The principal of a lower secondary school in Munich addresses this very openly and clearly in an interview:

> To [put] it bluntly, it fills the schools for us ... in Bavaria at least in the Mittelschulen [lower secondary schools] and actually nationwide with the dramatic drop in the number of schoolchildren accessing lower secondary school, it's wonderful for us.
>
> (Mr. Huber *[pseudonym]*, Principal, lower secondary school, Munich)

The lower secondary school in Germany is a type of school that is increasingly becoming socially marginalised. Due to demographic change, the expansion of education, and the limited future prospects of students at lower secondary schools, there is growing difficulty to maintain the number of students at such schools (Autorengruppe Bildungsberichtserstattung, 2018; Link, 2012). Opening to the new target group makes sense from a systems-theoretical point of view for the maintenance of the institution.

Discussion of the Results

A comparison of the two cities Munich and Toronto proves to be very fruitful for analysis. It sharpens the perception of the educational structures pertaining to young refugees and opens spaces for thinking ahead for both contexts. The results provide indications for increased educational opportunities for young refugees through an orientation toward diversity and an inclusive school system. However, a differentiated view also reveals limits and possibilities for different sub-groups in the two education systems.

System References and Marginalisation

In the sense of system references, there is an overlap in both cities between the asylum system and the education system, thus creating specific barriers and leading to the marginalisation of young refugees. Especially affected are those young people who do not (yet) have a permanent legal status. A central finding for the situation in Munich is that accompanied minor refugees as well as young adult refugees who are accommodated in mass shelters are particularly affected by information barriers, poor institutional ties, and stressful living conditions. Research shows that the initial admission system and housing in shelters for asylum seekers also represent direct educational barriers (Lechner & Huber, 2015; Vogel & Stock, 2017). In Toronto, the uncertain legal status leads to exclusion from tertiary education and to unstable living conditions that can favour educational drop out (Clark-Kazak, 2017).

Specialisation, Segregation, and Inclusion

In the two cities under consideration, very different educational systems have developed. The results of the analysis show that the Bavarian school system continues to attempt to homogenise students by separating them into different school types and migrant and refugee classes. Young refugees can only take part in lessons at medium-range secondary schools and academic tracks if they master the German language at a very high level. The current state of research problematises the restrictive and selective school system, which particularly affects refugees as a marginalised group (Crul et al., 2019). For older students, it poses great challenges in particular as they cannot complete their schooling at the specified age (Barth & Guerrero Meneses, 2012). According to international and European law, such as the *International Convention for the Rights of the Child* and the *European Reception Directive*, Germany is obliged to grant refugee children similar access to education as its nationals (Vogel & Stock, 2017).

Regulations on compulsory schooling differ between all federal States. They range from access to compulsory schooling at the very start of the stay to three or six months after arrival, or whenever the refugee student is transferred from the first reception centre to the municipality (Vogel & Stock, 2017). Youths and young adults have legal access to preparatory classes in vocational school until the age of 18 in most federal States. Some States extended the age range for access to vocational education training (VET) to 21 years and, in exceptional cases, to 27 years (Robert Bosch Expertenkommission, 2015). Even so, attendance rates of the younger cohorts are positive with 95% of the 10- to 17-year-old refugees attending schools. A Germany-wide study indicates a possible trend that, especially for older refugees, the integration is difficult to realise: Thirty-three percent of the 17-year-olds in a recent survey are not a part of a school anymore (Pavia Lareiro, 2019).

The study presented here clearly shows that young refugees benefit from the very broad access to secondary school in Toronto. Up to the age of 22, they have access to educational opportunities. In addition, due to the equity and diversity strategies of the school boards, evaluation mechanisms and enforcement strategies are developed to support equal access of different social groups to achievement levels and school-leaving qualifications. Within this inclusive school system, too, separation of certain groups is a topic of discussion and streaming and placement practices are criticised (Shakia et al., 2010). Nevertheless, there are indications that effective inclusion mechanisms are taking place within the school system (Stermac et al., 2013).

Practical and Scientific Implications

A comparison of the two research fields of Munich and Toronto provides an opportunity to highlight the weaknesses and strengths of the educational system for young refugees at the respective locations. In particular, the opportunities provided by inclusive schooling will be discussed.

There is no clear answer to the question of whether students with special educational needs should be responded to in the form of separate specialised school support or through supported inclusion in regular classes. There is evidence that both forms of support show positive and negative dynamics (El-Mafaalani & Massumi, 2019). Young refugees, for example, emphasise the feeling of belonging in specialised classes. On the other hand, they reject the separation from peers and from regular schooling (Korntheuer, 2016). The school authorities in Toronto are offering partially integrated provisions. The special needs of English Language Learners are met in separate classes or by parallel support in English as an additional language. However, they are only implemented as transitional systems and consistent participation in regular classes (such as sports and art education) is grounded in school policies. Nevertheless, even in this system, routines are consolidated, which can lead to the continuation of support systems and to segregation from regular schooling. Loewen (2006) concludes that inclusion in regular courses is the better option for most groups of second language learners. Separate schooling can lead to isolation, discrimination, and stereotyping and severely limits contact with native speakers. In some cases, however, there may be good reasons for specialised schooling:

> There may be occasions where withdrawing them is appropriate. Reasons for withdrawal might include helping total beginners with basic English literacy, focusing on specific problems or assignments, and allowing traumatised student to develop a trusting relationship with an adult.
>
> (Loewen, 2006, p. 45)

As Bunar (2018) criticises in his comparison of school provisions for refugee students in four European countries, school systems tend to segregate newly arrived students for organisational, hence system functional, reasons:

> Instead of making every effort to include newly-arrived children into the mainstream, schools prefer to segregate them in their own classes and groups, not because it is in the best interests of children, but because it is anticipated as an easier model for schools themselves. (p. 16)

Concrete implementation in practice is of great importance. At the point of educational transition, dysfunctional routines and bureaucratic processes can arise that significantly restrict access to further educational opportunities. In Munich, young refugees would be given significantly broader access to various educational qualifications through inclusion in regular programmes. However, effective support mechanisms from specialised programmes and their orientation towards life situations of the students would then also have to be implemented in the regular schooling. Cerna (2019) proposes a holistic model for the integration of refugee students, considering social, emotional, and learning needs as well as individual, interpersonal, and school-level factors.

This study leads to a substantial underpinning and extension of the state of research, both regarding the description of successful inclusion structures and mechanisms of institutional and structural discrimination. Indications of successful participation in education as well as educational inequalities become clear. First, results from quantitative longitudinal studies indicate that the majority of refugee youths are attending non-academic schooling-tracks in Germany and youth from age 17 onward have a higher risk of being excluded from educational institutions (Pavia Lareiro, 2019). Both the focus on VET programmes for youths and the provisions in lower secondary schools can have negative long-term impacts on the educational trajectories and labour market allocation of this population. High educational aspirations and resilience can be undermined by the lack of structure for educational opportunity.

Notes

1. The results presented in this chapter are excerpts from the publication of the dissertation by Korntheuer (2016).
2. *Formal education* includes formal schooling, vocational education, and tertiary education, which is regulated by the States. *Informal education* involves more student choice and often takes place outside of schools and other formal education institutions (e.g., sports and arts clubs). Characteristics of informal education include spontaneity, immersion in a social context, and engagement with tasks related to life; informal education does not lead to certification or credentials (Tippelt, 2010).
3. The SchlaU School is a state-approved alternative school for young refugees aged 16 and over in Munich. SchlaU stands for analogous teaching and learning, while the abbreviation also means "smart" in (see SchlaU Schule, 2017).
4. Settlement workers support students in Toronto's public school boards who have immigrated to Canada in the past four years.

References

Autorengruppe Bildungsberichterstattung (Hrsg.). (2018). *Bildung in Deutschland 2018. Ein indikatorengestützter Bericht mit einer Analyse zu Wirkungen und Erträgen von Bildung. Gefördert mit Mitteln der Ständigen Konferenz der Kultusminister der Länder in der Bundesrepublik Deutschland und des Bundesministeriums für Bildung und Forschung.* https://www.bildungsbericht.de/de/bildungsberichte-seit-2006/bildungsbericht-2018/pdf-bildungsbericht-2018/bildungsbericht-2018.pdf

Barth, S., & Guerrero Meneses, V. (2012). Zugang jugendlicher Asylsuchender zu formellen Bildungssystemen in Deutschland: Zwischen Kompetenzen und strukturellen Problemlagen. https://isissozialforschung.de/docs/BildungszugängefürAsylsuchende.pdf

Brenner, M. E., & Kia-Keating, M. (2017). Psychosocial and academic adjustment among resettled refugee youth. *Annual Review of Comparative and International Education, 30*, 221–249.

Bunar, N. (2018). Introduction. In N. Bunar (Ed.), *Education: Hope for newcomers in Europe* (pp. 1–23). Education International.

Castles, S., Haas, H. D., & Miller, M. J. (2014). *The age of migration: International population movements in the modern world* (5th ed.). Palgrave Macmillan.

Cerna, L. (2019). Refugee education: Integration models and practices in OECD countries (OECD Education Working Papers No. 203). https://doi.org/10.1787/a3251a00-en

Clark-Kazak, C. (2017). Structural context for refugee claimants in Canada. In A. Korntheuer, P. Pritchard, & D. Maehler (Eds.), *GESIS working papers. Structural context of refugee integration in Canada and Germany* (pp. 127–132). GESIS Institut für Sozialwissenschaften.

Crul, M., Lelie, F., Biner, Ö., Bunar, N., Keskiner, E., Kokkali, I.,. . . Shuayb, M. (2019). How the different policies and school systems affect the inclusion of Syrian refugee children in Sweden, Germany, Greece, Lebanon and Turkey. *Comparative Migration Studies*, 7(1). https://doi.org/10.1186/s40878-018-0110-6

Diehl, C., Hunkler, C., & Kristen, C. (2016). Ethnische Ungleichheiten im Bildungsverlauf: Eine Einführung. In C. Diehl, C. Hunkler, & C. Kristen (Eds.), *Ethnische Ungleichheiten im Bildungsverlauf: Mechanismen, Befunde, Debatten* (pp. 3–31). Springer VS.

El-Mafaalani, A., & Massumi, M. (2019). Flucht und Bildung: Frühkindliche, schulische, berufliche und non-formale Bildung (Internationales Konversionszentrum Bonn (BICC), (Hrsg.), State-of-Research Papier 08a, Verbundprojekt ‚Flucht: Forschung und Transfer.' Bonn.

Esser, H. (2016). Bildungssysteme und ethnische Bildungsungleichheiten. In C. Diehl, C. Hunkler, & C. Kirsten (Eds.), *Ethnische Ungleichheiten im Bildungsverlauf. Mechanismen, Befunde, Debatten* (pp. 331–397). Springer VS.

Feagin, J. R., & Feagin, C. B. (1986, ©1978). *Discrimination American style: Institutional racism and sexism* (2nd ed.). R.E. Krieger Pub. Co.

Gläser, J., & Laudel, G. (2009). *Experteninterviews und qualitative Inhaltsanalyse. Als Instrumente rekonstruierender Untersuchungen* (3rd ed.). Springer VS.

Gomolla, M. (2013). Fördern und Fordern allein genügt nicht! Mechanismen institutioneller Diskriminierung von Migrantenkindern und -jugendlichen im deutschen Schulsystem. In G. Auernheimer (Ed.), *Schieflagen im Bildungssystem: Die Benachteiligung der Migrantenkinder* (5th ed., pp. 87–102). Springer VS.

Gomolla, M., & Radtke, F.-O. (2009). *Institutionelle Diskriminierung* (3rd ed.). Springer VS.

Hasse, R., & Schmidt, L. (2012). Institutionelle Diskriminierung. In U. Bauer, U. H. Bittlingmayer, & A. Scherr (Eds.), *Bildung und Gesellschaft. Handbuch Bildungsund Erziehungssoziologie* (pp. 883–899). VS Verlag für Sozialwissenschaften.

Hormel, U. (2007). *Diskriminierung in der Einwanderungsgesellschaft. Begründungsprobleme pädagogischer Strategien und Konzepte.* Springer VS.

Hynie, M., Guruge, S., & Shakia, Y. B. (2012). Family relationships of Afghan, Karen, and Sudanese refugee youth. *Canadian Ethnic Studies*, *44*(3), 11–28.

Immigration, Refugees and Citizenship Canada. (2017). *IRCC dataset on the open data portal.* www.cic.gc.ca/english/resources/statistics/menu-fact.asp

Korntheuer, A. (2016). *Die Bildungsteilhabe junger Flüchtlinge: Faktoren von Inklusion und Exklusion in München und Toronto.* Waxmann.

Korntheuer, A. (2019). Cause we come with the spirit of coming to school. Die Bildungserfahrungen von jungen Geflüchteten in München und Toronto. In A. Eberle, U. Kaminsky, L. Behringer, & U. Unterkolfer (Eds.), *Menschenrechte und Soziale Arbeit im Schatten des Nationalsozialismus. Der lange Weg zu Reformen* (pp. 227–245). Springer.

Korntheuer, A., Gag, M., Anderson, P., & Schroeder, J. (2018a). Education of refugee youth in Germany: Systemic barriers to equitable participation in the vocational education system. In S. Shapiro, R. Farrelly, & M. J. Curry (Eds.),

Educating refugee-background students: Critical issues and dynamic contexts (pp. 191–207). Multilingual Matters.

Korntheuer, A., Korn, A., Hynie, M., Shimwe, B., & Homa, L. (2018b). Educational pathways: Policy implications for refugee youth in Germany and Canada. In S. Pashang, N. Khanlou, & J. Clark (Eds.), *Today's youth and mental health: Hope, power and resilience* (pp. 287–304). Springer International Publishing.

Korntheuer, A., Pritchard, P., & Maehler, D. (2017). The Canadian and German context for refugee integration. In A. Korntheuer, P. Pritchard, & D. Maehler (Eds.), *GESIS working papers. Structural context of refugee integration in Canada and Germany* (pp. 11–18). GESIS Institut für Sozialwissenschaften.

Korntheuer, A., Pritchard, P., Maehler, D., & Wilkinson, L. (2020). *Refugees in Canada and Germany. From research to policies and practice* (GESIS Working Paper No. 25). Institut für Sozialwissenschaften. https://cyrrc.org/wp-content/uploads/2021/02/ssoar-2020-korntheuer_et_al-Refugees_in_Canada_and_Germany.pdf

Kronauer, M. (2010). Inklusion – Exklusion. Eine historische und begriffliche Annäherung an die soziale Frage der Gegenwart. In M. Kronauer (Ed.), *Inklusion und Weiterbildung. Reflexionen zur gesellschaftlichen Teilhabe in der Gegenwart* (pp. 24–58). Bertelsmann.

Kruse, J. (2015). *Qualitative Interviewforschung. Ein integrativer Ansatz* (2nd ed.). Beltz Juventa.

Lechner, C., & Huber, A. (2015). *Ankommen nach der Flucht: Die Sicht begleiteter und unbegleiteter junger Geflüchteter auf ihre Lebenslage in Deutschland: Bericht.* DJI.

Link, J. (2012). *Schichttypische Benachteiligung im allgemeinen Bildungswesen. Ein Vergleich zwischen Kanada und Deutschland.* Springer VS.

Loewen, S. (2006). Second language concerns for refugee children. In R. J. Hamilton & D. Moore (Eds.), *Educational interventions for refugee children. Theoretical perspectives and implementing best practice* (2nd ed., pp. 25–52). Routledge Falmer.

Luhmann, N. (1997). *Die Gesellschaft der Gesellschaft.* Suhrkamp.

Maurice, J. von, & Will, G. (2021). *Geflüchtete Kinder und Jugendliche im deutschen Bildungssystem: Zentrale Befunde der Studie ReGES* (LIfBi Forschung kompakt No. 2). Bamberg.

Mayring, P. (2008). *Qualitative Inhaltsanalyse. Grundlagen und Techniken* (10th ed.). Beltz.

Merkens, M. (2006). Erziehungssystem im Wandel. Zu den Problemen der Veränderung seiner Grenzen und des Verhältnisses von Fremd-und Selbstreferenz. In Y. Ehrenspeck & D. Lenzen (Eds.), *Beobachtungen des Erziehungssystems. Systemtheoretische Perspektiven* (pp. 76–94). Springer VS.

Pastoor, L. de W. (2017). Reconceptualising refugee education: Exploring the diverse learning contexts of unaccompanied young refugees upon resettlement. *Intercultural Education, 28*(2), 143–164.

Pavia Lareiro, C. D. (2019). *Ankommen im deutschen Bildungssystem: Bildungsbeteiligung von geflüchteten Kindern und Jugendlichen* (BAMF-Kurzanalyse). Nürnberg.

Reinhoffer, B. (2008). Lehrkräfte geben Auskunft über ihren Unterricht. Ein systematisierender Vorschlag zur deduktiven und induktiven Kategorienbildung in der Unterrichtsforschung. In P. Mayring (Ed.), *Die Praxis der qualitativen Inhaltsanalyse* (2nd ed., pp. 123–141). Beltz.

Robert Bosch Expertenkommission. (2015). Themendossier. Zum Zugang zu Bildungseinrichtungen für Flüchtlinge: Kindertagesstätten, Schulen und Hochschulen. Stuttgart.

Rutokowsky, P. (2009). Vielfalt ist unsere Stärke: Das "equitable schools program" des Toronto District School Board. In Bertelsmann Stiftung (Ed.), *Integration braucht faire Bildungschancen* (pp. 51–65). Bertelsmann Stiftung.

Sachverständigenrat deutscher Stiftungen für Integration und Migration (SVR). (Ed.) (2017). *Fakten zur Asylpolitik 2017.* www.svr-migration.de/wp-content/uploads/2018/05/SVR_Fakten_zur_Asylpolitik.pdf

Sachverständigenrat deutscher Stiftungen für Integration und Migration (SVR). (2018). Schule als Sackgasse? Jugendliche Flüchtlinge an segregierten Schulen. Studie des SVR-Forschungsbereichs 2018-1. https://www.stiftung-mercator.de/media/downloads/3_Publikationen/2018/Maerz/SVR-FB_Bildungsintegration.pdf

SchlaU Schule. (2017). *Schulanaloger Unterricht für Flüchtlinge.* www.schlau-schule.de/

Schroeder, J. (2003). Der Flüchtlingsraum als ein „totaler Raum".Bildungsinstitutionen und ihre Grenzen. In U. Neumann, H. Niedrig, J. Schroeder, & L. H. Seukwa (Eds.), *Lernen am Rande der Gesellschaft. Bildungsinstitutionen im Spiegel von Flüchtlingsbiografien* (pp. 379–396). Waxmann.

Shakia, Y. B., Guruge, S., Hynie, M., Akbari, A., Malik, M., Htoo, S., Khogali, A., Mona, S. A., Murtaza, R., & Alley, S. (2010). Aspirations for higher education among newcomer refugee youth in Toronto: Expectations, challenges, and strategies. *Refuge,* 27(2), 65–78.

Stermac, L., Clark, A. K., & Brown, L. (2013). Pathways to resilience: The role of education in war-zone immigrant and refugee student success. In C. Fernando & M. Ferrari (Eds.) *Handbook of resilience in children of war* (pp. 211–220). Springer.

Stichweh, R. (2009). Leitgesichtspunkte einer Soziologie der Inklusion und Exklusion. In R. Stichweh & P. Windolf (Eds.), *Inklusion und Exklusion: Analysen zur Sozialstruktur und sozialen Ungleichheit* (pp. 29–42). Springer VS.

Tippelt, R. (2010). Bildung in Entwicklungsländern und internationale Bildungsarbeit. In R. Tippelt & B. Schmidt (Eds.), *Handbuch Bildungsforschung* (3rd ed., pp. 249–273). VS, Verl. für Sozialwiss.

UNESCO. (2018). *Global education monitoring report 2019.* https://en.unesco.org/gem-report/taxonomy/term/210.

Vanderplaat, M. (2017). Refugee access to education in Canada. In A. Korntheuer, P. Pritchard, & D. Maehler (Eds.), *GESIS working papers. Structural context of refugee integration in Canada and Germany* (pp. 53–58). GESIS Institut für Sozialwissenschaften.

Vey, J., & Gunsch, S. (Eds.). (2021). Unterbringung von Flüchtenden in Deutschland: Inklusion, Exklusion, Partizipation? Nomos Verlagsgesellschaft.

Vogel, D., & Stock, E. (2017). *Opportunities and hope through education: How German schools include refugees.* Education International. https://issuu.com/educationinternational/docs/vogel_stockv9

Will, G., Balaban, E., Dröscher, A., Homuth, C., & Welker, J. (2018). Integration von Flüchtlingen in Deutschland: Erste Ergebnisse aus der ReGEs Studie: LIfBi Working Paper No. 76. Bamberg.

Worbs, S., & Bund, E. (2016). *BAMF Kurzanalyse Asylberechtigte und anerkannte Flüchtlinge in Deutschland Qualifikationsstruktur, Arbeitsmarktbeteiligung und Zukunftsorientierungen.* BAMF.

8 On the Disappearance of Childhood

An Exploratory Interview Study of the Christian Homeschooling Milieu in Canada

David Jahr and Robert Kruschel

Introduction: Inclusion and Homeschooling in Canada

Unlike in Canada, homeschooling is a niche topic in Germany.[1] It comes to the public's attention mainly when courts deal with it and usually find that this educational practice is incompatible with German legislation. Recently, for example, the European Court of Justice issued such a ruling, stating that the children concerned are at risk because they grow up in a "symbiotic family system" and their social integration is thus impeded (Rath, 2019). In Germany, knowledge about homeschooling is limited to only a few studies and articles (see, among others, Fischer, 2009; Reimer, 2012; Spiegler, 2008). Although homeschooling is illegal in Germany due to compulsory schooling, it is still practiced by an estimated 1000 families (Ladenthin, 2018, p. 522). In Canada, on the other hand, there is no compulsory school attendance. Parents in Canada generally have the option to educate their children at home. Homeschooling has a certain tradition in Canada as an alternative to schooling. In detail, this practice is regulated differently in the ten provinces and 3 territories (overview in Van Pelt, 2015, p. 18). Official statistics show that, currently, about 0.5% of all Canadian students are home-schooled. The figure is probably higher, as Canadian families—although required by law—do not always disclose to public authorities that they are homeschoolers. This is a growing movement: between the 2006/2007 and 2011/2012 school years, the number of homeschooled children grew by 29% while, during the same period, the number of public school students grew by only 2%.

From the perspective of inclusive pedagogy, homeschooling may be of interest for several reasons. Elsewhere (Jahr & Kruschel, 2017), we have outlined how homeschooling can be evaluated from the perspective of inclusive pedagogy. In the normative account presented there, we do not pursue the empirical question of how homeschooling is implemented. We intend to make up for this with this exploratory study.

DOI: 10.4324/9781003204572-10

The question of why inclusive pedagogy, which is predominantly concerned with visions such as the "school for all" (Wocken, 2014) and with designing inclusive schools (Booth & Ainscow, 2011), should be concerned with educational practice beyond schools, and can be grounded in Boger's (2015, 2017) model of trilemmatic inclusion. One of the basic tenets of this meta-theory is that a society-based anti-discrimination approach such as inclusion cannot argue solely on the premise of taken-for-granted normative (such as compulsory education). For if one sees inclusion solely as a struggle for participation in societal institutions, or "if one fights for the right of children with disabilities to attend mainstream school, one affirms compulsory education with all its normalizing consequences" (Boger, 2015, p. 55). The discriminatory and exclusionary phenomena of this normativity are overlooked from this standpoint, which Boger labels inclusion as "empowerment" and "normalization." In terms of inclusion as "empowerment" and "deconstruction," however, it should be about "not demonizing self-chosen segregation but understanding it as part of inclusion" (Boger, 2015, p. 61). The decision to homeschool one's child is one such form of self-chosen segregation in which the norm of compulsory schooling is rejected. We see another reason for engaging with homeschooling from an inclusive pedagogical perspective in the constructive reconsiderations of the critical schooling perspective raised there. A look at families and social groups that prefer homeschooling to school-based learning can provide important clues about what is "wrong" for those milieus in the education system, whether and how they experience discrimination through the organisation of school (Sturm, 2016, pp. 37–40). In this way, important reform issues for the school system can be localised and work can be done on making it more inclusive.

For these reasons, we decided to take advantage of a two-week stay in Canada in connection with a study excursion in the fall of 2016 (see Boban et al., 2018) to conduct narrative interviews with two representatives of homeschooling associations from each of the two Canadian provinces of Ontario (pseudonym: Rick) and New Brunswick (pseudonym: Walter). Our research interest was focused on gaining access to the Christian homeschooling milieu to which the two interviewees belong. In this chapter, the results of the analysis of both interviews with the documentary method are presented and, finally, classified from the perspective of inclusive pedagogy.

Design: Explorative Interview Study and Evaluation with the Documentary Method

The contact with both homeschooling actors took place during the preparation of the field trip. For organisational reasons, we had to limit ourselves to two interviews. Both actors belong to Christian homeschooling associations and are part of the respective management level. Besides these similarities, there is the spatial difference between the more urban Ontario and the rural province of New Brunswick. Both interview partners are predestined for a deeper insight into homeschooling because they are doubly involved in this practice. On the one hand, they are in an executive position of a homeschooling association and thus experts in the organisation of homeschooling beyond their own life practice. At the same time, both are also fathers in families with four children each who practice homeschooling themselves. Here, both interviewees are of interest as individuals with life experience in homeschooling, both at the organisational level and at the family level. Both interviewees were interviewed by us in a guided manner in the sense of a narrative-based interview. Such interviews aim "not only to elicit opinions, assessments, everyday theories, and opinions of the interviewees, but to elicit narratives about their personal experiences grounded in their practice of action" (Nohl, 2017, p. 16). The interviews were designed to leave enough space for the interviewees to be able to elicit and process their themes and representations as autonomously as possible. For the analysis of the interviews, we used the documentary method (Bohnsack et al., 2010; Bohnsack, 2014, 2018).

The documentary method is based on the difference between communicative and conjunctive knowledge. Communicative knowledge corresponds to generalised knowledge, such as a formal definition of school or family. It can be empirically identified in the "general meaning of a textual content or action" (Nohl, 2017, p. 5). Conjunctive knowledge, on the other hand, refers to implicit, action-guiding knowledge that is documented between the lines due to the way that something is said. It is structured by practical life experiences and is evident in how a text or topic is produced and acted upon. This analytical setting allows us to explore both the interviewees' communicative knowledge, which we denote here as "common-sense theories" or as "actors' theories of their practice" (Bohnsack, 2017, p. 15; Bohnsack, 2018), as well as to reconstruct their tacit and conjunctive knowledge stocks—that is, "such knowledge stock[s] that have an action-guiding, a practice-orienting character" (Bohnsack, 2017, p. 7).

The documentary method aims to make orientations explicit. Orientations emerge in conjunctive spaces of experience, which are also called milieus in the documentary method. These milieus are formed by common (as in music groups or youth cliques) or structurally similar (as for occupational groups or generations) practices of action and connect those involved on a conjunctive level. We assume a specific milieu for the homeschooling actors we interviewed, since they practice a structurally similar educational concept in the same country and have to relate their action practices to similar social demands.

The documentary method works comparatively. In addition to within-case comparisons between different passages of an interview, our exploratory study allows at least one outside-case comparison between the two interviews. Our specific procedure involved full transcription of the interviews, making thematic progressions to identify the thematic structure raised, and deciding which passages to fine-interpret (formulating interpretation and reflecting interpretation). The results presented below are a summary of our documentary analysis of both interviews at the level of a comparative case description.

Aspects of Christian Homeschooling Milieus in Canada

In the interviews, both Rick (Ontario) and Walter (New Brunswick) turned out, as suspected, to be doubly involved in the practice of homeschooling. Both have *operating knowledge* related to the homeschooling association to which they each belong. They report on conferences they have attended or organised themselves and counseling sessions they offer to parents interested in homeschooling. In addition, both are also fathers in a homeschooling family. They talk about their own decisions to homeschool and about everyday experiences in the family. The content focus of both interviews is on the latter aspect. The overarching principle that emerges from both interviews is a promotion of homeschooling as a legitimate and functioning educational practice—a better alternative to schooling. There are passages in both interviews in which homeschooling is directly argued for. In addition, both produce numerous descriptions and narratives in which this advocacy is implicit. Since there are striking homologies in the argumentations of both interviews, these knowledge stocks, which can be summarised as common-sense theories in the sense of communicative knowledge, will be summarised in the first subsection. Knowledge stocks that are documented in the descriptions and narratives of both interviews in the sense of conjunctive knowledge and that orient the actors' practice of action will be summarised in the second subsection. In the sense of the method, only after the reconstruction are the results classified against the background of inclusive pedagogy.

Common Sense Theories about Homeschooling: About Homeschooling Mothers and Problematic Schools

In arguing for their educational practice, both homeschooling actors unfold their own specific theories. It is striking that some aspects are not argumentatively justified and thus staged as self-evident. These communicative knowledge stocks are aspects of the interviewees' common-sense theories, which are "selective and tautological constructions in the service of legitimizing action" (Bohnsack, 2017, p. 88). Not explicitly justified, a specific distribution of roles is stated: the domestic education and upbringing of children is largely the responsibility of mothers. Explicitly asked whether there are homeschooling fathers in addition to homeschooling mothers, too, both interviewees report only a few exceptions they are familiar with. Both see their own role—as well as that of (other) homeschooling fathers in general—as ensuring the family income and as a supplementary teacher to the mother for some teaching content. The descriptions of the daily routine at home are similar in both interviews, referring to the aspect that the morning hours are reserved for the more cognitive tasks, in which sitting at the table is occupied with textbooks and worksheets. For the afternoon hours, field trip-like excursions or projects take place. Both interviewees emphasise that this daily schedule is often deviated from to be flexible to things that are going on at home. Homeschooling is portrayed in both interviews as a deliberate financial sacrifice. In order to practice homeschooling, one has to do without an income, can only afford a small house, or an old car. Walter emphasises that this is a conscious renunciation of the "North American Dream," which he defines as "my two jobs, two kids, new car, new house" (Walter, personal communication, 2016).[2]

The statement that school is a problematic and, at the same time, in principle, replaceable place is a central argument in both interviews. Schools are rejected as organisations that are too large, destructive to peer relationships, and insufficiently responsive to the needs of the individual. Both interviewees cite two aspects as the most important general reasons why parents choose homeschooling: *special needs* and *bullying*. Regarding the former, it is argued that schools are too quick to make (special education) diagnoses that are not warranted. Walter argues here with reference to ADHD: "In Canada now boys don't do well in our system. Most boys are diagnosed ADHD. And they are on medication because boys want to be out and do things" (Walter, personal communication, 2016). Rick refers to special needs as a whole: "So, late maturing boys can get labeled as special needs in school and that label can stick with them" (Rick, personal communication, 2016).

In several passages, the relationships among peers that take shape in school are framed as problematic. In neither interview are there passages in which a positive, developmental role of peer relationships outside of the family or homeschooling network is addressed. An example of this negative interpretation of peers in school is a response by Walter when asked how he reacts when people accuse children in homeschooling settings of not having enough social contacts: "And I will say well, what happens with socialization in the public system? It's called peer pressure. And what comes out of peer pressure? Smoking, drinking, bullying, all the problems" (Walter, personal communication, 2016). The social pluralism found in schools is interpreted in a purely negative way.

In the perspective of both homeschooling actors, the family can easily replace this as well: "Most families have two adults and children of varying ages, so in the family unit, children are being socialized with a variety of ages" (Rick, personal communication, 2016).

Schools are also criticised for the homogenisation that goes hand in hand with year grouping. Connected to this is the criticism of schools for not being able to respond to the needs of the individual. Classes are too large and teachers are constantly overburdened. Families, on the other hand, have the flexibility to take a break from classes when their children are sick, for example. In terms of choice of learning content, homeschooling is also justified as much more flexible than school: "There's a lot of curriculum and you're not limited by this" (Walter, personal communication, 2016). Regarding working materials, Walter informs us that there are a lot of possibilities to get learning materials on the Internet and that one is not limited to the materials used in schools. As an example, he mentions the project *Tree of Life* (www.treeoflifeathome.com).

School is designed as a part of society in both interviews and the criticism of school in both interviews is mixed with a criticism of modern social conditions. This can be seen, for example, in the following quote from Walter:

> It's not so much the education system as it is society it's more of a society problem than it is an education problem. Because society is so centered in those things. We've raised generations of narcissistic people. It's all about me. And they not, they don't spend a lot of their time with their parents. They are not disciplined.
>
> (Walter, personal communication, 2016)

Elsewhere, Walter argues that the school system is not focused on educating "great people" but only on teaching subjects. The "North American Dream" he rejects and the associated obligation of both parents to obtain an income as high as possible is the real reason for him why children are sent to schools: "We do self-centre in North America and the kids are paying the price" (Walter, personal communication, 2016).

A noticeable difference in the argument for homeschooling between the two interviewees lies in the reasons why they themselves decided to homeschool. Walter states that he is convinced by the visible result ("outcome") of homeschooling. Explicitly asked what that outcome is for him specifically, he answers, "the behavior, the ability to carry on a conversation with people of all ages and their respect and they are smart kids" (Walter, personal communication, 2016). In contrast, Rick argues with literature and theoretical references. For him, the two most important advantages of homeschooling are learning content and relationship quality between teachers and learners. Regarding content, he leaves open what exactly this is, but he sees parents in the role of choosing it for their children due to the abundance of knowledge. The argumentative figure behind this is a distrust of the knowledge that is taught in school:

> The other thing of course is that the right learning takes place. If we search for something on the internet, we can often find many different answers and we have to make sure it is the right learning. So as a homeschool parent in the homeschool movement, we say that the parent is in the best position to not only deliver the education because of that relationship but also determinate what the right material is to learn.
>
> (Rick, personal communication, 2016)

Rick mentions several authors to justify the better quality of relationships in homeschooling. John Holt is cited as the starting point of modern homeschooling, since he popularised "unschooling" and "child-directed education." Raymond S. Moore is cited as the overarching inspiration for many homeschoolers. Gordon Neufeld and his research on the quality of relationships between teachers and students, and between parents and children, are also cited. The threat to the quality of relationships in the family posed by school is also addressed by Walter: "Well relationship matters in, in the families you never, we never want to compromise our relationship for, for school" (Walter, personal communication, 2016). Rick expresses this threat in this way: "When you go into schools, the age peers tend to become the best friends and home schooling it seems family remains best friends" (Rick, personal communication, 2016).

Orientation to Conformity and Parental Will in the Harmonious Family

In both interviews, the reconstructed orientations in the narrative and descriptive passages show up in parallel and reveal structurally identical experiences, which, in turn, suggest a shared milieu of both interviewees. The differentiation of three social spheres—family, homeschooling community, and society—is a striking overarching homologous figure in the manner of representation across different themes. The core of the life practices depicted is the family, around which there is the network of other homeschooling families (community), designed in a compensatory role for their own family. Society, with its institutions of school and authorities, stands in a diffuse negative counter-horizon. The actors' practice of action simultaneously moves away from and towards these.

The introductory passage from the interview with Walter shows orientation content that is structurally homologous to further passages. When we ask him how he came to homeschooling, he answers:

> ... it is not something that we set out to do. My wife knew friends that were homeschooling their children. And eh the children were very well behaved, very respectful, ehm very intelligent, ehm they had good manners. So that that impressed us. They could. The biggest thing, they could carry on a conversation with you and I very easily. And we find ... I was very involved in in New Brunswick coaching baseball and hockey and the kids couldn't talk, couldn't interact very well with me. They talked well with the kids their own age. But older people they they couldn't talk. You know Hi, couple words, that was it. So the homeschooled kids that could talk to me. That was really impressive.
>
> (Walter, personal communication, 2016)

The focus is on Walter's encounter with the observable behaviour of other homeschooled children, which is viewed as positive. It is emphasised that these homeschooling children can enter into exchanges with adults on the level of adults. This is not just a matter of being able to articulate oneself. Reference is made here to an eloquence that goes beyond what seems typical between peers. On the positive horizon, there are children who conform to the adult world and whose communicative behaviour marks them as *quasi-adults* and in difference to their peers who do not have homeschooling experiences. Walter lists several characteristics of homeschooling children that he sees as positive, all in the context of this conformity. Even the listed trait "intelligence" is not framed here (and in other passages) in terms of the children's critical attitude toward adults. Conformity of the (own) children to the adult world represents the overarching orientation of both interviewed actors. Rick puts this in the following formula: "We want the children to grow up to be adults and work in the adult world" (Rick, personal communication, 2016).

The family is designed as the centre of joint action practice. In both interviews, a representation aiming at harmony dominates: a family consisting of mother, father and four children each, which presents itself as united and free of conflict. Thus, neither Rick nor Walter shows any disagreements about the basic decision to homeschool or about the daily implementation of homeschooling. Even when explicitly asked, conflicts in the family are only dealt with superficially. In both interviews, the children appear only as those who are comprehensively satisfied with the decision to homeschool. This, too, reveals an orientation of the children's conformity to the adults' perspective. Neither contradiction nor the children's own perspective that can be distinguished from the adults' perspective is developed in any significant way. In response to our question whether his children wanted to attend public school, Walter answers, for example: "The only thing our kids wanted to do was ride the bus [laughing]" (Walter, personal communication, 2016). In this answer, there is an (assumed) lack of interest of the children in the contents and the life of the school.

Mothers, who are busy with the task of teaching the children and do not pursue their own professional gainful employment, are also uncritically enacted in the interviews. Asked whether his wife sometimes longs to pursue a career outside of homeschooling, Walter responds with a big picture formula that makes further inquiry on this topic seem inappropriate. With a reference to a metaphysical dimension, the question of professional activities is dismissed as earthly, transient, and unimportant:

> If you look at life in general, um, when people, when people die, they don't think, I should have spent more time at work, I should have spent more time working no one thinks that. They think I should have spent more time with my friends, with the people I love.
>
> (Walter, personal communication, 2016)

The harmonious family is held together by the will of the parents. This proves to be the central, decisive element (to the detriment of the child's perspective). This orientation towards the will of the parents is exemplified in the following passage, in which Rick describes a typical homeschooling day:

> It varied. But sometimes, my wife would sort out the books for what the children needed to do the night before and if they went to bed early, they could get up early and sometimes they finished the school work before breakfast. If they did that, we said okay, you finished your required work for the day. The rest of the day you can go and play. ... But those would be exceptions to the normal day. Mostly it would be breakfast and then start the schoolwork. The schoolwork would be done late morning. In the afternoon, especially in the early years, my wife would go for a walk with the children. We lived in a rural area, so they would identify wild flowers and trees. Sometimes she would have her afternoon nap of course and the children would play around her while she is having her nap. My wife really likes gardening, so she would have our children help her in the garden, do the weeding, pick the (?), and help get it ready for the freezer.
>
> (Rick, personal communication, 2016)

Here, we can see how both the varied and the typical daily routine depend on the will and needs of the parents or the mother: she appears as the linchpin of the activities. Her needs structure the schedule much more than those of the children. Following a similar narrative by Walter, we asked him what the role of children is in general in homeschooling. In his brief answer, "Um they do their work" (Walter, personal communication, 2016), there is also performative information about how little space the child's perspective has in the homeschooling practices presented.

In addition to this primary reference point of the family on nearly all aspects of the homeschooling practices depicted, the homeschooling community is situationally placed in position. This network consists of families who also practice homeschooling.

> So and there is lots of good things most homeschoolers feel a lot of pressure that their kids do well so we take a lot of effort to make sure we are doing a good job, cause a lot of people eh it's even though it's done in Canada it's not real common. … so parents really do make a lot of effort most the surveys and research that is done on home-educators shows … that the average education of homeschool families is quite high in our small group in [city A] we have doctors, lawyers, um, you know fairly well educated teachers, a lot of teachers that are homeschooling their kids. Which is surprising.
>
> (Walter, personal communication, 2016)

Here, too, there are orientation contents of conformity, this time related to social norms. The positive horizon is not to stand out socially, to "do a good job" and to meet social performance requirements. The homeschooling community sketched above is designed as an educationally oriented and socio-economic middle class formed by conforming people who are part of society. The educational practice of homeschooling appears as something socially conformed with the goal of fitting into society. The life trajectories of their own children after homeschooling, as described in the interviews, are also oriented toward social conformity.[3] The homeschooling community fulfils concrete functions for the homeschooling families. They serve primarily compensatory purposes: as a resource for learning and socialisation challenges that support the family. The role of the homeschooling community as peers is to compensate for any voids in the family. However, the family remains primary: all activities from the network to the children are narrated as contingencies. The family is designed as self-sufficient. This is exemplified in Rick's answer to our question about whether children who are homeschooled do not have too few social contacts with young people of other ages:

> Most families have two adults and children of varying ages, so in the family unit, children are being socialized with a variety of ages. The family will visit the grandparents, so you are visiting other older, wiser people.
>
> (Rick, personal communication, 2016)

Summary and Connection to Research Findings: The Christian Homeschooling Milieu as a Conservative Critique of Society

All in all, school is portrayed in both interviews as a place that is problematic and dangerous for children's learning, education, and socialisation, and that can be replaced by the family. What is striking is the criticism of society on a linguistic level, which is primarily directed to the institution of school with a simultaneous orientation towards social conformity. School is not threatening as an idea in itself but as a place of modern society and its problematic values, as a meeting place of different milieus, and the accompanying dangers for one's own children. In the orientation framework, society appears simultaneously both as a counter-model and as a reference point to which one must adapt.

Our findings can be placed in the research around homeschooling as follows. Most contributions on homeschooling distinguish between two social groups that practice homeschooling: "pious" and "alternative" (Spiegler, 2008, pp. 77–80), "leftist counterculture," and "Christian fundamentalism" (Gaither, 2008, p. 202), or "liberal left" and "conservative Christian right" (Murphy, 2012). Although religious motives do not explicitly emerge in the interviews, our reconstructed findings clearly indicate that the action practice Rick and Walter are involved in belongs to the "Christian fundamentalism" or "pious" group (Spiegler, 2008, pp. 78–80).[4] The motives why parents decide on homeschooling, such as those cited by Fischer and Ladenthin (2009), are also found in the two interviews, for example, "inaccurately perceived fit of the school system to the child," "protection from social and emotional overload of the children," or also the "strengthening of the family system" (Fischer & Ladenthin, 2009, pp. 165–166).

The promotion of homeschooling from the perspective of this Christian homeschooling milieu can be read as conservative social criticism. Values framed as current developments in society are rejected. The orientation is towards a conformist life in society within the primary frame of reference, the family. Both interviewees orient their educational practice at home strongly to the structure of conventional school lessons. Both actors repeatedly mention classical school subjects in the description of their practice. A conservative critique of society becomes clear, for example, in discourse figures that are not in the modern mainstream of social debates: the division of roles between man (job, earner) and woman (home) to the detriment of the woman as a non-employed person. This is described as self-evident by both actors.

Homeschooling Practice from the Perspective of Inclusive Pedagogy: Imitation of Structures, Rejection of Content, and Disappearance of Childhood

In the introduction of this chapter, we argued that a comprehensive concept of inclusion also includes a consideration of those educational practices that reject social norms, such as that of regular school attendance. Looking at our interviews, we see that while compulsory schooling is rejected in the homeschooling milieu we studied, the orientation toward formal education is also highly valued here. Structurally, this form of homeschooling imitates traditional school education. Other ideas of education, such as unschooling or democratic schools (Boban et al., 2012) were unknown to both interviewees. What is striking in the narratives about homeschooling practices is a ubiquity and dissolution of boundaries of education. In neither interview are there windows of *non-learning*. On the one hand, this is an opportunity to realise learning on the object and close to life. At the same time, such education, similar to gainful employment that is shifted to the so-called home office, seems to carry the danger that formal learning becomes the dominant structuring moment of life practice.

In contrast to this structural organisation of education, there is no imitation of school education regarding educational content in the homeschooling milieu studied. Educational content is rather deproblematised in both interviews. A homologous figure emerges, according to which school content can easily be compensated for by one's own knowledge, offers from the Internet, or with the help of social networks. The few explicit references to this in the interviews are rather sceptical. The source for learning material *Tree of Life* mentioned by Walter is a Christian-based platform with numerous materials that convey a creationist worldview. Rick argues that, with so much possible learning content, parents would have to decide what their children should learn. This must be seen sceptically from the point of view of any scientifically oriented education in general, and, in particular, from an inclusive point of view that upholds a socially shared minimal consensus for all relevant educational content (as drafted, among others, in the current *Index for Inclusion*; Booth & Ainscow, 2017). Questions follow about how societies relate to the question of the selection and legitimacy of educational content in homeschooling settings.

If one understands homeschooling as a conscious decision against school and thus as a symptom of a criticism of the difficulties of this institution to create a fit to heterogeneous social groups, which is also frequently found in inclusive pedagogy, some indications arise from the interviews. Both interviewees emphasise the same reasons why parents decide against schools and in favour of homeschooling: it is about the situation of children with special needs, about too early diagnoses and stigmatising labels, and about bullying in the sense of exclusion among peers. In addition, there is criticism of homogenisation and learning in lockstep. These reasons are very connectable to the discussion in inclusive pedagogy and its critique of schools and exclusionary practices there. However, the response to these problems is entirely different: while inclusive pedagogy advocates for school improvement in terms of minimising discrimination and exclusion, homeschooling families seem to prefer the exit option, thus evading the struggle for a more inclusive school. Critical from the perspective of inclusive education remains the one-sided negative interpretation of social heterogeneity in schools in both interviews—both regarding content issues and peers. It is precisely this opportunity of schools to allow heterogeneous social milieus to come into contact with each other (Sturm, 2016, pp. 139–141) that is explicitly rejected here.

We see a central point of criticism of homeschooling in the *disappearance of childhood*[5] that accompanies the orientation towards conformity and parental will. Values like self-determination or maturity of children are not in the foreground in the depictions but patriarchal family structures and conformity in society. The distrust of homeschooling actors is explicitly related to school, but implicitly, it is childhood or youth that disappears here. A strongly hierarchical and directive understanding of learning goes hand in hand with the parent orientation. Learning is produced as a knowledge transmission process from parents to children. Another expression of parental dominance is their ubiquity. They not only determine the daily routine, as shown above, but they are also the sole structuring factor on joint trips. In both interviews, trips, excursions, and vacations are described but not those that the children took alone. The picture sketched here assumes a hierarchy: The adult remains as he is and the child only appears positively if he behaves in an adapted manner. A child's own perspective—or at least an interest in it by the parents—is not opened up. The children literally disappear in the narratives of the interviews.

The documentary method ultimately aims to answer the question of in which milieus reconstructed orientations are located. In our explorative study, we remain in the context of Christian homeschooling milieus in Canada and cannot say anything about specifics of this homeschooling milieu due to the lack of contrast. Besides a necessary extension of the sample to other homeschooling actors in Canada itself and also to those belonging to the other large cluster of "alternatives," it would be further informative to contrast the results with homeschooling practitioners from other countries, other social milieus, as well as with representatives of other school-alternative educational concepts. For the latter, we find the discourse around democratic schools informative, in which at least rhetorically similar criticism of school is voiced. On an action-practical level, however, this is not related to orientations to family and conformity but much more to an empowering and participatory position of the child and the school democratic community (Hershkovitz et al., 2017). Researching such social milieus that are manifestly hostile to conventional schooling can, on the one hand, help to better understand the practices of those milieus and, on the other hand, support the opening of schools in the sense of inclusion.

Notes

1. We agree with Ladenthin's (2010) definition of homeschooling as the "(1) systematically planned (2) organization of (3) instruction and (4) education ('Bildung') for (5) school-age children and adolescents, which is provided with (6) specific teaching and learning materials and under the (7) target perspective of formal qualifications (8) exclusively or largely by (9) parents of these children in the (10) home environment and thus (11) wholly or partially replaces regular school instruction" (p. 21).
2. Excerpts from the interviews are indicated with pseudonym and year.
3. Rick's children have all studied and are pursuing careers in the technical field. Some of Walter's children are just beginning their studies. None of the children stands out with an "extravagant" profession or an "alternative" lifestyle.
4. Thus, Spiegler (2008, pp. 78–79) describes the "pious" in a strikingly similar way to our findings: Out of a deep Christian faith, parents take responsibility for a "loving" education through which children are led "to faith" and "to God." School, in this worldview, is an institution infiltrated by numerous anti-Christian influences. The decision to homeschool is made by the parents, who have authority over the child. The family image is characterised by biblical-traditional role patterns, in which the man has the main responsibility and the mother does the day-to-day child-rearing and educational work as a full-time job. The lifestyle is modest and the family is integrated into (Christian) communities.
5. With this expression we take up—rather unconsciously—the book title of a popular book by Postman (1987) in which he criticises the more intensive and earlier adaptation of children to the behaviours of adults, which finds its expression in language, clothing, posture, and so on. We do not subscribe here to the *medialisation* of childhood that he names as the cause of this process.

References

Boban, I., Hinz, A., Jahr, D., & Kruschel, R. (2018). Inklusive Schulsysteme in Kanada – Anregungen für den deutschsprachigen Raum? In E. Feyerer, W. Prammer, E. Prammer-Semmler, C. Kladnik, M. Leibetseder, & R. Wimberger (Hrsg.), *System. Wandel. Entwicklung. Akteurinnen und Akteure inklusiver Prozesse im Spannungsfeld von Institution, Profession und Person* (pp. 111–116). Klinkhardt.

Boban, I., Kruschel, R., & Wetzel, A. (2012). The marriage of inclusive and democratic education. In S. Seitz, N.-K. Finnern, N. Korff, & K. Scheidt (Eds.), *Inklusiv gleich gerecht? Inklusion und Bildungsgerechtigkeit* (pp. 174–179). Klinkhardt.

Boger, M.-A. (2015). Theorie der trilemmatischen Inklusion. In I. Schnell (Ed.), *Herausforderung Inklusion. Theoriebildung und Praxis* (pp. 51–62). Klinkhardt.

Boger, M.-A. (2017). Theorien der Inklusion – eine Übersicht. *Zeitschrift für Inklusion Online,* 1(12).

Bohnsack, R. (2014). Documentary method. In U. Flick (Ed.), *SAGE handbook of analyzing qualitative data* (pp. 217–233). SAGE.

Bohnsack, R. (2017). *Praxeologische Wissenssoziologie.* Budrich.

Bohnsack, R. (2018). Praxeological sociology of knowledge and documentary method: Karl Mannheim's framing of empirical research. In D. Kettler & V. Meja (Eds.), *The anthem companion to Karl Mannheim* (pp. 199–220). Anthem.

Bohnsack, R., Pfaff, N., & Weller, W. (Eds.). (2010). *Qualitative analysis and documentary method in international educational research.* Budrich.

Booth, T., & Ainscow, M. (2011). *Index for inclusion: Developing learning and participation in schools* (3rd. edition). Centre for Studies on Inclusive Education.

Fischer, R. (2009). *Homeschooling in der Bundesrepublik Deutschland. Eine erziehungswissenschaftliche Annäherung.* VKW.

Fischer, R., & Ladenthin, V. (2009). Gründe für bildenden Unterricht außerhalb der Schule. *PÄD-Forum, 4,* 165–167.

Gaither, M. (2008). *Homeschool: An American history.* Palgrave Macmillan.

Hershkovich, M., Simon, J., & Simon, T. (2017). Menschenrechte, Demokratie, Partizipation und Inklusion – ein (fast) in Vergessenheit geratenes Wechselverhältnis? In R. Kruschel (Ed.), *Menschenrechtsbasierte Bildung. Inklusive und demokratische Lern- und Erfahrungswelten im Fokus* (pp. 161–172). Klinkhardt.

Jahr, D., & Kruschel, R. (2017). Homeschooling als Alternative zur schulischen Bildung: Überlegungen zum Unterricht zu Hause aus der Perspektive inklusiver Pädagogik. In R. Kruschel (Ed.), *Menschenrechtsbasierte Bildung. Inklusive und Demokratische Lern- und Erfahrungswelten im Fokus* (pp. 197–215). Klinkhardt.

Ladenthin, V. (2010). Was ist Homeschooling? In V. Ladenthin (Ed.), *Homeschooling – Fragen und Antworten. Häusliche Bildung im Spannungsfeld zwischen Schulpflicht und Elternrecht* (pp. 21–27). VKW.

Ladenthin, V. (2018). Homeschooling. In H. Barz (Ed.), *Handbuch Bildungsreform und Reformpädagogik* (pp. 519–525). Springer VS.

Murphy, J. (2012). *Homeschooling in America: Capturing and assessing the movement.* Corwin.

Nohl, A.-M. (2017). *Interview und dokumentarische Methode. Anleitungen für die Forschungspraxis.* Springer VS.

Postman, N. (1987). *Das Verschwinden der Kindheit.* Fischer.

Rath, C. (2019). *Gericht für Menschenrechte fällt Urteil. Nicht in die Schule, sondern ins Heim.* www.taz.de/Gericht-fuer-Menschenrechte-faellt-Urteil/!5564588/

Reimer, F. (Ed.). (2012). *Homeschooling: Bedrohung oder Bewährung des freiheitlichen Rechtsstaats?* Nomos.

Spiegler, T. (2008). *Home Education in Deutschland.* Hintergründe – Praxis – Entwicklung. VS.

Sturm, T. (2016). *Lehrbuch Heterogenität in der Schule.* UTB.

Van Pelt, D. N. (2015). *Home schooling in Canada: The current picture.* Fraser Institute. www.fraserinstitute.org/sites/default/files/home-schooling-in-canada-2015-rev2.pdf

Wocken, H. (2014). Frei herumlaufende Irrtümer. Eine Warnung vor pseudo-inklusiven Betörungen. In H. Wocken (Ed.), *Im Haus der inklusiven Schule* (pp. 101–127). Feldhaus.

9 Structures That Inhibit and That Support Inclusive Education in Canada

A Response from a Canadian Scholar in Inclusive Education

Steve Sider

The concept of *structures* in inclusive education (IE) is an important one. In this chapter, I provide some general considerations for the idea of structures, one being more quantifiable and observable forms of structures and the other being more latent and invisible, although likely equally powerful and important. I then turn to an examination of the three chapters in this section that address structures. In the third section of this chapter, I provide an examination of research that I have been involved with in Canada that speak to the idea of structures particularly related to the work of school principals in fostering IE. I conclude by specifically addressing two issues that have very real pertinence to both observable and invisible structures of IE in Canada. First, I examine structural issues related to Indigenous students with disabilities on reserves as well as in relationship to the Truth and Reconciliation Commission's Calls to Action. Second, I consider recent research that is exploring the experiences of racialised and marginalised groups in relationship to disability. I use these issues to illustrate that although many Canadian jurisdictions have implemented structural supports for IE, there is much work yet to be done.

Thinking about Structures Both Visible and Invisible

On one level, we can quickly think of the structures that make IE effective. At this level, structures are typically things that can be observed and quantified. For example, we need human resources to meet the diverse needs of students; thus, we have processes to hire teachers and other educators who can help meet these needs. We also need educational facilities that enable all students to attend school without physical barriers. Schools are built or retrofitted to ensure that doors, halls, sidewalks, classrooms, washrooms, playgrounds, and other school facilities are accessible for all. We need

DOI: 10.4324/9781003204572-11

financial structures that provide clear revenue sources for programmes and services. In this case, governments and school systems put into place financial mechanisms that ensure the smooth transfer and application of funds to support IE. We also need policy structures that enable and foster IE. Policy structures at both government and school system levels can articulate processes for the identification of student needs, Individual Education Plans, teacher-to-student ratios, access to technology, and many more. For example, in Ontario, Bill 82, which was passed in 1980 and, federally, the *Canadian Charter of Rights and Freedoms* (1982), represent legal and policy frameworks which have shaped efforts to support IE.

A final example of observable or quantifiable structural aspects of IE includes pre-service and in-service teacher education. Teacher education programmes include courses on IE in their programmes. These provide training for new teachers on how to support students with disabilities in inclusive classrooms. Governments, school boards, and professional educational associations often provide in-service learning to help new and experienced teachers develop skills in IE. These structural aspects of IE are all quantifiable and observable to some degree. These types of structural aspects cannot be understated; they are critical to IE. They are important determinants of IE and, to varying degrees, are generally recognised aspects that have to be in place to enable inclusive education to exist in schools.

At another level, structures are sometimes invisible and difficult to quantify or measure. Yet these structures can be very real enablers or inhibitors of IE. In this case, structures might refer more to systemic and normative issues. We might refer to these types of structures as requiring dismantling or elimination in order for IE to effectively exist (Andrews et al., 2019; Fitzgerald, 2018). These types of structures could include practices such as inadequate or inequitable government funding for some types of disabilities. For example, in Ontario, Canada, where I am located, funding for autism services has had significant changes over the past three years. We might see this as a structural barrier for families who are trying to access programmes for children. I would consider this an invisible structural barrier because the general public has little understanding of how funding has shifted and how it is often applied inequitably (van Rensburg, 2020).

Further, I would argue that people's perceptions and stereotypes are another form of structure. These can be the attitudes of teachers, principals, parents, or the general public toward those with disabilities (Friedman & Owen, 2017). For example, if the general population stigmatises students with disabilities, this can serve as an invisible barrier for IE because it may influence the behaviours and resulting actions of teachers. Beliefs can influence teaching practices; for example, both individual and collective teacher efficacy can either support or inhibit the work of teachers (Fisher, 2017; Özokcu, 2017). Another example of invisible barriers could include teachers' perceptions of the other educators who work with students. In Ontario, these "other" educators might include educational assistants, child and youth workers, and social workers. Teachers have sometimes denigrated the work of these educators and see them as *second class citizens* in IE (Rämä et al., 2020; Takala, 2007). A further example of an invisible structural barrier is the perceptions that sometimes exist between families and educators. Mistrust or lack of communication between teachers and parents/guardians can be an invisible barrier to the effective inclusion of students with disabilities in schools (MacCormack & Matheson, 2017). These invisible issues provide another form of structure that can be a barrier to IE in schools.

Thus, we are left with two general conceptualisations regarding structures: Those which are observable and those which are more latent and often invisible. My point here is not to provide an exhaustive examination of the types of structures that support or inhibit IE but to highlight that we need to be cognizant not only of that which is easily described and observed but to also recognise the importance of exploring those structural aspects which are not as easily quantifiable. The three chapters in this section provide illustrations of these two important aspects of structures.

Reflecting on the Three Chapters

In this section, three chapters are provided which consider structures in IE. I thoroughly enjoyed reading the chapters because of the divergent ways in which the authors considered structures. One chapter was written by Dr. Markku Jahnukainen from the University of Helsinki and colleague Drs. Kimberly Maich, Sharon Penney, and Gabrielle Young from Memorial University of Newfoundland in Canada. In this chapter, entitled "Two Models of 'Education for All': Contrasting the Inclusive and Special Education Policies in Finland and Newfoundland and Labrador," Jahnukainen et al. describe and explore structures that support or inhibit IE in Finland and in one Canadian province, Newfoundland and Labrador. In the first half of the chapter, the authors focus on observable structures of IE in Newfoundland and Labrador, particularly related to policy changes. In the beginning of this chapter, the authors also identify other structural aspects of IE in Canada such as the federal system in Canada in which provinces and territories have responsibility for education, thus contributing to significant differences across the country. Jahnukainen et al. state that, as a result of the federal system and the provincial responsibility for education, "...policies, practices, and even definitions, remain vastly inconsistent across the country." This is helpful when considering how IE has been implemented across Canada.

Canada is a diverse country and, given the provincial responsibility for education, policies and programmes can look very different between the 10 provinces and three territories. It is important to note that significant differences can exist even within provinces even though school systems operate under the provincial authority. For example, Ontario has four publicly funded school systems (English Public, English Catholic, French Public, French Catholic). School boards that operate in the same geographic area can have different approaches to IE. For example, many Catholic school systems in Ontario have more of a full inclusion model where supports for students are provided in regular classrooms while Public school systems often rely more on congregated, specialised settings. In this regard, the chapter provides excellent insight into the Newfoundland and Labrador model of IE. Further, Jahnukainen et al. provide a very thorough overview of policy changes in Newfoundland and Labrador that have fostered IE. They also document teacher, parent, and general public responses to the move to IE.

In the second half of the chapter, Jahnukainen et al. provide an exploration of IE in Finland. Similar to the legislative overview that is provided for Canada, the authors trace the evolution of IE in Finland, including the *Basic Education Act* of 1998, which ushered in a spectrum of programmes, schools, and class settings for students with disabilities. Similar to Newfoundland and Labrador, a tiered system of supports and interventions has been implemented in Finland. Distinct from Newfoundland and Labrador, where approximately one in four students are identified as exceptional, in Finland, approximately 8.5% of students are identified. The authors discuss how funding changes in Finland may have contributed to this.

This chapter is particularly poignant for a number of reasons. First, it considers unique aspects of Newfoundland and Labrador, a small province with a significant urban-rural divide and which, as a result, has relied on distance education to support those students who live in low-population areas. This is a very important aspect of IE that is not often considered in the scholarly literature (Stenman & Pettersson, 2020). This may be a way in which the Newfoundland and Labrador model can be of value to other contexts: How can IE be implemented in regions where there is a low-density population and limited access to resources?

Second, the chapter documents how the province has developed policies that indicate a move from a model of special education (with segregated spaces for students with disabilities) to an IE model. For example, the authors state that: "In 2009, NL began its Inclusive Education Initiative with the goal of making schools places where all members of the school community feel safe, accepted and included." The authors discuss structural supports for this transition including the activities of itinerant IE teachers and changes to the identification model.

Third, the chapter is important because it identifies not only the quantifiable aspects of IE but also the importance of addressing those aspects which are more invisible, such as social norms. The authors note that, "however, there is still a difference between inclusivity as a societal norm in the province, and how to deliver supports for diverse groups of students in inclusive school settings." They identify five aspects related to the public perception of IE including, for example, "a generally positive view toward the philosophy of including students with disabilities in the classroom appears to exist; perhaps more so for those who tend to view inclusion as a right and responsibility."

Fourth, I found that Table 6.2 ("Components of Inclusion and Accompanying Issues with Implementation") in this chapter was very helpful in identifying aspects of IE and related issues for implementation. This table could be very helpful in other jurisdictions that are committed to an IE model. Of interest to my analysis of the chapter is the final row in the table which addresses systemic issues, particularly the challenge of providing an integrated system of policy and practice involving all stakeholders. This table is helpful in thinking about the observable, quantifiable structures that support IE.

Fifth, the authors include recent research that has examined the perceptions of educators in Newfoundland and Labrador and in Finland regarding IE. They identify challenges to IE including lack of resources, increasing class sizes, parental concerns, and issues related to complex and behavioural needs of students. It is interesting to note that in both jurisdictions, the authors point to how media portrays—and potentially exacerbates—negative attitudes towards IE. This section is helpful as we consider the intersection of the visible and invisible structures that support IE. For example, funding is a quantifiable, structural aspect of IE. However, the determination of funding is partially guided by the priorities of civil servants and elected officials. These priorities may be shaped by what these officials perceive as the public appetite for such funding. Thus, the invisible factor of societal norms can influence the visible structure of funding.

Sixth, funding is certainly a structural aspect of special education, and the Finnish example points to how funding changes can influence the formal identification process. This is important to consider, particularly if students are able to receive special education services and supports without formal identification. I return to the issue of funding later in the chapter as I raise structural barriers to equitable access to IE for Indigenous students on reserve due to the Canadian federal funding model.

Finally, a concluding statement in the chapter is particularly important to consider for how the authors' exploration of IE in Newfoundland and Labrador and Finland can be instructive:

> Although there might seem to be shared commitment between different countries and school systems at the ideological level, the local social-political context as well as the historical development will often play a major part in the final decision-making and in particular implementation of certain policies.

Thus, this chapter provides instructive insights into the experiences of IE in Newfoundland and Labrador and Finland, which may help in better understanding how IE can be implemented particularly in smaller and more rural communities.

In the second chapter, David Jahr and Robert Kruschel, scholars from Germany, write about "On the Disappearance of Childhood: An Exploratory Interview Study of the Christian Homeschooling Milieu in Canada." This chapter addresses an aspect of IE that is not greatly explored in Canadian research: Homeschooling. I have limited knowledge in this area, so I was particularly intrigued with this chapter. Jahr and Kruschel describe the differences between Germany and Canada concerning homeschooling. According to the authors, homeschooling is much more prevalent and socially accepted in Canada than Germany. Although the authors do not address homeschooling in relationship to the COVID-19 pandemic, I suspect that the pandemic has further solidified homeschooling in the Canadian context as some parents have opted out of public schools to ensure the health and educational progress of their children (Baxter, 2020).

Jahr and Kruschel raise a very intriguing question in this chapter: Should inclusive pedagogy be concerned with educational practices beyond schools? They reference Boger's (2015, 2017) model of trilemmatic inclusion to explore the intersection of homeschooling and IE. They state that "one of the basic tenets of this meta-theory is that a society-based anti-discrimination approach such as inclusion cannot argue solely on the premise of taken-for-granted normativities (such as compulsory education)." I was not familiar with Boger's work and this certainly caused me to reflect on a perception I had of homeschooling. It has made me question: Can those who engage in homeschooling also support IE?

Jahr and Kruschel interview two people in Ontario and New Brunswick who engage in Christian homeschooling. In their analysis of interviews with these participants, Jahr and Kruschel raise issues related to children with special needs and what the two interviewees thought about students with special education needs who are in traditional schools. For example, one participant comments "about too early diagnoses and stigmatising labels, and about 'bullying' in the sense of exclusion among peers." This provides fascinating insight into the reasons why families may choose to pursue homeschooling (among many others that the authors consider). Here, Jahr and Kruschel make a fascinating conclusion: "While inclusive pedagogy advocates for school improvement in terms of minimizing discrimination and exclusion, homeschooling families seem to prefer the exit option, thus evading the struggle for a more inclusive school."

This chapter provides compelling considerations for the intersection of homeschooling and disability. Specifically, the chapter raises insights into how families who pursue *alternative education* perceive programmes and services for students with disabilities and, at a deeper level, how they conceptualise issues such as inclusion. Although the chapter is limited in how much insight it provides into inclusive education for students with disabilities, it does raise important considerations. First, in my research on inclusive education in Canada, I have not considered the experiences of students with disabilities who are in homeschool or in other alternative education settings. This seems like a glaring gap in my own research. A quick exploration of scholarly databases indicated that there is in fact very limited research on the intersection of homeschooling and disability in Canada.

Second, the chapter provides insights into how the general public in Canada might view students with disabilities. The interviewees in the Jahr and Kruschel study described issues related to disability such as, "in Canada now boys don't do well in our system [and] boys want to be out and do things" and "late maturing boys can get labeled as special needs in school and that label can stick with them." These generalisations may be reasons why families choose homeschooling, but they may represent the views of parents who choose to send their children to neighbourhood public schools as well. These invisible structural aspects of stigma and stereotypes still exist with disability in Canada, despite 40 years of inclusive education practices (Waterfield & Whelan, 2017).

Finally, the chapter is poignant in considering the broader concept of inclusive education. As IE researchers, are we inclusive "enough" if we do not consider the experiences of families who choose alternative structures of education, particularly those that do not seem inclusive? At the core of inclusive education is a belief that all children should be able to engage fully in the educational and social experience of schooling in neighbourhood schools (Specht, 2013). How do we respond to families who choose alternatives to this concept, what we might consider a form of segregated setting? This chapter by Jahr and Kruschel has certainly made me reflect on this.

The third chapter is authored by Annette Korntheuer of the Catholic University of Eichstätt. In this chapter, entitled "Education for Young Refugees—Processes of Inclusion and Exclusion in Munich and Toronto," Korntheuer uses a systems-theoretical perspective to examine the extent to which people move within systems (inclusion) or are barred from systems (exclusion). Korntheuer uses this framework to examine educational components in Munich and Toronto that either facilitate or inhibit inclusion for young refugees. An example that Korntheuer shares is how school structural factors (e.g., assessments, ability tracking, etc.) and individual factors (previous educational attainment, socio-economic status of families, etc.) have influenced newcomer students in Germany.

This chapter is focused on the experiences of young refugee students in Canada and Germany but Korntheuer provides multiple opportunities to consider the inclusionary and exclusionary structures that these students face in relationship to other aspects of inclusion such as students with special educational needs. For example, Korntheuer describes and explores inclusion of newcomer students in specialised education contexts in Munich versus inclusive school systems in Toronto. She notes that that there are lots of wrap-around supports for students in Munich but that these are provided in segregated settings. In contrast, Toronto school settings provide similar supports while also including young refugee students in schools. This raises important questions about what authentic inclusion actually is.

As a former school administrator, and in the current research I do, I have been in lots of schools that are considered fully inclusive schools. However, when exploring what actually happens in classes, these schools often still practice segregation. This can be witnessed through specialised classes for students with complex needs who have little to no interaction with other students. It can also be seen in inclusive classes where students with developmental disabilities are working with an educational assistant but have limited interaction with their peers. This is a salient point in our work to support inclusive education: Are students authentically and fully included or just integrated with little meaningful interaction with peers?

Relatedly, Korntheuer raises another very important point about indirect discrimination and overt exclusion. She points to examples of indirect discrimination towards newcomer students in Toronto as a result of bureaucratic processes and other examples of overt exclusion in Munich due to things such as restrictive membership criteria. Again, I see similar parallels in situations involving students with disabilities and other special education needs. Bureaucratic barriers, such as long wait times for psycho-educational assessments can serve as a structural barrier to inclusion. As Korntheuer concludes, "High educational aspirations and resilience can be undermined by the lack of structure for educational opportunity." This statement is accurate for young refugee students as well as students with special educational needs.

I found the Korntheuer chapter really compelling in helping me think about intersectionality in inclusive education. For too long, we have focused on specific areas of inclusive education (e.g., disability, gender, language, socio-economics) instead of how the various aspects of a student's identity are considered as a whole. Recent work by David DeMatthews and colleagues (DeMatthews et al., 2020; DeMatthews et al., 2021) has emphasised the importance of this type of work going forward. This is an example of the ways in which the chapters have raised new considerations for me in my own research. I am deeply appreciative of this.

How the Chapters Intersect with My Research

The three chapters provide insights that are helpful for my own research and may be helpful in contexts beyond Canada. My research focuses on the intersection of IE, school leadership, and comparative and international perspectives. In this research, I have considered the issue of structures in a number of different ways. Examples in my research that include aspects of structure that support or deter from IE include: The influence of gender on school-based decisions in Haiti (Sider et al., 2019), how technology can be used to foster inclusive leadership competencies in Canada and Haiti (Sider, 2014), how the lack of supports during the COVID-19 pandemic influenced principals' work with students with disabilities (Sider, 2020), the fostering of professional learning through a peer coaching framework in Egypt (Sider, 2019), how civil society can engage to support inclusive education in alignment with Sustainable Development Goal 4 (Sider et al., 2021), and how training within principals' preparation programmes are limited in addressing IE (Sider et al., 2017).

A recent research project I led was completed in partnership with the largest principals' organisation in Canada, the Ontario Principals' Council, which represents more than 5000 principals. In this project, we examined the experiences of principals with IE, designed interactive, web-based case studies that highlighted some of these experiences, and piloted these cases to explore how this form of immersive learning could support principals' competencies for IE. This project included multiple aspects of structure. First, there was the formal partnership between participating universities and the Ontario Principals' Council. This required multiple collaborative meetings, developing memoranda of engagements, and ensuring appropriate signatories. Another structural aspect was identifying a suitable funding agency and developing the application materials. We received a Social Sciences and Humanities Research Council of Canada Partnership Engage Grant, thus necessitating further structural aspects such as oversight committees and funding channels. Many other tangible and observable aspects of structure included getting institutional Research Ethics Board clearance, developing a survey, interviewing participants, completing transcripts and member checking, developing cases, and writing reports. All of these structural aspects were necessary to complete the project and were easily quantifiable for developing metrics and submitting reports on the role of school principals in supporting IE.

In the midst of these observable structures, there were invisible, but equally important, structural aspects and outcomes. For example, we had to engage in multiple meetings between partners to develop a level of trust in the partnership. Trust is a critical aspect of research and certainly for research involving IE (Todd, 2007). In interviews, our research team had to probe responses to better understand the nuances of the experiences that participants shared with us. Thus, although the interview script and prompts were "visible" aspects of the methodology structure, we had to be attuned to comments that deserved further exploration. Comments made in interviews may have had latent meanings about IE. These might include generalisations, stereotypes, and biases. As noted earlier in the chapter, I consider these structural issues, even though they may not be easily observable, because they are a reflection of the values and beliefs that have been developed from people's experiences. Thus, this one research project intersected with both visible and invisible structures that significantly influence IE in Canada.

Raising Two Areas for Further IE Research in Canada and Beyond

When considering structural aspects of IE in Canada, whether those are policy frameworks as raised by Jahnukainen et al., those specific to a segment of the population who engage in home-schooling as discussed by Jahr and Kruschel, indirect or overt barriers for young refugee students as evidenced by Korntheuer, or how principals' organisations support the professional learning of school administrators related to IE, it is also important to think about other, largely unrepresented aspects of IE in Canada. In this section, I address two aspects of structures related to IE in Canada. Neither is an aspect of research that I have been significantly engaged with, but both are important as we consider the environment and structures of IE in Canada.

First, I turn to educational structures that involve Indigenous students with disabilities on reserves in Canada. Second, there is an increasing recognition in Canada of the intersection of IE and the experiences of students from racialised and marginalised populations. Particularly, I draw attention to the research of Gillian Parekh and colleagues in relationship to racialised students in Canada's most populous largest and most diverse city, Toronto.

Indigenous Students

A significant structural issue related to IE in Canada is how Indigenous students with disabilities are supported. To provide some context, according to the most recent available Canadian census data from 2016, there are approximately 1.7 million Indigenous peoples in Canada (Statistics Canada, 2021). About 44% of Indigenous peoples in Canada live on reserves while the balance lives off-reserve (Statistics Canada, 2021).

As noted in the chapter by Jahnukainen et al., education in Canada is a provincial responsibility. However, Indigenous students on reserve attend schools that are under federal government responsibility. Schools on reserves get significantly less funding that schools under provincial responsibility. This structural issue directly influences Indigenous students with disabilities on-reserve as less funding is available for supports and services. Kimberly Maich and I wrote about this unusual and problematic issue in 2018 and noted that:

> This arrangement is challenging with approximately 30 percent lower funding for these schools—including students with SEN (Porter 2016)—creating limited services for Indigenous students (e.g., educational assessments). High absentee rates, teacher recruitment, low literacy rates, and high drop-out rates further exacerbate the challenges faced by those students who have SEN (Normore 2015).
>
> (Maich & Sider, 2018, p. 4)

Indigenous students with disabilities on-reserve have access to less services and supports than Indigenous or non-Indigenous student off-reserve. This is a significant structural issue that contradicts principles of equity and human rights (Canadian Human Rights Commission, 2017).

A second issue related to Indigenous students is how Indigenous ways of knowing may be able to be leveraged as a model for supporting all students with disabilities. The Truth and Reconciliation Commission (TRC) of Canada investigated residential schools for Indigenous students and submitted 94 recommendations to address the harms caused to Indigenous families and communities. Although the TRC's Calls to Action addressed many educational issues including funding, curriculum development, and teacher training, it did not specifically address how Indigenous students with disabilities could be best supported through structures more aligned with Indigenous pedagogies (Truth and Reconciliation Commission, 2015). It is surprising that not more scholarly attention has been directed to this issue, although this may be partly due to the ways in which Indigenous groups conceptualise ability and disability (Velarde, 2018). As Indigenous, Canadian, and international scholars consider IE in Canada, increased focus should be given to how Indigenous ways of knowing could be used to effectively support students with disabilities. I see great opportunity for non-Indigenous educators to learn from a more holistic, community-oriented model that Indigenous scholars and elders could provide.

Racialised Students

A second structural area that is emerging in Canada and for which much more attention must be given is regarding the experiences of students with disabilities from racialised and marginalised communities. The work of Gillian Parekh is particularly instructive here as it is situated in Canada's most populous city, Toronto. Parekh has explored a wide variety of issues related to disability including how students from different racialised groups perceive and identify (or do not) with disability (Parekh & Brown, 2020) and how Canada's largest school board, the Toronto District School Board, has developed and adapted programming for students with disabilities from different equity-seeking groups (Parekh, 2020). Parekh's work exploring academic streaming is important in demonstrating the different pathways and outcomes that student from different racialised groups experience (e.g., Parekh et al., 2021). In Parekh and Brown (2019), they examine provincial and school board data sets to explore the linkages between racialised groups and placements in special education programmes. They state that their study "closely mirrors the findings of many international studies that find students enrolled in special education programs are more likely to be racialised, poor, and have limited access to resources" (p. 127). Parekh and Brown (2019) conclude that their study, "makes a strong case for how the congregation and segregation of students can shape how disability is, itself, constructed and how special education programs can further disable students' access and participation" (p. 130).

I highlight this work here to illustrate that, although Canada has made significant progress to implementing IE policies and practices, there is significant work yet to be done. The experiences of Indigenous students with disabilities on reserves, as well as that of racialised youth in Canada's most populous city, demonstrate the vast terrain requiring further IE research and advocacy in Canada. Structural aspects, whether these be formal in the sense of policy frameworks (e.g., federal funding for reserve schools) or informal in the ways in which students are streamed in Canada's largest city, provide insight into the complex and compelling work yet to be done in Canada.

This book, with its focus on blending different perspectives on IE from Europe and Canada, is an important way forward in problematising and shaping future IE research. Documenting both the visible and invisible structures that inhibit and enable IE will be important in ongoing research. Considering IE in Newfoundland and Labrador as well as Finland as provided by Jahnukainen and colleagues, the experiences of newcomers in Munich and Toronto as described by Korntheuer, as well as the unique area of Christian homeschooling in Canada and Germany as documented by Jahr and Kruschel, shed light onto both the observable and latent structural aspects related to IE. Exploring other aspects of IE in Canada, including the research I have engaged in with school principals, and emerging aspects related to Indigenous and racialised students, demonstrate that there is much work yet to be done to support research in inclusive education in Canada and beyond.

References

Andrews, D., Walton, E., & Osman, R. (2019). Constraints to the implementation of inclusive teaching: A cultural historical activity theory approach. *International Journal of Inclusive Education*, 1–16.

Baxter, M. (2020, September 10). *Parents are embracing home-schooling during COVID-19: What will that mean for kids?* TVO. https://www.tvo.org/article/parents-are-embracing-home-schooling-during-covid-19-what-will-that-mean-for-their-kids

Boger, M.-A. (2015). Theorie der trilemmatischen Inklusion. In I. Schnell (Ed.), *Herausforderung Inklusion. Theoriebildung und Praxis* (pp. 51–62). Klinkhardt.

Boger, M.-A. (2017). Theorien der Inklusion – eine Übersicht. *Zeitschrift für Inklusion Online, 1*(12). https://www.inklusion-online.net/index.php/inklusion-online/article/view/413

Canadian Charter of Rights and Freedoms, s 7, Part 1 of the Constitution Act, 1982, being Schedule B to the Canada Act 1982 (UK), 1982, c 11.

Canadian Human Rights Commission. (2017). *Left out: Challenges faced by persons with disabilities in Canada's schools.* Canadian Legal Information Institute. https://www.canlii.org/en/commentary/doc/2017CanLIIDocs3489#!fragment//BQCwhgziBcwMYgK4DsDWszIQewE4BUBTADwBdoByCgSgBpltTCIBFRQ3AT0otokLC4EbDtyp8BQkAGU8pAELcASgFEAMioBqAQQByAYRW1SYAEbRS2ONWpA

DeMatthews, D. E., Kotok, S., & Serafini, A. (2020). Leadership preparation for special education and inclusive schools: Beliefs and recommendations from successful principals. *Journal of Research on Leadership Education, 15*(4), 303–329.

DeMatthews, D. E., Serafini, A., & Watson, T. N. (2021). Leading inclusive schools: Principal perceptions, practices, and challenges to meaningful change. *Educational Administration Quarterly, 57*(1), 3–48.

Fisher, Y. (2017). Predicting teachers' perception of inclusion: What is the role of self-efficacy? *EC Psychology and Psychiatry, 2*(5), 157–171.

Fitzgerald, H. (2018). Disability and barriers to inclusion. In I. Brittain & A. Beacom (Eds.), *The Palgrave handbook of Paralympic studies* (pp. 55–70). Palgrave Macmillan.

Friedman, C., & Owen, A. L. (2017). Defining disability: Understandings of and attitudes towards ableism and disability. *Disability Studies Quarterly, 37*(1).

MacCormack, J., & Matheson, I. (2017). *Bear with me: Teaming up with parents of students with special needs.* Education Canada. https://www.edcan.ca/articles/bear-with-me/

Maich, K., & Sider, S. (2018). *Special education needs and disabilities in secondary education (Canada).* Bloomsbury Education & Childhood Studies.

Özokcu, O. (2017). Investigating the relationship between teachers' self-efficacy beliefs and efficacy for inclusion. *European Journal of Special Education Research, 2*(6), 234–252.

Parekh, G. (2020). How inclusive do we really want to be? In S. Winton & G. Parekh (Eds.), *Critical perspectives on education policy and schools, families, and communities* (pp. 123–139). Information Age Publishing.

Parekh, G., & Brown, R. S. (2019). Changing lanes: The relationship between special education placement and students' academic futures. *Educational Policy, 33*(1), 111–135.

Parekh, G., & Brown, R. S. (2020). Naming and claiming: The tension between institutional and self-identification of disability. *Canadian Journal of Disability Studies, 9*(5), 347–379.

Parekh, G., Brown, R. S., & Zheng, S. (2021). Learning skills, system equity, and implicit bias within Ontario, Canada. *Educational Policy, 35*(3), 395–421.

Rämä, I., Kontu, E., & Pirttimaa, R. (2020). Special education without teaching assistants? The development process for students with autism. *Journal of Education and Learning, 9*(6), 163–172.

Sider, S. (2014). School leadership across borders: Examining a Canadian-Haitian partnership to support educational capacity-building in Haiti. *International Studies in Educational Administration, 42*(1), 75–87.

Sider, S. (2019). Peer coaching in a school in Cairo, Egypt: Implementation, barriers, and pathways to effective adoption. *International Journal of Mentoring and Coaching in Education, 8*(1), 37–51.

Sider, S. (2020). School principals and students with special education needs in a pandemic: Emerging insights from Ontario, *Canada. International Studies in Educational Administration, 48*(2), 78–84.

Sider, S., Desir, C., Jean-Marie, G., & Watson, A. (2019). Exploring educational opportunities toward gender equity for girls in Haiti. In C. Sunal & K. Mutua (Eds.), *Transforming public education in Africa, Caribbean, and Middle East* (pp. 199–217). Information Age Publishing.

Sider, S., Maich, K., & Morvan, J. (2017). School principals and students with special education needs: Leading inclusive schools. *Canadian Journal of Education, 40*(2). https://journals.sfu.ca/cje/index.php/cje-rce/article/view/2417/2433

Sider, S., Morvan, J., & Borner, M. (2021). Inclusive and equitable education in Haiti: A case study of civil society organizations and international partnerships to reach the Sustainable Development Goals in a fragile state. *Compare: A Journal of Comparative and International Education.*

Specht, J. (2013). Introduction to the special issue: What is inclusive education in Canada? *Canadian Journal of Education, 36*(1).

Statistics Canada. (2021). *Statistics on Indigenous peoples.* https://www.statcan.gc.ca/eng/subjects-start/indigenous_peoples

Stenman, S., & Pettersson, F. (2020). Remote teaching for equal and inclusive education in rural areas? An analysis of teachers' perspectives on remote teaching. *International Journal of Information and Learning Technology, 37*(3), 87–98.

Takala, M. (2007). The work of classroom assistant in special and mainstream education in Finland. *British Journal of Special Education, 34*(1), 50–57.

Todd, L. (2007). *Partnerships for inclusive education: A critical approach to collaborative working.* Routledge.

Truth and Reconciliation Commission (2015). *Truth and reconciliation commission of Canada: Calls to action.* https://ehprnh2mwo3.exactdn.com/wp-content/uploads/2021/01/Calls_to_Action_English2.pdf

van Rensburg, M. J. (2020). *Autistics' perspectives of autism funding in Ontario* [unpublished Master's thesis]. Carleton University.

Velarde, M. R. (2018). Indigenous perspectives of disability. *Disability Studies Quarterly, 38*(4). https://dsq-sds.org/article/view/6114/5134

Waterfield, B., & Whelan, E. (2017). Learning disabled students and access to accommodations: Socioeconomic status, capital, and stigma. *Disability & Society, 32*(7), 986–1006.

Part III

Cultures around Inclusive Education

10 Cultural Challenges for School and Social Participation in Canada's Indigenous Reserves

The Example of the Atikamekw Community of Manawan in Québec

Nastasia Herold

Inclusion and Social Minorities

Inclusion in education is a highly complex term that has been interpreted and discussed very differently and controversially in Germany since its emergence in the early 2000s (Ahrbeck, 2014; Hinz, 2013; Wocken, 2010). One strand of discourse deals with the differentiation of the term into a *narrow* and a *broad* understanding. While the former is rather related to special education and focuses on disability, the broader understanding of inclusion is based on the human image of uniqueness, it avoids categorical demarcation from groups and respects the dignity of each individual child and young person (Wocken, 2015, p. 3). An explanation of the concept of inclusion in this broad understanding can be found in the *Index for Inclusion* where Boban & Hinz (2003, p. 10) state that Inclusion means change and a never-ending process of increased learning and increasing participation of all pupils. Thus, inclusion is not only about increasing participation in school life and the teaching-learning process but also about the resulting participation in society as a whole. This chapter subscribes to the broad understanding of the inclusion concept and increasing participation focusing on Indigenous minorities in Canada threatened by marginalisation.

Indigenous minorities—minority groups without a migration background—have so far been discussed very little in the context of inclusion discourse, although UNESCO (2005) explicitly addresses marginalised, excluded and vulnerable groups in its *Guidelines for Inclusion*, such as "ethnic" or "linguistic" minorities (p. 1). Indigenous people often must subordinate themselves economically, culturally and also educationally to the majority society, although they represent a majority in certain communities or regions. They advocate for an education policy that teaches their children, who are often bilingual, the language, culture, and values of the local group without obstructing their ability to connect

DOI: 10.4324/9781003204572-13

with the majority society. Examples of such groups in Germany are the Sorbs in eastern Saxony and Brandenburg and, in Italy, the German-speaking Tyroleans in South Tyrol.

With respect to linguistic minorities in Canada, it is French-Canadian society which is often thought of first, whose language in Canada is an official language equivalent to English but is spoken by significantly fewer people. French is the dominant language only in the province of Québec. There are numerous studies and school models for dealing with both languages in education (Boudreau & Dubois, 1998; Conseil de la langue française, 1990; Landry, 2014; Morcos, 1989). But what about the approximately 50 Indigenous languages that are still spoken in Canada? They have no political recognition at a federal or provincial level although, according to the 2011 Canadian Census, for 7.7% of the First Nations, their first language is their Indigenous language (Leclerc, 2015).[1]

Since a language always goes hand in hand with a history, culture, and values, the integration of the Indigenous first language into schooling can only take place with the simultaneous teaching of the Indigenous culture. In the following sections, problems, opportunities and implementation in the design of institutionalised education for First Nations children and adolescents will be explained and discussed using the example of the Atikamekw in Québec. The aim of the chapter is to analyse which problems the Canadian reserves must face in educational questions and which culturally sensitive measures can be undertaken with the aim of increasing participation. My linguistic and sociographic field studies in the Atikamekw community Manawan, which lasted several months, and the resulting master's thesis on the bilingual language situation in the reserve are the basis of this chapter.

In Canada, more than 1.4 million Indigenous people live. The Atikamekw are one of 11 Indigenous nations in Québec. The approximately 8.200 Atikamekw (as of January 2022; CIRNAC, 2022) live on their ancestral territory north of the St. Lawrence River between Montreal and Québec City in the three isolated reserves of Manawan, Opitciwan and Wemotaci. Each community is administered and politically represented by a council elected democratically every four years, headed by an elected chief. In 1982, the three reserves founded a joint Conseil de la Nation Atikamekw (Council of the Atikamekw Nation) as an official and joint representation of the Atikamekw at regional, provincial and federal levels. The head of the National Council is the Great Chief, who is elected every four years by all members of the nation. The Atikamekw speak the most vital Indigenous language in Canada with 96% native speakers (Leclerc, 2015). Their second language is French. Although all First Nations in Canada struggle with the same or similar historical, political, economic and social conditions, they differ from each other not only linguistically and culturally but also in their political commitment to preserve their language and culture. The specific situation of the Atikamekw described below can therefore only be transferred to other First Nations of Canada to a limited extent.

Historical Educational Structures of Indigenous People in Canada

With the colonisation of Canada and the Indigenous people living there, the European understanding of education was introduced into North America. In the Jesuit reports of 1634, it is noted about the Indigenous people by the St. Lawrence River: "La seule education et instruction leur manque" (Coté, 1858, pp. 1634/28).[2] What remains unmentioned is that education in other cultures contains different values and teachings from those in Europe or Canada, which was shaped by Europe. To survive and to live together, the Indigenous people of Canada had their own ideas for bringing up their children. With the arrival of the Europeans, these ideas were increasingly repressed and lost in some cultures. The Atikamekw in Québec were able to largely preserve their language, traditions and values despite Canada's assimilation policy, which, according to Lavoie and Vaugeois (2010, p. 27), peaked in the period of the late 19th century up to the beginning of the second half of the 20th century. However, the gains in political autonomy in the field of education are still relatively recent and must overcome both the historical events and the economic and socio-economic situation, as well as respecting today's post-secondary educational structures of Québec and Canada so that young Indigenous people can participate fully in Canada's post-secondary education system and thus in Canadian society as a whole.

The Holistic Learning Model of the Atikamekw

The upbringing and socialisation of Indigenous children in North America has traditionally been the responsibility of the family (Arens & Braun, 2008, p. 42). Children mainly learned by watching, trial and error, or were individually instructed in gender-specific skills, such as handicrafts, hunting and food preparation. For the Atikamekw, Audy and Lemay (2009) state that the children's education used to take place within extended families on the Atikamekw territory following the rhythm of the seasons. Traditional activities included hunting, fishing, trapping, and gathering. The values of the community were traditionally taught to them by women. The grandparents, whose opinions were highly valued, also had a strong influence on the education of the Atikamekw children. Until they grew up, the girls and boys had to undergo several rites and ceremonies that influenced their developing education (Audy & Lemay, 2009).

The traditional educational model of the Atikamekw and other First Nations in Canada, as Audy and Lemay (2009) state, is *holistic* in nature for education has been seen here as a process of integration in which the whole person is involved, implying the physical, emotional, mental and spiritual aspects of life and continues throughout life.

Boarding Schools as a Central Institution for Social Assimilation

With the first expedition of the Frenchman Jacques Cartier in 1534/1535, the (French) colonisation of the territory of the Atikamekw and their neighbouring peoples began. In the first centuries, the Atikamekw's contact with Europeans was regionally limited to the south of their territory, the region on the St. Lawrence River between Montreal and Québec City. *The British Constitution Act* of 1867 created the Canadian government and its constitution without the inclusion of Indigenous peoples (Lepage, 2009, p. 22). In section 91(24) of the *Constitution Act* it was stipulated that the Indigenous people and the land reserved for them are the sole responsibility of the federal government (Government of Canada, 2017). Following this was the *Indian Act* passed in 1876, about which Lepage (2009, p. 22) claims that it sealed the legal impotence of the Indigenous peoples of Canada in almost all areas and completely undermined their autonomy, including the education of their children and young people. The law is still in force today.

By the middle of the 19th century at the latest, Canada began to pursue a more aggressive policy towards First Nations which, according to Lavoie and Vaugeois (2010, p. 27), officially aimed at settlement, education, Christianisation and instruction in agriculture and trades. In 1892, an alliance was formed between the Canadian government and various churches to jointly establish and administer so-called Residential Schools (French: pensionnats), which were boarding schools for Indigenous children (Ottawa, 2010, p. 7). Between 1874 and 1996, there were 130 of these Residential Schools in Canada (Ottawa, 2010, p. 9). In the province of Québec, there were six such schools but only from 1934 to 1990 (Ottawa, 2010, p. 9). As the reason for the much later introduction of these Residential Schools, Goulet (2016, p. 26) states that Québec, in contrast to the Anglophone provinces of Canada, only decided in the 1940s to make money available for the schooling of Indigenous children.

The Indigenous children in Québec were separated from their families at the age of five or six years and taken to one of the six Residential Schools, which were 200 kilometres or more away from their family homes (Ottawa, 2010, p. 25). Manawan and Opitciwan, two of the Atikamekw reserves, had primary schools, so the families were "lucky" that their children were "only" snatched from their familiar surroundings at the age of 12 (Ottawa, 2010, p. 25). Usually, the pupils were separated from their families for ten months a year (Ottawa, 2005, p. 39). The school subjects were French or English, the history of Canada and the world, geography, mathematics, natural sciences, and religious education (Ottawa, 2010, p. 33). The children were separated according to gender and age, which meant that siblings hardly ever saw each other (Ottawa, 2010, p. 29). Everyday life followed strict rules not only with regard to the timetable but also with regard to clothing, hygiene, sport and food (Ottawa, 2010, p. 52). Those who opposed the strict rules or achieved poor results in class risked being beaten (Ottawa, 2010, p. 53). According to a testimony quoted by Ottawa (2010, p. 98), some children were forced to eat soap if they dared to use their first language. A certain number of Residential School pupils, especially orphans, the "weak," and girls, were mentally and physically abused, including sexually. Talking about it would have only brought them even more punishment, which is why many have only begun to talk about their experiences in recent years, when the subject of the Residential Schools finally began to be reappraised in Québec (Ottawa, 2010, p. 99).

The ban on the first language, the subjects taught, the standardisation of clothing and hairstyles, the separation of girls, boys, and age groups as well as the strict daily schedule in the Residential Schools did not correspond to the traditional customs of the Atikamekw children, who communicated with their families exclusively in their Indigenous language, received individual lessons or learned together with their siblings, cousins and friends, and whose everyday life was marked by survival in the forests north of the St. Lawrence River. There was no consideration taken of their origin; on the contrary, the Residential Schools system was devised to uproot the children and to assimilate them into the Euro-Canadian way of life so that they could give up their status as "Indian" laid down in the *Indian Act.*[3] According to the Fondation autochtone de guérison (2003, as cited in Pronovost et al., 2010, p. 3), the social problems in the Indigenous communities that still exist today can be attributed to the massive social after-effects of the decades-long policy of compulsory boarding. According to Pronovost et al. (2010), these long-term effects include family violence and alcohol and drug abuse, which can lead to physical and sexual abuse, loss of parental care and self-destructive behaviour.

Indigenous people today intend to overcome the decades of deprivation of their rights and the associated loss of culture through political, economic, and cultural self-determination.

Increasing Educational Autonomy since the 1970s

In 1969, the partnership between state and church was abolished, heralding the end of the Residential Schools in Canada (Lepage, 2009, p. 39). More and more reserves were equipped with elementary schools and older children were encouraged to enrol in secondary schools and Cégeps (senior high school) in cities in the region. The teachers, both on the reserves and in the cities, were paid by the government and followed the Canadian education system, where French or English was the sole language of instruction and the subjects taught were prescribed by the government. At the beginning of the 1970s, the National Indian Brotherhood declared the creation of its own education system as a priority for its movement and published the *Indian Control of Indian Education* (Lepage, 2009, p. 40). Today, almost all primary and secondary education is under the control of the reserve councils. The agreements on autonomy are also considered concluded for health and social services as well as for leisure, housing, public safety and economic development (Lepage, 2009, pp. 39–40). Thus, it has been increasingly possible for the Atikamekw to develop and establish their own educational system in order to adapt it to the conditions on their communities.

The Bilingual Primary School System of the Atikamekw

The education of the First Nations children on the reserves is funded today by the Ministry of Indigenous Services, which approves the monies dedicated to elementary and secondary school management and provides financial support to students in post-secondary education.

When the Conseil de la Nation Atikamekw (Council of the Atikamekw Nation) was founded in 1982, an education department was set up which is responsible for developing and revising the Atikamekw's own school system in which the Indigenous language is now established as the language of instruction and which at the same time respects their values and culture. According to Audy and Lemay (2009), all three Atikamekw reserves stated that the provincial school system adopted in their villages was not adapted to their needs: The children were learning French, but the quality of the knowledge of this second language was poor, and the schools were using Québec teaching materials in which the children did not recognise their culture. Many pupils stayed away from classes and almost nobody graduated from secondary school. The Atikamekw called for the development of an educational system that would meet the needs of their children and enhance and protect their language and culture (Audy & Lemay, 2009). In 1992, the bilingual education programme developed for the Atikamekw was introduced for the first grades of primary schools. In 1998, the first graduates of this programme completed primary school and switched to secondary school. The bilingual school programme of the Atikamekw provides for literacy in the first language (i.e., in Atikamekw Nehiromowin). Since this language was traditionally a purely oral language, a written norm had to be created beforehand and neologisms had to be developed, introduced and enforced in the various subject areas. In addition, it was necessary to incorporate Atikamekw values into the teaching and learning materials (Audy & Lemay, 2009).

During my research stay in Manawan, I was able to observe many examples of the inclusion of the Atikamekw culture in everyday elementary school lessons. Many stories in the work materials deal with situations in the forest or in the Atikamekw community. The pictures in the books show Atikamekw children in the forest instead of Euro-Canadian children in a city. The science lessons mainly cover the flora and fauna of the Atikamekw territory. There is a cultural week in May and October, during which the Atikamekw children do not attend school in order to engage in the traditional activities in the forest with their parents (Guèye, 2017). The teachers, who are Atikamekw themselves, teach the primary school children patiently and peacefully, which follows on from the traditional interaction between adults and children outside school.

The *programme bilingue* (bilingual school programme) covers preschool up to Grade 6. The programme is structured so that, year by year, the language of instruction changes from Atikamekw to French. The children are alphabetised in Atikamekw and 90% of the first grade is taught in Atikamekw and 10% in French. This ratio changes from school year to school year in favour of French, until the majority of Grade 5 and 6 classes are taught in French (Castonguay, 1997, p. 44). The aim of this programme is to do justice to the local traditions of the Atikamekw while at the same time making it possible for the children to participate in social life outside the community by learning the majority language of Québec.

With an alphabetisation programme in the Indigenous language Atikamekw, the use of French as a second language, the establishment of the Atikamekw culture and its values in teaching and materials, an environment could be created in the Atikamekw primary schools which takes greater account of the realities on the Indigenous communities than the Québec educational programme. In Manawan, according to Audy and Lemay (2009), parents now have a choice between the Atikamekw and French-Canadian programmes so that the few children who already know French or speak it as their first language before they go to school are not disadvantaged.

Nevertheless, the drop-out rate on reserves such as Manawan remains worryingly high, not only because of the language of instruction, French, especially in secondary schools, but also because of the interplay of historical and socio-economic factors that complicate everyday school life, as will be explained in more detail in the following section.

Current Educational Problems in the First Nations Reserve of Manawan

From secondary school onwards, the Conseil de la Nation Atikamekw (1992, p. 35) defined French as the language of instruction and English as a second language in its working protocol for the "école Atikamekw" (Atikamekw school). This fact poses a problem because it does not correspond to the language situation in Manawan, since 97% of Manawans speak Atikamekw as their first language and not French (Leclerc, 2015). French is the second language and English is the first foreign language. Another problem at the secondary school in Manawan is that several francophone teachers do not come from Québec but, as Tremblay (2010, p. 3) says, from Europe and North and Central Africa. The pupils are therefore confronted with different varieties of the French language in class, although they are not yet fully proficient in the language itself.

Addressing the alarmingly high drop-out rate in Manawan, Moar published a study in 2011 dealing with this topic. His report shows that 48% of Manawans drop out of school between the ages of 14 and 19. Only 6% of the under-20s in Manawan have a secondary school diploma, while the rate in Québec as a whole is around 80% (Moar, 2011, p. 4).

Moar's (2011) statistics show that since the opening of the École secondaire Otapi (Manawan Secondary School) in 1992, an average of 4.4 pupils per year gain their secondary school diploma. Among pupils repeating grades, the study found that it did not matter whether students participated in the bilingual programme (75%) or in the francophone programme (73%) in elementary school (Moar, 2011). However, the drop-out rate among 14- to 16-year-olds is somewhat higher among children from the bilingual programme than among those from the francophone programme (37.6%–22.4%; Moar, 2011, p. 7), which may also be due to the better social situation of some parents of the children coming from the francophone programme. From these figures, it can be concluded that the current elementary school programme and the accompanying linguistic and cultural adaptation of the teaching system in primary education are not yet sufficient. The question is, therefore, what other factors need to be taken into account and what measures need to be taken in Manawan to improve children's real opportunities?

As Moar (2011, p. 20) states, from the point of view of the teachers at the secondary school in Manawan, the pupils' main difficulty is reading and writing French as the language of instruction. Family problems, such as a lack of support from parents or alcoholism in the household, also make everyday school life more difficult for adolescents (Moar, 2011, p. 31). Over 23% of school dropouts surveyed stated that they did not know why they had dropped out of school. The main reasons for the other young people interviewed were school problems, such as difficulties with the content of the lessons or having to re-take grades multiple times, which embarrassed them. Other reasons cited for dropping out include early pregnancy, peer group influence, the school climate (lack of respect between pupils and teachers), a stable relationship or drug use (Moar, 2011, pp. 9–10). There are several professional contact points in Manawan (e.g., psychologists, nurses, social workers), but these are often non-Indigenous people who do not speak Atikamekw, so that young people who learn French at school but use Atikamekw as their first language of communication usually do not seek professional help (Pronovost et al., 2010, p. 6).

Various models have been established in recent years to facilitate secondary education for young people in Manawan. For example, children can insert a pre-school year for secondary school (an additional seventh grade) between elementary and secondary school, which prepares them intensively for the methods and language of instruction used there (Conseil des Atikamekw de Manawan, 2016, p. 24). In addition, Otapi Secondary School has set up so-called MSS classes (formation de métiers semi-spécialisés, i.e., semi-specialised vocational training), which helps young people who have completed primary school but do not meet secondary school requirements. In the MSS class, pupils can continue to participate in lessons and, at the same time, be integrated into certain fields of work in the village (Conseil des Atikamekw de Manawan, 2016, p. 11). In addition, extracurricular excursions to the forest and the city are organised for all students and, as already mentioned, cultural weeks are organised in spring and autumn, during which the children have no schooling in order to learn traditional activities from their parents (Conseil des Atikamekw de Manawan, 2016, pp. 25, 33).

Since the 2017/2018 school year, Atikamekw lessons have been introduced for secondary Grades 7 and 8 so that the pupils now learn in secondary school about the structure of their first language as well as the oral and written distinctions between Atikamekw and French. This is an important step towards the recognition of Atikamekw Nehiromowin as the first language of these young people.

Despite conceptual restructuring in certain areas in recent years, the number of secondary school graduates in Manawan is increasing only slowly, so much remains to be done to make life easier for Manawan's pupils and to ensure their full participation in the education system and the majority society. As a measure to create a school that is better adapted to the cultural conditions in Manawan, not only should an Atikamekw secondary school education programme be developed and established that, like the elementary school programme, is responsive to the linguistic and cultural realities, but at the same time, schools need to work more closely with parents to actively involve them in their children's school careers. Since the children of the Atikamekw as well as many other Indigenous people were removed for many decades from the reserves to be taught in the Residential Schools and the secondary schools on the reserves have only existed for just a few decades, parents have not yet had the opportunity to learn how important their own role is in supporting their children at school.

Two Educational Projects to Enhance the Appreciation of the Language and Culture in Manawan

In view of the still limited financial resources in Manawan, two initiatives undertaken there will be presented in the following, which, although they involve additional expenditure for teaching staff, young people, parents and public institutions, hardly require any financial resources from the Atikamekw schools and enjoy lively participation. The first is a film project and the second is an online encyclopaedia project.

The Wapikoni mobile project was launched in 2003 by the Québec film director Manon Barbeau, the Council of the Atikamekw Nation and the First Nations Youth Council of Quebec and Labrador. It is a mobile studio that brings together young people of the First Nations to create audio-visual and musical works. The mobile studio travels to Indigenous villages in Québec, Labrador and beyond, and is sponsored by several official and private institutions. Volunteers teach the young Indigenous people how to use digital tools to make short films and create musical compositions. Twice a year, on average, Wapikoni mobile also stops in Manawan and welcomes about 30 young participants who are trained and supported for all stages of their film and musical creations. Some short films of Manawan's Atikamekw have already been screened and awarded prizes at international film festivals. For the young Atikamekw, Wapikoni mobile is not only an opportunity to express themselves artistically and to work with their own language, culture, personality and imagination, but they are also motivated and supported both by the volunteers and by the village community, which is encouraged by the fact that all newly created works are shown publicly on a large screen in the village at the end of each visit by the mobile studio (Wapikoni, 2017).

Another project is Wikipetcia Atikamekw Nehiromowin. It is a Wikipedia project that started in 2013 as a school project at Otapi Secondary School in Manawan. The online encyclopaedia Wikipedia belongs to the non-profit Wikimedia Foundation and is a collaborative encyclopaedia on the Internet that already has editions in many languages. Wikipedia works with wikis (i.e., websites that can be read and edited by their users). The Wikipetcia project was started after the pupils' council of Otapi Secondary School had approved the project in May 2013, as it is always consulted before school projects are initiated (Wikipetcia, 2018). In their computer classes, the students in the higher grades of the school learned about how a wiki is structured and about the Wikipedia guidelines. In accordance with Wikimedia Foundation regulations for a Wikipedia in a new language, the pupils initially wrote their articles in Atikamekw in a test wiki, the Wikimedia Incubator (Wheeler, 2017). A main goal of the project was the use of the Atikamekw Wikipedia as an encyclopaedia for elementary schools in the communities, which is why the secondary school students were encouraged to limit their articles to topics reflecting the Atikamekw culture (local flora and fauna, traditional activities or important Atikamekw personalities; Wheeler, 2017). Since the pupils had not practiced writing their first language correctly since elementary school, they were assisted by an Atikamekw language specialist who checked the syntax, grammar and spelling of the articles (Wikipetcia, 2018). Within the first school year, more than 160 articles were written in Atikamekw using the Wikimedia Incubator (Wheeler, 2017). In 2016, the project was extended to the other two reserves, Wemotaci and Opitciwan. Due to the lively participation of the Atikamekw population and about 1000 translations for the Wikipetcia interface, the articles and related pages were transferred from the Incubator to the publicly accessible Wikipedia by the Wikimedia Foundation in June 2017 (Wheeler, 2017).[4] Atikamekw is a traditionally purely oral language, now standardised in the written form but hardly represented at all on the Internet, a medium also heavily used by the Atikamekw (Wheeler, 2017). Thanks to the Wikipetcia project, which was started at the secondary school in Manawan, Atikamekw is now the language of an online encyclopaedia for the first time, thus contributing to the preservation and promotion of this language. At the same time, the wiki principle will enable all Atikamekw to participate in the project.

The two projects presented here have a lot in common: Within a certain framework, the young people have the freedom to work on a topic of their own choice, in their own language, with continuing support and with a sustainable result (i.e., a film accessible online or a contribution to an encyclopaedic article). The high level of media interest shown to both initiatives also contributes to motivation. Both projects enable children and young people to get to know and cultivate their culture of origin better and to learn certain skills for participation in society outside their community.

Conclusion

The example of educational structures in Manawan shows that the needs and cultural conditions of local communities—such as linguistic, cultural, socio-economic and historical factors and traumas—need to be taken into account in order to reduce the school drop-out rate and create a participatory schooling environment. Atikamekw's traditional education system is holistic and responsive individually to all children and young people. The fact that this traditional model still exerts a strong influence is demonstrated by the MSS classes, the cultural weeks, the wide-ranging participation of the pupils' council, a pre-secondary seventh grade, the choice between the bilingual and the francophone programme in the elementary school, as well as the school and extra-curricular projects to promote pupils' self-image and cultural preservation using modern means.

Nevertheless, the Atikamekw have to follow certain guidelines in order to enable their young people to obtain a school diploma recognised in Québec and Canada as a whole. This challenge requires a high level of financial resources and the will of the school authorities and parents to change the existing education system which is still predominantly culturally insensitive. Once this path has been taken, then further steps will be possible that, taking full account of the special cultural and linguistic situation of the Indigenous people, will create the greatest possible opportunities for each individual child and all young people.

Notes

1. First Nations is the term used to refer to the Indigenous nations or peoples in Canada with the exception of Métis and Inuit in the north of the country.
2. English "They lack even the most basic elements of education and instruction."
3. The status as Indian used to be mainly disadvantageous as First Nations, for example, were not allowed to vote at federal level until 1960 and were not allowed to slaughter and sell livestock until 1951. Meanwhile, however, the status as Indigenous people now also provides advantages, such as certain tax concessions on the reserves.
4. The website of the project can be found at atj.wikipedia.org

References

Ahrbeck, B. (2014). *Inklusion. Eine Kritik.* Kohlhammer.

Arens, W., & Braun, H. M. (2008). *Die Indianer Nordamerikas – Geschichte, Kultur, Religion* (2nd ed.). Beck. Prospects, *49*(3), 313–328.

Audy, N., & Lemay, J. (2009). *Pochette d'information – Pour les enseignants d'apprenants atikamekws* (unverkäufliches Werk). La Tuque: Conseil de la Nation Atikamekw.

Boban, I., & Hinz, A. (Eds.). (2003). *Index für Inklusion – Lernen und Teilhabe in der Schule der Vielfalt entwickeln.* Martin-Luther-Universität Halle-Wittenberg.

Boudreau, A., & Dubois, L. (Eds.). (1998). *Le français, langue maternelle, dans les collèges et les universités en milieu minoritaire. Actes du colloque.* Les Éditions d'Acadie.

Castonguay, C. (1997). *Rapport d'évaluation du processus d'implantation du programme bilingue – Parler ma langue à l'aube du XXIe siècle, c'est un privilège.* Conseil de la nation Atikamekw.

CIRNAC (Crown-Indigenous Relations and Northern Affairs Canada). (2021). *Tribal Council Detail. Atikamekw Sipi – Conseil de la Nation Atikamekw.* https://fnp-ppn.aadnc-aandc.gc.ca/fnp/Main/Search/TCMain.aspx?TC_NUMBER=1064&lang=eng

Conseil de la Langue Française (Ed.). (1990). *Dix études portant sur l'aménagement de la langue au Québec.*

Conseil de la Nation Atikamekw. (1992). *L'école atikamekw – Énonce de politique éducative. Document de travail. La Tuque: Conseil de la nation Atikamekw.* Services documentaires de la Nation Atikamekw.

Conseil des Atikamekw de Manawan. (2016). *Rapport des activités, 2015-2016.* Secteur Éducation. http://manawan.com/pdf/rapport-2015-2016-education.pdf

Coté, A. (Ed.). (1858). *Relations des Jésuites. Ce qui s'est passé de plus remarquable dans les missions des pères de la Compagnie de Jésus dans la Nouvelle-France.*

Government of Canada. (2017). *Constitution Act, 1867.* https://lois.justice.gc.ca/eng/Const/page-1.html

Goulet, H. (2016). *Histoire des pensionnats indiens catholiques au Québec – Le rôle déterminant des pères oblats.* Les Presses de l'Université de Montréal.

Guèye, J. (2017). *École secondaire Otapi – Calendrier scolaire, 2017-2018.* www.otapi.ca/

Hinz, A. (2013). Inklusion – von der Unkenntnis zur Unkenntlichkeit?! *Zeitschrift für Inklusion Online, 1.*

Landry, R. (Ed.). (2014). *La vie dans une langue officielle minoritaire au Canada.* Les Presses de l'Université Laval.

Lavoie, M., & Vaugeois, D. (2010). *L'impasse amérindienne – Trois commissions d'enquête à l'origine d'une politique de tutelle et d'assimilation – 1828–1858.* Septentrion.

Leclerc, J. (2015). Les langues et les droits linguistiques des autochtones – Canada féféral. In J. Leclerc (Ed.), *L'aménagement linguistique dans le monde.* TLFQ, Université Laval.

Lepage, P. (2009). *Mythes et réalités sur les peuples autochtones* (2nd ed.). Commission des Droits de la Personne et des Droits de la Jeunesse.

Moar, C. (2011). *Enquête auprès des décrocheurs de Manawan – Rapport, 2011* (2nd ed.). Services éducatifs et culturels de Manawan.

Morcos, G. (Ed.). (1989). *Bilinguisme en enseignement du français.* Méridien.

Ottawa, G. (2010). *Les pensionnats indiens au Québec – Un double regard.* Cornac.

Pronovost, J., Plourde, C., & Alain, M. (2010). *Qu'en pensent les ADOS? Les problèmes psychosociaux qui touchent les jeunes atikamekw/Tan e ici wapatakik? E ici arimiparitcik ka ocki pimatisitcik Atikamekw otenak ka aitaciketcik.* Université du Québec à Trois-Rivières.

Tremblay, B. (2010). Enseigner à Manawan. *Viateurs Canada,* 125(Juin 2010), 1–3.

UNESCO. (2005). *Guidelines for inclusion: Ensuring access to education for all.* unesdoc.unesco.org/images/0014/001402/140224e.pdf

Wapikoni. (2017). *Wakiponi.* www.wapikoni.ca

Wheeler, M. (2017). *Web-savvy Atikamekw communities bring mother tongue to life online.* CBC. https://www.cbc.ca/news/canada/montreal/quebec-wikipedia-atikamekw-nastasia-herold-1.4135833

Wikipetcia. (2018). *Projet pédagogique Wikipetcia* Atikamekw.atj.wikipedia.org/wiki/Wikipetcia:Wikipetcia_Atikamekw#Description_du_projet

Wocken, H. (2010). Über Widersacher der Inklusion und ihre Gegenreden – Essay. *ApuZ*, 23–31.

Wocken, H. (2015). *Inklusion im Nebel. Kritik des Konzepts "Vielfalt schulischer Angebote" in einer "inklusiven Bildungslandschaft."* Online-Magazin Auswege – Perspektiven für den Erziehungsalltag. www.magazin-auswege.de/data/2014/04/Wocken_Inklusion_im_Nebel_ Printausgabe_Magazin_Auswege.pdf

11 Indigenous Cultural Inclusivity in Canadian Schools

Considerations and Imperatives

Jenn de Lugt

Introduction

Microcosms of Canadian society, K to 12 schools in Canada are becoming increasingly diverse. According to Statistics Canada (2010), approximately three Canadians in 10 could be a member of a visible minority group in 2031. Furthermore, a projection by Statistics Canada (2017) indicates that the proportion of Canada's foreign-born population could be as high as 30.0% by 2036. Adding to the growing immigrant population, Indigenous populations are also increasing, especially the youth age group (Chiefs Assembly on Education, 2012).

Before beginning this conversation, we must clarify what we mean by *inclusion* and *culture*. Since the signing of the *Salamanca Statement* (UNESCO, 1994), schools globally have committed to becoming more inclusive—recognising both just and ethical reasons for doing so. Very broadly, the framework was intended to include all students, celebrate differences, support learning, and respond to individual needs. In alignment with the chapter by Herold, this chapter will use the broad definition of inclusion and will focus on cultural considerations and imperatives specific to Indigenous populations in Canada. Herold specifically refers to the Atikamekw peoples of Quebec, and while recognising and respecting the diversity of the various Indigenous nations, I will refer more broadly to Indigenous peoples across Canada.

It is important to consider culture beyond ethnicity, race, and/or faith, to include social identities, and ways of knowing and being. The Canadian Human Rights Act (1985) is meant to ensure that all Canadians are afforded an equal opportunity and should, in no way, be discriminated against for their race, national or ethnic origin, colour, religion, age, sex, sexual orientation, gender identity or expression, marital status, family status, genetic characteristics, disability or conviction for an offence which has been suspended. Considering the diversity in Canadian classrooms, it is crucial that, as educators, we deliberately reassess to align our pedagogical practices to better represent the

DOI: 10.4324/9781003204572-14

learning needs of all students regardless of ability, learning needs, socio-economic status, and cultural identity.

An Overview of Indigenous Education in Canada

In Canada, Indigenous peoples and organisations are responsible for managing and delivering education programmes and services for students who are ordinarily living on reserve lands, with Indigenous Services Canada (ISC) providing funding for students who are 4–21 years of age, and who are enrolled in an eligible elementary or secondary programme. Reserve lands, are Crown lands held in trust for the use and benefit of the local Indian bands—or First Nations groups. These bands do not own the lands, but have governing rights and are responsible for band affairs such as education, band schools, housing, water and sewer, roads, and other community assets, businesses, and services. In 2010, 64% of Indigenous students attended reserve schools—with the majority (75%) attending Kindergarten or elementary schools and 25% enrolled in secondary on-reserve schools. The same report (Chiefs Assembly on Education, 2012) indicated that approximately 31% of Indigenous students attended off-reserve, provincially-funded schools, and the remaining 5% attended a private or federal school.

Through the *Calls to Action* of the Truth and Reconciliation Commission (TRC) of Canada (TRC, 2015) our attention has been drawn to our responsibility as a society to work towards reconciling the deep historical wrongs and injustices that have marginalised Indigenous peoples for too long. The *Calls to Action* specifically related to education are twofold in purpose: (1) to raise awareness of non-Indigenous learners of Indigenous peoples, their histories, traditions, and philosophies, and (2) to simultaneously include Indigenous learners through meaningful, relatable, and accessible learning opportunities. Historically, the mandatory boarding or Residential Schools, as described by Herold, decimated families, destroyed Indigenous ways of knowing and being, and has impacted the lives of generations, and generations to come. Through stories of survivors and from recent heart wrenching discoveries of unmarked graves of young Indigenous children, harrowing realities are being exposed. Now, more than ever, we are morally and ethically *obligated* to attempt to support Indigenous students in their learning so that their ways of knowing and being are restored and celebrated, in a way that honours their individual and collective identities.

This chapter will reflect and expand upon Herold's chapter entitled *Cultural Challenges for School and Social Participation in Canada's Indigenous Reserves.* Using the framework of self-determination theory as posited by Ryan and Deci (2000) and guided by the Medicine Wheel and Seven Grandfather Teachings, this chapter presents an opportunity to begin the process of reconciliation in education.

Challenges and Considerations

A considerable challenge to the educational attainment of Indigenous students is visible through the graduation rate disparity that is in stark contrast to that of the general Canadian population. In 2018, about 44% of Indigenous students on-reserve completed high school, compared to 88% of the remaining student population in Canada (Indigenous Services Canada, 2021). This clearly has implications for post-secondary education opportunities and future employment. Call to Action 10 calls for legislation that is aimed to close the achievement gap between Indigenous and non-Indigenous students.

Language

Ancestral languages across Turtle Island—the name traditionally used by many Indigenous groups for the landmass we call North America—are unique and hold valuable truths and realities of the cultures and nations to whom they belong. Further honouring Call to Action 10, which requires that teachers be trained to teach Indigenous languages, would see deliberate and sustained efforts to revive Indigenous languages.

Culture

As Herold and other authors (e.g., Gomashie, 2019; Morcom & Freeman, 2018) have articulated, "language goes hand in hand with a history, culture, and values" (In this volume), and should therefore be integrated with simultaneous teachings of Indigenous cultures. Calls to Action 62 and 63 call for provincial, territorial, and federal schools to adjust curriculums to include age-appropriate teaching and learning on residential schools, Treaties, and Indigenous peoples' historical and contemporary contributions to Canada—a mandatory education requirement for all students in the Kindergarten to Grade 12 schooling system. The intent is to build capacity for "intercultural understanding, empathy, and mutual respect" (TRC, 2015, p. 7).

TAKING THE CLASSROOM OUTSIDE

In a study by Hansen (2018), six Cree Elders from northern Manitoba discussed the importance of land-based education in promoting the well-being of Indigenous peoples in Canada. Herold, in her chapter, mentions how she witnessed instances of cultural inclusion with the Atikamekw teachings in everyday primary school lessons. This was done naturally and importantly through stories and work that were relevant to the Atikamekw children, picturing them in forest settings and situations. Science lessons were about the flora and fauna in the Atikamekw territory, and during a cultural week in both May and October students had the week off so they could be in the forest with their parents.

Implications

As highlighted in this volume, the traditional educational model of the Atikamekw people and, in fact, of most Indigenous peoples in Canada, was traditionally holistic in nature. Education was a shared responsibility and encompassed the physical, mental, emotional, and spiritual dimensions of the whole person in an integrated way. In addition, as stated by Herold, education and learning was not static and confined to 12 years of schooling but rather was ongoing and lifelong.

Self-Determination Theory as a Framework

Self-Determination Theory (SDT) is a macro theory related to human motivation, development, and wellness (Ryan & Deci, 2000). In short, the theory proposes three basic and universal psychological needs—autonomy, relatedness or belonging, and competence—essential and vital for optimum human functioning. Autonomy in Indigenous education would allow and encourage Indigenous groups to align their curriculums with the traditional teachings that are considered to be essential in their cultural ways of knowing and being. Relatedness is the sense of community that can result with understanding, appreciation, and celebration of a uniting culture. Day-to-day honouring of culture, as well as designated cultural days and weeks and seasonal celebrations is uniting and creates an important sense of community. Competence comes with successes in learning—the more autonomous and culturally relevant the curriculum is, the more likely students will be motivated to engage, persist, and succeed (Nalipay et al., 2020).

Holistic Education and the Medicine Wheel

A holistic approach to education considers the whole student—their mental condition (north), their spiritual well-being (east), their physical self (south), and their emotional self (west). Although variations exist, we are innately drawn to the four (cardinal) directions and many Indigenous nations across Canada use the Medicine Wheel as a fundamental framework for living, learning, being, and thriving. The Medicine Wheel is viewed as a guide to understanding that all things are interconnected and interrelated. The Medicine Wheel is divided into four teachings, four cardinal directions, four winds, etc. (see Figure 11.1). Although colours, orientation, quadrant titles, and keywords all can vary across nations, the teachings are focused on the

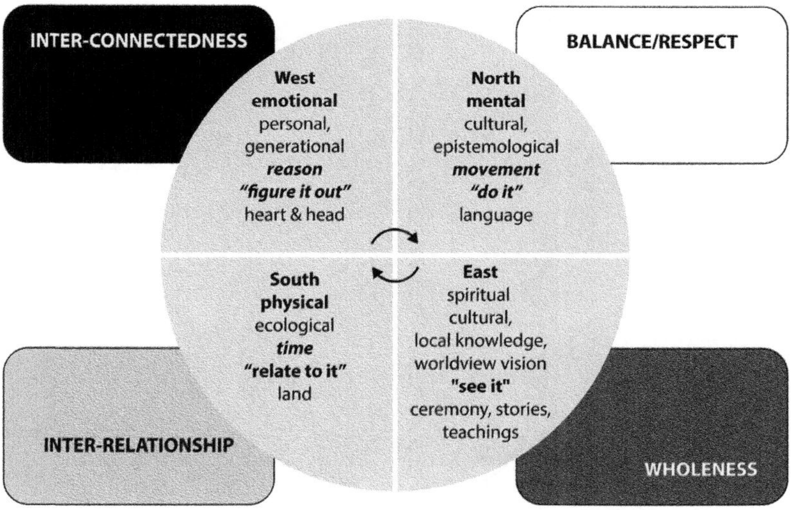

Figure 11.1 An Example of a Medicine Wheel (Bell, 2014).

idea that we are positioned in a relational way to all things, and through it, we can be guided to follow a good path (Morcom & Freeman, 2018).

By providing educational opportunities in the four areas, a more balanced, holistic, and culturally sensitive and appreciative approach is achieved. In a learning context, through the teaching and learning of traditional ways, as well as learning Indigenous languages, the mental aspect (north) of the Medicine Wheel is targeted. Student spiritual well-being (east) can be supported daily through ceremonies such as morning circles (similar to sunrise ceremonies) and seasonal celebrations and ceremonies. Traditional storytelling and teachings can also support students' spiritual learning and being. The physical dimension of the student (south) can be supported by land-based activities and learnings such as berry, herbal medicine, and wild rice picking, tree tapping, and maple syrup making, and other traditional interactions with the land. The emotional aspect and learning of the student (west) can be enhanced and supported through individual or group activities and ceremonies that emphasise healing and connecting the heart and the head. Also, through learning and following the seven sacred teachings—or core values (also known as the *Seven Grandfather Teachings*)—emotional wellness can be strengthened.

A multitude of feasts, powwows, dances, and ceremonies across Canada reflect the diversity of the Indigenous peoples. Some ceremonies, however, such as smudging, are widely practiced both in Canada and around the world. This fairly ubiquitous practice is frequently used for spiritual, emotional, physical, and mental well-being, along with cleansing a space or place, and for other restorative purposes.

Figure 11.2 Seven Grandfather Teachings.

Source: https://www.southernnetwork.org/site/seven-teachings

Seven Grandfather Teachings

There are numerous versions of the *Seven Grandfather Teachings* and all are considered to be foundational to an Indigenous way of life. The seven sacred teachings are considered to be core ways of interacting with others, and are deemed essential for the survival of communities and the way to live a good life in peace and without conflict. These teachings include: wisdom (beaver), bravery/courage (bear), honesty (Sabe/raven), respect (buffalo), truth (turtle), humility (wolf), and love (eagle; see Figure 11.2).

Although the Teachings are originally a set of Anishinaabe guiding principles passed down from generation to generation, they have been widely adapted by many Indigenous organisations and communities across Canada to align with their community values and morals (Seven Generations Education Institute, 2021).

The Seven Sacred Teachings are as follows:

- *Wisdom* (Nibwaakaawin): To cherish knowledge is to know Wisdom. Wisdom is given by the Creator to be used for the good of the People. In the Anishinawbe language this word expresses not only *wisdom* but also means *prudence* and *intelligence*. In addition to *wisdom*, this word can also mean *intelligence* and *knowledge*.

- *Love* (Zaagi'idiwin): To know love is to know peace. Love must be unconditional. When people are weak they need love the most.
- *Respect* (Manaaji'idiwin): To honour all Creation is to have respect. All of Creation should be treated with respect. You must give respect if you wish to be respected.
- *Bravery* (Zoongide'ewin): Is to face the foe with integrity. In the Anishinawbe language, this word literally means *state of having a fearless heart*. To do what is right even when the consequences are unpleasant.
- *Honesty* (Gwayakwaadiziwin): In facing a situation is to be brave. Always be honest in word and action. Be honest first with yourself, and you will more easily be able to be honest with others. This word can also mean *righteousness*.
- *Humility* (Dabasendiziwin): Is to know oneself as a sacred part of Creation. This word can also mean compassion, calmness, meekness, gentility or patience. You are equal to others, but you are not better.
- *Truth* (Debwewin): Is to know all of these things. Speak the truth. Do not deceive yourself or others (Northern College, 2020).

Cultural Identity and Relatedness and Mental/Emotional Health

Over the years, historically overt and covert inequalities have led to a range of negative health outcomes, including a disproportionately high rate of depression and suicidality among First Nations, Métis, and Inuit (FNMI) youth in Canada. Importantly, recent studies have shown that *cultural connectedness*, or the extent to which someone feels embedded in their cultural group, is a strong protective factor. A keen, positive sense of cultural identity has been shown to be associated with positive functioning and well-being (Crooks et al., 2017). Another study by Snowshoe and colleagues (2017) that looked at identity, traditions, and spirituality of cultural connectedness found that there was a strong and positive relationship to Indigenous well-being. Furthermore, Indigenous youth who are able to maintain positive family and school connections experience less emotional distress and are also less likely to participate in risk-taking behaviours (van der Woerd et al., 2005).

The Path Forward

Being cognizant of the challenges to equitable and inclusive educational experiences for Indigenous children and youth in Canada, we are morally and ethically obligated to make changes. It is undeniably a human rights issue if we are not providing for the needs of our Indigenous students in a way that is fully inclusive. In order to drive positive change, there are essential elements to consider—Indigenous autonomy, linguistic sovereignty, and cultural connectedness. These aspects can and should guide curricula, in order to resurrect and revive what has been depleted or lost over the years.

Indigenising Education in Canada—Federal, Provincial, and Territorial Initiatives

Preliminary, changes and initiatives have begun at all levels of government—federal, provincial, and territorial. In their draft report, Archibald and colleagues (2016) highlighted some of the challenges and considerations related to indigenising Kindergarten to Grade 12 education in Canada: the need for legislation and implementation of self-governance in education that includes urban Indigenous peoples; the ongoing challenge of insufficient funding; systematic and widespread change to make Indigenous knowledge and history a mandatory learning requirement; and, addressing Indigenous language teaching and learning more comprehensively. The following is a brief sampling of evolving programmes and initiatives across the country.

FEDERAL INITIATIVES

The Aboriginal Head Start Program began in 1995 and provides early intervention programming for FNMI children between the ages of three to five years and their families who live off-reserve. The programme is federally funded but locally delivered. The six elements of the programme include: Indigenous culture and language, education and school readiness, health promotion, nutrition, social support, and parental involvement. A few years later, a similar programme was offered on-reserve for young Indigenous students and their families. With the off-reserve students, it was found that culture and language fostered a positive sense of identity for both the children and their families. For the on-reserve students in the Head Start Program, Kindergarten teachers noted that they had better developed basic skills, were more independent, more confident, and had greater self-esteem compared to the students who didn't attend the Program (Archibald et al., 2016). Importantly, the benefits of the Head Start Program were further enhanced when learning was done from and on the land, and with family members (Peterson et al., 2018).

BRITISH COLUMBIA (BC) INITIATIVES

In 2015/2016, the BC Ministry of Education redesigned the K-9 curriculum to embed Indigenous perspectives and resources into each subject area at each grade level, with the intent to do the same for the Grades 10–12 curriculum as well. In addition, the First Nations Education Steering Committee has led the development of Indigenous curricula (Archibald et al., 2016).

ALBERTA INITIATIVES

Since 2006, the federally funded Alberta Initiative for School Improvement (AISI), has been attempting to close the gap in completion rates of Indigenous versus non-Indigenous students. Forty-eight funded projects targeted all grade levels and addressed areas of concern including literacy, cultural awareness, attendance, and Indigenous language and culture courses. The key findings of the review of the programmes revealed that, by involving Indigenous parents and Elders in meaningful ways, and by focusing on Indigenous language, culture, and history as an integral part of their curricula, Indigenous students were more likely to stay in school (Gunn et al., 2011).

SASKATCHEWAN INITIATIVES

In 2013, with extensive consultation with First Nations and Métis peoples, and through a literature review and research project, a joint Indigenous and provincial task force released a comprehensive report entitled: *Voice, Vision, and Leadership: A Place for All.* Since then, further research and consultation with scholars in New Zealand led to *Seeking Their Voices* and, subsequently, a programme entitled *Following Their Voices (FTV).* This programme is still active and gives autonomy to the schools participating in the programme but also emphasises engaging and meaningful pedagogies, Indigenous languages, learning from the land, developing relationships, and cultural activities, spaces, and events. Importantly, several schools have a devoted Indigenous space, smudge at the beginning of each day, and have an Elder in School to support their Indigenous student populations.

MANITOBA INITIATIVES

Manitoba has developed a curriculum and resources to support the learning of Indigenous languages and cultures for K to 12 students—the *Manitoba Curriculum Framework of Outcomes.*

ONTARIO INITIATIVES

Ontario's *Indigenous Education Strategy* was released in 2007 to support FNMI students and consists of three primary overarching goals: (1) to improve FNMI student achievement and well-being, (2) to close the achievement gap between Indigenous and all students, and (3) to increase public confidence in publicly funded education. In addition, Indigenous curriculum resources have been developed and teacher professional development enhanced (Archibald et al., 2016).

QUEBEC INITIATIVES

Although not a province-wide initiative, Herold (In this volume) has highlighted some positive changes to the educational experiences and options for the Atikamekw students. For students in Kindergarten to Grade 6, parents have the option to enrol their children into the programme bilingue (bilingual school programme), a programme that progressively changes from Atikamekw to French through these grades. In this way, the home language is honoured, while they increasingly get exposure to the French language, which will support them in the province as a whole. Atikamekw students are supported culturally through the two annual cultural weeks and curricular excursions to the forest, and are academically supported in their transition to high school by having the option of taking an additional year prior to beginning—in essence, a second Grade 7 year. Finally, two educational projects, a film project and an online encyclopaedia project, have been introduced to enhance the appreciation of the Atikamekw language and culture. These projects serve to support, validate, and engage the Indigenous students who are involved in them, often through to high school completion (In this volume).

NOVA SCOTIA INITIATIVES

Since 1999, the Mik'maq communities in Nova Scotia have had full responsibility of their K to 12 school programming and services. According to Simon (2014), graduation rates have increased markedly from 75% for the 2010/2011 school year to 92% for the 2013/2014 school year. Another initiative, Nova Scotia's Action Plan for Education 2015 entitled *The 3 Rs: Renew, Refocus, Rebuild* incorporates the language, history, and culture of Acadians, African Nova Scotians, Gaels, and Mi'kmaq peoples. In addition, there is an emphasis on entrepreneurship and math throughout the grades (with math mentors), as well as a deliberate teacher recruitment campaign to attract culturally representative teachers.

NUNAVUT INITIATIVES

Since 2000, there has been an attempt to create an educational system embedded within the Inuit culture. In 2007/2008, three foundational documents were published that focused on Ilitaunnikuliriniq (assessment), Inuglugijaittuq (inclusive education), and Inuit Qaujimajatuqangit (traditional knowledge) Nunavut curriculum. In addition, some approved aspects from the Northwest Territories (NWT), British Columbia, Alberta, Saskatchewan, and Manitoba curriculums have been adopted—including an Elder in schools. It is these Elders who generally teach the local Indigenous language, their traditional culture, land-based teachings, environmental knowledge, and navigation skills (Archibald et al., 2016).

NORTHWEST TERRITORIES (NWT) INITIATIVES

More than 50% of the students in the Northwest Territories are Indigenous (Archibald et al., 2016). Within this context, an *Aboriginal Student Achievement Education Plan* 2011–2021 was developed. This multi-pronged programme was designed to support Indigenous languages and the cultural curriculum. In addition, a territorial holistic action plan (Action Plan, 2014–2017) included commitments to developing community/school relationships, student academic learning and sense of identity, professional knowledge and training for teachers, as well as accountability measures (Archibald et al., 2016).

YUKON TERRITORY INITIATIVES

The First Nations Programs and Partnerships Unit (FNPP) was established to build relationships with Indigenous communities, to increase the Indigenous perspectives in schools, to revitalise Indigenous languages, and to increase Indigenous academic progress.

Conclusion

Although we undeniably have only begun the journey towards Reconciliation in education, there has been progress. At all levels, from federal to provincial to community, and in all sectors, changes are being made. Teacher preparation programmes and professional development opportunities have been redesigned to include Indigenous education. There has been increased funding for Indigenous resources and services. Curriculums are being upgraded to include Indigenous histories, with information on Residential Schools, philosophies, and ways of being. Cultural and land-based pedagogies are being expanded for both Indigenous and non-Indigenous students alike. However, with these positive gains, we must also recognise gaps and areas where more change is needed. There is still a disproportionate representation of Indigenous teachers in most schools—even in many reserve schools. More Indigenous mentors and models would be inspiring and validating. In provincial schools, there needs to be more emphasis on honouring Indigenous ways of being to include spaces where Indigenous students can gather and perhaps smudge. Having an Elder in school, even on a periodic basis, would be highly valued and supportive of the Indigenous students in those schools. Finally, and importantly, cross-cultural activities, events, and celebrations will help bridge a divide and facilitate a greater understanding, respect, and appreciation of diversity, which will benefit *all* students and, ultimately, the greater society.

In teacher education, this is an exciting time in Canada. There is opportunity, awareness, and consciousness. But along with these comes responsibilities and obligations. To be fully inclusive, we can no longer ignore and neglect the needs of our Indigenous students. Words are no longer enough. In order to move forward as a society and as a united nation, reconciliation needs to be enacted. We can no longer remain idle and have no excuse to remain ignorant. Through education, we are in a privileged position to support Indigenous students, learn from their ways of knowing and being and, as a nation, we now have the opportunity to grow stronger and wiser. In an inclusive classroom setting, this means all students benefit—both Indigenous and non-Indigenous students. Honouring those who came before us and to truly and genuinely reconcile means learning, teaching, and embracing Indigenous philosophies. If Indigenous knowledge and understandings are integrated authentically into the Kindergarten to Grade 12 Canadian schooling system, there is considerable potential for a societal change that is deep, sustainable, and very real.

References

Archibald, J., Xiem, Q., Hare, J. (2016). Indigenizing education in Canada. Background Paper for: The (RCAP) Forum *Sharing the Land, Sharing a Future: Realizing the Promise, Facing the Challenge of Reconciliation*, November 2–4, 2016.

Bell, N. (2014). *Teaching by the Medicine Wheel: An Anishinaabe framework for Indigenous education.* EdCan Network. https://www.edcan.ca/articles/teaching-by-the-medicine-wheel/

Canadian Human Rights Commission. (1985). The Canadian Human Rights Act. Canadian Human Rights Commission. https://laws-lois.justice.gc.ca/eng/acts/H-6/

Chiefs Assembly on Education. (2012). *A portrait of First Nations and education.* https://docplayer.net/1817377-A-portrait-of-first-nations-and-education.html

Crooks, C.V., Exner-Cortens, D., Burm, S., Lapointe, A., & Chiodo, D. (2017). Two years of relationship-focused mentoring for First Nations, Métis, and Inuit adolescents: Promoting positive mental health. *The Journal of Primary Prevention, 38*(1–2), 87–104.

Gomashie, G.A. (2019). Kanien'keha/Mohawk Indigenous language revitalization efforts in Canada. *McGill Journal of Education, 54*(1), 151–171.

Gunn, T.M., Pomahae, G., Striker, E.G., & Tailfearthers, J. (2011). First Nations, Métis, and Inuit education: The Alberta initiative for school improvement approach to improve Indigenous education in Alberta. *Journal of Educational Change, 12*(3), 323–345.

Hansen, J. (2018). Cree Elders' perspectives on land-based education: A case study. *Brock Education Journal, 28*(1), 74–91.

Indigenous Services Canada. (2021). *Key priority: Quality education.* https://www.sac-isc.gc.ca/eng/1523814808542/1523815053376?wbdisable=true#wb-cont

Morcom, L., & Freeman, K. (2018). Niini – Kiinwa – Kiinwi: Building non-Indigenous allies in education through Indigenous pedagogy. *Canadian Journal of Education, 41*(3), 808–833.

Nalipay, M. J., King, R. B., & Cai, Y. (2020). Autonomy is equally important across east and west: Testing the cross-cultural universality of self-determination theory. *Journal of Adolescence,* 78, 67–72.

Northern College. (2020). The teachings of the Seven Grandfathers. http://www.northernc.on.ca/indigenous/teachings-seven-grandfathers/

Peterson, S. S., Jang, S. Y., Miguel, J. S., Styres, S., & Madsen, A. (2018). Infusing Indigenous knowledge and epistemologies: Learning from teachers in a Northern Aboriginal head start classroom. *Revue Des Sciences de L'Education de McGill, 53*(1), 26–46.

Ryan, R. M., & Deci, E. L. (2000). Self-determination theory and the facilitation of intrinsic motivation, social development, and well-being. *American Psychologist, 55*(1), 68–78.

Seven Generations Education Institute. (2021). *Seven Grandfather Teachings.* http://www.7generations.org/seven-grandfather-teachings/

Simon, L. (2014). *Mi'kmaw Kina'matnewey Supporting Student Success.* Inspire: Indigenous Education, Canada's Future. https://www.google.com/url?sa=t&rct=j&q=&esrc=s&source=web&cd=&ved=2ahUKEwiBiJ_XlcvzAhV-GDQIHaWBCI4QFnoECAIQAw&url=https%3A%2F%2Findspire.ca%2Fwp-content%-2Fuploads%2F2019%2F10%2Findspire-nurturing-capacity-mk-2014-en-v2.pdf&usg=AOvVaw1RSMxJgqN2Y6b5sbCNh5fR

Snowshoe, A., Crooks, C. V., Tremblay, P. F., & Hinson, R. E. (2017). Cultural connectedness and its relation to mental wellness for First Nations youth. *The Journal of Primary Prevention, 38*(1–2), 67–86.

Statistics Canada. (2010). *Projections of the Diversity of the Canadian Population,* 2006–2031. http://www.statcan.gc.ca/pub/91-551-x/91-551-x2010001-eng.pdf

Statistics Canada. (2017). *Immigration and ethnocultural diversity: Key results from the 2016 Census.* https://www150.statcan.gc.ca/n1/daily-quotidien/171025/dq171025b-eng.htm?indid=14428-1&indgeo=0

Truth and Reconciliation Commission of Canada (TRC). (2015). *Calls to action.* Truth and Reconciliation Commission of Canada. https://www.google.com/url?sa=t&rct=j&q=&esrc=s&source=web&cd=&ved=2a-hUKEwjsy5mhl8vzAhVSDzQIHRwFAu8QFnoECAcQAQ&url=https%3A%2F%2Fwww.irsss.ca%2Fdownloads%2Ftrc-calls-to-action.pdf&usg=AOvVaw2ae3w68N286O6Zo_fL6Fcw

UNESCO. (1994). *The Salamanca statement and framework for action on special needs education.* https://unesdoc.unesco.org/ark:/48223/pf0000098427

van der Woerd, K. A., Dixon, B. L., McDiarmid, T., Chittenden, M., & Murphy A. (2005). *Raven's children II: Aboriginal youth health in BC.* The McCreary Centre Society. http://mcs.bc.ca/pdf/Ravens_children_2-web.pdf

12 Reclaiming Disability

Of *Mino-Pimatisiwin*, Belonging, and Gentle Teaching

Margaret Kress

Setting the Context

The author recognises the healing territories of the Nehiyawak and Michif as her homelands, and acknowledges with gratitude the gifts and teachings of the ancestors and elders across Turtle Island.

One in five Canadians over the age of 15 claims to have a disability and for Aboriginal peoples, this statistic may be more than double (Canadian Survey on Disability [CSoD], 2017; Durst, 2006).[1] Further, while many individuals carry the categorisation of a mild disability, more than one million Canadians are pathologised as persons with *severe* disabilities (Durst, 2006).[2] Added to this, "Demas (1993) states that in some native communities it is estimated that 40% of people live with some kind of disability. [And most notable,] lifestyle diseases associated with socio-economic conditions are quite prevalent amongst First Nations people" (Frideres & Gadacz, 2001, as cited in Durst, 2006, p. 15). It comes as no surprise that failing mental health is connected to high incidences of disability and disease, and that addictions, substance abuse, homelessness, and malnutrition exist as factors revealing secondary impairments (Canadian Federation of Nurses Unions [CFNU], 2011; Kress, 2015). In addition, individuals and families who are isolated or marginalised in communities without supports often experience far greater impacts of health decline than do others (Durst & Bluechardt, 2001; Kress, 2015; Loppie et al., 2009).

First, while recognising the disparities of higher rates of injury, accidents, violence, and suicidal ideation among Indigenous peoples globally, I point to colonial violations experienced by those forced into residential and Indian day schools in Canada.[3] Some refer to this colonial infraction by both the Canadian government and churches as genocide, and each day we see a clearer truth in this designation. Today, the residue of settler colonisation contributing to a loss of place, culture, language, identity, and life among Indigenous peoples and nations correlates with the colossal mountain of statistics in trauma-related health issues, disorders, disabilities, and deaths among First Nations, Inuit, and

DOI: 10.4324/9781003204572-15

Métis peoples (CSoD, 2017; Kress, 2015, 2017). And as instances of discord, hopelessness, and trauma escalate, we should be most alarmed by the suicide statistics of Indigenous children and youth, with Inuit cited at a frequency of 11 times higher than all other Canadians; these numbers and the numbers of children entering child welfare in greater rolls than children institutionalised at the height of the residential school era should urge all of us to move beyond settler policy and practice in respect to care and educational processes for Indigenous children (Kress, 2015; McKenzie et al., 2016). Globally, poverty, poor economic and social conditions, and environmental injustice, all cited as causations in a demise of health and wellness, must be considered in the context of a disability profile for Indigenous children, youth, and adults (Avery, 2020; CFNU, 2011; Fernández-Llamazares et al., 2020; Kress, 2015, Sugla, 2020). There is no doubt that ongoing colonial traumas affect the mental health, security, and well-being of all Indigenous peoples, and those with disabilities in Canada, seemingly to a greater degree than non-disabled persons (Avery, 2020; Durst, 2006; Durst et al., 2007; Canada et al., 1996).

> As far as Aboriginal people with disabilities [are concerned] ... we are less recognized and the most violated against by both races, both sexes, and both communities. We are raped by disabled men; we are raped by disabled women; we are raped by Aboriginal women; we are raped by Aboriginal men; we are raped by white women; we are raped by white men. And believe you me we have been raped by our medical attendants, doctors, nurses, occupational therapists—you name it, we've had it. We know what it is like to be down low, but for God's sake, you don't have to keep us there either'.
>
> (J. Johnny, November 18, 1992,
> as cited in RCAP, Vol. 3, 1996, p. 56)

This quote presents a sliver of the oppression Indigenous peoples with disabilities have endured in Canada, and throughout history. The cycle of abuse, tyranny, paternalism, and genocide has not ended with the cessation of residential schools or pass system enforcements; rather, its prevalence in today's western systems and particularly in education, health, and social services (child welfare), and in judicial, policing and penal structures, requires a profound disruption and a restock to move forward (Allan & Smylie, 2015; Blackstock, 2009; Boyer, 2014; Durst, 2006; Kress, 2015; Ross, 2006; Sobey, 1994). The redress of this cycle demands an approach which highlights and adopts Indigenous knowledges, natural laws and principles of balance within teacher education and human services—all done in a good way through the guidance of Indigenous peoples. Nehiyaw or Cree concepts of wellness and other Indigenous philosophies lend their voices to this reform within homes, schools, institutions and communities.

A Short History of Disability, Pathology, and the Indigenous Body

Quoting directly from a Lakota woman, Pengra & Godfrey (2001) write:

> *[The] real disability is racism. Our people are crippled by racism. If my family had a good place to live, had enough food, so would I ... We want our treaty rights.*
>
> (p. 46)

Although I cannot expose every digression found within the disability history of Indigenous peoples, I point to the relationship between residential school policies and the eugenics movement of the early 1900s.[4] While Canadian officials carved out components of the eugenics framework to promote a *fitter family* ideology, the underlying policies of this movement were principled on providing access to colonisers' quests for the privilege of settlement through measures of genetic profiling, whiteness, and patriarchy. Persons classified as poor, mentally ill, feebleminded, or those demarcated as homosexuals, promiscuous women, or *Indians*, Romas, or Jews, were rounded up and segregated, institutionalised, sterilised, and even euthanised (Dyck, 2013; Kress-White, 2009). Knowingly, the German Nazis used the pseudo-science of eugenics extensively, and not surprisingly, throughout Europe persons with disabilities became their first experiential group of humans to encounter genocide prior to World War II (Dyck, 2013). Recently, alarming evidence in Canada reveals Indigenous women with and without disability classifications were also scrutinised, examined, and eventually sterilised by eugenics boards during the residential school era, and in the years following their departures from these institutions (Boyer, 2014). Today, "the coerced sterilization of Indigenous women [continues], and [in] what some have termed the 'new eugenics'—genetic editing and the screening of foetuses for disabilities" is normalised as standard (Marshall & Robertson, 2006/2019, para. 1). In what is known as the slippery slope argument,[5] persons with disabilities continue to be scrutinised and controlled by those manning scientific and medical research; and respectfully, the ethics guiding this research deserve to be examined. Certainly, much evidence exists in this measure of "new eugenics" to show the disregard and elimination of the disabled foetus, and particularly those with Down syndrome (Graham, 2018; Quinones, 2017; Zhang, 2020). Here, in this analysis, questions remain whether the ethical constitution of research encompassing genetic screening and engineering collectively support diversity and health within the human condition, or if this science is simply advancing a new version of the *fitter family* ideology found within the old eugenics era.

Upon deeper investigation of the stories found within testimonies and archival records, a much broader picture of racial profiling, coercion, relocation, and marginalisation of Aboriginal children, youth, and adults, perpetuated by colonial white privileging, is found in today's society—realities of systemic racism, sexism, homophobia, and ableism[6] are entwined (Campbell, 2008; Kress, 2017). Although the practices of eugenics in British Columbia and Alberta were essentially dissolved in the mid-1970s, specifically with the eradication of the *Sexual Sterilisation* Acts of these provinces, a wider Canadian residue prevailed, and the ideologies bound within the movement live on in present day policies of medicine, genetic engineering, rehabilitation, educational psychology, and special education (Kress, 2017; Kress-White, 2009). Further to this analysis are discourses within social, economic, and legal frameworks pathologising Indigenous peoples, where disabled or designated abnormal categorisations often set them aside as marginalised figures subsisting in poverty and dismay. International media too often portrays First Nations, Inuit, and Métis as peoples reeling from an internalised strife, and while journalists attempt to take ethical steps to project fair assessments of truth, many Indigenous peoples are often racialised and demeaned in some of these stories. Often, Indigenous peoples are unfairly exposed to discourses of pathologies in which westerners and their governments place upon them. Frankly, these pathologies centre normalcy as a "cure" for disability, deviance, and disease, and they continue to be forcibly or insidiously imposed upon Indigenous populations today (Davis, 1995, 1997; Durst, 2006; Dyck, 2013; Kress, 2017; Kress-White, 2009).[7]

As part of a colonised discourse, educators often rely on a pathology of the Indigenous body, and as they cling to labels of *at risk, disruptive, abnormal, angry,* and *dis-engaged,* they go about the business of assessment and placement (Greensmith, 2012; Wotherspoon & Schissel, 2001). Still, confusion abounds because although these labels do not reflect the truths of all Indigenous youths or communities, cases of child and youth health traumas, homicides, and suicides in, for example, Saskatchewan, Manitoba, and Ontario, show us these stories are not simply perceptions. Moreover, appalling realities of historical trauma have come to light. Most recently, Tk'emlúps te Secwépemc First Nation announced the horrific uncovering of 215 children in a mass grave at the former residential school site in Kamloops, British Columbia, and Chief Cadmus Delorme is attempting to ground his community of Cowessess in Saskatchewan, as members grapple with emotions of sorrow, anger, grief, and hopelessness upon the confirmation of more than 700 graves at the nearby former Marieval Indian Residential School. These uncoverings and confirmations, and the mourning, and even re-storying of these experiences instigate traumatic memories and deep sadness among survivors and families right across our nation state. The physical and psycho-emotional traumas associated with these occurrences, and with other realities of settler and lateral violence towards Indigenous peoples, may present significant despair for residential school survivors and their relations (National Inquiry in Missing and Murdered Indigenous Women and Girls [MMIWG], 2019; Truth and Reconciliation Commission [TRC], 2015a, 2015b).

Finally, media images and discourses of *the other* interface daily within the making of a school culture. The culture of today's schooling upholds a medicalisation of the child (Petrina, 2006) and ensures a default for the protection of pathological labelling and separating (Wotherspoon & Schissel, 2001). While the psycho-educational frameworks of schooling and assessment are of some value, the consistent elevation and reinforcement of pathological referencing by administrators justifying funding and services for Indigenous children with disabilities and mental health needs often dims the socio-economic inequalities these same children experience—and many educators see these issues as beyond the scope of school investigation, or as those requiring transformative recourse, so they are dismissed. Additionally, we are reminded that a normalising of current social policy drives and widens socio-economic inequalities between Indigenous and settler societies, and in doing so, it increases the incidences of systemic racism, ableism, sexism, and homophobia found in our schools, and in the larger society (Devandas-Aguilar, 2019; Kress, 2015).

Also prevalent in schools and communities around the globe is an internalised fear of disability by both persons with and without disabilities (Charlton, 1998; Davis, 1997; Kress-White, 2009). For those with disabilities, there is the added realism of neglect, abhorrence, and abuse by those without. Although some individuals may benefit from forms of disability labelling, they too recognise the damage such an identity carries, and they may reveal aspects of shame within the circumstance of their experience. Sometimes, the notion of *disability as abject* becomes so pervasive, persons with disabilities themselves, and very often their parents, carry these fears as internalised oppressions (Campbell, 2008; Kress-White, 2009). Historical and contemporary narratives show the impact of colonial violence on Indigenous bodies, and for Two Spirit and trans children and youth, and women and girls with disabilities, it is twofold. These individuals are often targets of violence and genocide within both settler and Indigenous communities in Canada (Disabled Aboriginal Women's Network, 2021; Durst & Bluechardt, 2001; Gehl, 2020; MMWIG, 2019; Ott, 2016; Sunuwar, 2019; TRC, 2015a, 2015b). Further, when Indigenous peoples with disabilities leave northern reserve communities and move to larger urban settlements to access western medical supports, they often experience accentuated forms of racism and the compounding effects of isolation (Durst, 2006; Durst & Bluechardt, 2001). It is known these hurtful encounters, dismissals, and acts of violence toward persons with disabilities are directly tied to prejudices and fears attached to a western ideology of disability and the myth of normalcy (Charlton, 1998; Davis, 1995; Linton, 1998). Well-known disability activists are not convinced that Indigenous persons with disabilities have either a voice in or acceptance by the larger society (Gehl, 2020; Kress, 2017; Sunuwar, 2019). Throughout the history of industrialisation and in today's colonial experience, persons with disabilities are "isolated, incarcerated, observed, written about, operated on, instructed, implanted, regulated, treated, institutionalized, and controlled to a degree probably unequal to that experienced by any other minority group" (Davis, 1997, as cited in Barnes & Mercer, 2003, p. 41).

Globally, negative correlations associated with disabilities and ill health often project the reality of marginalisation, human rights infractions, and even genocide placed upon a peoples (Kress, 2015; Sunuwar, 2019). It may seem cliché, however, ableism is alive and well, particularly in the western world. Reliant on the protected phenomena of normalcy, settler patriarchy, and white saviourism, disability classifications impact Indigenous peoples in the most significant of ways; and not surprising, the studying of trauma is another reality of settler colonialism (Bex & Craps, 2016; Davis, 1997; Durst, 2006; Kress, 2017; Tuck, 2009).

The complexity found in an Indigenous disabled identity must be thoughtfully analysed to grasp how the constraints of both a disabled reality and the discrimination one endures may impact their search for *mino-pimatisiwin*.[8] In an attempt to gain understanding, one questions whether intergenerational trauma is the largest contributor to the causation of disability, and to other states of ill health and marginalisation for Indigenous peoples today. As an educator, I wonder: have we simply followed the colonial "wisdoms" of westerners and placed all persons with disabilities into a convenient package for the benevolent settler humanitarian to care for? (Bex & Craps, 2016; Tomlinson, 2014; Slee, 2001). We all know the realities of manifested traumas, disrupted family systems, and children being placed in welfare and juvenile institutions that have direct ties to settler colonialism (TRC, 2015a; Wesley-Esquimaux & Smolewski, 2004). In addition, we see more Indigenous youth experiencing mental health and addiction-related disabilities (including those such as Fetal Alcohol Spectrum Disorder [FASD]) and higher rates of suicide and suicide ideation than non-Indigenous youth (Kress, 2015). Further, because of ableist constraints and neo-colonial barriers within their own communities, we realise many of these young people with various designations do not often complete their high school education or obtain access to employment or other vital amenities important to their economic and social capital (Kress, 2015, 2017). Regardless of what we gather in these reports, observe in communities, or appreciate from the stories of Indigenous peoples, as those studying and serving Aboriginal peoples living with disabilities or traumas, we must acknowledge our roles as part of a settler capital coming from a process of "damaged centred research" (Tuck, 2009), which in of itself needs unpacking.

I urge educators to examine these realities—and to grab onto the courage required to deconstruct neo-colonial remnants of settler humanitarianism so they learn to confront the current racist and ableist dogmas found in western pedagogical policy and practice. In this regard, educators seeking a full delivery of services for all children must acknowledge there currently exist a lack of justice to ensure equity for Indigenous children with disabilities (Blackstock, 2012). I suggest the truth telling which comes before the setting down of justice, through both policy and practice, must be led by both Indigenous peoples and persons with disabilities to certify that they and their family members are afforded the necessary measures of cultural protection, space, and ongoing safety to engage fully in an inclusive and culturally relevant education (Durst, 2006; RCAP, 1996; TRC, 2015a, 2015b). For educators to move to a conscientisation of gentleness and elevate *mino-pimatisiwin* (the good life) as foundational, it seems all must gain an understanding of Indigenous knowledge, justice, and ethics.[9] By inserting a lens with a Cree or Nehiyawak worldview, for example, I am hopeful educators might open the door to an ethic of care which elevates both an Indigenous philosophy and the psychology of Gentle Teaching to understand disability ontology, equity and inclusion within schools. While this writing calls for all schools and communities to take up the challenge of ethical engagement with Indigenous families, it provides only a slice of what *mino-pimatisiwin* could mean for children with disabilities and their families.

Of Spatial Injustice, Truth, and "the Other"

Canadian histories show how we have consistently used space to confine and subjugate Indigenous peoples, persons with disabilities, and those living in poverty, through the extraction, appropriation, and manipulation of resources and knowledges, bodies and lands (Kress, 2014). Many civic or governmental practices can be dubbed as reinforcers of spatial injustice, as each operando potentially protects a measure of space set aside for *the other*. As LaRoque (2010) reveals how Aboriginal peoples continue to move in and out of spaces preserved for *the other*, she points to the gaze of the coloniser. With this gaze of control, perspectives of romanticism, deviance, and exaggerated difference exist, and simultaneously, the reality of internalised racism raises its head to all watching (Razack, 1998a, 1998b). Psycho-educational practices often make use of this gaze to demarcate Indigenous children and adolescents as *the other*, especially those with intellectual disabilities, behavioural differences, gender variances, or other positionalities distinct from the definitive construct of normalcy (Davis, 1997; Wotherspoon & Schissel, 2001). Disability experts themselves frequently uphold space for *the other*, and, in doing so, take on the roles of settler humanitarianism or white saviourism (Bex & Craps, 2016; Wolfe, 2006). Rather than seeing themselves in a place of fluidity similar to that of their students or their patients, these experts are complicit in protecting their personal and professional spaces of privilege (Kress-White, 2009). Very often, they control political, economic, and social policies and practices of their organisations, and when they decide who is placed in the categorisation of *the other*, they concoct when and how that occurs. Under the guise of settler humanitarianism or benevolent humanitarianism, (Maxwell, 2017; Tomlinson, 1982), those who dominate fields of human service and education protect discourses of *the other*, and while ensuring their own powers and livelihoods remain intact, they continue to uphold and promote abjected views of a disabled ontology (Ferri & Conner, 2006; Wotherspoon & Schissel, 2001). Sally Tomlinson (1982) and others draw attention to the bureaucracy and growth of special education, the financial resourcing of schools within the processes of diagnoses and placement, the expanding mandates of those who hold power over youth with disabilities, the profitability of the pharmaceuticals and nuero-scientific professionals, and the fragmentation of parent-educator relations (Allan, 2015; Kress, 2017; Tomlinson, 2014).

In their analysis of *at-risk* Indigenous children, Wotherspoon and Schlissel's (2001) posits a full stop on this view of *the other* by drawing attention to processes of hegemonic positioning. They warn educators who aspire to the duties of assessing, labelling, placing, and keeping Indigenous children in special education environments and other institutions to proceed with caution. In working for the disabled, the reality of settler humanitarianism (Maxwell, 2017; Wolfe, 2006) "comes perilously close to nineteenth century eugenic theories, [in which] … medical textbooks … confidently showed pictures of the warped brains of criminals and the mentally retarded" (Tomlinson, 2014, p. 71). It comes as no surprise that psychopathology processes found in schools follow youth to outside agencies where they are often institutionalised or incarcerated, "the mentally abnormal child is now principally represented as presenting danger and risk, and with these new identifications come a set of practices which are concerned with control, containment and governance and are aimed at protecting the securing of the school and societal population" (Allan, 2015, p. 44).

While the ideology of normalcy (Davis, 1995, 1997) works to conceal the humanity of a disabled child, his deficit identity, sharpened by educational psychology, supersedes the revealing of all other human characteristics and often becomes the child in his entirety. In this regard, worldviews presented by Indigenous parents depicting both their child's challenges and gifts are invariably diminished, rejected, or ignored altogether by governmental providers in education and social services (Blackstock, 2009; Durst & Bluechardt, 2001). Not surprisingly, while few researchers show authentic interest in learning more about peoples with disabilities from the perspective of the family, it seems getting down to the difficult task of creating authentic "boots on the ground" supports diminishes (Durst & Bluechardt, 2001). Here, government systems most often perpetuate inadequacies around funding, and many Indigenous children with disabilities and their families become some of the most marginalised within today's society (Blackstock, 2011, 2012; Wotherspoon & Schissel, 2001)

And so, we ask: how might educators come to understand a spatial justice, an Indigenous interdependence which honours peoples, their humanities, their bodies, their kinships, their lands, and their ways of knowing? Is it through an embracement of Indigenous knowledge and an acceptance of diversity, along with a deconstruction of bias, privilege, and history? Or is it in the creating of safe spaces for all learners? What must educators consider in this realm of justice and truth? While there are no simple answers, I point to spatial justice as a route that reveals "simply the intersection of space and social justice" (Design Studio for Social Intervention, 2015, p. 2). Embedded in this context is a critical approach to social, cultural, and environmental interactions, and the upholding of self-determining practices. Here, Cree scholar Willie Ermine calls for practitioners to learn about an ethical space of engagement (2007). When educators begin to have "the capacity to know what harms or enhances the well-being of sentient creatures" (Ermine, 2007, p. 195), and "how our actions may infringe upon or violate the spaces of others," (p. 195) they may then begin to see the necessity of two worldviews (Bartlett et al., 2012).

The attention given to this form of justice—a spatial justice—signals educators to create spaces of all types, those in which peoples enter by choice and which promote equity, access, safety, and healthy living. In these spaces, all peoples have the right to be safe regardless of ability, gender variance, sexual origination or racial, cultural, or tribal positionality (Soja, 2010). Critically, these ethical aspects of spatial justice are connected to Indigenous identity and growth: (1) the right to be and become; (2) the right to thrive and express; and (3) the right to access and connect (Design Studio for Social Intervention, 2015, p. 14/15). In this learning, educators must begin to see how images and realities of Indigenous peoples with disabilities are protected and/or manipulated by western interests, settler colonialism, and ableist notions, and moreover, how freedoms, value, respect, and recognition for every living being must be advanced in the spaces we occupy, live, work, and play in. In this analysis, one must become conscious of the incidences of discrimination that Indigenous peoples face each day in our country; most critically one must recognise systemic oppression and systemic racism in its multiple forms as an infused societal reality: "As Indigenous peoples, we have lost our most precious of all human rights—the freedom to be ourselves. Our existence is reduced to a meaningless and marginal part of broader Canadian life to be silent and ultimately controllable" (Ermine, 2007, p. 199).

Creating Space for Indigenous Ethics and Gentle Teaching

In my lifetime, I have come to understand "thinking spatially about justice can uncover significant new insights that extend our practical knowledge into more effective actions to achieve greater justice and democracy" (SOJa, 2015, as cited in Design Studio for Social Intervention, 2015, p. 3). This notion of justice gives educators the opportunity to recognise links between our colonial history and practices of today's schooling for Indigenous children with disabilities. It encourages all of us to look at the knowledges we hold in esteem and the spaces in which we relegate Indigenous children and youth. When Willie Ermine (2007) calls for the merging of western and Indigenous principles to "entertain the notion of engagement" (p. 202), I know we must all come together, including educators, traditional knowledge holders, disability practitioners, and parents, to begin conversations to explore Indigeneity and disability—and when Willie speaks of freedoms, I know this conversation must move far from the ideologies which uphold the pathologising of Indigenous bodies, to one in which we learn about and embrace Indigenous worldviews and positionality. As this negotiation moves forward, I call for a mutually agreed-upon change process which accepts companionship and community as paramount for the participation of Indigenous peoples and their families. This negotiation must be lead and formed within a leadership of Indigenous peoples, educators, and families.

With the acceptance of disability as a physical reality (involving aspects of biological impairment), and also a positionality holding a social construct in which attitudinal and environmental barriers may impact or oppress a person, I advance moving from old notions of disability—including charity and deficit models of disability—to the teaching of the social model of disability in pre-service teacher education. As time and critique have stretched this model to recognise kinship, personhood, and ontology, I believe it to carry a depth of disability knowledge that beginner teachers must take to their classrooms. Regardless of evolution, it continues to enlighten new communities as it creates a shift in thinking from that of "fixing" a person with disabilities, to one of supporting their needs. In this way, it exists as a model which encourages transformation by teachers and practitioners in upholding a culture of acceptance and belonging—one where all persons are viewed as diverse and valued beings receiving respectful treatment, equal opportunities, and equitable services (Linton, 1998; Pothier & Devlin, 2006;

Slee, 2001). With care, this model has the potential to exist as a decolonising tool as it "involves recognizing, then shedding the mindset associated with colonial processes by which one culture subjugates another and defines it as inferior" (Weaver, 1999, p. 222). Not only does it provide a space for a collective opposition to ableist discourses and systems perpetuating derogatory imagery, hegemonic positioning, and blatant human rights infractions against persons with disabilities within education and human services, it simultaneously builds upon equitable service. By accepting an Indigenous *way of being* within the social model of disability, educators learn to appreciate the need for safe spaces in which to honour the person(s) and their/his/her embodiments (Martin & Mirraboopa, 2003). The entirety of this grand shift calls for ethical, moral, and legal considerations mandating a respect for the traditional worldviews of Indigenous peoples with disabilities as they determine, create, and occupy chosen spaces, and embrace particular ways of being and knowing (Devandas-Aguilar, 2019; Ermine, 1995, 2007; Martin & Mirraboopa, 2003; Sunuwar, 2019). Additionally, it helps educators appreciate a pathway to connect disability and impairment as one within an "embodied ontology ... [and it shows them how] the reality of one's disability [is held] within a complex social network" including that of school culture (Mcilroy, 2005, para. 4). Within this embodied ontology, there is fluidity in the ever-growing social networks and changes found in day-to-day lives of all peoples, like those found in Indigenous knowledge systems (Ermine, 2007).

How Then Do We Move Forward?

As Indigenous and non-Indigenous peoples of Canada, we are entwined within treaty relationships (Cardinal & Hildebrandt, 2000) and in this, we are obligated to learn from and to support one another. It is within the *we* rather than the *you-I* dichotomy of western thinking that foundations of Indigenous ethics and Gentle Teaching can be advanced. Cree scholars, Willie Ermine (1995) and Kim Anderson (2000), and inclusion activists, Julie Allan (2005) and Roger Slee (2004), advocate for all individuals, Indigenous and non-Indigenous alike, to take responsibility for personal growth and change. Like Freire (1970), I believe they encourage self-reflection and conscious action to help us discover the *we*, as *we* reach for a society built on equity and belonging. These types of reflections and conversations activate responsibility in helping us understand treaty obligations and support actions that come with healing, growth (Cardinal & Hildebrandt, 2000), and ultimately by forming a pathway to *mino-pimatisiwin* ensuring access for all. *Mino-pimatisiwin,* loosely translated as living the good life, describes a "state of harmony, well-being, and comprehensive health based on relationships, cultural identity, and connection to the land" (Landry et al., 2019, para. 5). The concept of *mino-pimatisiwin* moves beyond a biomedical notion of health, which in western terms signifies the absence of illness, to a reality of fluidity within the human condition, and fullness within a life, with a focus on balance and harmony. It is noted that similar concepts of the good life are carried by some Algonquian peoples here in Canada (Mi'kmaq, Algonquin, Ojibwe, Nehiyawak and Niitsitapi or Blackfoot), as well as many others around the globe. As always, in this learning from knowledge keepers or elders, one must adhere to the protocols defined by the Indigenous nation they support.

Many Indigenous peoples, guided by factors of spirit, recognise the principles of *mino-pimatisiwin, kanawayhitowin, wahkohtowin* and other intuitive Indigenous knowings are both necessary and complex in this reach for harmony, and that it takes time to know them: "Life is experienced as a series of circles, in which change is not an irreversible line but a curve bending backwards toward its beginning. Time extends from far in the past to far into the future," (Nelson et al., 1990, p. 237, as cited in Hart, 2002, p. 99). These circular principles of learning come from ancestral wisdoms, oralities, languages, and land knowings, and they are connected to *wahkotowin*—this *being in relationship* not only ensures a type of kindredness, but it offers the giving of space to those who wish to enter the circle and learn. In addition, I was taught that as an ethic of Indigenous care, *kanawayhitowin* implies we are responsible to protect the spirit of all other living beings within the cosmos and *Earth Mother* herself (Kress, 2014). In this teaching, life extends beyond the human and connects us to the sustainability of all. It should be no surprise then, that *mino-pimatisiwin* is a type of actualisation in which "native cultures emphasize cooperation, harmony, interdependence, the achievement of socially oriented and group goals, and collective responsibility. [And it] ... is more akin to family and tribal self-actualization" (Herring, 1996, p. 74, as cited in Hart, 2002, p. 96). It seems this search for *mino-pimatisiwin* is a process by which one is required to manoeuvre through oppressive states impacting the *being* of all who are alive. On a spiritual level, Nehiyawak internalise a belief in wellness and balance through a reclaim of worldview, culture, language, and the teachings of the land (Michell, 2005). Additionally, the late Blackfoot elder Narcisse Blood (2015) draws our attention to the notion of *wahkotowin* or relatedness in this way:

> you are a person first ... your career should not be your identity, in western world it becomes your identity, for us no. You are a Niitsitapi first, that is a doctor first, that is a teacher, not the other way around. If we can get this back to this then we can teach the new comers of what they should have paid attention to then ... the whole notion of citizenship and community would be prevalent. We are, in fact, all related, and we should take care of one another, and not look down

> on each other. That goal of Blackfoot throughout your life, it's not about being Blackfoot, it is about becoming Blackfoot throughout your life. In other words, becoming a human to its fullest.

The sentiment of Blood's (2015) reflection helps us learn about others, and ourselves, through non-judgment, love, and service. Careful attention to Indigenous cultures and languages helps one discover ways of knowing as cycles of teaching through ceremony, natural law, and Indigenous ethics. Renewal and wellness, harmony, and health, can only exist in a culture of balance, interdependence, and synergy (Blackstock, 2011; Boyer, 2014); and in my examination of Gentle Teaching (McGee & Brown, 2007), I believe it to be a psychology aligned with the ethics and natural laws of Indigenous peoples. By spending time with Mi'kmaq Elder Albert Marshall, I have also come to see the benefits of *etuaptmumk* or two-eyed seeing (2015). As I have learned, "... to see from one eye with the strengths of Indigenous knowledges and ways of knowing, and from the other eye with the strengths of mainstream knowledges and ways of knowing, and to use both these eyes together, for the benefit of all" (Bartlett et al., 2012, p. 335), is life-altering. While Albert elevates *etuaptmumk* as a mode of hope and cooperation between settlers and Indigenous peoples, he lives his life with *netukulimk* (sustainability) at the forefront. When teaching about this Mi'kmaq principle of community actualisation, he encourages youth and elders alike to embrace life by protecting the diversity of all living within the natural environment for the next seven generations to come (McMillan & Prosper, 2016; Prosper et al., 2011).[10] This wisdom of protecting diversity is one that many Indigenous peoples hold in esteem, and we can easily see its transference to the protection of humanity's diversity.

A shift to *etuaptmumk* or two-eyed seeing, allowing for the receiving of acumen and balance found in Mi'kmaq teachings, and similarly within Blackfoot and Nehiyaw natural laws, is paramount for outsiders to understanding the depth of Indigenous ontologies or *ways of being*. Global Indigenous knowledge systems often hold similar directives for both insiders and outsiders; and one is obliged to become aware of the established protocols of the traditional territories they occupy or visit. Yet another aspect of relationality is shown in Blackstock's *Breath of Life* theory—where Indigenous ontology and ethics merge with western physics and the theory of everything. She proclaims if "relational worldview[s] ... are out of balance within the framework of community culture and context, then risks to the child's safety and well-being will increase" (Blackstock, 2011, p. 3). Blackstock provides a comparative of the Gitxsan *Breath of Life* to the Blackfoot law of *Cultural Perpetuity,* both founded within the fluidity of ancestral notions defining harmony, balance, and spirit. In reference to these teachings, I share a short story about Albert Maslow and his research. Of special note are the actions of both the governments of Canada and the United States—in their attempt to submerge the true roots of Maslow's work and dim the complexity of Blackfoot spiritual and intellectual tradition found within it. In the late 1930s, Albert Maslow took a trip to Blackfoot territory (in southern Alberta) to visit friends who were conducting anthropological research. While there, Maslow began to rethink his notions of human development and need, and it seems, he took generous liberties with some sources saying he appropriated from the Blackfoot as he formed a new impression of theory from his personal observations of Blackfoot life. Today, we know this developmental psychology as *Maslow's Hierarchy of Needs* (Maslow, 1943). During the last decade, Ryan Heavy Head and Narcisse Blood (2007) began to dismantle the notion of Maslow's hierarchy (Maslow, 1943) holding all the answers to developmental wellness, particularly for Blackfoot.. Although we know some similarities of the human condition existed within the triangular shapes of Maslow's work and those of the Blackfoot model of life, Blood, Heavy Head, and other researchers believe(d) Maslow mistakenly inverted the knowledges of the Blackfoot—for in Maslow's work, the teepee was actually converted into a triangular model of varying notions defining a western human condition relative to need (Heavy Head & Blood, 2007).

In Indigenous reality, the teepee, with its poles reaching up to the skies, signifies Blackfoot's ongoing search for community actualisation and cultural perpetuity through ancestral teachings. Here, the notion of reaching for the good life or *mino-pimatisiwin* comes from tribal knowings and a reclaim of Blackfoot culture as wellness. The three foundations of this Blackfoot knowledge from the bottom to top of this life model are 3) self-actualisation, 2) community actualisation, and 1) *Cultural Perpetuity*. This notion of *Cultural Perpetuity* gifts humanity with an understanding that we are whole—when and if we honour our teachings and our ancestors. If we recognise both the Blackfoot's teaching of *Cultural Perpetuity* and the Gitxsan notion of *Breath of Life* as vital teachings, we may begin to see the significance of Indigenous intellectual and spiritual tradition, and the elevation of ancestral knowledges being shared in schools with all children—and only then will we begin to see how balance, harmony, and wellness are premised on and within community, and how the protection of kinship, culture, and diversity is vital to each member in a search for belonging and love. As Blackstock (2011) implies, the *Breath of Life* asks us to breath in and keep searching for the knowledges of our ancestors, and the ancestors of those we serve. Cross's (1995) Indigenous interpretation of the Blackfoot knowledge system which includes this teaching, references the elevation of spirituality, love, belonging, and relationships above those of physical and security needs. Similarly, within the model of the medicine wheel, the harmony of the circle exists for all—here the physical, emotional, spiritual, and cognitive needs of a child or young person are equally significant to holistic human development, with none overpowering others (Fitznor, 1998). Both intergenerational trauma and the reality of a life experience with disability may disrupt a child or youth's cultural encounters within a kinship; therefore, educators must begin to analyse their actions, and the needs of Indigenous children and youth with disabilities through the contexts of culture, seven generations thinking, and relationality (Blackstock, 2011; Fitznor, 2006). Indigenous peoples call for educators to accept:

1. Recognition of our worldviews, our knowledges and our realities as distinctive and to our existence and survival;
2. Honouring our social mores as essential processes through which we live, learn and situate ourselves as Aboriginal people in our own lands and when in the lands of other Aboriginal people;
3. Emphasising social, historical and political contexts which shape our experiences, lives, positions and futures;
4. Privileging the voices, experiences and lives of Aboriginal people and Aboriginal lands (Martin & Mirraboopa, 2003, p. 5).

More than two decades ago, when I first had the opportunity to listen to the late Dr. John McGee, I learned something about the spirit, and about relationality. I observed his presence, his connection, and the way in which he spoke to persons with disabilities, in a genuine and open manner, somewhat similar to elders I know today. I learned that McGee's life experiences with Brazilian street kids and those with developmental disabilities warehoused in institutions around the globe solidified his push for an interdependent psychology—one to give life back to those who needed it most. Premised on notions of being safe and being loved, becoming loving and becoming engaged, in his understanding of the human, John McGee recognised gentleness to be the core of support for all peoples everywhere. His lifework gave opportunity for caregivers to reflect, and really begin to understand what it means to feel and be safe, loved, loving, and engaged through the experiences of those they cared for, and through their own interactions and lives (McGee, 2000).

On my journey, I discovered First Nations elders on the west coast utilising these gentle principles and those of their own culture to assist staff from the H.O.M.E. Society in British Columbia (Dore & Tsa-Me-Gahl, 2011). Although we recognise that understandings of safety and love may vary among Indigenous and non-Indigenous peoples, and particularly with those who work or live within lands apart from urbanity, the teachings of Indigenous peoples world over elevate the assertion of patience and modelling, first and foremost. In serving adults with developmental disabilities, together elders and supporting staff displayed respect, compassion, honesty, unconditional love, tenderness, consistency, and reciprocity to facilitate Indigenous knowings, community inclusion, and kinship integration. In coming to what I know as *wahkotowin*, the Gentle Teachers in this instance, sharpen their sensibilities by listening, sensing, conceptualising, assessing, modelling, engaging, and applying knowledge that was shared with them by other knowledge keepers (Martin & Mirraboopa, 2003); only then did they begin to gain the trust and respect of the individuals, and their larger collectives, culminating in the building of authentic relationships (McGee, 2000). As educators, we are obligated to learn about the people we serve and the mores of the behaviours they hold; we must learn about Indigenous ethics and protocols, and other relational notions that influence the responses a child or youth exhibits (Blackstock, 2011; Brant Castellano, 2006; Ermine, 2007; Ross, 2006). As we consciously take time to learn, we simultaneously enlarge our capacities to understand Indigenous non-interference, collective sharing and gratitude, modelling and observation in learning, and withdrawal until the time is right (Brant, 1990). When this learning occurs, cultural safety grows, and children and adults alike see the environments they occupy as places of gentleness. Educators can learn from this British Columbian example—to discover how kitchen talks become sharing circles, and how the cultural practices of smudging, dancing, singing, and drumming may be vital in the everyday lives of Indigenous men, women, and children.

Gentle Teaching, of course, is not just about the person in need, or those we serve. It is also about the caregiver as "it calls for transformation in our inner lives, the way we see ourselves and others, and the recognition that unfolding interdependence is a vital and central dimension of our life-condition" (McGee & Menolascino, 1991, p. 4). Through a careful examination of Ermine's (1995, 2007) directives for ethical engagement, I believe educators may begin to see how imposing western values, beliefs, and actions may be detrimental to an inclusionary practice. *Conscientisation* (Freire, 1970) helps aspiring Gentle Teachers recognise how they are conditioned to hold on to the fears associated with ableist constructs of disability, and how an expression of person's ontology and/or behaviour is essentially an individual's call for support, love, and gentleness (McGee, 2000). While challenging behaviours may incite fear, angst, anger, and frustration (Morris, 1991), it is important for educators to acknowledge how bias and negative emotions have weighty influences on those they serve (Allan, 2015; Slee, 2001, 2004). Ultimately, the job of a Gentle Teacher is to provide measures of unconditional love, safety, and equity so all students feel they belong and are loved. And although these measures vary among peoples, only with the elements of safety and love will young people eventually learn to return love, and to become fully engaged with their classmates and kins (McGee, 2000). The natural law of *sakihiwawin*, that is, showing love in your actions (Wilson, 2014), is critical for those who have experienced traumas of any kind. As a gentle educator, one shows actions with presence, words, hands, and eyes—always with soft, slow, predictable, quiet, calm, warm, relaxed, generous, compassionate, and loving responses. Persons teaching or supporting students with disabilities must learn to enter with humility, knowledge, and faith in what they are learning from others. In this interdependent model, recognition and love of "the other" is generated through conscious support, inclusive thought, and mindful action (Creative Options Regina, 2015; McGee, 2000; Vincent, 2015).

Wahkohtowin highlights human cries for nurturing, companionship, and acceptance in this search for *mino-pimatisiwin*. Collectively, as educators and allies, we hold a responsibility to carve out space, and to protect the very spaces Indigenous peoples with disabilities occupy. In the process of dismantling oppression and modelling safety, love, and engagement, those who carry the role of Gentle Teacher must adopt a stance which ensures cultural humility. Here, we learn that we are never finished evolving as caring humans, and as self-critiquing and Gentle Teachers, we begin to recognise this form of giving as that of humility—a lifelong endevour (Tervalon & Murray-García, 1998). We come to know that in order to achieve an understanding of those we serve, an infusion of humility is required to reach aspects of cultural competence, and of course, cultural safety— it is our role to examine power imbalances that create barriers and unsafe circumstances, and to instigate change in our personal stance, by grabbing on to a piece of conscientisation (Freire, 1980) so this may occur. Finally, we agree that working in tandem with others, and especially elder keepers, ensures a stance of cultural humility; and as we become those who are ethically aware and critically engaged, this stance allows us to advocate with and for parents, kinships and communities of Indigenous peoples, as their allies (Tervalon & Murray-García, 1998). The processes and spaces that we that we are obligated to provide and protect for those most vulnerable, can only achieve a foothold of cultural safety with the sanction of the larger community. We know that in this search for *mino-pimatisiwin*, we must teach others in our classrooms, courtyards, gymnasiums, and pools, that worldviews elevating interdependence, choice and love are foundational and necessary for persons with disabilities to experience spatial justice, growth, inclusion, self-determination and peace. In creating a culture of gentleness, I ask all educators to take on *kanawayhitowin* as an ethic of care—if one sees the spirit of another in their humanity, one learns to truly value the person whom one serves. Lastly, we must allow Indigenous children and their families to reach for *mino-pimatisiwin* by ensuring an ethical and safe space for them to be in their own way (Ermine, 2007); this means no impending bias, barriers, or blockades will be placed within the entrance or upon their paths as they enter and move through and within a particular space. I encourage all to learn from the elders and the gentle ones so together we can begin to offer *sakihiwawin* and "become fully human" (Blood, 2015).

Mina ka waapamatin. Until we meet again, I leave you with the words of Ponca Chief White Eagle: Go forward with courage.

> When you are in doubt, be still, and wait; when doubt no longer exists for you, then go forward with courage. So long as mists envelop you, be still; be still until the sunlight pours through and dispels the mists—as it surely will. Then act with courage.
>
> (Chief White Eagle, 1840–1914)

Notes

1. Aboriginal peoples of Canada include First Nations, Inuit, and Métis as defined by the *Constitution Act, 1982*, Section 35(2). It also refers to persons who are registered under the *Indian Act of Canada* as having Treaty Indian status and to those with Aboriginal ancestry who may be considered as non-status peoples. In this work, the designation is used interchangeably with the global term signifying Indigenous peoples.
2. Severe disability is defined by the Government of Canada as that which has a factor of limitation impacting an individual's capacity to live and to complete daily tasks in the defined categories signifying "often or always" in this state.
3. Self-identifying persons who are culturally distinct, multigenerational occupants of a specific land base; as a group or kinship, they are protected by specific rights-based legislation related to geographical territory, culture, language, and oral tradition. The lands of ancestral territories most often support Indigenous peoples or they have a historical alliance to subsistence-oriented production. Many speak an Indigenous language, often a minority language within their recognised state country, and honour and practice traditional ancestral teachings and ceremony. Indigenous peoples include Aboriginal peoples of Canada—First Nations, Inuit, and Métis—legal and colonial construct produced by the state (Kress, 2014).
4. Eugenics is a belief system and/or a set of practices used to improve the genetic qualities of the human or a group of humans. Its operando examined, excluded, segregated, and euthanised those who were judged to be biologically inferior. As such, people with intellectual or physical disabilities, those described as deviants, criminals, or minorities, including Jews, Romas, Sikhs, or Indians were targeted.
5. Found in case law and political rhetoric, this form of argument leads to a chain of events usually culminating into a negative effect for persons with disabilities.
6. A pervasive and systemic form of discrimination and exclusion impacting those with physical, emotional, cognitive, or sensory disabilities. Similar to racism and sexism, ableism impacts individuals whose positionalities fall outside of what is deemed "normal" within our society. Values and beliefs about health, beauty, productivity, and value of life itself, are propagated through the societal constructs of normality within fields of medicine, rehabilitation, law, education, and others (Kress, 2017, p. 51).

7. A profiling of the able-bodied person as one who holds a normal or standardised body, while disabled individuals, and the bodily variances they present, are considered deficit entities. Normalcy (also normality) privileges the able-bodied position through a series of medicalised categorisations and systems. Intersections of heterosexuality, maleness, and whiteness may attach themselves to the construct of able-bodiedness.
8. In their understanding of wellness and life balance, *mino-pimatisiwin* is a Cree concept shared by many Indigenous nations (in a variety of Indigenous languages and/or spellings). Safe spaces and access to traditional and/or cultural ceremonies and teachings, ancestral knowledges, lands, and waters are deemed critical to the fullness of the experience.
9. Brazilian educationist Paulo Freire is responsible for the study of conscientisation, which began with his teaching in Latin America. Here with those most oppressed by the regime, he guided their resistance through an awareness to a state of critical consciousness and critical action. The adults he taught soon recognised that existing power structures could not be changed by awareness alone, and that one must take critical action to do so. Details of this movement can be found in *Pedagogy of the Oppressed*, one of the foremost and influential writings in today's education of teachers.
10. Seven generations forward implies one considers both ancestors' wishes and wisdoms as well as the needs of the seven generations yet to be born while making decisions that impact the future of a nation.

References

Adelson, N. (2000). *"Being alive well": Health and the politics of Cree well-being*. University of Toronto Press.

Allan, J. (2005). Inclusion as an ethical project. In S. Tremain (Ed.), *Foucault and the Government of Disability* (pp. 281–297). University of Michigan Press.

Allan, B., & Smylie, J. (2015). *First Peoples, second class treatment: The role of racism in the health and well-being of Indigenous peoples in Canada*. The Wellesley Institute.

Allan, J. (2015). Stealth bureaucracy in Sally Tomlinson's irresistible rise of the SEN industry. In P. Jones & S. Danforth (Eds.), *Foundations of inclusive education research* (Vol. 6). Emerald Group Publishing.

Anderson, K. (2000). A recognition of being: Reconstructing native womanhood. Sumach Press.

Avery, S. (2020). *"Something stronger": Truth-telling on hurt and loss, strength, and healing, from First Nations people with disability*. Royal Commission on the Violence, Abuse, Neglect, and Exploitation of People with Disability. https://disability.royalcommission.gov.au/system/files/202010/Research%20Report%20%20Something%20Stronger_Truthtelling%20on%20hurt%20and%20loss%2C%20strength%20%20and%20healing%2C%20from%20First%20Nations%20people%20%20with%20disability.pdf

Barnes, C., & Mercer, G. (2003). *Disability*. Blackwell Publishers Ltd.

Bartlett, C., Marshall, M., Marshall, A., & Iwama, M. (2012). Integrative science and two-eyed seeing: Enriching the discussion framework for healthy communities. In L. K. Hallstrom, N. Guehlstorf, & M. Parkes (Eds.), *Beyond intractability: Convergence and opportunity at the interface of environmental, health and social issues*. UBC Press.

Blackstock, C. (2009). *Opening statement* [Speech transcript]. https://fncaringsociety.com/sites/default/files/opening_statement_by_cindy_blackstock.pdf

Blackstock, C. (2011). The emergence of the breath of life theory. *Journal of Social Work Values & Ethics, 8*(1), 1–16.

Blackstock, C. (2012). Jordan's Principle: Canada's broken promise to First Nations children? *Paediatrics & Child Health, 17*(7), 368–370. https://doi.org/10.1093/pch/17.7.368

Blood, N. (2015). *Identity. Vimeo and multi-sense media* [Video]. Vimeo. https://vimeo.com/119367676

Bex, S., & Craps, S. (2016). Humanitarianism, testimony, and the white savior industrial complex: What is the what versus Kony 2012. *Cultural Critique, 92*, 32–56.

Boyer, Y. (2014). *Moving Aboriginal health forward: Discarding Canada's legal barriers.* Purich Publishing Ltd.

Brant, C. (1990). Native ethics and rules of behaviour. *Canadian Journal of Psychiatry, 35*(6), 534–539.

Brant Castellano, M. (2006). *Final report of the Aboriginal healing foundation, Volume 1: A healing journey: Reclaiming wellness.* https://www.ahf.ca/downloads/final-report-vol-1.pdf

Campbell, F. A. K. (2008). Exploring internalized ableism using critical race theory. *Disability & Society, 23*(2), 151–162.

Canada, Erasmus, G., & Dussault, R. (1996). *Report of the Royal Commission on Aboriginal Peoples.* The Commission.

Canadian Federation of Nurses Unions. (2011). *Aboriginal health Backgrounder.* Canadian Federation of Nurses Unions. http://www.nursesunions.ca/sites/default/files/2011.backgrounder.aboriginal.health.e.pdf

Cardinal, H., & Hildebrandt, W. (2000). *Treaty elders of Saskatchewan: Our dream is that our peoples will one day be clearly recognized as nations.* University of Calgary Press.

Charlton, J. I. (1998). *Nothing about us without us: Disability oppression and empowerment.* University of California Press.

Creative Options Regina. (2015). *Creative Options Regina.* https://creativeoptionsregina.ca/

Cross, T. (1995). Understanding family resiliency from a relational view. In H. I. McCubbin, E. A. Thompson, A. I. Thompson, & J. E. Fromer (Eds.), *Resiliency in ethnic minority families: Vol. 1. Native and immigrant American families* (pp. 143–157). University of Wisconsin Press.

Davis, L. J. (1995). *Enforcing normalcy: Disability, deafness and the body.* Verso.

Davis, L. J. (1997). The need for disability studies. In L. J. Davis (Ed.), *The disability studies reader.* Routledge.

Design Studio for Social Intervention. (2015). *Spatial justice—The Praxis project.* http://www.thepraxisproject.org/sites/default/files/Miles/201201/SpatialJustice_ds4si.pdf

Devandas-Aguilar, C. (2019). *End of mission statement by United Nations special rapporteur on rights of person with disabilities, Ms. Catalina Devandas-Aguilar, on her visit to Canada.* United Nations Human Rights, Office of the High Commissioner. https://www.ohchr.org/en/NewsEvents/Pages/DisplayNews.aspx?NewsID=24481&LangID=E

Disabled Aboriginal Women's Network. (2015). *DAWN Canada.* https://www.dawncanada.net/

Dore, C., & Tsa-Me-Gahl, B. (2011). *Gentle teaching: A Canadian perspective.* http://acid2011-korea.org/kaidd_abs/pds/20110600313_16th_A_9.pdf

Durst, D. (2006). *Urban aboriginal families of children with disabilities: Social inclusion or exclusion.* National Association of Friendship Centres.

Durst, D., & Bluechardt, M. (2001). *Urban Aboriginal persons with disabilities: Triple jeopardy.* http://www.uregina.ca/spru/spruweb/durst.html

Durst, D., Morin, G., Wall, S., & Bluechardt, M. (2007). A First Nations woman with disabilities: "Listen to what i am saying!" *Native Social Work Journal. Resistance and Resiliency: Addressing Historical Trauma of Aboriginal Peoples, 6*(1), 57–77.

Dyck, E. (2013). *Facing the history of eugenics: Reproduction, sterilization and the politics of choice in 20th century Alberta* (1st ed.). University of Toronto Press.

Ermine, W. (1995). *Ethical space: Transforming relations.* http://www.traditions.gc.ca/docs/docs_disc_ermine_e.cfm

Ermine, W. (2007). Ethical space of engagement. *Indigenous Law Journal, 6*(1), 194–201.

Ferri, B. A., & Connor, D. J. (2006). Reading resistance: Discourses of exclusion in desegregation & inclusion debates. Peter Lang.

Fernández-Llamazares, Á., Garteizgogeascoa, M., Basu, N., Brondizio, E. S., Cabeza, M., Martínez-Alier, J., McElwee, P., & Reyes-García, V. (2020). A state-of-the-art review of Indigenous peoples and environmental pollution. *Integrated Environmental Assessment and Management, 16*(3), 324–341.

Fitznor, L. (1998). The circle of life. Affirming Aboriginal philosophies in everyday life. In D. C. McCance (Ed.), *Life ethics in world religions* (pp. 21–39). Scholars Press.

Fitznor, L. (2006). The power of indigenous knowledge: Naming and identity and colonization in Canada. In J. E. Kunnie & N. I. Goduka (Eds.), *Indigenous peoples' wisdom and power: Affirming our knowledge through narratives* (pp. 51–77). Ashgate Publishing Limited.

Freire, P. (1970). *Pedagogy of the oppressed.* The Continuum Publishing Company.

Gehl, L. (2020). *Indigenous women and girls with disabilities are targets of sexual violence.* https://dawncanada.net/news/idam-

Graham, R. (2018, May 31). *Choosing life with Down syndrome.* Slate.

Greensmith, C. (2012). Pathologizing indigeneity in the Caledonia "crisis". *Canadian Journal of Disability Studies, 1*(2), 19–42.

Hart, M. A. (2002). *Seeking mino-pimatisiwin: An Aboriginal approach to helping.* Fernwood Publishing.

Heavy Head, R., & Blood, N. (2007). *Blackfoot influence on Abraham Maslow, presented by Narcisse Blood and Ryan Heavy Head at the University of Montana.* Blackfoot Digital Library. https://digitallibrary.uleth.ca/digital/collection/bdl/id/1285/

Kress, M. (2014). *Sisters of Sasipihkeyihtamowin—Wise women of the Cree, Denesuline, Inuit and Metis: Understandings of storywork, traditional knowledges and eco-justice among Indigenous women leaders* [Unpublished dissertation]. University of Manitoba.

Kress, M. (2015). *Mental health strategy and feasibility study for a wellness, health and recovery centre for the Lac La Ronge Indian band.* Lac La Ronge Indian Band.

Kress, M. (2017). Reclaiming disability through *Pimâtisowin:* Of Indigenous ethics, spatial justice and gentle teaching. In *International Perspectives on Inclusive Education* (Vol. 1, pp. 23–57). Emerald Group Publishing Ltd.

Kress-White, M. (2009). *The quest of inclusion: Understandings of ableism, pedagogy and the right to belong* [Unpublished master's thesis]. University of Saskatchewan.

Landry, V., Asselin, H., & Lévesque, C. (2019). Link to the land and *Mino-Pimatisiwin* (Comprehensive Health) of Indigenous people living in urban areas in Eastern Canada. *International Journal of Environmental Research and Public Health, 16*(23), 4782. https://doi.org/10.3390/ijerph16234782

LaRoque, E. (2010). *When the other is me: Native Resistance Discourse, 1850 – 1990.* University of Manitoba Press.

Linton, S. (1998). *Claiming disability: Knowledge and identity.* New York University Press.

Loppie Reading, C., & Wien, F. (2009). *Heath inequalities and social determinants of aboriginal peoples' health.* National Collaborating Centre for Aboriginal Health. http://www.nccah-ccnsa.ca/docs/social%20determinates/NCCAHLoppie-Wien_Report.pdf

Marshall, A. (2001). *Taking charge of the Bras d'Or: Ecological politics in the "Land of Fog".* In W. Hipwell [Unpublished doctoral dissertation]. Carleton University.

Marshall, T., & Robertson, G. (2019). Eugenics in Canada. In *The Canadian encyclopedia.* (Original work published 2006). https://www.thecanadianencyclopedia.ca/en/article/eugenics

Martin, K. L., & Mirraboopa, B. (2003). Ways of knowing, ways of being and ways of doing: A theoretical framework and methods for Indigenous re-search and Indigenist research. *Journal of Australian Studies, 27*(76), 203–214.

Maslow, A. H. (1943). A theory of human motivation. *Psychological Review, 50*(4), 370–396.

Maxwell, K. (2017). Settler-humanitarianism: Healing the Indigenous child-victim. *Comparative Studies in Society and History, 59*(4), 974–1007.

McGee, J. (2000). *Feeling at home is where the heart must be.* www.GentleTeaching.com

McGee, J., & Brown, M. (2007). *A gentle teaching primer.* http://cdn.gentleteaching.com/wp-content/uploads/2014/02/GTPrimerFinal7-08-07.pdf

McGee, J., & Menolascino, F. J. (1991). *Beyond gentle teaching: A non-aversive approach to helping those in need.* Springer Publishing.

McIlroy, G. (2005, August 1–4). *Embodied ontology model: A way forward.* Inclusions: Celebrating diversity? International Special Education Conference, Glasgow, Scotland.

McKenzie, H. A., Varcoe, C., Browne, A. J., & Day, L. (2016). Disrupting the continuities among residential schools, the sixties scoop, and child welfare: An analysis of colonial and neocolonial discourses. *The International Indigenous Policy Journal, 7*(2), 1–27.

McMillan, L. J., & Prosper, K. (2016). Remobilizing netukulimk: Indigenous cultural and spiritual connections with resource stewardship and fisheries management in Atlantic Canada. *Reviews in Fish Biology and Fisheries, 26*(4), 629–647

Michell, H. (2005). Nehithawak of Reindeer Lake, Canada: Worldview, epistemology and relationships with the natural world. *Australian Journal of Indigenous Education, 34,* 33–43.

Morris, J. (1991). *Pride against prejudice: Transforming attitudes to disability.* New Society Publishers.

National Inquiry into Missing & Murdered Indigenous Women and Girls. (2019). *Reclaiming power and place: The final report of the national inquiry into missing and murdered Indigenous women and girls.* https://www.mmiwg-ffada.ca/final-report/

Ott, M. (2016). *A walk in two worlds. Digital project.* Ryerson School of Journalism. https://trc.journalism.ryerson.ca/taking-a-walk-in-two-worlds/

Pengra, L. M., & Godfrey, J. G. (2001). Different boundaries, different barriers: Disability studies and Lakota culture. *Disability Studies Quarterly, 21*(3), 36–53.

Petrina, S. (2006). The medicalization of education: A historiographic synthesis. *History of Education Quarterly, 46*(4), 503–531.

Pothier, D., & Devlin, R. (2006). *Critical disability theory: Essays in philosophy, politics, policy and law.* UBC Press.

Prosper, K., McMillan, L. J., Davis, A. A., & Moffitt, M. (2011). Returning to Netukulimk: Mi'kmaq cultural and spiritual connections with resource stewardship and self-governance. *International Indigenous Policy Journal, 2*(4), 7.

Quinones, J., & Lajka, A. (2017, August 14). *"What kind of society do you want to live in?" Inside the country where Down syndrome is disappearing.* CBSN on Assignment. https://www.cbsnews.com/news/down-syndrome-iceland/

Razack, S. H. (1998a). From pity to respect: The ableist gaze and the politics of rescue. In S. H. Razack (Ed.), *Looking white people in the eye: Gender, race and culture in courtrooms and classrooms* (pp. 130–156). University of Toronto Press.

Razack, S. H. (1998b). The gaze from the other side: Story telling for social change. In S. H. Razack (Ed.), *Looking white people in the eye: Gender, race and culture in courtrooms and classrooms* (pp. 36–55). University of Toronto Press.

Ross, R. (2006). *Returning to the teachings: Exploring Aboriginal justice.* Penguin Canada.

Royal Commission on Aboriginal Peoples. (1996). *Report of the Royal Commission on Aboriginal Peoples* (Vol. 3. Gathering Strength). Minister of Supply and Services Canada.

Slee, R. (2001). Driven to the margins: Disabled students, inclusive schooling and the politics of possibility. *Cambridge Journal of Education, 31*(3), 385–397.

Slee, R. (2004). Meaning in the service of power. In L. Ware (Ed.), *Ideology and the politics of (in)exclusion* (pp. 46–60). Peter Lang Publishing.

Sobsey, D. (1994). *Violence and abuse in the lives of people with disabilities: The end of silent acceptance?* Paul H. Brookes Publishing Company.

Soja, E. (2010). *Seeking spatial justice.* University of Minnesota Press.

Statistics Canada. (2017). *Canadian survey on disability.* https://www150.statcan.gc.ca/n1/daily-quotidien/181128/dq181128a-eng.htm

Sugla, R. (2020, July 30). *A study of nearly 700 studies makes it clear: Environmental injustice is rampant around the world.* Ensia.

Sunuwar, D. K. (2019). *Nothing about us without us: The struggle for inclusion of Indigenous women with disabilities.* https://www.culturalsurvival.org/publications/cultural-survival-quarterly/nothing-about-us-without-us-struggle-inclusion-indigenous

Tervalon, M., & Murray-García, J. (1998). Cultural humility versus cultural competence: A critical distinction in defining physician training outcomes in multicultural education. *Journal of Health Care for the Poor and Underserved, 9*(2), 117–125.

Tomlinson, S. (1982). *A sociology of education.* Routledge & Kegan Paul.

Tomlinson, S. (2014). *The politics of race, class and special education.* Routledge.

Truth and Reconciliation Commission of Canada. (2015a). *Honouring the truth, reconciling for the future. Summary of the final report of the Truth and Reconciliation Commission of Canada.* Government of Canada. www.trc.ca/websites/trcinstitution/File/2015/Findings/Exec_Summary_2015_05_31_web_o.pdf

Truth and Reconciliation Commission of Canada. (2015b). Truth & reconciliation: Calls to action. https://www.irsss.ca/downloads/trc-calls-to-action.pdf

Tuck, E. (2009). Suspending damage: A letter to communities. *Harvard Educational Review, 79*(3), 409–427.

Vincent, M. (2015). *Key competencies of a gentle mentor.* Creative Options Regina. creativeoptionsregina.ca/what-makes-a-gentle-mentor/

Weaver, H. N. (1999). Indigenous people and the social work profession: Defining culturally competent services. *Social Work, 44*(3), 217–225.

Wesley-Esquimaux, C., & Smolewski, M. (2004). *Historic trauma and aboriginal healing.* Aboriginal Healing Foundation. https://www.ahf.ca/downloads/historic-trauma.pdf

Wilson, A. (2014). *The movement needs to keep moving.* https://socialistworker.org/2014/04/15/the-movement-needs-to-move

Wolfe, P. (2006). Settler colonialism and the elimination of the native. *Journal of Genocide Research, 8*(4), 387–409.

Wotherspoon, T., & Schissel, B. (2001). The business of placing Canadian children and youth "at-risk". *Canadian Journal of Education, 26*(3), 321–339.

Zhang, S. (2020, December). The last children of Down syndrome. *The Atlantic.* https://www.theatlantic.com/magazine/archive/2020/12/the-last-children-of-down-syndrome/616928/

13 Why Decolonisation Is So Important[1]

A Comment to the Paper of Margaret Kress

Ines Boban and Andreas Hinz

During our first visit to Canada in 2004, Gary Bunch, Professor for Inclusive Education at York University, showed us a property with unnamed gravestones in Toronto where the city wanted to build a shopping centre. He explained that in earlier times, on this site, there had been an institution for people with disabilities. This reminded us of the ill-advised plan that the city of Hamburg had in the 1970s for the building of a shopping centre, which similarly, was planned on the site of a former Jewish cemetery. Now, while reading the text of Margaret Kress, disturbing information and images of children's graves at the sites of residential institutions in Canada resurfaced.

During our visit to Canada in 2016, we were looking forward to seeing democratic, human rights-based education; instead, we found a great deal of behaviouristic education (Boban & Hinz, in this volume). We saw many inclusive structures (some in New Brunswick) but—in relation to our expectations of what Canada professes—a lot of problematic processes.

In many places and moments, we witnessed the immense challenge of recognising the suppressive and genocidal history of Indigenous peoples in Canada. Then, we had a meeting with Jack Pearpoint, a self-professed "old white man," who told us about his experiences growing up in Saskatchewan on Indigenous land (Pearpoint, 2019); in thinking back to 2004, we joined a vernissage at the Marsha Forest Center in Toronto for the publication of a book which included the paintings of Randy Charbonneau, an Indigenous artist who acknowledged his marginalisation and trauma (Lockhart & Clarke, 2016), even though at the time we did not understand the dimensions or significance of what Canadians refer to as Reconciliation. And we met Dr. Margaret Kress again at the University of New Brunswick (UNB) and learned she is a person with multiple ethnicities, including being a Michif woman with a disabled daughter and Mi'kmaq ancestry. At UNB, we reconnected with our colleague who supports Indigenous students to organically transform and decolonise teaching and research methods. Dr. Kress offered profound analyses and critiques of inclusive education in Canada from an Indigenous perspective,

DOI: 10.4324/9781003204572-16

including an introduction to "Gentle Teaching" (Kress, 2017), an anti-colonial form of pedagogy.

As scholars who live and work far away from Canada, and as white Europeans in particular, we react to Dr. Kress's chapter as we might to a boomerang, associating our learning to our past interactions with the scholar. We understood better how white Europeans who once went to a region that became "Canada" established education systems that reminded us of our experience in schools in the 1970s (Miller, 1997; Rutschky, 1977;), which aimed to produce loyal subjects with a servile spirit. Now, the narrative about the history of Indigenous peoples in Canada being victims of this genocide has arrived in Germany (Braune, 2020; Menrath, 2020). These scholars also reflect on the problematic attitude in connection with "Indian games," following Karl May and his romanticised fantasies. All this is happening while Germans work on healing from the effects of the Nazi regime including elements of eugenics, even as these roots are once again nurturing populistic movements.

Following the example of Laloux (2015, p. 227), we see that there are two basic narratives about human development, psychology, and education. Laloux analyses the individual and collective dimensions of a situation or structure through inner (subjective) and outer (objective) lenses and connects them for the reflection of organisational development (these four lenses are represented in the rows of Table 13.1). Thinking about educational attitudes and cultures, including the picture of children, we came to clear results (Boban & Hinz, 2017, p. 185): there are educators, who(se):

Table 13.1 Two Ways of Thinking about Children and Consequences for Education

—Either—	*—Or—*
• Ways of thinking and beliefs mean that children are *born as egocentric beings* and who have to be educated towards social acting, will try to install systems of stimulus and sanction.	• Ways of thinking and beliefs mean that all people are *born as "socially talented,"* are oriented to harmony and relations, and "education" is rather disturbing empathy and so can cause an anti-social behaviour.
• Actions will be affecting in a restricting way against *impulses of the child labelled compulsive,* and will be following plans, concepts and curricula in an assimilating and adjusting way.	• Actions will aim to exchange on equal level, presence, and resonance for widening openly, facing, and acknowledging spaces for *impulses of a child which are understood as expression of liveliness and individuality.*
• Will ask for and support such structures, processes and practices which *set strict rules and requirements* with praises and rewards or humiliation and punishment.	• Will contribute to such structures, processes and practices which *develop rules for living together in dialog* and emphasise on democratic negotiation processes.
• Worldview leads to a *hierarchical organisational culture,* which will be based on competition, the tendency of orientation to individual success and structures for assimilation.	• Worldview leads to a *consensus-orientated organisational culture,* which will be based on the orientation to the community, agreements and the tendency to mutual complement for common action as a team.

In this comparison, we represent how worldviews, behavioural logics, systems, and cultures correspond one to another and how they can lead to opposite consequences. The model on the left contains traditional, colonial thinking, including behavioural conditioning and punishment by rewards (Kohn, 1993). It will seek optimisation, which comes at the cost of a reduction in complexity. In contrast, the model on the right builds on a democratic- and partnership-based approach, which we see as having a strong connection to the basic attitude of Gentle Teaching. This approach values sufficiency and complexity, including emerging contradictions. Because these worldviews are fundamentally contradictory, either/or thinking predominates over a both/and approach to expressions in pedagogy.

For us, it is hard to imagine how we might link the model on the left with inclusive education, and yet it is quite obvious that the Canadian system is an example of this possibility (Boban & Hinz, in this volume). Riane Eisler (2015; 2017) would call this framework much more a domination model than a partnership model on her "domination-partnership-scale." It is so contradictory: On the one hand, inclusion is seen to be a normal thing to do, while on the other hand, this is framed in terms that entrench white, Christian, behaviouristic, hierarchical, and colonial systems and practices. In this sense, while the Canadian history of Residential and Day Schools, which sought to extinguish Indigenous children's culture, heritage, and language, also entailed killing all curiosity in children and, more tragically, killing children.

In this sense, Canadian education can be seen as one of many educational systems worldwide that are suppressive, as opposed to inclusive. Yet another example is shown in the film, "Schooling the World—the Whiten Man's Last Burden," by Carol Black (2010). In this film, the colonial tradition of schooling is apparent, violence is visible, and native language is suppressed. This language, Ladakhi, is forbidden, everyone has to speak English, and so-called well-educated youth are entirely disconnected from their lands and their traditions, along with their ecology and the wisdom of their elders. This pattern immediately draws a similarity to the situation of Indigenous peoples in Canada and elsewhere, as we reflect on the crimes European colonialists executed not only in Europe (with Sami, Sinti, and Roma), but in Africa and all over parts of Asia, or in Australia and New Zealand as well. This comparison is not meant to relativise genocide, but it makes clear that the destructive effects of colonialism in education can be seen across the world.

Therefore, as a last aspect, we would like to highlight the necessity of an intersectional approach in fighting against oppression. As the founder of the Center for Intersectional Justice in Berlin, Emilia Roig (2021) writes, it is necessary to make minorities visible, as Margaret states in her chapter. It is also necessary to reflect suppression in suppression. To fight against racism seems to be futile without also fighting against sexism, ableism, classism, capitalism, and more. The fight against suppression as a complex whole is needed, with all its diverse aspects. This is especially important for people working in the educational field, and maybe, it is even more important for people who are presumably working in inclusive education and advancing the grounding concept of diversity on the basis of equality; obviously and contradictory, it can also be practiced as a domination system with a simple and suppressive right-wrong-scheme (Hinz, 2021). Instead, the main obligation of inclusive educators is to nurture human rights by helping other educators become increasingly conscious. It is all about biases and awareness, avoiding comparisons and competitions which lead to frustration and building of hierarchies. So, at last, Margaret does not just describe the situation of Indigenous persons with disabilities in Canada, she highlights a society and its educational system which suppress and marginalise children. We believe, as we see Margaret arguing, that we must create spaces for invisible populations to be seen, also creating spaces for voices to be heard and narratives to be told. In this way, we invite other invisible and silenced groups also to the conversation. We are guided here in part by Jacob Holdt (2007), whose research on poverty and race in the United States revealed depths of marginalised human suffering.

The fight for a democratic and inclusive education system will be a long one, which will not be concluded anytime soon. But as adults who professionally accompany the development processes of young persons by mentoring through dialogue (Simri & Hinz, 2021), we hope that one day there will be more and more children not experiencing adultist colonialism. This the songwriter Randy Newman (1988) sums up in his album "Land of Dreams." He describes nightmares, as exemplified by the song "Four eyes." For our four eyes and our four ears, it provokes us to see the destructive, "ungentle" roots of settler narratives and cowboy traditions.

We were five years old when Malvina Reynolds (1962) wrote the song "Little Boxes." Pete Seeger went public with the song, telling a story about how schools "ticky-tacky" try to produce homogenous elements, "and they all look just the same." As long as children's individuality and curiosity are seen as inappropriate, causing "bypasses" and "serpentines" on the intended standard mainstream highway to an "appropriately assimilated [Canadian] citizen," many more songs of this kind will, sadly, be written.

Note

1. We dedicate this paper to Esther Bejarano. She survived the Holocaust as a member of the Woman's Orchestra of Auschwitz and worked her whole life against old and new Nazis. The day we wrote this paper, she passed away at the age of 96 in Hamburg.

References

Black, C. (2010). *Schooling the world. The white man's Last burden.* Schooling the World. www.schoolingtheworld.org

Boban, I., & Hinz, A. (2017). Gemeinsame Potenziale unterschiedlicher Zugänge für inklusive Bildungsprozesse. In I. Boban & A. Hinz (Hrsg.), *Inklusive Bildungsprozesse gestalten – Nachdenken über Horizonte, Spannungsfelder und mögliche Schritte* (pp. 168–190). Klett Kallmeyer.

Braune, G. (2020). *Indigene Völker in Kanada. Der schwere Weg zur Verständigung.* Ch. Links.

Eisler, R. (2015). Nurturing children's humanity: Partnership education. *Interdisciplinary Journal of Partnership Studies,* 2(2)

Eisler, R. (2017). Building a caring democracy: Four cornerstones for an integrated progressive agenda. *Interdisciplinary Journal of Partnership Studies, 4*(1), 1–23.

Hinz, A. (2021). Update Theorie integrativer Prozesse. Wie der Inklusionsdiskurs Vitalisierung aus ihrer Weiterentwicklung erfahren könnte In H. Wocken (Ed.), *Dialektik der Inklusion. Inklusion als Balance dialektischer Qualitäten* (pp. 177–199). Feldhaus.

Holdt, J. (2007). *United States 1970–1975: American pictures.* Steidl.

Kohn, A. (1993). *Punished by rewards. The trouble with gold stars, incentive plans, A's, praise, and other bribes.* Houghton Mifflin.

Kress, M. (2017). Reclaiming disability through *Pimâtisowin:* Of Indigenous ethics, spatial justice and gentle teaching. In *International Perspectives on Inclusive Education* (Vol. 1, pp. 23–57). Emerald Group Publishing Ltd.

Laloux, F. (2015). *Reinventing organizations. Ein Leitfaden zur Gestaltung sinnstiftender Formen der Zusammenarbeit.* Vahlen.

Lockhart, A. R., & Clarke, M. (2016). *Community lost and found: A conversation between two dreamers.* Inclusion Press.

Menrath, M. (2020). *Unter dem Nordlicht. Indianer aus Kanada erzählen von ihrem Land.* Galiani.

Miller, A. (1997). *Das Drama des begabten Kindes und die Suche nach dem wahren Selbst [The drama of the gifted child: The search for the true self].* Basic Books.

Newman, R. (1988). Four eyes. In *LP land of dreams.* Reprise Records.

Pearpoint, J. (2019). Wegwerfbare Menschen; Vom Aufdecken kanadischer 'Nicht-Menschen' und ihrer 'Nicht-Geschichte'. In D. Jahr & R. Kruschel (Eds.), *Inklusion in Kanada. Internationale Perspektiven auf heterogenitätssensible Bildung* (pp. 426–444). Beltz Juventa.

Reynold, M. (1962). Little boxes. https://en.wikipedia.org/wiki/Little_Boxes

Roig, E. (2021). *Why we matter. Das Ende der Unterdrückung.* Aufbau.

Rutschky, K. (Hrsg.). (1977). *Schwarze Pädagogik. Quellen zur Naturgeschichte der bürgerlichen Erziehung.* Ulstein

Simri, D., & Hinz, A. (2021). Mentoring durch Dialog – Begleitung und Beratung von Schüler*innen in Demokratischen Schulen in Israel. *Schule Inklusiv,* 12, 39–41.

Part IV

Practices of Inclusive Education

14 Individual Reference Norm Orientation and Motivation

Perspectives from Germany, Finland, and Canada

Britta Klopsch, Katharina Reschke, and Anne Sliwka

Introduction: What Is Reference Norm Orientation?

Thinking about students and their learning progress is something that every teacher must do every day. However, teachers do not perceive learning outcomes in a vacuum. They usually put it in some context to which they can refer. This is how *reference norms* arise. Teachers and learners compare their outcomes on a *social* level with their peers, on an *individual* level with their previous skills, and *criterion-based* on standards or competencies.

Initial discussions about reference norms can be traced back to the early 20th century. The first systematic studies appeared on individual (also: temporal) and social reference norm orientation within the field of educational psychology (Fischer, 1912). Nonetheless, initial ideas on individual reference norms appeared almost a century earlier when Herbart (1831) suggested that educators do not compare students with others but with themselves.

A distinction between social and criterion-based reference norms occurred in the 1960s in educational diagnostics (Ebel, 1962; Glaser, 1963). *Social comparisons* usually refer to the children in a particular class. *Criterion-based comparisons* are oriented to a specific competence that should be achieved. Although the use of reference standards slowly became established, the term "reference standard" was not coined until the 1970s by Heckhausen (1972, p. 957).

Heckhausen embeds the term in the context of motivational psychology, assuming that when students have different reference norm orientations, they show different levels of *motivation*. He explicitly contrasts social and individual reference norm orientation, speaking of interindividual cross-sectional comparisons and intraindividual longitudinal comparisons.

DOI: 10.4324/9781003204572-18

Similar substantive arguments in English-speaking countries can be found in the concepts of Dweck and her colleagues (Dweck & Leggett, 1988; Elliot & Dweck, 1988) as well as in those of Nicholls (1984). Dweck (1990) argues that learning or *mastery goal orientation* leads to students being interested in increasing their competence (Kaplan & Maehr, 2007). *Performance orientation* leads students to demonstrate skills and knowledge for others to perceive them without considering their own growth in learning (Dweck & Legget, 1988).

In his *achievement goal setting theory*, Nicholls (1984) distinguishes *task* and *ego* goals. Similar to the theory of reference norm orientation, he refers to the theoretical relationship between goal orientation and performance comparisons. According to the social norm orientation, performance goals lead to showing others one's own competence, while an ego goal orientation can be compared to the individual reference norm orientation (Dickhäuser & Rheinberg, 2003, p. 48).

Today, reference norm orientation is internationally seen as very important (Elliot et al., 2011) to give a multifaceted perspective on learning outcomes and, considering this, to improving individual learning. However, "research specifically focusing on teachers' reference norm orientations has mainly been conducted in Germany and published mainly in German" (Dickhäuser et al., 2017, p. 206).

This chapter aims to broaden the mainly German view and compare individual reference norms and motivation in an international perspective, namely in Germany, Finland, and Canada. Before taking this international perspective, we give an overview on effects of reference norms and its connection to motivation.

Why Are Reference Norms Important?

Research shows that individual, social, and criterion-based reference norms "have a demonstrable influence on academic self-concepts" (Atzert et al., 2020, p. 90). For this, the role of the teacher is very important. Their reference norm orientation affects students' beliefs of their abilities and whether they can change them or not (Dickhäuser et al., 2017, p. 215).

Research on different teacher preferences shows that teachers who evaluate their students using social comparison create motivationally less favourable conditions. Teachers who also considered individual references motivated their students significantly more than those who chose not to use them (Rheinberg, 1982). Krug and Lecybyl (2005) even show that students in classrooms with a strong individual reference norm orientation (IRN) performed better than students in classrooms with a strong social reference norm orientation (SRN).

Similar findings emerge when comparing the individual reference norm orientation with a criterion-based norm orientation. Meece and

Holt (1993) reported that learning-oriented students have a very positive achievement profile, being very engaged and having high achievement expectations. Setbacks do not make them stop learning. Even if the IRN is the teacher's attitude, they manage to keep their confidence in success, willingness to make an effort, and show self-reliance (Rheinberg & Krug, 1999).

Performance-oriented students attribute failure to the lack of their own ability. This leads to low engagement and low achievement expectations after negative feedback on their learning outcome (Meece & Holt, 1993). Rising or falling performance tends to have a particularly large impact on students' motivation to continue to engage with the subject matter.

We can thus assume that the individual reference norm is motivationally promoting while the social reference norm or the criterion-based norm orientation is motivationally inhibiting (Rheinberg, 2014) whether we consider students or teachers. Nonetheless, it is important to note that there is not necessarily an "either/or": "A teacher can, for example, take the view that good achievement is indicated by temporal [individual] improvement and by being better than others" (Dickhäuser et al., 2017, p. 206).

But why is the individual norm orientation so important for students' achievements? Research suggests that an IRN enhances the motivation to learn. This could be because an IRN goes along with feedback on individual learning outcomes and individual learning processes. Learners notice their progress, they see that their effort is "worth it," and they can enjoy their learning process much more (Jagacinski & Nicholls, 1987, p. 110). Students get used to a realistic level of aspiration, expectation, and their effort attribution (Brunstein & Heckhausen, 2018, p. 281). This especially helps students who struggle (Krampen, 1987).

Learning behaviour and performance are positively affected by the belief that students have the ability to succeed, which leads to a reduced fear of failure (Brunstein & Heckhausen, 2018, p. 279). Failure is connected to learning as a natural part of it without feeling bad about it and reducing efforts to learn. On the teacher's side, closer attention to individual performance developments leads to the design of appropriate task requirements. The individual RNO thus supports individualisation of requirements wherever possible. Consequently, increased use of the individual reference standard is desirable in schools to encourage all students to reach their potential.

Germany, Finland, and Canada—Basis of Research and Hypotheses

This chapter aims to show whether teachers and students in different countries perceive individual reference norms differently and thus if the students' motivation is also seen as different.

The differences between Germany, Finland, and Canada seem to be interesting. In Germany, there is a long tradition of dealing with reference norms in education, though social reference norms and criterion-based norms seem to exceed the use of individual norms (Sliwka & Klopsch, 2018). Nationwide performance tests and a strongly selective school system may be the reasons for this.

In Finland, there is no national inspection of schools or assessments of students (Vainikainen et al., 2017). Based on the national core curriculum, every Finnish municipality draws up its own curriculum "taking into consideration the special circumstances and needs of local children and families" (Kupiainen et al., 2009, p. 19). This strong role of local needs is supported by a three-tiered model of support that helps students with learning difficulties catch up at a very early stage (Thuneberg et al., 2013, p. 69). Evidence-informed decisions are therefore part of everyday teaching (Tatto, 2015).

The third country is Canada with its horizontally and vertically aligned[1] accountability system that leads to detailed, data-informed decision-making (Klopsch & Sliwka, 2020). These decisions lead to supporting students individually. The Canadian Response to Intervention Model (Government of Alberta, 2019) is quite similar to the Finnish 3-tiered model. Both countries also work with individual programme plans for students with special needs (Kupiainen et al., 2009; Sliwka & Klopsch, 2018; Vainikainen et al., 2017). These structural differences lead to the following hypotheses:

a In Finland and in Canada, individual norm orientation is stronger than in Germany—especially regarding the perspectives of teachers.
b The strong focus on the individual school might even cause a stronger individual norm orientation in Finland compared to Canada.
c The students' motivation is higher in Canada and Finland than in Germany.

Methods

This study used the Trends in International Mathematics and Science Study (TIMSS) 2015 dataset, an international assessment of mathematics and science in Grades 4 and 8 that has been conducted every four years since 1995 (Mullis & Martin, 2013). TIMSS 2015 is the sixth assessment in the TIMSS series, monitoring 20 years of trends in educational achievement together with comprehensive data on students' contexts for learning mathematics and science. The data were created under the direction of the International Association for the Evaluation of Achievement (IEA), its TIMSS, and the Progress in International Reading Literacy Study (PIRLS) at the International Study Center at

Boston College (Mullis & Martin, 2013) and are publicly available for secondary analysis.

Sample and Procedure

Overall, 57 countries participated in TIMSS 2015. In our study, we focus on the following three countries: Germany, Canada, and Finland. The German TIMSS sample is fully representative of the German population of Grade 4 students in elementary school (M = 10.4 years old). In Germany, elementary school is the first level of the compulsory education system and generally comprises Grades 1 to 4 (ages six to ten). The sample comprised 3460 students enrolled in 210 schools. Forty-nine percent of the students were female. The Canadian TIMSS sample is representative of the Canadian population of Grade 4 students in elementary school (M = 9.9). In Canada, the elementary level ranges from Grades 1 to 6 or from Grades 1 to 8 (depending on the province or territory). The sample consisted of 12,019 students from 441 schools (49% female). The TIMSS sample from Finland is fully representative of the Finnish population of Grade 4 students in elementary school (M = 10.8). Compulsory education in Finland usually starts the year in which a child turns seven. The basic education syllabus spans nine years, which nearly all children complete by attending comprehensive school. This sample included 5793 students from 158 schools (48% female).

In addition to students, teachers also completed a questionnaire in mathematics classes. In Germany, 224 teachers participated, whereas in Canada, 841 teachers took part in TIMSS. The number of Finnish teachers could not be found.

Internationally, a test procedure is specified that provides all participating students with sufficient time to complete the test items and answer the questions in the student questionnaire (Wendt et al., 2016). The testing and questioning of the students took place on a morning. On the test day, the students first solved test items from the areas of mathematics and science, as they are prescribed internationally. The test day ended for the participating students with the completion of the student questionnaire, which was divided into two parts so that the students could take another break. The students had a total of 45 minutes to complete the questionnaire.

Measures

Teacher Questionnaire

The participating teachers were given a self-report questionnaire assessing their teaching behaviour and their own confidence for motivating their students in the classroom. All items were assessed specifically for mathematics. We used two items as indicators of the use of an individual reference norm answered on a 4-point scale (1 = very high, 4 = low; e.g., "In teaching mathematics to this class, how would you characterise your confidence in doing the following? ... Improving to understand of struggling students"). The motivating teaching scale assessed teachers' confidence to inspire students to learn mathematics and foster their motivation answered on a 4-point scale (1 = very high, 4 = low; e.g., "In teaching mathematics to this class, how would you characterise your confidence in doing the following ... Making mathematics relevant to students?").

Student Questionnaire

Besides the tests of mathematical and scientific competence, students filled out a questionnaire on their motivation and perceptions of math teaching. Students' perspectives of the use of an individual reference norm were assessed using two items (e.g., "My teacher tells me how to do better when I make a mistake") answered on a 4-point scale (1 = agree a lot; 4 = disagree a lot). Two items were used as a measure of students' perspectives of motivating teaching (e.g., "My teacher gives me interesting things to do") answered on a 4-point scale (1 = agree a lot; 4 = disagree a lot).

Statistical Analysis

For analysing our data, we used the IEA International Database Analyzer (IDB Analyzer). This is a free tool to combine and analyse data from all IEA's large-scale assessments (Foy, 2017). Within the IDB Analyzer, we computed descriptive statistics and analyses of variance to determine whether there were any systematic differences between the three countries in the examined variables, such as use of the individual reference norm (from teachers' and students' perspectives) and motivating teaching (from teachers' and students' perspectives). Moreover, we computed effect sizes (Cohen's *d*) to interpret the magnitude of differences between countries.

Results

Descriptives

Means (*M*) and standard deviations (*SD*) for all measures from the teachers' samples are presented in Table 14.1. Table 14.2 shows all means and standard deviations for all measures from the students' samples. In both tables, lower values symbolise agreement with the construct in the sense of better and more adaptive behaviour/teaching.

Table 14.1 Descriptive Statistics for the Use of an IRN and Motivation Teaching from Teachers' Perspectives among Canada, Finland, and Germany

	Canada		*Finland*		*Germany*	
Variable	*M*	*SD*	*M*	*SD*	*M*	*SD*
Individual RN 1	2.09	.76	1.96	.67	1.95	.72
Individual RN 2	2.00	.71	2.07	.72	1.94	.67
Motivating teaching 1	1.83	.66	1.72	.63	1.86	.63
Motivating teaching 2	1.90	.69	2.03	.70	2.02	.59
Motivating teaching 3	1.87	.71	1.83	.65	1.81	.61
Motivating teaching 4	1.84	.68	2.02	.69	1.97	.64

Note. RN = reference norm. Lower values symbolise agreement with the construct.

Table 14.2 Descriptive Statistics for the Use of an IRN and Motivation Teaching from Students' Perspectives among Canada, Finland, and Germany

	Canada		*Finland*		*Germany*	
Variable	*M*	*SD*	*M*	*SD*	*M*	*SD*
Individual RN 1	1.59	.81	1.68	.76	1.68	.85
Individual RN 2	1.34	.64	1.33	.60	1.40	.69
Motivating teaching 1	1.51	.75	1.97	.86	1.72	.85
Motivating teaching 2	1.25	.56	1.26	.53	1.39	.66

Note. RN = reference norm. Lower values symbolise agreement with the construct.

Country Differences in the Use of the Individual Reference Norm

Teachers' Perspectives on Their Use of the Individual Reference Norm

For our first item of the use of an individual reference norm from teachers' perspectives, we found German ($d = 0.18$) and Finnish ($d = 0.19$) teachers to score significantly lower compared to Canadian teachers. The teachers from Germany and Finland did not significantly differ in their use of an individual reference norm. For our second item of the use of an individual reference norm from teachers' perspectives, we also found significant differences between the three countries (Finland versus Canada, $d = 0.10$; Canada versus Germany, $d = 0.09$; Finland versus Germany, $d = 0.19$). This time, teachers from Germany showed the lowest values followed by teachers from Finland and Canada showing the highest values.

Students' Perspectives on Their Teachers' Use of the Individual Reference Norm

For our first item of the use of an individual reference norm from students' perspectives, we found no differences between German and Finnish students. Furthermore, German and Finnish students scored higher compared to Canadian students (Germany versus Canada, $d = 0.11$; Finland versus Canada, $d = 0.11$). For our second item of the use of an individual reference norm from students' perspectives, we also found significant differences between the three countries: insofar that German students scored significantly higher than Finnish students ($d = 0.11$) and Canadian students ($d = 0.09$). Students from Finland and Canada did not significantly differ on this indicator.

Country Differences in Motivating Teaching

Teachers' Perspectives on Their Motivating Teaching

Teachers from Finland showed lower values (higher agreement) on the item measuring confidence in inspiring students to learn mathematics versus teachers from Canada ($d = 0.17$) and Germany ($d = 0.22$). Teachers from Canada showed higher confidence compared to teachers from Germany ($d = 0.05$). In relation to teachers' confidence in adapting their teaching to students' interests, Canadian teachers outperform teachers from Finland ($d = 0.18$) and Germany ($d = 0.19$) with no significant difference between Germany and Finland. Regarding teachers' confidence in demonstrating the usefulness of mathematics to their students, Canadian teachers scored significantly higher than German ($d = 0.09$) and Finnish ($d = 0.06$) teachers with no significant difference between the latter. Furthermore, teachers from Canada showed higher confidence in making mathematics relevant to students compared to teachers from Germany ($d = 0.19$) followed by teachers from Finland ($d = 0.26$).

Students' Perspectives on Motivating Teaching

Students from Canada stated that their teachers gave them more interesting things to do compared to students from Germany ($d = 0.27$) and compared to Finnish students ($d = 0.58$). Moreover, students from Canada ($d = 0.22$) and Finland ($d = 0.24$) reported higher agreement on the question of whether their teachers do a variety of things to help them learn compared to students from Germany with no significant difference between Canada and Finland.

Discussion

In this chapter, we analysed teachers' and student's self-disclosure in relation to different items. All items were related to individual norm orientation or motivation.

Analysis showed that the individual reference norm orientation among teachers seems to be strongest in Germany from the perspective of teachers. The first hypothesis, a stronger IRN orientation among Finland's and Canada's teachers, can therefore be discarded. However, it is interesting that Canadian students rate the IRN the highest. Thus, it can be surmised that teachers may actually care more about individual students than the teachers themselves perceive. This could be because of the different perspectives: The description of the teachers is very much their attitude; the students describe their own perceptions based on the level of the teacher behaviour they observe. This suggests that teachers in Canada are more critical of themselves and perhaps more self-reflective in terms of individual student orientation than, for example, teachers in Germany. The latter group seem to have more confidence in individual IRN, but this is less perceived by the students they are teaching.

An explanation of this difference could be that German teachers provide answers on a much more superficial level. Canadian teachers regularly work in collaborative teams on supporting every child. This could lead to a very specific and detailed idea of individual support, which might lead to more self-reflection and self-criticism than it does among teachers in Germany who do not regularly have to deliberate and collaborate about providing individual support to students.

Finnish teachers' and their students' perceptions fall in between the findings from Germany and Canada. From both perspectives, they are, in some items, closer to Germany and, in other items, closer to Canada. The argument that teachers who delve deeper into concepts of individual support are more critical of themselves can again be seen here. The Finnish teachers also describe that they support struggling students less than the German teachers, although they invest a lot of time in diagnostics and individual programme plans, which are rarely used in Germany. Finnish students stress this argument as they confirm that teachers tell them how to do better when they make mistakes. German teachers do not rate this item very highly.

Our second hypothesis, that the strong focus on the individual school causes stronger individual norm orientation in Finland compared to Canada cannot be confirmed. Strengthening schools and their connection to local needs does not automatically lead to more individualised learning.

The third hypothesis looks at motivation. We assumed that students' motivation is higher in Canada and Finland than in Germany. In Canada, teaching seems to be more motivating. Teachers are more confident in their ability to engage students and demonstrate the importance of school subjects. Students also agreed on this. Canadian students are the most motivated in the entire dataset. We assume that the high motivation is related, among other things, to individualised instruction, although this was not the subject of the present analysis.

The only aspect in which the German and Finnish teachers rate themselves more positively is showing the students the value of learning.

In addition, the Finnish teachers are most convinced that they can inspire their students.

The Finnish students show a mixed picture. They emphasise the wide-ranging support they receive from their teachers, but they show the weakest interest in the subject matter. This shows a clear difference to the teachers' assessed ability to inspire the children.

Conclusion

The data analysis clearly shows that we should not trust first impressions when looking at teacher perception data from different countries. How teachers perceive the use of reference norms in their teaching depends on what they value and what they learn in their daily professional life. It is only through triangulation with students' perceptions that a more accurate picture emerges. Only when student perceptions of what teachers do overlap with teachers' own perceptions of the use of reference norms can we assume that the data paint a clear picture. If German teachers are not aware of strategies for the use of individual norm referencing in providing individual student support, they may overestimate their own competencies in this regard, whereas teachers in Canada and Finland, where individual student support is seen as a core concept of the teaching profession, may be overly critical of their own success. The study shows how complex cross-cultural research is, because in addition to the data, we always need to take systemic factors and cultural context into account.

Note

1. The horizontal and vertical alignments describe that all actions in the school system are interlinked, on the one hand, by the different levels, and on the other hand, procedures within the individual levels, for example, at school level or school board level, are also coordinated with each other.

References

Atzert, R., John, R., Preisfeld, A., & Damerau, K. (2020). Der Einfluss kriterialer, sozialer und individueller Bezugsnormen auf das experimentbezogene Fähigkeitsselbstkonzept. *Zeitschrift für Didaktik der Naturwissenschaften, 26*(1), 89–102.

Brunstein, J., & Heckhausen, H. (2018). Achievement motivation. In J. Heckhausen & H. Heckhausen (Eds.), *Motivation and action* (pp. 221–304). Springer.

Dickhäuser, O., Janke, S., Praetorius, A.K., & Dresel, M. (2017). The effects of teachers' reference norm orientations on students' implicit theories and academic self-concepts. *Zeitschrift für Pädagogische Psychologie, 31*(3–4), 205–219.

Dickhäuser, O., & Rheinberg, F. (2003). Bezugsnormorientierung: Erfassung, Probleme, Perspektiven. In J. Stiensmeyer-Pelster & F. Rheinberg (Eds), *Diagnostik von Selbstkonzept, Lernmotivation und Selbstregulation* (pp. 41–55). Hogrefe.

Dweck, C. (1990). Self-theories and goals: Their role in motivation, personality, and development. In R. Dienstbier (Ed.), *Perspectives on motivation: Nebraska Symposium on motivation* (pp. 38, 199–235). University of Nebraska Press.

Dweck, C., & Leggett, E. (1988), A social cognitive approach to personality and motivation. *Psychological Review, 95*(2), 256–273.

Ebel, R. L. (1962). Content-standard test scores. *Educational and Psychological Measurement, 22*(1), 15–25.

Elliot, A. J., Murayama, K., & Pekrun, R. (2011). A 3 × 2 achievement goal model. *Journal of Educational Psychology, 103*(3), 632–648.

Elliot, E. S., & Dweck, C. S. (1988). Goals: An approach to motivation and achievement. *Journal of Personality and Social Psychology, 54*(1), 5–12.

Fischer, A. (1912). Über die Faulheit. *Zeitschrift für Pädagogische Psychologie und Experimentelle Pädagogik*, 8, 507–516.

Foy, P. (2017). *TIMSS 2015 user guide for the international database.* https://timssandpirls.bc.edu/timss2015/international-database/downloads/T15_UserGuide.pdf

Glaser, R. (1963). Instrumental technology and the measurement of learning outcomes. *American Psychologist, 18*(8), 519–521.

Government of Alberta. (2019). *Response to intervention.* https://www.alberta.ca/response-to-intervention.aspx

Heckhausen, H. (1972). Die Interaktion der Sozialisationsvariablen in der Genese des Leistungsmotivs. In C. F. Graumann (Ed.), *Handbuch der Psychologie* (pp. 955–1019). Hogrefe.

Herbart, J. F. (1831). *Pädagogische Briefe oder Briefe über die Anwendung der Psychologie auf die Pädagogik.* Osterwick.

Jagacinski, C. M., & Nicholls, J. G. (1987). Competence and affect in task involvement and ego involvement: The impact of social comparison information. *Journal of Educational Psychology, 79*(2), 107–114.

Kaplan, A., & Maehr, M. L. (2007). The contributions and prospects of goal orientation theory. *Educational Psychology Review, 19*(2), 141–184.

Klopsch, B., & Sliwka, A. (2020). Schulqualität als Resultat eines “komplexen adaptiven Systems”. In D. Fickermann, V. Manitius, & M. Karcher (Eds.). *“Neue Steuerung” – Renaissance der Kybernetik? Die Deutsche Schule* (pp. 58–74). Waxmann.

Krampen, G. (1987). Differential effects of teacher comments. *Journal of Educational Psychology, 79*(2), 137–146.

Krug, S., & Lecybyl, R. (2005). Die Veränderung von Einstellung, Mitarbeit und Lernleistung im Verlauf einer bezugsnormspezifischen Motivationsintervention. In F. Rheinberg & S. Krug (Eds.), *Motivationsförderung im Schulalltag* (pp. 95–114). Hogrefe.

Kupiainen, S., Hautamäki, J., & Karjalainen, T. (2009). *The Finnish Education System and PISA.* Ministry of Education Publications.

Meece, J. L., & Holt, K. (1993). A pattern analysis of students' achievement goals. *Journal of Educational Psychology, 85*(4), 582–590. https://doi.org/10.1037/0022-0663.85.4.582

Mullis, I. V. S., & Martin, M. O. (2013). *TIMSS 2015 assessment frameworks.* http://timssandpirls.bc.edu/timss2015/frameworks.html

Nicholls, J. G. (1984). Achievement motivation: Conceptions of ability, subjective experience, task choice, and performance. *Psychological Review, 91*(3), 328–346.

Rheinberg, F. (1982). *Bezugsnormen zur Schulleistungsbewertung: Analyse und intervention.* Schwann.

Rheinberg, F. (2014). Bezugsnorm. In M. A. Wirtz (Hrsg.), *Dorsch: Lexikon der Psychologie.* Hans Huber.

Rheinberg, F., & Krug, S. (1999). *Motivationsförderung im Schulalltag.* Hogrefe.

Sliwka, A., & Klopsch, B. (2018). Schule in Kanada. In M. Harring, C. Rohlfs, & M. Gläser-Zikuda (Eds.), *Handbuch Schulpädagogik* (pp. 63–77). Waxmann.

Tatto, M. (2015). The role of research in the policy and practice of quality teacher education: An international review. *Oxford Review of Education, 41*(2), 171–201.

Thuneberg, H., Vainikainen, M.-P., Ahtiainen, R., Lintuvuori, M., Salo, K., & Hautamäki, J. (2013). Education is special for all—The Finnish support model. *Gemeinsam Leben, 21*(2), 67–78.

Vainikainen, M.-P., Thuneberg, H., Marjanen, J., Hautamäki, J., Kupiainen, S., & Hotulainen, R. (2017). How do Finns know? Educational monitoring without inspection and standard setting. In S. Blömeke & J.-E. Gustafsson (Eds.), *Standard setting in education, methodology of educational measurement and assessment* (pp. 243–259). Springer.

Wendt, H., Bos, W., Selter, C., Köller, O., Schwippert, K., & Kasper, D. (Eds.). (2016). *TIMSS 2015. Mathematische und naturwissenschaftliche Kompetenzen von Grundschulkindern in Deutschland im internationalen Vergleich.* Waxmann.

15 Human Rights-Based Education—Inclusive and "Appropriate"?

Some Questions after Visits to Toronto and New Brunswick

Ines Boban and Andreas Hinz

In this chapter, we try to deal with our doubts and questions arising from our visits to Toronto and New Brunswick in September 2016. Both Toronto and New Brunswick have a positive reputation as global "lighthouses" or even as "guiding lights" of inclusive education (Hinz, 2006a, 2007; Köpfer, 2013a, 2013b, about New Brunswick; Reich, 2012, about Toronto); also, UNESCO's Lena Saleh recommended in the 2000s looking at New Brunswick on the question of the most inclusive educational system. In 2016, New Brunswick received an international award for its continuing commitment to inclusive education (Department of Education and Early Childhood Development New Brunswick, 2016). We, the authors, have also had many positive inspirations, but here we address our doubts and questions, which can become a specific source of learning, especially in an international context (Boban & Kruschel, 2015). In this respect, formulations like *appropriateness* that are used by many people in practice and that appear in official documents play a central role in leading us to have our critical questions.

Canada is regarded as a country which, with its long tradition as a country of immigration, welcomes diversity and difference among communities (Polat, in this volume). It cannot be overlooked, however, that the federal system results in the provinces of Ontario and New Brunswick having two very different educational systems, both of which reflect internationally dominant but very differently assessed models: the *cascade model*, which is described as differentiated or selective, and the *full inclusion* model, which is regarded as consistent or total (Bunch et al., 2015; Hinz, 2006a). Canada is therefore by no means uniformly structured; in this respect, it is also more than questionable to denigrate positive concepts as unrealistic idealisations of *full inclusion* (Schroeder, 2016). A "swarm of discourses" (Schroeder, in this volume) also seems to be an expression of a limited view of Canada: People who travel to

DOI: 10.4324/9781003204572-19

provinces that use the *cascade model* should not really be surprised if they find the whole spectrum of integrative, partially integrative, and segregative forms of school organisation; in our view, however, the question arises as to what extent this is still inclusion; Bunch et al. (2015, p. 16) identify it as "fundamental to a special education model."

However, the unconscious tendency to project one's own desires and expectations can go hand in hand with a frequently occurring positive orientation function—as already happened with Finland as the "winner" of the PISA study or before that also with Italy—so that an *inclusive paradise* is expected that leads to frustration when reality is finally encountered. After our stay of several months in 2004, we highlighted the inclusive support structures as internationally exemplary (Hinz, 2006a, 2007; Köpfer, 2013b); with regard to the pedagogical processes, we were less forthcoming. In a publication in Canada, however, in addition to highlighting strengths, we also asked some critical questions about inclusive practices, for example, about the high priority given to *appropriate behaviour* by children, which already, at that time, seemed to us to be almost more important than *authentic being*, or about the high value of *respect*, which often seemed to us more like control and could result in individual work lasting several days in a room with a speaking ban (Hinz, 2006b).

More than 10 years later, we now return to these two regions on a university excursion with students and colleagues and realise that our questions at the time have come to a head: What we noticed then in specific situations as questionable practices in the truest sense of the word now condenses into an overall picture raising fundamental questions. Apparently, the massive behaviourist tradition in North America also continues in inclusive education—a considerable area of tension for us, but one that is apparently not perceived as such there, so that university colleagues who are inquiring about it cannot name for us any texts that present such a discussion; we are also not sure whether we were able to make clear our "problem" at all.

This area of tension between the behaviourist tradition and the claim to inclusion will be examined in the following section. To this end, we will first make transparent some situations we actually experienced in which these phenomena became clear to us. Next, we work out their possible backgrounds, and finally, we consider as a conclusion how this possible conflict can be explained, and which counterforces can be found.

Some New "Oops-Stories"

In an article from the 1990s, in which we discussed the changed developments of children with special needs, we focus on intellectual development in integration classes that had not been thought possible before (Boban & Hinz, 1993) and we told some "Oops-Stories" about them.

With this, we wanted to clarify when and by what means we were astonished to observe things which we thought were not possible and contradicted everything we had learned before in the study of the *education of the mentally impaired.*

We take up this approach here and tell a few new "Oops-Stories." These are specifically selected examples to draw attention to certain tendencies; we are by no means interested in disparaging in its entirety educational practice that conceives itself as inclusive. That is why we report another story beforehand: At the end of a long conversation, the head of a school support team asks why we should actually make such a huge effort to come all the way to Canada—as, after all, they were not doing anything special. When we tell her, among other things, that children in Germany go to different types of schools after primary school, she is so astonished that she calls out to her colleague working at the back of the room: "Did you hear that? In Germany, after a few years, they separate the children by sending them to different types of schools—that's unbelievable! Why do you do that?" Now she has an idea why we are there (Hinz, 2004, 2009, 2010).

"Special Support" for Life at Work

In a high school, we are led into a special room in which hundreds of consecutively numbered Tupperware boxes are stacked against a wall (see Figure 15.1). The support teacher in charge proudly informs us how *autonomy* is taught in this room: Young people with *special educational*

Figure 15.1 The Tupperware Boxes. Photographer: I. Boban (2016).

needs come to the room once a week, receive a small book with their name on it and six numbers, look for the correspondingly numbered box, open it, take out the materials, read the task written on the lid, for example "put the blue squares together with the other blue squares, the yellow squares with the yellow squares, the red squares with the red ones etc." Then, they perform this task without talking to anyone, put the materials back in the box, and take them back to their place. In accordance with the numbers written down, they complete all the tasks and finish their work after one hour. It is irrelevant whether these tasks make any sense—it is just important that they are done correctly and independently according to the instructions. Because (as we are told) if the young people are to have a chance on the job market, it is important that they can inform a potential employer in their job application that they are able to carry out an assigned task for one hour independently and reliably and, therefore, *appropriately*.

We find another room like this with the same equipment and use in another high school, but the approach is described differently with varying degrees of conviction—the spectrum ranges from pride to clear doubts about what this exercise can achieve in view of the obvious degree of apathy largely noticeable in the young people.

Attendance Check and the National Anthem

In the Kindergarten group of a school, the four-year-old children gather at hexagonal group tables and have apparently been instructed to do this in silence. They are in "play time," which apparently means they are allowed to busy themselves with materials on their segmented table section marked out with red tape. At a signal from the teacher, they all gather on carpet tiles in front of a touch screen showing a list of the names of all the children. The teacher turns to the list and begins to read out the names. A child replying promptly and with a loud "here!" accompanied by a broad smile receives a sympathetic nod; if this response lacks these attributes, the teacher spreads out her index and middle finger, pushes up the corners of her own mouth, and demands a repetition with "give me a smile!" After the list has been completed, the Canadian flag appears on the screen to the music of the national anthem. The children are now required to stand on their carpet tiles, put their hands on their hearts, sing along, and adopt an appropriate attitude, namely: "Stand like a soldier!" A child who does not adopt the required posture is grabbed by the shoulders and placed in the *appropriate* position.

Integration Assistance for "New Canadians"

In a Kindergarten group in a school, a *parental training course* is taking place to help parents deal with their children. It is offered to *newcomers* or *new Canadians* (i.e., people who have recently immigrated to Canada):

They should learn how to introduce their children to reading in the *appropriate* manner. Contrary to what seems to be a widespread tradition, here, it is not one teacher sitting in a rocking chair but two adults on a small bench while all the children and their parents sit cross-legged on carpet tiles on the floor. The two colleagues have an extraordinarily large picture book on their knees and leaf through it together, visible to all. Before this, animal pictures on paper were distributed to the children and they were instructed to pay exact attention and hold up the relevant picture as soon as the animal appeared in the story. And then the teachers begin to read the story from the book with theatrical intensity to elicit appropriate statements from the children prompted by unfinished sentences. For about a third of the children, this seems to be exactly what fascinates them and where they are willing to participate, and a smile is visible on several mothers' faces. Another third of the children seem to be more oriented towards their own mothers and seem to wait patiently until this phase is over. The faces of some mothers leave much room for interpretation. And about a third of the children seem uninterested and look in other directions; some ask if they can go out. Then, they receive the emphatically smiling answer: "No! You know: first we read the book together, then we all have breakfast together, and then we decide who can go out." Some of the mothers' facial expressions seem to suggest that they are thinking they would never read a book to their child in this way or express themselves in such an artificial way.

Walking through the School Building

In a school with a school-aged population ranging from Kindergarten to Grade 8, there are two photographers who today take the annual class photos. The students are told by their principal via loudspeaker to come to the relevant room, class by class. We see the students walking in single file with their hands on the seam of their trousers, silently walking through the school building to be photographed. It is therefore all the more striking that a teacher in the company of a child is also walking through the school building—and the child is singing loudly and moving along with dance movements. Later in the day, the principal asks us if we saw an individual child who—*inappropriately*—was singing while walking through the building: "That's our autist—we just can't stop him."

By the way, in this school, as in many others, there are various commercially distributed posters on the walls in corridors and classrooms with slogans like: "You are unique because you are you," "Dance as if nobody was watching you," or "Respect is not a gift, it's something you have to earn." What is striking, too, is the high proportion of graphic decoration using Indigenous symbols. There are also homemade posters, such as the one with five rules for crossing the recreation hall (see Figure 15.2).

Figure 15.2 Rules for Crossing the Recreation Hall. Photographer: Kruschel (2016).

Professional Clothing

All the female teachers at the school wear skirts, nylon stockings, and pumps with heels; no matter what age group they work with, from Kindergarten groups to Grade 8. This is considered *appropriate*, professional clothing from Monday to Thursday. Friday is considered a transition to the weekend; on this day, a *casual day*, jeans are also allowed. Wearing jeans on all other days is subject to the payment of a fine. When asked critically to what extent this is professional clothing, the principal explains that appropriate adult clothing is a prerequisite for being able to demand *appropriate clothing* from the children.

Forming a Community

In a large elementary school, every morning the vice principal makes various announcements throughout the school using the central audio system. On this particular day, the visitors from Germany are welcomed, birthday children are invited to his office for a personal congratulations, and it is pointed out that this school is located on the territory where Cree once lived; until these members of a First Nation were expelled.

On request, we learn that the daily reminder of the oppression of the First Nations and of this injustice towards the Indigenous Peoples has been newly introduced in this district following the example of New Zealand with its decision to come to terms with the reappraisal of the crimes committed against the Maoris. This is connected with a new willingness during Justin Trudeau's leadership to confront the historical treatment of the Indigenous peoples, intensifying the processing of this social genocide and the consequences for its survivors, among other things, also with the help of *truth and reconciliation committees*, as are familiar from South Africa (Metcalfe-Chenail, 2016; Pearpoint, 2019; Truth and Reconciliation Commission of Canada, 2015).

A Systematic Approach to Support

During a full day introduction to New Brunswick's education system at the Ministry responsible in Fredericton, it is emphasised by various speakers, among other things, that the basis of the justification for inclusive education consists of various facets. In addition to aspects familiar to us such as relying on team structures, the use of methods of cooperative problem-solving or *Universal Design for Learning*, new ones are emerging, such as data-supported decision-making and scientific, research-based interventions with three different levels. When asked, it turns out that New Brunswick, as do many countries (Jahnukainen & Itkonen, 2021), now also uses *Response to Intervention* (RTI) as a central element of its practice of inclusive education (Department of Education and Early Childhood Development New Brunswick, 2015, p. 1f.; 2017). In response to our intervention, our question as to why this is helpful, the following explanation is given: it is by no means a question of assigning children to different levels and labelling them—RTI helps them by providing the systematic, rapid selection of support approaches, which then contributes to appropriate responses to appropriate intervention.

Background to the "Oops-Stories"

From our point of view, the "Oops-Stories" help to recognise a basic attitude that is characterised by various aspects related to notions of normality and clear definitions of what is regarded as *appropriate*. In the following section, we characterise them as a mixture of interrelated, discriminatory tendencies:

- *Normalism*: Educators know exactly what they expect from young people and what goals they set for them—be it in the area of performance or *appropriate behaviour* even including *appropriate clothing* (Link, 1998).

- *Adultism*: Adults see themselves as having the right and the obligation to bring all this, in the form of praise and criticism, to the attention of young people who have to submit to these requirements—unless they have *special educational needs* and appear to be only adaptable to a limited extent (Liebel, 2020; Rempel, 2017).
- *Canadaism* (a working concept created here on an experimental basis): Representatives of the Canadian majority society know exactly which attitudes and actions distinguish *good Canadian citizens* and how the associated values are embodied and made clear in everyday behaviour. Refugees and other immigrants are also taught assertively how to become *new Canadians*. In keeping with Canada's positive self-image, symbols of the Indigenous peoples are also used for this purpose—to be found widely on commercial posters in schools. And it is to be hoped that the daily announcement in Toronto's schools that the school in question is located on First Nations land, from where they were expelled by whites, will contribute to a platform of equal dialogue (Pearpoint, 2019) and not descend into the mere staging of a chore.
- *Colonialism*: White Canadians from Europe follow a binary logic that labels behaviour and achievement as *right* or *wrong*, *appropriate* or *inappropriate*, and *better* or *worse*, and thus constructs and stabilises a "two-group theory" (Hinz, 2004, p. 45). It is criticised in Canada as a form of colonialism since Indigenous peoples do not practice such a mode of thought and, when confronted with it, are turned into losers in white Canadian society (Herold, in this volume; Kress, in this volume, 2017; Pearpoint, 2019).
- *Ableism*: Especially in high school with the increasing proximity to school diplomas and social connections, ableism is increasingly assigned to different sets of specific course offerings, such as those for future university students, future trainees, and future workers. As a result, the stimulating potential of heterogeneous learning groups is receding behind the specific nature of the offerings. This specificity can be understood as "systemic ableism" (Kress, 2017, p. 39) and is increasingly approaching separate and distinct forms of special educational support and is also accompanied by corresponding *protective ideas*: Supposedly, it seems better for everyone if a young person with a clear support need learns *autonomy* on an individual basis rather than being confronted with the conversations with peers who exchange dates, relationships, hip music and concerts, etc. Thus, the question of how their participation in such activities can be facilitated seems not to be given much attention.
- *Behaviourism:* Both at the concrete level in schools and structurally at the level of the province or district, in many statements, the belief that the behaviour and development of young people can be

> directed in a more or less linear form. This tendency of adultism, with its conception of normalcy, is a necessary prerequisite for *appropriate* performance development and *appropriate* behaviour. Both learners and teachers are under massive pressure—they *play* this difficult *game*, but many of them are also dissatisfied, as becomes evident repeatedly in conversations (Kohn, 2015). In this respect, it is not surprising that RTI is being increasingly used as such an approach and is now being used extensively for the area of behaviour (Department of Education and Early Childhood Development New Brunswick, 2015, 2017) even though a high level of systemic attention has long been paid to development processes using various other tools (Porter & Crawford, 2004) and North American results from the evaluation of RTI are by no means as consistently positive (Balu et al., 2015) as they are often presented. Nevertheless, in the school psychological literature, RTI is regarded as a "promising model of service delivery and special education identification" (McIntosh et al., 2011, p. 19) which, explicitly understood as a special educational concept, obviously fits in well with one's professional self-image (McIntosh et al., 2011).

As critical as automatic data-based assignment of students to schools—in Toronto, Ontario, the *inner city model* schools serve as an example (Boban et al., 2018)—socio-political programmes can also be seen as expressions of a behaviourist form of control that neglects social and contextual difference.

Presumably, the tendency towards a behaviourist educational culture is the central pedagogical basis for all the other aspects listed—*Canadaism* is a linguistically used term that we are trying to extend with critical meaning here. The overall situation becomes contradictory because, according to Canadian self-understanding, it is equally *appropriate* to value diversity and thus to think and act in an accepting and inclusive way—and all this in a domination manner (Eisler, 2017).

Conclusion—Possible Backgrounds and Countertendencies

Of course, the *promised land of inclusion* cannot be found in Canada either. In both Canadian regions which were examined more closely, there are tendencies which point to a contradictory basic situation: On the one hand, a strong behaviourist attitude with very clear expectations and monitoring of them; on the other hand, the internationally acclaimed acceptance of diversity.

The backgrounds to this contradictory basic situation can only be speculated on here. With some probability, however, what could play a role is that:

- The second empirical turn has also led—especially in Canada—to massive pressure on teachers, students, as well as on education administration and policy, which makes the international comparison extremely important. As employees of the University of British Columbia state: "Schools are bombarded with demands to do more," and this is in the context of reduced resources (McIntosh et al., 2011, p. 19). New Brunswick is regularly at the bottom of the Canadian rankings but still ahead of almost all German federal states.
- Accountability has a very high priority in the Canadian education system—not least because of the logic of the North American legal system, which can quickly lead to litigation and compensation demands going into the millions. Here, reliability and security are necessary conditions.
- Education in Canada has also been widely taken into neoliberal service by society (Dannenbeck & Hinz, 2017). Even the Secretary of State in New Brunswick's Ministry of Education pointed out in 2016 during our visit in his statement that *employability and education*—in this order—are decisive factors for the further economic development of the province.
- Inclusive education is being re-contextualised in connection with the strong behaviourist tradition in North America (Fend, 2008). And it seems to be located quite to the side of the domination model and not to the partnership model in the partnership-domination-scale (Eisler, 2017; Eisler & Fry, 2019).

Nevertheless, Canada's city of Toronto and province of New Brunswick do not simply have a normative, dogmatic educational system based on normalcy. Structural guidelines can only define the participants to a limited extent, as neo-institutionalism shows (Sieber, 2006). Already in the "Oops-Stories" it becomes clear that there are different degrees of satisfaction with existing structures and practices. And there are also tendencies that can be interpreted as contrary to the dominant behaviourist logic. Finally, two of these will be discussed.

Toronto has a whole series of state schools with alternative concepts, one of which is the Democratic Alpha School (Alpha Alternative School, n.d.). It refuses to exercise massive control inherent in the collecting of performance, social, and other data. Nevertheless, it has been publicly funded for about 40 years and has no sanctions to fear. In this school—as is customary internationally in democratic schools—individual decisions are made as to what is learned together or individually. The school rules are in a permanent state of development; here, too, violations are dealt with by a "juridical committee," in which adults play an exclusively moderating role (Hershkovich et al., 2017, p. 167). The pressure on education policy is apparently not so great that such schools would be closed, but they are under pressure to assert themselves in the education market and to be selected by parents—and that is, then again, compatible with neoliberal market logic in the education sector.

From the context of the work on the situation of Indigenous peoples, attention is increasingly drawn to the *gentle teaching* approach, which can be traced back to working with street children in Brazil (Boban & Hinz, 2019; Kress, 2017).[1] In accordance with this and under Canadian conditions, its primary concern is to gain insight into the sociocultural background of the Indigenous peoples in order to work out reasons for the failure of the behaviourist system of white Canadian colonialism. So, in this way decolonising—in fact, inclusive—alternatives with acceptance of the cultural backgrounds of Indigenous students (Kress, 2017, p. 39, in this volume) can be developed. At the same time, it is important to avoid establishing a new special pedagogy for Indigenous students most severely threatened by marginalisation. Rather, with this sensitive perception of such marginalisation processes, an appreciative, inclusive understanding of education in theory and practice in the sense of decolonisation needs to be developed and thus *Pimatisiwin* (Boban & Hinz, 2019; Kress, 2017, in this volume), a life in well-being and in self-realisation for all people, needs to be cultivated.

In this respect, it may be comforting to find that there are also clear controversies in Canada between different understandings of education—and also of inclusive education. Inclusive education is integrated into all social mechanisms—including those that form hierarchies—and remains highly contradictory (Tiedeken, 2017), above all with regard to the aspect of how stimulating the relationship between inclusive and *appropriate* tendencies can be shaped when they are brought together. It remains extremely doubtful and worth discussing whether respect is "not a gift" but must first be "earned." The dignity of the child plays a central role here; in accordance with the *Convention on the Rights of the Child* it is protected from any punishment "which belittles, humiliates, denigrates, scapegoats, threatens, scares or ridicules the child" by someone (Committee on the Rights of the Child, 2006, p. 4) and children should rather be heard in all matters concerning them (Bundesministerium für Familie, Senioren, Frauen und Jugend (BMFSFJ), 2014, p. 15), as practised in the Alpha School. Inclusive education in Canada too continues to face the challenge of reflecting and cultivating its human rights basis beyond—at least in New Brunswick—the undisputed right to institutional membership of the neighbourhood school.

Note

1. Following APA style, we have to be the first in this citation—of course, Margaret Kress was the first and we learned from her.

References

Alpha Alternative School. (n.d.). Homepage. Alpha Alternative School. https://www.alphaschool.ca/new/

Balu, R., Zhu, P., Doolittle, F., Schiller, E., Jenkins, J., & Gersten, R. (2015). *Evaluation of response to intervention practices for elementary school reading*. National Center for Education Evaluation and Regional Assistance & US Department of Education. www.mdrc.org/publication/evaluation-response-intervention-rti-practices-elementary-school-reading

Boban, I., & Hinz, A. (1993). Geistige Behinderung und Integration: Überlegungen zum Begriff der "Geistigen Behinderung" im Zusammenhang integrativer Erziehung. *Zeitschrift für Heilpädagogik, 44*(44), 327–340.

Boban, I., & Hinz, A. (2019). "Gentle Teaching" – ein radikaler Impuls für eine inklusive Haltung. In D. Jahr & R. Kruschel (Hrsg.), *Inklusion in Kanada. Internationale Perspektiven auf heterogenitätssensible Bildung* (pp. 138–153). Beltz Juventa.

Boban, I., Hinz, A., Jahr, D., & Kruschel, R. (2018). Inklusive Schulsysteme in Kanada – Anregungen für den deutschsprachigen Raum? In E. Feyerer, W. Prammer, E. Prammer-Semmler, C. Kladnik, M. Leibetseder, & R. Wimberger (Hrsg.), *System. Wandel. Entwicklung. Akteurinnen und Akteure inklusiver Prozesse im Spannungsfeld von Institution, Profession und Person* (pp. 111–116). Klinkhardt.

Boban, I., & Kruschel, R. (2015). "Thinking outside the box" – produktive Irritationen durchein internationales Kooperationsprojekt. In I. Schnell (Ed.), *Herausforderung Inklusion – Theoriebildung und Praxis* (pp. 313–321). Klinkhardt.

Bunch, G., Finnegan, K., Humphries, C., Dore, R., & Dore, L. (2015). *Crucial terms final report. Finding a way through the maze: Crucial terms used in education provision for Canadians with disabilities*. The Marsha Forest Center. https://inclusion.com/site/wp-content/uploads/2017/03/crucialterms.pdf

Bundesministerium für Familie, Senioren, Frauen und Jugend. (2014). *Übereinkommen über die Rechte des Kindes: VN-Kinderrechtskonvention im Wortlaut mit Materialien*. BMFSFJ.

Committee on the Rights of the Child. (2006). General Comment No. 8. The right of the child to protection from corporal punishment and other cruel or degrading forms of punishment. https://resourcecentre.savethechildren.net/library/general-comment-no-8-2006-right-child-protection-corporal-punishment-and-other-cruel-or#:~:text=The%20Committee%20is%20issuing%20this%20General%20Comment%20No.,awareness-raising%20and%20educational%20measures%20that%20States%20must%20taking.

Dannenbeck, C., & Hinz, A. (2017). Das Politische (in) der Gestaltung inklusionsorientierter Bildungsprozesse. In I. Boban & A. Hinz (Eds.), *Inklusive Bildungsprozesse gestalten – Nachdenken über Horizonte, Spannungsfelder und mögliche Schritte* (pp. 52–69). Klett Kallmeyer.

Department of Education and Early Childhood Development New Brunswick. (2015). *Guidelines and standards. Educational planning for students with diverse learning needs.* https://www2.gnb.ca/content/dam/gnb/Departments/ed/pdf/K12/curric/Resource/GuidelinesStandardsEducationalPlanningStudentsWithExceptionalities.pdf

Department of Education and Early Childhood Development New Brunswick. (2016). *New Brunswick receives international award for inclusive education.*

Department of Education and Early Childhood Development New Brunswick. (2017). *Response to intervention in behaviour: A PBIS resource guide for school-based teams.* https://www2.gnb.ca/content/dam/gnb/Departments/ed/pdf/K12/Inclusion/ResponseToInterventionForBehaviour.pdf

Eisler, R. (2017). Building a caring Democracy: Four cornerstones for an integrated progressive agenda. *Interdisciplinary Journal of Partnership Studies, 4*(1), 1–23.

Eisler, R., & Fry, D. P. (2019). *Nurturing our humanity. How domination and partnership shape our brains, lives, and future.* Oxford University Press.

Fend, H. (2008). *Schule gestalten. Systemsteuerung, Schulentwicklung und Unterrichtsqualität.* VS.

Hershkovich, M., Simon, J., & Simon, T. (2017). Menschenrechte, Demokratie, Partizipation und Inklusion – ein (fast) in Vergessenheit geratenes Wechselverhältnis? In R. Kruschel (Ed.), *Menschenrechtsbasierte Bildung. Inklusive und demokratische Lern- und Erfahrungswelten im Fokus* (pp. 161–172). Klinkhardt.

Hinz, A. (2004). Vom sonderpädagogischen Verständnis der Integration zum integrationspädagogischen Verständnis der Inklusion!? In I. Schnell & A. Sander (Eds.), *Inklusive Pädagogik* (pp. 41–74). Klinkhardt.

Hinz, A. (2006a). Kanada – ein 'Nordstern' in Sachen Inklusion. In A. Platte, S. Seitz, & K. Terfloth (Eds.), *Inklusive Bildungsprozesse* (pp. 149–158). Klinkhardt.

Hinz, A. (2006b). A world of difference: Inclusive education in Canada and Germany. *Education Canada, 46*(1), 22–24.

Hinz, A. (2007). Inklusion – Vision und Realität! Herausforderungen in Deutschland und Praxis in Kanada. In D. Katzenbach (Ed.), *Vielfalt braucht Struktur. Heterogenität als Herausforderung für die Unterrichts- und Schulentwicklung* (pp. 81–98). Goethe-Universität.

Hinz, A. (2009). Models of inclusion: Germany. In M. Alur & V. Timmons (Eds.), *inclusive education across cultures. Crossing boundaries, sharing ideas* (pp. 299–317). Sage.

Hinz, A. (2010). Towards inclusive education in Germany – Structures, practical and theoretical development of joint education. In G. Bunch & A. Valeo (Eds.), *Inclusive education: Emergent solutions. England, Germany, Croatia, Canada, India, Spain, Malta* (pp. 40–73). Inclusion Press.

Jahnukainen, M., & Itkonen, T. (2021). Steps to inclusion? The role of tiered intervention in Finland and in the United States. In A. Köpfer, J. W. Powell, & R. Zahnd (Eds.), *International handbook of inclusive education. Global, national and local perspectives* (pp. 345–356). Barbara Budrich.

Kohn, A. (2015). *Der Mythos des verwöhnten Kindes. Erziehungslügen unter die Lupe genommen.* Beltz.

Köpfer, A. (2013a). *Inclusion in Kanada. Analyse inclusiver Unterrichtsprozesse, Unterstützungsstrukturen und Rollen am Beispiel kanadischer Schulen in den Provinzen New Brunswick, Prince Edward Island und Quebec.* Klinkhardt.

Köpfer, A. (2013b). Inclusive Unterstützungsstrukturen und Rollen am Beispiel kanadischer Schulen in den Provinzen New Brunswick, Prince Edward Island und Québec. *Zeitschrift Inklusion Online, 4*(8).

Kress, M. (2017). Reclaiming disability through *Pimâtisowin:* Of Indigenous ethics, spatial justice and gentle teaching. In *International Perspectives on Inclusive Education* (vol. 1, pp. 23–57). Emerald Group Publishing Ltd.

Liebel, M. (2020). *Unerhört. Kinder und Macht.* Beltz Juventa.

Link, J. (1998). *Versuch über den Normalismus. Wie Normalität produziert wird.* Vandenhoeck & Ruprecht.

McIntosh, K., MacKay, L. D., Andreu, T., Brown, J. A., Mathews, S., Gietz, C., & Bennett, J. L. (2011). Response to intervention in Canada: Definitions, the evidence base, and future directions. *Canadian Journal of School Psychology, 26*(1) 1, 18–43.

Metcalfe-Chenail, D. (Ed.). (2016). *In This Together – 15 Stories of Truth and Reconciliation.* Brindle & Glass.

Pearpoint, J. (2019). Wegwerfbare Menschen; Vom Aufdecken kanadischer "Nicht-Menschen" und ihrer "Nicht-Geschichte". In D. Jahr & R. Kruschel (Eds.), *Inklusion in Kanada. Internationale Perspektiven auf heterogenitätssensible Bildung* (pp. 426–444). Beltz Juventa.

Porter, G. L., & Crawford, C. (2004). *Teachers helping teachers: Problem solving teams that work.* The Roeher Institute.

Reich, K. (2012): Fünf notwendige Standards der Inklusion. In K. Reich (Ed.), *Inklusion und Bildungsgerechtigkeit. Standards und Regeln zur Umsetzung einer inklusiven Schule* (pp. 54–90). Beltz.

Rempel, E. (2017). "Dafür bist du noch zu klein!" – Sprache und Adultismus. In R. Kruschel, (Ed.), *Menschenrechtsbasierte Bildung. Inklusive und demokratische Lern- und Erfahrungswelten im Fokus* (pp. 231–237). Klinkhardt.

Schroeder, J. (2016). Kanada kann auch anders. Vielfältige Schulangebote im "gelobten Land der Inklusion." *Zeitschrift für Inklusion Online, 4*(11).

Sieber, P. (2006). *Steuerung und Eigendynamik der Aussonderung. Vom Umgang des Bildungswesens mit Heterogenität.* Edition SHZ/CSPS.

Tiedeken, P. (2017). *Musik und Inklusion – Zu den Widersprüchen inklusive Musikproduktion in der Sozialen Arbeit.* Beltz Juventa.

Truth and Reconciliation Commission of Canada. (2015). *Truth & reconciliation: Calls to action.* https://www.irsss.ca/downloads/trc-calls-to-action.pdf

16 Curriculum Design in Inclusive Education

Comparison of Curricular Approaches to Diversity at School in Prince Edward Island (Canada), Finland, and South Tyrol

Andreas Köpfer, Marcel Veber, and Anna Bollesen

Introduction: Inclusive Education and the Function of Curricula

The ratification of the United Nations *Convention on the Rights of Persons with Disabilities* in 2006 firmly anchored the human right to inclusive education in Germany, and "required [changes to be made] by the schools to their structures, ethos and practices" and the removal of "barriers (which may be environmental, structural or attitudinal) to children's participation" (Allan, 2012). For schools and teaching, this requires considering not only the formal roles and practices of the professional actors but also structural, administrative, and legal framework conditions. These are examined in our analysis with a focus on the curriculum. In contrast to the partial narrowing of an understanding of inclusion to disability (Hinz, 2013), the following takes as its basis a holistic, support-oriented approach to inclusion in which intersectional influences can be identified.

To shed light on normative structures in schools and teaching that are affected by inclusion, we can focus on control instruments such as curricula since they act as links between school structure, school organisation, and teaching, and they contain classification systems for dealing with diversity (e.g., disability). However, a look at other school systems, which are often cited as role models in the discussion on inclusion in Germany (Arbeitsgruppe Internationale Vergleichsstudie, 2007), reveals a different picture: In South Tyrol, Finland, and the Canadian province of Prince Edward Island, for example, no causal relationship can be discerned between the degree of categorisation in curricular frameworks and inclusive structures. Therefore, the question of whether and how barriers to learning are understood or generated in the curriculum becomes central: How do different, selected school systems deal with diversity in

DOI: 10.4324/9781003204572-20

groups? The question arises as to what forms of selection this is translated into against the background of the reform mandate of inclusion.

Methodology

The following analysis is based in the field of international comparative education (Adick, 2008). The aim is to identify explanatory correlations and potential ambivalences in relation to the target perspective of *curricular framework conditions for dealing with diversity in schools*. To gain an overview of the specifics of school systems in different regions, we first carried out an explorative analysis of documents and literature, which included educational policy and administrative guidelines, as well as the relevant discussion and state of research in each country. With support in the literature and document analysis by students in a research workshop at the University of Münster during the winter semester of 2015/2016, as well as an MA thesis, the following two questions were considered: What structures does the state school system have in terms of dealing with students' diversity? What role does the curriculum play and how is it used formally and structurally? As is customary with participatory processes in research-based learning workshops (Grell, 2013, pp. 888–890), the countries and regions to be investigated were selected based on students' previous knowledge and specific interests. Language skills were also considered, so that the following 10 countries or regions were considered in the first phase of the study: England, Finland, Flanders, France, Ireland, Iceland, the Netherlands, Norway, South Africa, and Turkey. The selection of countries focused on educational systems that are not (yet) predominantly at the centre of the research discourse in Germany and also reflect a plurality of cultural, political, and social forms. The variety is particularly advantageous for comparative documentary analyses (Glaser, 2013, pp. 365–366). The aim of this research phase was to identify international differences regarding the structural implementation of curricular guidelines in education systems and to develop an initial analytical template of formal curricular structures.

For this purpose, a differentiated analysis of specific countries and their overall social and curricular structures was completed with the students at the end of the induction-deduction process with the analysis then being operationalised in a three-step process (analysis structures based on Rühle, 2015):

1. Documentation of the basic (education policy) framework conditions of each country;
2. Presentation of country-specific empirical findings on diversity, education, and equal opportunities; and
3. Differentiated analysis of (selected) curricular structures in each country.

The function of curricula to link the school system and its everyday practices with constantly changing social conditions was of particular importance. This research phase was completed in spring 2016. A synopsis of the results of the student research work gradually revealed the interactive relationship between opportunities for participation among groups of people affected by exclusion on the one hand, and (linguistic-) cultural diversity on the other.

Curricular Approaches to Diversity in Selected School Systems

In the following section, three regions are selected as examples. The selection was made based on the curricular analysis and the expositions provided by the MA thesis and research.

Prince Edward Island (Canada)—Adaptation and Modification of the Curriculum

Canada was selected as the first country for the curricular analysis for two reasons. First, Canada is ascribed a pioneering role in the inclusive pedagogical discourse regarding the implementation of inclusive structures, practices, and cultures (including Hinz, 2008). Second, being non-selective, the school framework conditions provide suitable structural prerequisites for a horizontal examination of diversity (Arbeitsgruppe Internationale Vergleichsstudie, 2007; Köpfer, 2013). As in Germany and Austria, the individual provinces and territories determine educational policies in Canada, leading to the development of different forms of implementation and organisation of inclusive education. In the following sections, we will examine the province of Prince Edward Island as an example, focusing particularly on Special Educational Needs (SEN). Prince Edward Island is a small maritime island province with an area of 6000 km^2. Although it is small compared to large provinces such as Alberta and Québec, it has geo-historical significance due to the founding of the confederation of the former colonies into one nation of Canada—formalised by the *Canadian Charter of Rights and Freedoms* (Government of Canada, 2018). There are three school boards serving the province, two anglophone and one francophone. These are subordinated to the Department of Education and Early Childhood Development (DEECD), which covers the areas of education and early childhood and provides a joint minister. The legal regulations on school development and school organisation are laid down in the *School Act* (Legislative Counsel Office [LCO] Prince Edward Island, 2010). The province's 64 schools are divided into two school districts, an anglophone and a francophone sector.

Regarding inclusive education, the analysis of curricular documents reveals two strands of content. Firstly, inclusive education is strongly associated with aspects of lifelong learning. This can be seen, for example, in the so-called *Vision Statement* (DEECD Prince Edward Island, 2009), in which access to education and lifelong learning are interconnected.

Secondly, inclusive education in the Canadian province of Prince Edward Island is related to students with SEN. For example, the *School Act* of Prince Edward Island, Section O (LCO Prince Edward Island, 2010) stipulates a *one school for all* system for the province without a separate school for students with special educational needs. In addition, the *Minister's Directive on Special Education* (DEECD Prince Edward Island, 2009) describes the support measures and structures for students with SEN and specifies the terminology relevant for the support. It is necessary to emphasise that the understanding of special education does not take the form of assigning students with special educational needs to a specialised institution; rather, special education is seen as an auxiliary support measure that is organised in accordance with the curriculum. As in the province of New Brunswick (Köpfer, 2013), a support system has been established that defines various individual support measures for students with special educational needs depending on the form of the disability, which also includes the teacher as someone who requires support (Horne et al., 2008).

As in the province of New Brunswick, the so-called *special education plans*, which are presented here in exemplary form (for more detailed information, see Horne et al., 2008), are the central instrument for providing support for students with special educational needs in the classroom. There is also a three-tier structure in Prince Edward Island, characterised as *adapted, modified,* and *individualised* (DE Prince Edward Island, 2005; DEELC Prince Edward Island, 2011).

Whereas an *adapted education plan* merely involves a change in the curriculum in the sense of adapting the learning content, teaching, or monitoring channels, and does not entail a change to the content of the curriculum, a *modified education plan* does lead to curricular change, which is also noted in the student's file as a modified course. For each type of education plan, all participants and, in particular, the parents of the child concerned must be involved in a collaborative approach (DE Prince Edward Island, 2005). This also applies to the preparation and implementation of an *Individualised Education Plan,* which contains far more comprehensive changes regarding learning content and therefore requires more far-reaching and extensive planning steps. These steps were prepared in great detail for the actors in the schools as a joint product of the former Department of Education (prior to the merger with the Early Childhood Development Department) and all the existing school boards (DE Prince Edward Island, 2005). The term *Individualised Education Plan* refers to "a process by which educators, support personnel and parents collaborate to ensure that students' needs are addressed in a systematic manner" (DE Prince Edward Island, 2005, p. 5). The requirements of an *Individualised Education Plan* include methodological proposals for teaching design and further monitoring of the child's learning status (DE Prince Edward Island, 2005). In addition, measures such as the use of support materials and assistive technologies are explained, as are proposals for planning the transition to higher grades or secondary schools (DEELC Prince Edward Island, 2013). Overall, the curriculum in Prince Edward Island is designed as universal, offering a starting point for different forms of differentiation and modification.

Finland: Multiculturality Anchored in the Curriculum

Our investigation of the Finnish curricular framework focused on the aspect of *multiculturality*. First, multiculturality seems to be a "new phenomenon in Finnish society" (Riitaoja et al., 2010, p. 90) since Finnish culture is described historically as more homogeneous. At present, however, it is increasingly being pointed out that Finnish society is made up of different cultural backgrounds (e.g., the Sami people, an ethnic group that inhabits the north of Scandinavia as an Indigenous people, the Roma minority, Swedes, and immigrants).

With around 5.5 million inhabitants and an area of 338,432 km^2, Finland is one of the most sparsely populated countries in Europe. One of Finland's distinguishing features is that it is officially bilingual. According to the *Finnish Language Act* No. 423/2003, both Finnish and Swedish are official languages (Ministry of Justice Finland [MJ] Finland, 2003, p. 1) with Swedish being a minority language. The *Constitution* explicitly mentions both those who speak Sami or Romani as their mother tongue and those who use sign language as having the right to preserve their language and culture (MJ Finland, 2003, p. 15). Thus, Finnish language legislation can be considered "a model for good treatment of linguistic minorities" (Mikkola, 2008, p. 13). Since Finland's social development was "characterised by emigration until the 1980s and by almost no labour migration until the 1990s" (Hortsch, 2015, p. 57), Finland was not regarded as a classic immigration country until a few years ago. Since the 1990s, however, the number of migrants has risen sharply so that, by the end of 2015, 6.2% of the population was deemed to have a migrant background. Even though the proportion of immigrants has so far been relatively low in European terms, it has risen rapidly since 2000 (Statistics Finland, 2015). Although Finland was not initially regarded as a country of immigration, and the majority of the Finnish population sees itself as monolingual (Nikula et al., 2012, p. 24), it can be said that Finland is developing into a multicultural country. Consequently, Finland's increasingly heterogeneous population is also reflected in schools.

As Finland gains worldwide recognition as a successful school system in which students have equal opportunities (see, for example, the 2001 PISA results [Rühle, 2015]), it has also become a focus of education research and comparative studies. A basic characteristic of the Finnish school system is that there are "comparatively small performance differences between pupils" (Fischer et al., 2015, p. 90). Furthermore, the educational participation of the entire population is among the highest in an Organisation for Economic Co-operation and Development (OECD) comparison (2016). But there are also performance differences in Finland in the context of multiculturality, with Holm and Mansikka (2013) pointing out that "immigrant students do better than immigrant students in other countries [but] they still do less well than ethnic Finnish students" (p. 67). It should also be mentioned, in this context, that unemployment among people with a migrant background is relatively high in Finland (OECD, 2016).

In Finland, the same binding goals and guidelines apply to school education nationwide. These are laid down in a national framework curriculum (Vitikka et al., 2012). Finland's school system has evolved within a "process of continuous educational development over a period of decades" (Skiera & Matthies, 2009, p. 16) from a structured school system to a nine-year primary comprehensive school (the *peruskoulu*). Compulsory education for all children begins at the age of seven, with the requirement that they attend the nine-year school. Classes take place in mixed-age groups (Ratzki, 2007). According to Domisch (2008, p. 199), who was significantly involved in the reform processes of the Finnish school system, the nine-year comprehensive primary school sees itself as "a comprehensive school for different learners in which promotion, support and motivation are the most important elements." Each student is granted "free and equal basic school education—regardless of gender, social background, or ethnicity" (Domisch, 2009, p. 622). The free, basic school education for each student not only includes a basic access to schooling but also the provision of textbooks and teaching materials, as well as lunch, transport, healthcare, and student counselling (Domisch & Klein, 2012). These various measures clearly show that an attempt is being made by the Finnish curriculum to anchor equal opportunities in the education system (Finnish National Board of Education, 2014).

In addition to analysing the conditions of the school structure, the curriculum was also examined relative to multiculturality based on the categories described earlier and listed as follows. The main categories were *target-group orientation*, learning *objectives and learning contents*, as well as *methodological-didactic aspects*. The analysis was based on Finland's national curriculum from 2014.

Finland is considered "very supportive of a multicultural education" (Holm & Mansikka, 2013, p. 63), particularly regarding the legal framework and the curriculum with the relevant documents emphasising the individuality of the student. It should also be emphasised that multiculturality is considered in a separate chapter titled *Special Questions of Language and Culture,* which stresses the promotion of students' cultural competences and the strengthening of their cultural and linguistic identity (Finnish National Board of Education, 2014).

Regarding anchoring multiculturality in the curriculum, a "wide range of languages and cultures" (Finnish National Board of Education, 2014, p. 126) is assumed. In this context, the inclusion of the Sami and Romani languages should be pointed out. Another indicator is the wide range of languages on offer with this range being an integral part of the curriculum. The aim of this is to enable students to gain knowledge and understanding of the different cultures and languages as well as their significance (Finnish National Board of Education, 2014, p. 484). The Finnish National Board of Education (2014) has firmly established 12 different curricula for the subject of first-language learning and literature. It also emphasises that all students whose first language is not Finnish or Swedish have the right to be taught in their first language. This right is also emphasised for students with a migrant background (Finnish National Board of Education, 2014, p. 14ff). Classes in "Finnish/Swedish as a second language" (Finnish National Board of Education, 2014, p. 120) are also offered to enable students to learn the language in which other subjects are taught. Regarding methodological-didactic implementation, it is also noticeable that importance is attached to the active use of the respective language in the teaching of the various languages, so that students are encouraged to use their first language in other subjects as well as in school activities (Finnish National Board of Education, 2014, p. 116). Furthermore, students are also encouraged to consolidate their knowledge of the language and culture by means of literature that typifies the language and culture (e.g., relative to Sami teaching; Finnish National Board of Education, 2014.). In addition, it is also important when dealing with multiculturality in class that there is concrete reference to the real world (Finnish National Board of Education, 2014) and that, for example, students learn the various languages and subject matter in relation to cultural aspects in an interdisciplinary process (p. 38, p. 349). It is therefore not surprising that multiculturality is explicitly highlighted in the Finnish curriculum as "richness" (Finnish National Board of Education, 2014 p. 19) and as a "positive resource" (p. 25). It is conveyed as "normal" that different identities, languages, religions, and worldviews exist together (Finnish National Board of Education, 2014, p. 33). One of the primary learning objectives of Finnish education is to ensure that students treat each other respectfully, and thus to prevent bullying, discrimination, and racism as best it can (Finnish National Board of Education, 2014, p. 32).

Finally, the multiculturality of students has a positive connotation in Finland's national curriculum and the linguistic and cultural identity of students is strengthened mainly by the anchoring of different languages within the curricula. Moreover, many additional support procedures promoting multiculturality are firmly embedded in the curriculum.

South Tyrol: Curricular Recognition of Diversity in Structural Selection Patterns

From a German perspective on how students with and without special educational needs are taught, the contrast between different assessments of how the school structure has developed in South Tyrol regarding inclusion could hardly be greater. There are representatives of the first generation of German researchers on integration who hold up the small officially trilingual region in northern Italy as a model of inclusion for Germany. At the same time, though, those wishing to preserve the institution of special schools have long warned against precisely these developments. South Tyrol was included in the comparison made here precisely due to this tension between the very different evaluations of the abolition of special schools for students with an ascribed special educational need, as well as the very distinctive multicultural structures that have developed over time (reflected, for example, in separate educational institutions for the German, Italian, and Ladin language communities).

In South Tyrol, as in Finland, the focus on curricular structures is based on multiculturality. This view will be operationalised with the help of primary and secondary school curricula, with the comparison being based on the core curriculum for the subject of social studies at the comprehensive school in North Rhine-Westphalia (NRW Nordrhein-Westfalen, 2011). Five levels will be considered:

1. Curricular framing and target-group orientation;
2. Linkage of curricular frameworks with categorisations;
3. Curricular control of resource allocations;
4. Curricular changes since the ratification of the UN-FCCC; and
5. Curricular steering of the requirement to take account of multiculturality.

South Tyrol is a region with about half a million inhabitants, which has grown historically and consists of three language and cultural groups (70% German, 26% Italian, and 4% first-language Ladin; Heissl-Deporta, 2016, pp. 59–60). Due to migratory movements, the proportion of citizens from other countries has increased to about 10%. In accordance with the first-language distribution, the province has three separate educational administrations and school structures (German, Italian, and Ladin). These separate structures stand in contrast to the statement found in comparable form in the literature that there is a school for all in South Tyrol (Brugger-Paggi, 2015, pp. 23–24), a statement that relates to the unsegregated teaching of students with and without ascribed special educational needs. This discrepancy between what is regarded as a progressive school system in the sense of an unrestricted understanding of the concept of inclusion, and the separation of students in the sense of a comprehensive understanding of the concept, makes the focus on multiculturality at the curricular level more important.

Having looked at the framing of the school structure, we now consider curricular framing in terms of our research interests (Autonomous Province of Bolzano, 2009) and outline the results of our analysis below. Migrant people are not mentioned explicitly at the curricular level in South Tyrol, which might be interpreted as meaning that multiculturality is being neglected. At the same time, though, the curriculum explains throughout the opportunity of increasing educational success through multilingualism, thus making one aspect of multiculturality (i.e., multilingualism) the focus of curricular interest.

There seems to be a contradiction in the curricular guidelines, however, between separating students into different language groups while at the same time stressing the positive connotations of linguistic diversity.

The tripartite division of the school authorities in South Tyrol has far-reaching consequences. On the one hand, the selection tendencies determined by the school structure (based on a language division and thus also a cultural categorisation) contradict general pedagogical efforts at inclusion and viewpoints critical of categorisation (e.g., Hinz & Köpfer, 2016). On the other, a structural level of selection is being implemented here, which will almost certainly have an impact on the acceptance of cultural diversity at both the cultural and practical levels—including the curricular focus on multilingualism.

At the same time, questions arise concerning the expressed need for support after special schools for students with special educational needs were abolished 40 years ago and replaced by a school for all students. Regarding differing pre-conditions vis-à-vis students' learning outcomes, the requirements at the competence level are not differentiated by the curriculum, a fact which can be assessed in different ways. Using the taxonomy of Fischer's integrative aptitude model (Veber & Fischer, 2016), we can criticise the fact that sufficient adjustments have not been made to individual needs either at the potential or the performance level. At the same time, with the aim of providing inclusive support, the curricular anchoring of (high) demands on all students can be understood as positive and stimulating.

Whereas in South Tyrol, different schools are planned for different language groups (German, Italian, and Ladin speakers), in Germany, other forms of special groups are formed after the primary level by means of selection based upon academic level (*Hauptschule*, *Realschule* and *Gymnasium*, each with its own curriculum).[1] In view of the link in Germany between social origin and educational success, this transition barrier appears incompatible with an inclusive system, which would enable all students to participate fully in the life of society. From a curricular-comparative viewpoint, it is first noticeable that the term *social theory* alone mitigates against an egalitarian-inclusive society and could thus also stand in the way of multiculturality in society as a whole. The curriculum in Germany does indeed address the existence of diversity, but it does not explicitly consider the positive interdependence of different cultural groups and no explicit reference is made to divergent pre-conditions. For example, the basis of German understanding of disability as expressed in the Social Security Statute Book is that of an ecosystem. One consequence of this is that the manifold aspects of individual promotion are not directly addressed here. Finally, a verbal appreciation of individuality can be found in the curricula for primary and secondary schools in South Tyrol, whereby the selective pattern in the school structural framework (in the form of management and control) must be considered.

Comparison

This short analysis shows that the curriculum can take different forms in addressing and dealing with diversity. In addition, a latent emphasis on the normative implementation of inclusion becomes apparent in the respective countries. Thus, Finland showed how multilingualism can be addressed proactively and from a curricular viewpoint as a productive resource. In Prince Edward Island (Canada), on the other hand, the universal curriculum served to address all students in a differentiated way according to their level of achievement, with the focus being on the distinctive feature of disability. In South Tyrol, there is a pronounced ambivalence in curricular terms relative to the handling of diversity: on the one hand, recognition should be given to the diversity of all students without segregation and, on the other, the different school systems practised selection based on linguistic-cultural affiliation (German, Italian, and Ladin).

Overall, the curriculum can be designed as a governance tool for dealing with heterogeneity in an inclusive and educationally appropriate way, and it enables differentiation. At the same time, differentiation also creates differences (Budde & Hummrich, 2013) so that latent norm-setting can be maintained. This becomes clear in South Tyrol, where the selection process places students in different school systems. Adjustments and individualisations (as in Prince Edward Island), for example, offer possibilities for adapting curricular requirements to students' level of learning and development. At the same time, modifications indirectly make restrictive norms relevant or strengthen them. This is particularly relevant in the case of powerful instruments of control, such as curricula, where the fundamental question can be asked as to whether curricula are suitable control instruments for diversity, or whether they increase opportunities for operationalisation and mechanisation with the aim of measuring competence via performance.

This is particularly relevant in view of developments in Germany. The empirical findings gained here offer an occasion for reflection partly because of a questionable approach to competence orientation in Germany, an approach that is currently receiving attention and is coupled with models of evidence-based measurement that are difficult to combine with the requirement for inclusion (e.g., Rödler, 2013). Because of the diverse and partly ambivalent control of diversity exercised by curricula on the learning side—as has become clear in the insights into the three countries—the question arises as to how the central tasks of school, upbringing, and education, which currently receive little public consideration, can be adopted (again) for all students in the sense of an egalitarian-inclusive participative space. If this reflection on the relationship between upbringing and education as well as control (e.g., through curricula) is developed further, this will affect not only school practice but also educational science (Bellmann, 2015).

Although only a brief comparison could be made here, there are indications that a systematic consideration and comparative investigation of how different countries deal with school diversity through curricula is significant in many respects. A look beyond national borders can serve as an opportunity for reflection (Fuchs & Berg, 1993) on Germany's efforts to implement inclusive education. The ability to participate in this international discourse is of great importance, especially for Germany, with its performance-related, multipartite school system, which is one of the most selective in the world.

Note

1. At secondary level 1 (after the fourth grade of primary school), Germany has a multitrack system comprising *Hauptschule* (lower secondary), *Realschule* (middle school), and *Gymnasium* (upper secondary).

References

Adick, C. (2008). *Vergleichende Erziehungswissenschaft: Eine Einführung.* Kohlhammer.

Allan, J. (2012). Inclusion: Patterns and possibilities. *Zeitschrift für Inklusion Online, 4*(7), n.p.

Arbeitsgruppe Internationale Vergleichsstudie (Ed.). (2007). *Schulleistungen und Steuerung des Schulsystems im Bundesstaat: Kanada und Deutschland im Vergleich.* Waxmann.

Autonome Provinz Bozen. (2009). *Rahmenrichtlinien des Landes für die Festlegung der Curricula für die Grundschule und die Mittelschule an den autonomen deutschsprachigen Schulen.* www.bildung.suedtirol.it/files/4313/7706/6525/druckfassung_rahmenrichtlinien_gs-msdt09.pdf

Bellmann, J. (2015). Symptome der gleichzeitigen Politisierung und Entpolitisierung der Erziehungswissenschaft im Kontext datengetriebener Steuerung. *Erziehungswissenschaft, 26*(1), 45–54.

Brugger-Paggi, E. (2015). Etappen auf dem Weg zu einer inklusiven Schule. Herausforderungen und Gelingensbedingungen – Das Beispiel Südtirol. In D. Blömer, M. Lichtblau, A.-K. Jüttner, K. Koch, M. Krüger, & R. Werning (Eds.), *Perspektiven auf inklusive Bildung. Gemeinsam anders lehren und lernen* (pp. 23–32). Springer.

Budde, J., & Hummrich, M. (2013). Reflexive Inklusion. *Zeitschrift für Inklusion Online, 4*(8), n.p.

Department of Education Prince Edward Island. (2005). *Individualized educational planning (IEP). Standards and guidelines. A handbook for educators.* gov.pe.ca/photos/original/ed_ieplanning.pdf

Department of Education and Early Childhood Development Prince Edward Island. (2009). *Annual report. April 1, 2008 to March 31, 2009.* https://www.gov.pe.ca/photos/original/EducECDAnnual.pdf

Department of Education and Early Childhood Development Prince Edward Island. (2013). *Transition planning.* www.gov.pe.ca/eecd/index.php3?number=1027875&lang=E

Department of Education, Early Learning and Culture Prince Edward Island. (2011). *Individual educational planning (IEP) for students.* www.gov.pe.ca/eecd/index.php3?number=1027859&lang=E

Domisch, R. (2008). Die am häufigsten von Besuchern aus Deutschland gestellten zehn Fragen – und zehn Antworten darauf. In J. Sarjala & E. Häkli (Eds.), *Jenseits von PISA. Finnlands Schulsystem und seine neuesten Entwicklungen* (pp. 199–201). BWV.

Domisch, R. (2009). Keine Mythen, sondern fundierte Schulreformen. *Zeitschrift für Erziehungswissenschaft, 4*, 617–632.

Domisch, R., & Klein, A. (2012). *Niemand wird zurückgelassen: Eine Schule für Alle.* Hanser.

Finnish National Board of Education. (2014). *National core curriculum for basic education, 2014.* https://kosovo.finnish.school/wp-content/uploads/2020/11/Basic-Education-Grades-1-9.pdf

Fischer, C., Rott, D., Veber, M., Fischer-Ontrup, C., & Gralla, A. (2015). *Individuelle Förderung als schulische Herausforderung* (3rd ed.). Friedrich-Ebert-Stiftung.

Fuchs, M., & Berg, E. (1993). Phänomenologie der Differenz. In E. Berg & M. Fuchs (Eds.), *Kultur, soziale Praxis, Text. Die Krise der ethnographischen Repräsentation* (pp. 11–108). Suhrkamp.

Glaser, E. (2013). Dokumentenanalyse und Quellenkritik. In B. Friebertshäuser, A. Langer, & A. Prengel (Eds.), *Handbuch Qualitative Forschungsmethoden in der Erziehungswissenschaft* (4th ed., pp. 365–375). Beltz Juventa.

Grell, P. (2013). Forschende Lernwerkstatt. In B. Friebertshäuser, A. Langer, & A. Prengel (Eds.), *Handbuch Qualitative Forschungsmethoden in der Erziehungswissenschaft* (4th ed., pp. 887–896). Beltz Juventa.

Government of Canada. (2018). *Constitution Act, 1982.* lois.justice.gc.ca/eng/Const/page-15.html

Heissl-Deporta, R. (2016). Südtirol – ein Land auf dem Weg zur Inklusion. Wie geht das? In W. Schönig & J. A. Fuchs (Eds.), *Inklusion: Gefordert! Gefördert? Schultheoretische, raumtheoretische und didaktische Zugänge* (pp. 59–76). Klinkhardt.

Hinz, A. (2008). Inklusion – historische Entwicklungslinien und internationale Kontexte. In A. Hinz, I. Körner, & U. Niehoff (Eds.), *Von der Integration zur Inklusion. Grundlagen – Perspektiven – Praxis* (pp. 33–52). Lebenshilfe.

Hinz, A. (2013). Inklusion – von der Unkenntnis zur Unkenntlichkeit?! *Zeitschrift für Inklusion Online, 1,* n.p.

Hinz, A., & Köpfer, A. (2016). Unterstützung trotz Dekategorisierung? Beispiele für Unterstützung durch Dekategorisierung. *Vierteljahresschrift für Heilpädagogik und ihre Nachbargebiete, 1,* 36.

Holm, G., & Mansikka, J.-E. (2013). Multicultural education as policy and praxis in Finland: Heading in a problematic direction? *Recherches en Education, 16,* 63–73.

Horne, P., Timmons, V., & Adamowycz, R. (2008). Identified teacher supports for inclusive practice. *Exceptionality Education Canada, 18*(3), 82–94.

Hortsch, W. (2015). *Sprachliche Bildung im Elementar- und Primarbereich: Ethnographische Feldstudien zur Transition von Kindern mit Migrationshintergrund in Deutschland und Finnland.* Klinkhardt.

Köpfer, A. (2013). *Inclusion in Canada. Analyse inclusiver Unterrichtsprozesse, Unterstützungsstrukturen und Rollen am Beispiel kanadischer Schulen in den Provinzen New Brunswick, Prince Edward Island und Québec.* Klinkhardt.

Legislative Counsel Office Prince Edward Island (LCO). (2010). Office consolidation of the school act 2018. www.gov.pe.ca/law/statutes/pdf/s-02_1.pdf

Mikkola, A. (2008). Finnland und die Finnen. In J. Sarjala & E. Häkli (Eds.), *Jenseits von PISA. Finnlands Schulsystem und seine neuesten Entwicklungen* (pp. 13–27). BWV.

Ministry of Justice Finland. (2003). *Finnish Language Act (423/2003).* www.finlex.fi/fi/laki/kaannokset/2003/en20030423.pdf

MSW Nordrhein-Westfalen (Ministerium für Schule und Weiterbildung des Landes Nordrhein-Westfalen). (2011). *Kernlehrplan für die Gesamtschule – Sekundarstufe I in Nordrhein-Westfalen. Gesellschaftslehre.Erdkunde, Geschichte, Politik.* www.schulentwicklung.nrw.de/lehrplaene/upload/klp_SI/GE/GL/KLP_GE_GL.pdf

Nikula, T., Saarinen, T., Pöyhönen, S., & Kangasvierei, T. (2012). Linguistic diversity as a problem and a resource – Multilingualism in European and Finnish policy documents. In J. S. Blommaert, P. Leppänen, & T. Räisänen (Eds.), *Dangerous multilingualism. Northern perspectives on order, purity and normality* (pp. 41–66). Palgrave Macmillan.

Organisation for Economic Cooperation and Development. (2016). *Foreign-born unemployment.* data.oecd.org/migration/foreign-born-unemployment.htm

Ratzki, A. (2007). Chancen der Vielfalt: Wie Schülerinnen und Schüler in Europa erfolgreich lernen. In S. Boller, E. Rosowski, & T. Stroot (Eds.), *Heterogenität in Schule und Unterricht* (pp. 67–77). Beltz.

Riitaoja, A.-L., Poulter, S. & Kuusisto, A. (2010). Worldviews and multicultural education in the Finnish context: A critical philosophical approach to theory and practices. *Finnish Journal of Ethnicity and Migration, 5*(3), 87–95.

Rödler, P. (2013). Inklusion ist evident begründbar, aber nicht evident machbar. Das Problem pädagogischer Praxis mit Ergebnissen "evidenzbasierter" Wissenschaft. *Behindertenpädagogik, 4*, 381–387.

Rühle, S. (2015). *Diversität, Curriculum und Bildungsstrukturen.* Waxmann.

Skiera, E., & Matthies, A.-L. (2009). Einleitung: Das Bildungswesen Finnlands in mehrperspektivischer Sicht. In A.-L. Matthies, E. Skiera, & M. Sorvakko-Spratte (Eds.), *Das Bildungswesen in Finnland* (pp. 13–22). Klinkhardt.

Statistics Finland. (2015). *Swedish-speakers' and foreign-language speakers' proportion of the population in 1900–2015.* www.stat.fi/til/vaerak/2015/01/vaerak_2015_01_2016-09-23_kuv_001_en.html

Veber, M., & Fischer, C. (2016). Individuelle Förderung in Inklusiver Bildung – eine potenzialorientierte Verortung. In B. Amrhein (Ed.). *Diagnostik im Kontext inklusiver Bildung* (pp. 98–117). Klinkhardt.

Vitikka, E., Krokfors, L., & Hurmerinta, E. (2012). The Finnish National Core Curriculum: Structure and development. In A. Toom, A. Kallioniemi, & H. Niemi (Eds.), *Miracle of education. The principles and practices of teaching and learning in Finnish schools* (pp. 83–96). Sense Publishers.

17 Advancing Inclusion in Education Systems

Insights from New Brunswick

Cecilia Simón, Yolanda Muñoz-Martínez, and Gordon L. Porter

Introduction

New Brunswick is one of the 10 provinces of Canada and the only one that has both English and French as official languages. New Brunswick has a policy of full inclusion educational systems that began in the 1980s and has been a precursor to the concept of inclusive education for more than 30 years. This is reflected through legislation, local authority policies, and professional guidelines (UNESCO, 2020a). The province has sustained the inclusion effort over time and continues to focus and evolve school and classroom practices toward more effective ways to respond to the needs of all students and their families (Echeita et al., 2021). New Brunswick's approach to inclusive education is strongly rooted in a rights-based approach and was recently recognised as a world leader and pioneer in inclusive education by UNESCO (2020b) in the *Global Education Monitoring Report*. It was previously recognised in 2014, when it received the UNESCO/Emir Jaber Al Ahmad Al Jaber Al Sabah Prize (Kuwait) for promoting quality education for people with intellectual disability.

The process of transformation towards a fully inclusive education system began in the 1980s. The first initiatives in 1983/1984 were in specific local education authorities (Porter & Richler, 1991) with subsequent provincial legislation through Bill 85 in 1986. This legislation established an inclusion mandate for all primary and secondary schools. At the time Bill 85 was passed, there were approximately 25 special education schools in New Brunswick that served almost all students with intellectual disability and other special needs who were receiving education—many were not in school. Most of the programmes were not operated by local education authorities but by NGO parent groups that were part of the Canadian Association for the Mentally Retarded (CAMR). Subsequently, in 1985, CAMR changed its name to the Canadian Association for Community Living (CACL). Most of the

DOI: 10.4324/9781003204572-21

funding for these programmes, including operations, facilities, and transportation, was provided by charity donations. The Ministry of Education only funded the cost of teachers and educational assistants according to an established formula (Echeita et al., 2021).

The approval of Bill 85, which focused on equality issues, allowed New Brunswick to establish Canada as an international leader in inclusive education (Calder & AuCoin, 2018; Porter & Richler, 1991). For example, Section 45(2)1 of Project Bill 85 (1986) addresses student placement considerations and is particularly significant:

> A school board will place "exceptional students" in such a way that they receive special education programs and services in circumstances that may engage non-exceptional students in the regular classroom, to the extent the board deems appropriate taking into account the educational needs of all the students.

Over a period of three years ending in 1989, the implementation of Bill 85 saw the province close all special education schools. It was a process that was full of challenges and difficulties; however, from that moment until today, more than 30 years later, there have been no special education schools in New Brunswick (Echeita et al., 2021).

In the 1990s, as the transformation process continued, a number of procedures to systematise inclusion in classroom and school practices were developed and carried out. At that time, critical challenges were identified and resulted in increased investments to support teachers and students. Over time, resources and strategies necessary for inclusive education to be successful emerged and were strengthened. Several documents and protocols were published that guided the work of school staff. In 1994, the Education Department published a guide on *Best Practices for* Inclusion; in the same year, it also released *Teacher Assistant Guidelines*. In 2000, a resource manual called *Resource for Assisting Struggling Learners* was published. These publications helped consolidate practice in schools and across school districts.

In 2013, the Minister of Education issued *Policy 322 – Inclusive Education*, representing the first time that all provincial public schools followed a consistent set of practices and strategies to strengthen inclusion. This was a breakthrough since it removed what had been discretion over practices previously left to individual school districts. New Brunswick's full inclusion model, formalised by *Policy 322*, mandates the provision of effective supports through trained and skilled personnel. This is considered essential to make it possible for teachers to be successful with students with a full range of diverse needs. These regulations established clearly defined requirements consistent with best practices. Among them: designing and implementing education support teams, defining personalised learning plans for students, forbidding the use of segregated settings, and ensuring inclusion and accommodation of all children, not only those with disabilities.

To meet this challenge, schools and districts (local education authorities) developed new approaches to build networks of support for teachers, a topic we will describe in more detail later. However, the fact that these networks of support exist should not distract us from the central element of the New Brunswick inclusive education model: the focus on the classroom teacher as the staff member primarily responsible for the success of each learner. Thus, both the pre-service training and ongoing professional learning of classroom teachers is vitally important. Each teacher needs to acquire competency in making accommodations to instructional strategies and resources when they are essential for the inclusion of individual learners.

While classroom teachers are primarily responsible for each student's learning, *Policy 322* makes it clear that they must be assured of the support they need to meet this challenge. This is the mandate of the school-based education support team. Led by the school principal, the support team assists classroom teachers to develop and implement instructional and/or management strategies, and to coordinate support resources for students with diverse needs. This is how Bunch (2015) explains it:

> The central support for all students is the regular classroom teacher. The teacher's tools are the regular classroom curriculum and a repertoire of Enabling Adjustments. Also, the development of an in-class team led by the teacher and supported by Special Education Teachers, Educational Assistants, other professionals, and by the parents and other students is fundamental. (p. 8)

In this chapter, we describe key features of the inclusion programme in New Brunswick that may be informative for other state or local educational systems considering a transition towards a more inclusive educational model. We will share the perspectives of New Brunswick stakeholders based on their experience working in a model with a long tradition of full inclusion.

If we look at the recommendations that different authors make to facilitate the advancement of educational systems and contexts to be more inclusive, we find similarities with respect to what to change, how to change, and, who should be involved in the change. In Table 17.1, we show an outline of the analyses carried out by Porter and Towell (2017) as an example.

In order to illustrate these proposals to the reader, we will now detail the recommendations made by Porter and Towell (2017).

Table 17.1 What Do We Need to Do?

WHAT TO CHANGE	• Education for life • Promoting inclusion	
HOW TO CHANGE	• Addressing barriers to participation • Learning from experience • Investing in equity • Charting the path to inclusion	Strengthen inclusive pedagogy
WHAT IS NEEDED	• Prioritize professional development • Establish alliances • Foster transformational leadership	

In Relation to "What to Change"

- *Education for life*: Those involved must develop a shared vision of what inclusive education is and how all students can benefit from it, as well as families, teachers, schools, and society as a whole.
- *Promote a culture of inclusion:* The aim is all students, not specific groups. The benchmark is that every person has the opportunity to be educated in regular classrooms in their community schools.

Regarding "How to Change"

- *Addressing barriers to participation:* Schools end exclusion and address the barriers that limit the participation of all students.
- *Learning from experience:* Take advantage of cross-system learning as a whole—both *vertically* and *horizontally*—so policies respond to classroom experience and vice versa, and that innovation in one area becomes a guide or inspiration for innovation in others.
- *Investing in equity:* Governments invest resources in development of the education system as a whole; they ensure that expertise, evidence-based practices are directed to support regular schools to adequately perform their functions. In this regard, it is important to recognise that while more resources are always useful, it is first necessary to make more effective use of the resources that already exist (UNESCO, 2020a).
- *Charting the path to inclusion:* Leaders at all levels of the education system establish a *captivating vision* of inclusive education, they obtain the necessary support for change, they mobilise mutually reinforcing actions at different levels and in different parts of the education system, and they ensure that all efforts are directed towards achieving the same objectives.

In short, the strategies described are about strengthening inclusive pedagogy and the success of the learning process—*for all students.* This means ensuring a welcoming culture defined by the goal of equity and equal participation for every student.

On "What Is Needed"

- *Prioritise professional learning*: Teachers, as well as other professionals involved in the teaching and learning processes, must have the necessary skills to implement inclusive practices in the school and in the classroom.
- *Establish alliances*: Improving education implies working in alliance with students and their families, as well as with all the people, entities, and groups involved directly or indirectly with education (UNESCO, 2020a).
- *Fostering transformational leadership*: It is necessary to move beyond isolated innovations and make necessary transformations on a systemic level where the new ways of thinking are reflected in actions at all levels of the educational system and are focused on concrete outcomes in the classroom.

With these concepts in mind, we will now look more deeply into the three aspects mentioned above (what to change, how to change, and what is needed). The result of the discussion between the three authors is presented, considering that both Spanish authors have undertaken research visits to New Brunswick and the third author is the host of those visits, as well as one of the promoters of the inclusive educational system in New Brunswick. We will incorporate the opinions and visions of important actors in this process.

Keys to the Development of Inclusive Educational Systems

A Coherent Legislative Framework Based on a Rights Perspective

The fundamental benchmark in New Brunswick has been the defence of human rights and, as such, has been present in the speeches of all the people who were involved in the process. While they vary in their intensity, passion, and conviction, political leaders, families, and associations, as well as teachers, school principals, and educational officials, share this vision and commitment. There are two laws that provide the context for each child's right to education. First, the *Canadian Charter of Rights and Freedoms* (*CCRF*) is part of the Constitution of Canada. It was adopted in 1982 and came into effect in 1985. It provides constitutional protection of the rights and freedoms of all Canadians and applies to the laws, policies, and actions of all levels of government. Section 15(1) of the Charter provides that every person is equal before and under the law and has the right to the equal protection and equal benefit of the law without discrimination based on race, national or ethnic origin, colour, religion, sex, age, or mental or physical disability

(Minister of Justice, 1982). The Charter has been generally used to promote human rights and dignity of people with disabilities in many areas of life.

Secondly, we find the *New Brunswick Human Rights Act*, the aim of which is to protect the rights of New Brunswickers and prohibit discrimination and harassment in employment, housing, public services (schools, hospitals, police, and most government services), and publicity. It prohibits discrimination on several grounds, including "physical and mental disability." People who believe that they are being discriminated against can file a complaint with the Human Rights Commission, which investigates and tries to settle complaints of discrimination and harassment. If a complaint cannot be settled, a human rights tribunal can hear the evidence. If the judge decides that there was discrimination, they can issue orders to correct it. Citizens have full access to the process and there is no cost to filing a human rights complaint.

For this, as Echeita et al. (2021) assert, leaders from both the administration and from the school must be trained and prepared to argue and show the benefits of education from this perspective. In order to build this shared vision by the entire community, it has been important to devise and sustain a continuous awareness-raising process, directed not only at the educational sphere but also at the general public by sharing successful experiences, inspiring practices, and positive benefits.

One of the fundamental features of the New Brunswick education system is the consistency of its legislative framework and the alignment with a rights-based approach. As Ainscow (2020) concludes, policies should be based on clear and widely understood definitions of what the terms "inclusion" and "equity" mean (p. 8). In 2009, the Government of New Brunswick published an important document that established a definition, vision, and guiding principles for inclusive education (Province of New Brunswick, 2009). This mandates that the New Brunswick public education system will ensure compliance with both the *Canadian Charter of Rights and Freedoms* and the *New Brunswick Human Rights Act*. This means schools must make accommodations to ensure the success of students with disabilities and other special needs to the point of undue hardship due to cost, risk to safety, or impact on others, particularly on other students. In the discussion of accommodations in the same document, it is asserted that every student has the right to expect accommodations, interventions, supports, and adaptations to make possible full participation in the common learning environment, meaning an environment that is designed for all students, is typical for the student's age and grade, and is shared with his/her neighbourhood peers.

In New Brunswick, *Policy 322* (2013) defines the fundamental elements of an inclusive education system that supports students in common learning environments and assures help to teachers. It establishes clear requirements for school practice, such as procedures for the development of personalised learning plans, inclusive graduation, and school learning procedures, as well as strict guidelines for determining when a variation of the common learning environment may be necessary (UNESCO, 2020a). The New Brunswick definition of inclusive education clarifies the conditions to which we have previously referred, and which would explain what we understand by *all means all* (Bunch, 2015; UNESCO, 2020a). In New Brunswick, inclusive education is:

> the pairing of philosophy and pedagogical practices that allows each student to feel respected, confident and safe so he or she can participate with peers in the common learning environment and learn and develop to his or her full potential. It is based on a system of values and beliefs centered on the best interest of the student, which promotes social cohesion, belonging, active participation in learning, a complete school experience, and positive interactions with peers and others in the school community. These values and beliefs will be shared by schools and communities. Inclusive education is put into practice within school communities that value diversity and nurture the well-being and quality of learning of each of their members. Inclusive education is carried out through a range of public and community programs and services available to all students. Inclusive education is the foundation for ensuring an inclusive New Brunswick society.
>
> (Province of New Brunswick, 2013, p. 2)

In this sense, we show the different stakeholders' approaches to the concept of inclusive education in New Brunswick.

An Educational Leadership for Inclusion

Research has shown the central role of leadership in fostering inclusive cultures (Billingslet & McLeskey, 2014; Causton & Theoharis, 2014; Kugelmass, & Ainscow, 2005; Shogren et al., 2015; UNESCO, 2017). According to Ainscow and Sandill (2010), leadership practice is a key factor in moving education systems towards inclusive values (Booth & Ainscow, 2011) and bringing about sustainable change. Previous analyses about organisational conditions that can help schools to become more inclusive agree on the crucial role of the school principal in providing leadership for such processes (Ainscow et al., 2006; Dolmage et al., 2009; McLeskey, et al., 2014; Slee, 2011). UNESCO (2017) observes that:

> Leaders at all levels need to establish the conditions within their organizations for challenging non-inclusive, discriminatory and inequitable educational practices. From the complementary perspective, leaders need to establish the conditions that build consensus and commitment towards putting the universal values of inclusion and equity into practice. (p. 26)

As Hoppey and McLeskey (2014) point out, the principal's role is critical in creating the conditions for effective inclusive schools. School principals not only must provide administrative and teacher support but also facilitate the development of cultural and organisational qualities, such as building a unifying vision for inclusion. By doing so, they are able to promote improved collaboration, shared decision-making, and distributed leadership. These actions embed data-based decision-making into daily practice and create an efficient and flexible use of resources. The result is a school focused on becoming a problem-solving organisation able to address the challenges of being inclusive.

Another important role for a school principal is impacting the quality of classroom instruction and ensuring learner-centred professional development for teachers. They play a very important role in the development of high-quality education for all students (Bryk et al., 2010; Sider, et al., 2017).

The European Agency for Special Needs and Inclusive Education (2018) argues that inclusive leadership goes beyond the school:

> It aims to address inequity to build community and full participation. It focuses on developing an inclusive culture where all stakeholders are supported to work together, value diversity and ensure that all learners, including those most vulnerable to exclusion, receive a high-quality education. (p. 20)

This leads to the questions of: What are the characteristics of leadership capable of promoting inclusion as a core value of a school? What must a leader do to create the conditions in a school to set this process in motion and make it sustainable?

Leithwood and colleagues (2006) argue that successful leaders share a repertoire of basic leadership practices: building vision and setting direction, understanding and developing people, redesigning the organisation, and managing the teaching and learning programme. Cobb (2015), as a result of his meta-analysis, identifies three core elements of the principal's role in the development of an effective inclusive school: inclusive programme delivery, staff collaboration, and parental engagement.

In addition, this research indicates seven key roles that must be played by principals within these three domains as they work to foster inclusion: visionary, partner, coach, conflict-resolver, advocate, interpreter, and organiser: "While principals encourage inclusive programme delivery, they also facilitate staff collaboration to enrich school-wide inclusion and foster parental engagement to establish an inclusive atmosphere in the school community" (Cobb, 2015, p. 220). As Sider and colleagues (2017) have shown, effective school leadership has another important feature: recruiting and managing the talents and energies of school community members (educators, students, parents, and community stakeholders) towards achieving shared educational goals.

It is clear that fulfilling these tasks requires highly trained principals with the skills necessary to develop and sustain inclusive schools. Education systems can promote this kind of supportive school leadership in three ways: (1) selecting and training school leaders based on their commitment to inclusive and equitable values, and their capacity to promote the style of management that is necessary for this task; (2) providing teachers with opportunities to pool their professional experience and expertise so as to re-examine and enhance their practices; and (3) sharing the values that underpin inclusion and equity thus promoting the development of "inclusive cultures" within school communities (UNESCO, 2017, p. 26).

> An NB school principal considers that when a school has teachers who are uncertain or resistant to inclusion, principals need to help them develop a more positive attitude. One principal builds confidence by engaging teachers in intensive and sustained planning on the needs of one or two specific students. Success with these individual students leads to a change in attitude and increased motivation for inclusion generally. Learning opportunities with peers in their own school have the greatest impact and are highly valued

Most Important Implications of Becoming Inclusive for a School

As Cobb (2015) points out, "while principals encourage inclusive programme delivery, they also facilitate staff collaboration to enrich school-wide inclusion and foster parental engagement to establish an inclusive atmosphere in the school community" (p. 220). Welcoming inclusion in our schools has a positive impact on different stakeholders and in areas related to both the school and the community beyond. First, we want to highlight how inclusive schools can contribute to the construction of a more equitable society. It is an essential step a community can take to fulfil the fundamental human right of an education that prepares an individual for life as a citizen in society (United Nations, 1948).

As Casanova points out, education in a democratic society is either inclusive or it is not education.

In order to have success with all students in our schools, it is necessary to develop an inclusive pedagogy (Florian & Beaton, 2018). This in part relies on developing synergy from activities both within and beyond the school (Ainscow et al., 2012). Moving forward with inclusion also enhances the movement towards meeting the mandate of international commitments (e.g., Objective 4 of the United Nations *2030 Agenda for Sustainable Development*), a step that people with disabilities have long been demanding as a fundamental element of their rights (UN, 2006).

While these factors should be sufficient justification to build an inclusive public education system that embraces diversity in all its forms, unfortunately, in too many jurisdictions, this is not the case. However, it is important to point out that actions to build inclusive schools can have a positive impact on the entire educational community. That includes students, professionals, and families served by the school as well as the community as a whole (Kefallinou et al., 2020).

For classroom teachers, focusing on meeting the needs of a specific student can involve learning new skills and strategies that become embedded in instructional practice and result in improving learning for all students (Hehir et al., 2016). Meeting the challenges of inclusion requires greater collaboration between professionals, and this collaboration benefits teachers by strengthening their performance from both an academic and an emotional perspective (Drossel et al., 2019). When teachers are fully engaged in making inclusion a success in their classrooms, they have the opportunity for both professional growth and increased personal satisfaction that results in stronger perception of professional competence (Finke et al., 2009; Jordan et al., 2010).

As for students, research has demonstrated that, for the most part, including students with disabilities in regular education classes does not diminish the learning of non-disabled students, and may in fact confer academic and social benefits. Hehir et al. (2016) carried out a systematic review of 280 studies from 25 countries, 89 of which provide relevant scientific evidence of this fact. Based on their research, they concluded that "there is clear and consistent evidence that even educational settings can confer substantial short and long-term benefits for students with and without disabilities" (Hehir et al., 2016, p. 2).

The effect of inclusion on peers without disabilities is often mentioned as a concern of increasing inclusion in schools. The available data demonstrates that the inclusion of students with disabilities does not interfere with the academic performance of their peers and, most notably, if there is an impact on them, it is more likely to be positive (Hehir, et al., 2016; Szumski et al., 2017). Specifically, in their meta-analysis of the academic achievement of students without special educational needs in inclusive classrooms, Szumski, et al. (2017) conclude that attending inclusive classrooms is positively, though weakly, associated with the academic achievement of students without SEN. They have also found that inclusion has a positive effect on the emotional and social development of these peers (Hehir et al., 2016), facilitating the development of positive attitudes towards inclusion, the acceptance and appreciation of diversity, and the development of interpersonal skills (Alnahdi, 2019; Cologon, 2019).

With respect to students with disabilities, research has also demonstrated important positive impacts. Inclusive education can provide a range of academic and social benefits for students with disabilities, such as higher achievement in language and mathematics, improved rates of high school graduation, and more positive relationships with non-disabled students (Hehir et al., 2016).

Similarly, as noted by Causton-Theoharis et al. (2011), learners with SEN, educated in ordinary contexts compared with segregated education settings, benefit from increased maintenance of their learning as well as stronger generalisation of learning between and across settings. In addition, some papers point out that these benefits are not limited to only specific degrees of disability. "Inclusive Education has benefits for the academic, communication, positive behavioural and social development of students labelled with "severe' and 'multiple' 'disabilities'" (Cologon, 2019, p. 8).

With respect to families, in many cases, they have been the prime advocates of inclusion. Their struggle for the right of their children to be educated in the same schools as their siblings or neighbours has been fundamental in mobilising changes in the educational systems, and this has also been the case for New Brunswick as well as other jurisdictions (Echeita et al., 2021; Moliner, 2008). When inclusive education works, there is a positive impact on parents' perception of personal and family well-being (Cologon, 2019).

Share the Perspective

As UNESCO (2020a) points out, "clarity of purpose" is one of the basic assumptions that should guide policies to support the change to inclusive educational environments. A clear and shared vision of the rationale and purpose for the changes is essential. This is essential for mobilising broad support from stakeholders throughout the process. Likewise, to make our schools inclusive,

> "first we need to state clearly that our goal is to have 'inclusive, effective, community schools' that are both committed to inclusion and able to effectively carry it out. Once the goal is set and before us, we can make plans to move ahead"
>
> (Porter & Richler, 1991, p. 26).

> A principal in a K–5 school in NB says the starting point for successful inclusion is a vision shared by school leaders, teachers, and parents. She emphasises that teachers make the difference. They implement the vision in the classroom. She provides common planning time for teachers so they can assist each other in learning new strategies to use in their teaching. Time for joint reflection and planning for any student the teacher needs help with is important (NB Principal).

This will require, among other things, a clear definition of what is meant by inclusive education (Simón et al., 2019). In this regard, Kozleski et al. (2015) as well as Schuelka et al. (2019) highlight the conceptual confusion surrounding this term, which may be one of the factors that hinders sustained progress towards this goal on an international level.

Discourses on inclusive education range from those that refer to the inclusion of students with (dis)abilities in ordinary classrooms; some speak of the transformation of the curriculum, classrooms, or pedagogies; others focus on the transformation of the education system in general and of schools in particular (Kozleski et al., 2015). Within these discussions, the assumption that inclusion is only concerned with a specific group of students (SEN) has caused significant confusion and has been an obstacle to progress. Inclusion is not just about students labelled with special educational needs and, more specifically, with those linked to (dis)ability.

As Schuelka et al. (2019) note, this perspective has meant a lack of visibility and awareness of other factors linked to economic, social, and origin factors that place individual students at an enormous disadvantage. This may result in a limited understanding of students' needs, which perpetuate traditional practices that do not contribute to success in diverse classrooms.

In this sense, policies must be formulated at all levels of the national education system, not just at the classroom level (UNESCO, 2020a). Further, there must be shared meaning and coherence when speaking of inclusion. In this sense, we find the New Brunswick expressed in a document published by the Department of Education (Ministry of Education, New Brunswick Department of Education, 2009). In this document, a vision of an inclusive school is spelled out and concepts such as equity and accommodation are articulated. It introduces the concept of serving all students in a "common learning environment" in the community school. It includes discussion of a quality education for each student, student-centred services, appropriate curriculum and assessment, as well as the role of educators and support personnel, the involvement of community, and the need to build partnerships.

At the school level, among the factors critical for the transition to an inclusive approach is creating opportunities for teachers to reflect on their practices, both individually and in teams (Powell et al., 2019). These opportunities to be thoughtful and reflective are essential for important elements of the schools' operation to be changed and for sharing a common vision. Among them: the meaning of inclusion and equity, the implications for school practices, what inclusion means for classroom instruction, barriers to inclusion (culture, policies, and practices), strategies for improvement, ensuring professional learning, defining support for teachers, and assessing progress.

However, we should not forget that the catalyst for these reflections must be the evidence gathered from these different levels (culture, policies, and practices) and through different sources (students, teachers, and families). For this to happen, those involved must have "time" that is purposefully set aside from ongoing tasks. This is a challenge in schools, but it is an obstacle that must be overcome if the transition to inclusion is to have a chance to succeed. While allocating time is necessary, it is not by itself sufficient. Creating the conditions for the school to be successful requires sustained commitment and leadership by the school principal.

The principal, as the leader of the school, must engage the participation of the entire educational community in its broadest sense (teachers, students, administration and service personnel, families, community, and external services, etc.) in the process. For that, it is necessary to value and recognise the importance of all the voices and ensure that participation in the decision-making process is real. Teachers must feel involved, recognised, valued, and supported (Porter & Richler, 1991). In the same way, processes to make students' and families' voices heard can make a big difference. Voices (silenced on many occasions) can be powerful resources for the improvement of the school in general and for teaching practice (Messiou, 2019).

As Ainscow (2020) points out, planning for change must be rigorously carried out and be based on evidence collected, considering all those involved in the process. New Brunswick schools have used several tools to facilitate the change process. They provide a context for reflection and for stakeholders to develop proposals for improvement to overcome identified barriers. One of the tools used emphasises the overall culture of the school and focuses on strategies to motivate school communities to promote, create, and sustain inclusive schools throughout New Brunswick (Porter, 2011).

Caring for Teacher Professional Development

The European Agency for Development in Special Needs Education (2012) identifies four core values relating to teaching and learning as the basis for the work of all teachers in inclusive education. These four core values are: (1) valuing learner diversity—learner difference is considered as a resource and an asset to education; (2) supporting all learners—teachers have high expectations for all learners' achievements; (3) working with others—collaboration and teamwork are essential approaches for all teachers; and finally, (4) continuing personal professional development (CPD)—understanding that teaching is a learning activity and teachers take responsibility for their own lifelong learning (European Agency for Development in Special Needs Education, 2012, p. 11).

We want to focus on the importance of collaboration by the school team in the continuing professional development (CPD) of teachers on the knowledge and skills needed for successful inclusion. Collaboration entails teachers working in teams and sharing experiences with other professionals where each participant feels their contribution and input is valued (Hutchinson 2017, p. 38). Teachers learn to work together to reflect on their practices, make changes as needed, and thus improve their effectiveness with students who experience obstacles to learning. Hargreaves and O'Connor (2017) have described this concept as "collaborative professionalism." For inclusion to work in the classroom, we know that teachers and other educators need to transform teaching and learning so all students can feel purpose and experience success. Teachers working alone are not sufficient for success of all students but, by developing solidarity with each other, they can strengthen their effectiveness. Professional collaboration permits them to be responsive to and inclusive of the learning needs of their students while being respectful of the cultural conditions in their community and the society (Hargreaves & O'Connor, 2017, p. 81).

According to Hay Group (2012, as cited in the European Agency for Special Needs and Inclusive Education, 2019) when they talk about the different CPD strategies, teacher performance is likely to improve when the following conditions are present: opportunities for teacher self-reflection and objective setting; regular classroom observation and the provision of constructive feedback from both their school leader or manager, as well as their peers; frequent feedback on classroom performance as an ongoing dialogue; shadowing, coaching, and mentoring from peers and leaders; and opportunities to contribute to and engage in teamwork, collaboration, and action learning with other teachers to obtain the best possible outcomes for students. Throughout this process, principals and other school leaders play a fundamental role in ensuring that educators develop and use social capital to support each other in understanding and undertaking improvement and innovation (Hargreaves & Shirley, 2019, p. 92).

Support among teachers with different levels of knowledge and experience, together with making use of expert knowledge when it is needed, is another essential element of teacher professional development for inclusive education. Professional learning must also be provided for educators who provide support to classroom teachers, such as learning support teachers and school leaders (European Agency for Special Needs and Inclusive Education, 2019, p. 34). They too encounter challenges they have not experienced before as they attend to the instructional needs of a widely diverse student population (UNESCO, 2020b).

UNESCO's (2020b) review of New Brunswick's inclusion practices notes that, while training on inclusion often tends to focus on teaching skills for specialists, a quarter of all teachers in the province were trained to help students with autism spectrum disorder (p. 136). This reinforces the principle that classroom teachers with the necessary supports are the key players in an inclusive classroom and school. In that report, it was also observed that inclusion-focused teacher education can have a positive impact on attitudes about inclusion. This was reported in a study comparing Canadian and German pre-service vocational teacher education that found Canadian teachers more likely to have positive attitudes regarding inclusion and their capacity to create inclusive classrooms, partly because of the more prominent role inclusion played in their pre-service training (Miesera & Gebhardt, 2018).

Monitor and Sustain the Process

How to Get Stronger to Face the Barriers?

In the previous sections, we have referred to elements necessary to strengthen the school. As Porter and AuCoin (2012) point out, strengthening inclusion helps strengthen the school. They assert that each investment that increases a school's capacity to succeed with inclusion will develop and reinforce knowledge and skills that are transferable to school success. In the same way, UNESCO (2017, p. 7) defines inclusive education as a "process of strengthening the capacity of the education system to reach out to all learners."

For classroom teachers, without doubt, the most compelling plea is that they be provided with "support." The traditional view of support is often not actually working with the teacher as instruction is delivered but rather relieving the teacher of the responsibility for instruction, in whole or in part. From the perspective of several researchers, support must be understood from a broad perspective and include all the activities that increase the capacity of a school to respond to diversity (Booth & Ainscow, 2011). Let's reflect on what this support might be and how it can be provided.

First, support for inclusion is not dependent on teachers surrendering their role to an educational assistant or a special education support or resource teacher. For inclusion to be a reality, the student must share educational experiences in the *common learning environment* with peers. As a consequence, each classroom teacher needs to be ensured of the professional and practical help needed to deliver on this commitment.

Looking at the school environment itself, one of the nodes of this network of support that is often overlooked are the students themselves. Barkley et al. (2005) as well as Pujolas (2008) describe ways that students can assist and empower each other through cooperative and collaborative learning structures, peer tutoring, circles of friends, and by acting as mediators. In fact, as Porter (2014) states, the fact that inclusion makes it possible for students themselves to engage and communicate as they learn, play and live together, is one of the most important "ingredients" in creating a successful inclusive school.

Just as importantly, support is also provided when teachers collaborate and support each other (e.g., when they plan activities or design materials collaboratively, when they carry out shared teaching, when they use group structures that bring teachers together, when they observe each other, and when they share experiences or knowledge). Furthermore, the participation of families is also a critical factor. Effectively involving families can make them part of the team working for school success by helping identify areas for improvement and serving as partners in the process.

However, it is useful to recognise that no school needs to stand alone. It can come from collaboration with other schools in the area or region (Ainscow, 2020; Ainscow et al., 2012). Support can also come from individuals and agencies beyond the school through involvement with the local community. There are typically a number of community services provided by organisations, professionals from different fields, and universities that can be engaged as partners. We should bear in mind, as Parrilla et al. (2013) state, that the school itself can become a resource for the community.

It is important to reiterate that, for a teacher to be successful in an inclusive classroom, it is not necessary to be an expert in everything. However, they do have to use their skills effectively and be open and responsive when a new approach or strategy may be needed. This means a teacher will welcome collaboration and support and ask for help when it is needed. Effective inclusive schools have developed approaches to deliver these flexible supports to teachers through what some call a *network* of supports. It is the teacher's responsibility to collaborate with the colleagues and partners who make up their school's network.

New Brunswick schools have established a support network that emerged from the school practice in supporting teachers. In this case, practice preceded theory. Here is the description of the model used in that province (Province of New Brunswick, 2016):

> School-Based Education Support Team: it is the central core of the support system in New Brunswick. It is a team led by the school principal that helps classroom teachers develop and implement instructional and/or administrative strategies and coordinate support resources for students with diverse educational needs. The main professional profiles of this team for each school are:
>
> - Educational Support Teacher (EST)
> - Educational Assistant
> - Guidance Counsellor
> - School Intervention Workers
> - First Nation (Aboriginal) Enhancement Practitioner
> - Itinerant Teacher for hearing/visually impaired
> - Other Related Service Providers (language therapist, educational psychologist, social workers, etc.).
>
> District Education Support Service/District ESS: supports the "School-Based ESS Teams." The District ESS Team is made up of district educational support teachers (PMR, literacy, numeracy, French), subject coordinators, psychologists, speech therapists, social workers, and other district staff members who support the School-Based ESS Team.

Other examples of guidelines for inclusive schooling can be found in other parts of Canada, such as the Northwest Territories (Government of Northwest Territories, 2016), which provides direction to education bodies from the Minister of Education, Culture and Employment to ensure that schools in the Northwest Territories are implementing inclusive schooling.

How to Maintain the Process of Continuous Review and Improvement of the Schools?

Every innovation or improvement plan must include provisions for evaluation and review. Assessing the success of actions taken to introduce improvements is the only way to determine whether goals and objectives are being met. The process of review and planning for improvement has been a critical feature of inclusive education efforts in New Brunswick. Four formal studies have been carried out over the years, focusing on legislation and policy, funding, legal and philosophical issues, and finally on classroom, school, and school district implementation. The most thorough of the studies was carried out by Porter and AuCoin (2012) in *Strengthening Inclusion, Strengthening Schools: Report of the Review of Inclusive Education Programs and Practices in New Brunswick Schools*. This report responded to the request of the Minister of Early Childhood Education and Development to conduct a review of the current situation of inclusive education in the province of New Brunswick. The Minister appointed Gordon L. Porter to lead the review process in partnership with Angela AuCoin (Echeita et al., 2021). The aim was to make recommendations to improve the development of an inclusive education system for all New Brunswick students. The ultimate purpose of the work was to strengthen the New Brunswick public education system by developing an updated action plan referencing the *MacKay Report* (2006). Based on more than 50 school visits and engagement with scores of education stakeholders, Porter and AuCoin (2012) set out 12 action areas with specific recommendations for improvement. They include leadership, roles and responsibilities, instruction and learning, professional learning (for teachers), collaboration structures, equity, financing and responsibility, personalised learning plans, positive learning environment, higher education, alternative education, and conflict resolution.

As can be seen from the analyses carried out, although many steps have been taken in New Brunswick schools to ensure the success of all their students, without exclusions of any kind, improvements were still found to be necessary in the 12 different areas indicated in the report. But this fact is a reflection that reinforces what we understand about the process to create and sustain an inclusive education system (UNESCO International Bureau of Education, 2016).

Ensuring that a continuous review process is in place that results in goals for change and improvement is essential to making the process sustainable. As an example, the UNESCO (2020a) report specifically noted that, after the study carried out by Porter and AuCoin (2012), it was found that professional development in some areas, including supporting students with autism spectrum disorder, needed to be strengthened. In response to that need, the Department of Education and Early Childhood Development created the *Autism Learning Partnership* in 2012. A training course consisting of online introductory and advanced learning programmes and continued education opportunities, it is supported by a team of behaviour analysts, psychologists, researchers, and educators. As a result, about 25% of all education personnel, including education assistants, and behaviour interventionists, completed the course and preliminary research found that introductory learning programme participants had increased confidence in their ability to: understand how autism characteristics affect learning, provide support to students with autism spectrum disorder, and recognise adaptation and response strategies to help students (UNESCO, 2020b, p. 145).

> For an NB school principal, inclusion is enhanced when teachers are supported to develop a more flexible approach to curriculum and instruction based on a thorough understanding of the student's needs. Holding high expectations for each student and assessing success in learning on daily classroom work are critical practices. Teachers must set realistic goals but to always look for a way to go forward by raising the bar. Sharing experiences with colleagues is a big help for teachers. Efforts are more successful when teachers want to be part of "the inclusion team"
>
> —NB Principal

A clear example of planning the process, actions, and review is the report *Expecting the Best from Everyone* (Province of New Brunswick, 2016), where we find recommendations for the next educational plan from the results of a study carried out to find out those aspects that need attention, followed by the *Ten Year Education Plan: Everyone at their Best 2016–2025* (Province of New Brunswick, 2016a) taking into account the recommendations from the previous report.

Conclusion

While the process of change involved in developing an inclusive education system is complex (Kefallinou et al., 2020), it is a challenge that must be taken up to meet current commitments to human rights. Even though inclusive schooling was accepted as an international objective in the *2030 Agenda for Sustainable Development* (UNESCO, 2015), evaluations carried out so far offer discouraging results (UNESCO, 2020b). However, we can say that while difficult and disappointing, the evidence is that it is possible (UNESCO, 2020a). In this chapter, we have used the experience in New Brunswick, Canada over the more than three decades they have worked toward an inclusive education system. The context of these efforts in New Brunswick and indeed elsewhere in Canada where they have occurred must be seen in the context of the *Canadian Charter of Rights and Freedoms* (1982). The Charter provided the context for the province's first official step towards inclusive education with the passage of Bill 85 in 1986. As a result, they continue to be the Canadian province furthest along the path to inclusion (AuCoin et al., 2020). In fact, the province has been recognised as a leader in the effort to make schools inclusive on a global level (UNESCO, 2020a; Zero Project, 2016). Although we know that there is no one model that will work in diverse political and cultural contexts, the experience in New Brunswick does serve as an inspiring example. The experience there reveals the principles, circumstances, and actions that have facilitated the implementation and sustainability of the process and thus has provided an example for evaluation that strengthens the international analyses that have been carried out (Kefallinou et al., 2020; UNESCO, 2020a).

As AuCoin et al. (2020) noted, inclusive education has been identified as one of the principal trends in Canadian education. Yet, as the EdCan Network explained a year earlier, in 2019, inclusion remains an unfinished process, as well as a continuing challenge across most of Canada.

For schools to achieve systemic transformation it is necessary for stakeholders to develop a shared, human-rights based vision of what inclusive education is. In addition, Echeita et al. (2021) conclude they must devise and sustain a continuous awareness-raising improvement similar to the decades-long effort that has been seen in New Brunswick. The case for this is strengthened by evidence cited previously that inclusion benefits all students (Kefallinou et al., 2020), teachers, schools, and indeed, society as a whole.

We have highlighted factors that our analysis indicates are critical in facilitating school improvement focused on strengthening inclusion. They provide important lessons for other education systems and national efforts. We share the conclusion of Aucoin et al. (2020) that leadership, collaboration, and personalised instruction are three critical principles of the success achieved in New Brunswick. We also highlight important aspects such as establishing clear educational policy, building support structures, providing for teachers' professional development, and engaging in ongoing monitoring processes.

The New Brunswick experience demonstrates that a shared vision must be accompanied by a legislative and policy framework that is coherent in terms of the meaning of inclusion and provides clear and purposeful requirements at the school and classroom level that facilitate and support inclusive practice. The need for a strong and well-designed support structure for inclusion has been discussed previously. It is especially needed to focus on supporting classroom teachers who are directly responsible for children's learning if inclusion is to be a reality.

The professional development and learning of teachers in areas relevant to inclusive education is a fundamental element for success. This applies to both initial or pre-service teacher training as well as continuing or in-service teacher education. Developing and continuing actions that ensure that teachers have successful experiences as they begin to use inclusive practices can be an important first step. All these actions are dependent on strong inclusive leadership not only in establishing and sustaining a vision but more practically in terms of the distribution of functions and responsibilities among school staff so that teachers are supported, and students benefit from a coordinated and effective instructional team. New Brunswick's emphasis on the role of the school-based support team is especially relevant in this context.

For New Brunswick's inclusion model to have been sustainable over time, it has been essential that it be embedded in a process of ongoing monitoring (see MacKay, 2006; Porter & Aucoin, 2012) that identifies what has been achieved as well as improvements that are needed. This has resulted in specific proposals for action to be undertaken by educational administrators.

New Brunswick's recent educational history demonstrates that it is possible to undertake and make sustainable processes for educational improvement consistent with the principles of inclusive education. Although the elements that make this possible may be consistent in a variety of contexts, each educational system will need to seek its own way based on its strengths identified through collaborative planning. Since inclusion is so strongly connected to recognised human rights, we can be confident that meeting this challenge is worthwhile. The effort can contribute to the construction of a more just society in which each person is important, each person is necessary, and each person matters.

References

Ainscow, M. (2020). Promoting inclusion and equity in education: Lessons from international experiences. *Nordic Journal of Studies in Educational Policy, 6*(1), 7–16.

Ainscow, M., Booth. T., & Dyson, A. (2006). *Improving schools, developing inclusion.* Routledge.

Ainscow, M., Dyson, A., Goldrick, S., & West, M. (2012). *Developing equitable education systems.* Routledge.

Ainscow, M., & Sandhill, A. (2010). Developing inclusive education systems: The role of organisational cultures and leadership. *International Journal of Inclusive Education, 14*(4), 401–416.

Alnahdi, G. H. (2019). The positive impact of including students with intellectual disabilities in schools: Children's attitudes towards peers with disabilities in Saudi Arabia. *Research in Developmental Disabilities, 85*, 1–7.

AuCoin, A., Porter, G. L., & Baker-Korotkov, K. (2020). New Brunswick's journey to inclusive education. *Prospects, 49*(3), 313–328.

Barkley, E. F., Cross, K. P., & Major, C. H. (2005). *Collaborative learning techniques: A handbook for college faculty.* Jossey Bass.

Billingsley, B. S., & McLeskey, J. (2014). What are the roles of principals in inclusive schools? In J. McLeskey, N.L. Waldron, F. Spooner, & B. Algozzine (Eds.), *Handbook of effective inclusive schools. Research and practice* (pp. 67–79). Routledge.

Booth, T., & Ainscow, M. (2011). *Index for inclusion. Developing learning and participation in schools* (3rd ed.). Centre for Studies on Inclusive Education.

Bryk, A., Sebring, P., Allensworth, E., Luppescu, S., & Easton, J. (2010). *Organizing schools for improvement: Lessons from Chicago.* University of Chicago Press.

Bunch, G. (2015). An analysis of the move to inclusive education in Canada: What works. *Revista Electrónica Interuniversitaria de Formación del Profesorado, 18*(1), 1–15.

Calder, K., & AuCoin, A. (2018). History of inclusive education. In *Inclusive education. Stories of success and hope in a Canadian context* (pp. 9–24). Pearson.

Causton, J., & Theoharis, G. (2014). *The principal's handbook for leading inclusive schools*. Paul H. Brookes Publishing.

Causton-Theoharis, J., Theoharis, G., Orsati, F., & Cosier, M. (2011). Does self-contained special education deliver on its promises? A critical inquiry into research and practice. *Journal of Special Education Leadership, 24*(2), 61–78.

Cobb, C. (2015). Principals play many parts: a review of the research on school principals as special education leaders 2001–2011. *International Journal of Inclusive Education, 19*(3), 213–234.

Cologon, K. (2019). *Towards inclusive education: A necessary process of transformation*. Children and Young People with Disability Australia (CYDA). file:///C:/Users/CS.5021580/Desktop/Documents%20for%20moving/C.Sim%C3%B3n/Cecilia/Documentos/Inclusi%C3%B3n/BENEFICIOS%20DE%20LA%20INCLUSI%C3%93N/Inclusion+Report+Oct2019_P5.pdf

Dolmage, M., Young, G., Stuart, H., Specht, J., & Strickland, J. (2009). *Evidence of effective high schools inclusion: Research, resources and inspiration*. http://www.edu.gov.on.ca/eng/policyfunding/memos/april2009/IAI_EDU_research_report.pdf

Drossel, K., Eickelmann, B., van Ophuysen, S., & Bos, W. (2019). Why teachers cooperate: An expectancy-value model of teacher cooperation. *European Journal of Psychology of Education, 34*(1), 187–208.

Echeita, G., Simón, C., Muñoz, Y., Martín, E., Palomo, R., & Echeita, R. (2021). The role of special education centers in the process towards more inclusive educational systems. Four case studies: Newham (UK), New Brunswick (Canada), Italy and Portugal. *Ministerio de Educación y Formación Profesional/Inclusion International*: https://sede.educacion.gob.es/publiventa/descarga.action.

EdCan Network. (2019). *Trends in Canadian education 2018–2019*. https://www.edcan.ca/wp-content/uploads/Trends-in-Education-1.pdf

European Agency for Development in Special Needs Education. (2012). Profile of inclusive teachers. https://www.european-agency.org/sites/default/files/Profile-of-Inclusive-Teachers.pdf

European Agency for Special Needs and Inclusive Education. (2018). *European agency statistics on inclusive education: 2016 dataset cross-country report* [Dataset]. https://www.european-agency.org/data/cross-country-reports

European Agency for Special Needs and Inclusive Education. (2019). *Teacher professional learning for inclusion: Literature review* (A. De Vroey, S. Symeonidou, & A. Watkins, Eds.). https://www.european-agency.org/sites/default/files/tpl4i_literature_review.pdf

Finke, E. H., McNaughton, D. B., & Drager, K. D. (2009). All children can and should have the opportunity to learn: General education teachers' perspectives on including children with autism spectrum disorder who require AAC. *Augmentative and Alternative Communication, 25*(2), 110–122.

Florian, L., & Beaton, M. (2018). Inclusive pedagogy in action: Getting it right for every child. *International Journal of Inclusive Education, 22*(8), 870–884.

Government of Northwest Territories. (2016). NWT ministerial directive on inclusive schooling. Guidelines for inclusive schooling: Supporting the NWT ministerial directive on inclusive schooling. Department of Education, Culture and Employment, Government of Northwest Territories. https://www.ece.gov.nt.ca/sites/ece/files/resources/inclusiveschoolingmanualandguidelines-educatorversion-english.pdf

Hargreaves, A., & O'Connor, M. T. (2017). Cultures of professional collaboration: Their origins and opponents. *Journal of Professional Capital and Community, 2*(2), 74–85. https://doi.org/10.1108/JPCC-02-2017-0004

Hargreaves, A., & Shirley, D. (2019). Leading from the middle: Its nature, origins and importance. *Journal of Professional Capital and Community, 5*(1), 92–114.

Hehir, T., Grindal, T., Freeman, B., Lamoreau, R., Borquaye, Y., & Burke, S. (2016). *A summary of the evidence on inclusive education.* ABT Associates.

Hoppey, D., & McLeskey, J. (2014). What are qualities of effective inclusive schools? In J. McLeskey, N. L. Waldron, F. Spooner, & B. Algozzine (Eds.), *Handbook of effective inclusive schools. Research and practice* (pp. 17–29). Routledge.

Hutchinson, N. L. (2017). *Inclusion of exceptional learners in Canadian schools.* Pearson.

Jordan, A., Glenn, C., & McGhie-Richmond, D. (2010). The supporting effective teaching (SET) project: The relationship of inclusive teaching practices to teachers' beliefs about disability and ability, and about their roles as teachers. *Teaching and Teacher Education, 26*(2), 259–266.

Kefallinou, A., Symeonidou, S., Meijer, C. J.W. (2020). Understanding the value of inclusive education and its implementation: A review of the literature. *Prospects, 49*(3), 135–152.

Kozleski, E. B., Artiles, A. J., & Waitoller, F. R. (2015). Equity in inclusive education. Historical trajectories and theoretical commitments. In A. J. Artiles, E. B. Kozleski, & F. R. Waitoller (Eds.), *Inclusive education. Examining equity on five continents* (pp. 1–14). Harvard Education Press.

Kugelmass, J., & Ainscow, M. (2005). Leading inclusive schools: A comparison of practices in three countries. *Journal of Research in Special Needs Education, 4*(3), 3–12.

Leithwood, K., Harris, A., & Hopkins, D. (2006). *Seven strong claims about successful school leadership.* National College for School Leadership.

MacKay, A. W. (2006). *Connecting care and challenge: Tapping our human potential—Inclusive Education: A review of programming and services in province.* New Brunswick Department of Education and Early Childhood Development.

McLeskey, J., Waldron, N. L., Spooner, F., & Algozzine, B. (2014). *Handbook of research and practice for inclusive schools.* Routledge.

Messiou, K. (2019) Understanding marginalisation through dialogue: A strategy for promoting the inclusion of all students in schools. *Educational Review, 71*(3), 306–317.

Miesera, S., & Gebhardt, M. (2018). Inclusive vocational schools in Canada and Germany. A comparison of vocational pre-service teachers' attitudes, self-efficacy and experiences towards inclusive education. *European Journal of Special Needs Education, 33*(5), 707–722.

Minister of Justice. (1982). Canadian Charter of Rights and Freedoms. https://laws-lois.justice.gc.ca/eng/const/page-12.html

Ministry of Education, New Brunswick Department of Education. (2009). Inclusive education: Definition, vision and guiding principles. https://www2.gnb.ca/content/dam/gnb/Departments/ed/pdf/K12/Inclusion/DefinitionOfInclusion.pdf

Moliner, O. (2008). Condiciones, procesos y circunstancias que permiten avanzar hacia la inclusión educativa: retomando las aportaciones de la experiencia canadiense. *Revista Electrónica Iberoamericana sobre Calidad, Eficacia y Cambio en Educación, 6*(2), 27–44.

Parrilla, A., Muñoz -Cadavid, A., & Sierra, S. (2013). Proyectos educativos con vocación comunitaria. *Revista de Investigación en Educación, 11*(3), 15–31.

Porter, G. L. (2011). *School principals: Leading the way to inclusive schools: Implementation steps for moving forward.* Canadian Association for Community Living.

Porter, G. L. (2014). A recipe for successful inclusive education: Three key ingredients revealed. *Interacções,* 10(33), 10–17.

Porter, G. L., & AuCoin, A. (2012). *Strengthening Inclusion: Strengthening schools.* Province of New Brunswick.

Porter, G. L., & Richler, D. (1991). *Changing Canadian schools: Perspectives on disability and inclusion.* Roeher Institute.

Porter, G. L., & Towell, D. (2017). *Advancing inclusive education. Keys to transformational change in public education systems.* Inclusive Education Canada—Centre for Inclusive Futures. https://inclusion-international.org/wp-content/uploads/2017/05/Porter-and-Towell-Advancing-IE-2017-Online-FINAL.pdf

Powell, J. J. W., & Merz-Atalik, K. (2019). Teaching diverse learners in Europe: Inspiring practices and lessons learned from Germany, Iceland, Lithuania, Luxembourg, Spain and Sweden. In M. Schuelka, C. Johnstone, G. Thomas, & A. J. Artiles (Eds.), *SAGE handbook of inclusion and diversity in education* (pp. 321–337). Routledge.

Province of New Brunswick. (2013). Policy 322: Inclusive education. Department of Education and Early Childhood Development.

Province of New Brunswick. (2016). *Expecting the best from everyone. Recommendations for a 10-year education plan (Anglophone sector): Final report.* Department of Education and Early Childhood Development.

Pujolàs, P. (2008). El aprendizaje cooperativo como recurso y como contenido. *Aula de Innovación Educativa, 170,* 37–41.

Schuelka, M. J., Johnstone, C. J., Thomas, G., & Artiles, A. J. (2019). Introduction: Scholarship for diversity and inclusion in education in the 21st century. In M. J. Schuelka, C. J. Johnstone, G. Thomas, & A. J. Artiles (Eds.), *The SAGE handbook of comparative studies in education* (pp. 31–41). SAGE.

Shogren, K., McCart, A., Lyon, K., & Sailor, W. (2015). All means all: Building knowledge for inclusive schoolwide transformation. *Research and Practice for Persons with Severe Disabilities, 40*(3), 173–191.

Sider, S., Maich, K., & Morvan, J. (2017). School principals and students with special education needs: Leading inclusive schools. *Canadian Journal of Education, 40*(2), 1–31.

Simón, C., Barrios, Ángela, Gutiérrez, H., & Muñoz, Y. (2019). Equidad, Educación Inclusiva y Educación para la Justicia Social. ¿Llevan Todos los Caminos a la Misma Meta? *Revista Internacional de Educación para la Justicia Social, 8*(2), 17–32. https://doi.org/10.15366/riejs2019.8.2.001

Slee, R. (2011). *The irregular school. Exclusion, schooling and inclusive education.* Routledge.

Szumski, G., Smogorzewska, J., & Karwowski, M. (2017). Academic achievement of students without special educational needs in inclusive classrooms: A meta-analysis. *Educational Research Review, 21,* 33–54.

UN General Assembly (2006). *Convention on the Rights of Persons with Disabilities,* 13 December 2006, A/RES/61/106. https://www.un.org/development/desa/disabilities/convention-on-the-rights-of-persons-with-disabilities.html

UNESCO. (2015). *UNESCO and sustainable development goals.* https://en.unesco.org/sustainabledevelopmentgoals

UNESCO. (2017). *A guide for ensuring inclusion and equity in education.* http://www.unesco.org/new/en/media-services/single-view/news/a_guide_for_ensuring_inclusion_and_equity_in_education/

UNESCO. (2020a). *Towards inclusion in education: Status, trends and challenges. The UNESCO Salamanca Statement 25 years on.* https://reliefweb.int/report/world/towards-inclusion-education-status-trends-and-challenges-unesco-salamanca-statement-25

UNESCO. (2020b). *Global education monitoring report 2020: Inclusion and education: All means all.* https://en.unesco.org/gem-report/report/2020/inclusion

UNESCO International Bureau of Education. (2016). *Reaching out to all learners: A resource pack for supporting inclusive education.* UNESCO. http://www.ibe.unesco.org/sites/default/files/resources/ibe-crp-inclusiveeducation-2016_eng.pdf

United Nations. (1948). *The Universal Declaration of Human Rights,* 10 December 1948, 217 A (III). https://www.un.org/en/about-us/universal-declaration-of-human-rights

Zero Project. (2016). *Zero project report 2016.* https://bit.ly/3fvV4y3

18 Response from Canadian Scholar in Inclusive Education

What Can Comparative Views of Inclusive Practices Teach Us?

Jeffrey MacCormack

Taking a note from Slee (2001), who opened his discussion of four papers on inclusion with the candid admission: "It is with trepidation that I commence my discussion of the papers that follow" (p. 113), I would like to open this chapter by admitting that I am also feeling a little trepidation. What about inclusion might cause trepidation? Despite the glowing and warm descriptions of the hope, evidence, and success of inclusive practices that often precede manuals for educators (e.g., Stegemann & AuCoin, 2018), inclusive education is a politicised and polemic issue (e.g., Ainscow, 2000; Boyle et al., 2012; Boyle et al., 2020; Imray & Colley, 2017), considered a *wicked problem* by some (Armstrong, 2017) and a "radical intellectual movement" (Kauffman et al., 2020, p. 74) by others. What might be controversial about the idea that children and youth need to be educated in neighbourhood classrooms with same-age peers? Unfortunately, not all students are well served in inclusive spaces, a point that I will expand through my responses to these four papers. But first, I want you to meet my former student, Allen (pseudonyms used throughout). He will be a useful touchpoint as we work through these papers. But before we meet Allen, I want to tell you about a lavish conference in Salamanca, Spain that changed the world.

Salamanca Statement

In June of 1994, more than 300 representatives from 92 nations and 25 organisations met in the city of Salamanca, Spain for the United Nations Educational, Scientific, and Cultural Organisation (UNESCO) World Conference on Special Needs Education. Apparently, the conference was quite lovely. Attendees raved about the "splendid social programme organised each evening for the delegates, with banquets, receptions and lots of splendid Spanish wine" (Ainscow et al., 2019, p. 673).[1] In spite of (or perhaps *because of*) the opulent and comfortable setting, the constituents accomplished something important at that conference.

DOI: 10.4324/9781003204572-22

The resulting consensus report, known as the Salamanca Statement (UNESCO, 1994), that is considered to be one of the most influential tools in the abolishment of segregated and unequal education. Not to dismiss the contribution of other significant policy documents (e.g., *United Nations Convention on the Rights of Persons with Disabilities* [CRPD]), but the Salamanca Statement is considered to be the most unequivocal statement about inclusion and the foundation of modern inclusive practices (e.g., Imray & Colley, 2017).

The fundamental contribution of the Salamanca Statement was its message that "all children should learn together, wherever possible, regardless of any difficulties or differences they may have" (p. 11). The Statement also recommended that schools identify and respond to the range of needs of their students through appropriate curricula, organisational structures, teaching practices, resource use, and collaborations with local communities. According to the Statement, inclusive education is the "most effective means of combating discriminatory attitudes, creating welcoming communities, building an inclusive society and achieving education for all [and can] improve the efficiency and ultimately the cost-effectiveness of the entire education system" (p. ix). In short, inclusive education will do what other forms of education had hitherto failed to accomplish (provide education for all, particularly the most vulnerable) and all for a cheaper price.

To understand the contribution of the Salamanca Statement, it is helpful to understand its historical context. While a full review of the history of special education would be far beyond the scope of this chapter (for such a review, see Gerber, 2017; Winzer, 2009), a brief primer of special education will help to explain the context of the Salamanca Statement. In early societies, the lives of people with intellectual or physical differences might be summed with one word: exclusion. With few exceptions, those were people outcast from the community entirely or, for those who remained within the community, they were excluded from marriage, livelihood, and other facets of functional society.

Describing people with special education needs can be very difficult for those of us who would like to avoid sounding imprecise, exclusionary, or cruel. I mention this because I will leave the heavy task of choosing language to frame this discussion to Winzer. In her chapter about the history of special education, Winzer (2007) opens with this statement: "Across the range of human behaviour, there is some point at which different societies and cultures make a judgement as to whether an individual is normal or abnormal" (p. 21). The people whom society considered abnormal have been given many labels throughout history (e.g., cripple, simpleton, exceptional), but one commonality of all of those individuals is that throughout the span of history, and until quite recently, they were usually considered valueless and uneducable drains on society's resources. This perspective continued until about the mid-18th century, when some European nations gradually began to work towards the education of people with disabilities.[2] While the history of Deaf schooling dates back many centuries, the beginning of the 20th century brought the first surge of students who attended school in segregated settings. Our social appetite to support and educate people with disabilities increased along with the advent of progressive education. During the first half of the 20th century, the fields of psychology, social work, and healthcare improved in their capacities to support child development. More money and resources were available after the First World War and by the middle of the century, almost 200 institutions across the United States trained teachers to support "special education" students. In most special education classrooms, educators provided a hybrid programme of academic courses (with alternative curriculum) and work skills and practical handwork (sewing, weaving, knitting, woodwork).

While the establishment of programmes designed for students with special education needs was an effort to address the staggering loss of opportunity for those students, the establishment of special education programmes led to new problems. In many jurisdictions, teacher training was delineated between general education and special education. As special education classes became the preferred placement for certain students, the schism between the schooling streams widened, both in terms of programme planning and school culture. The different approaches of special and general education streams amplified the perceived differences between the students of those systems. Students in the special education system had very little, if any, interaction with their general stream peers. As many of them have reported, students with special education needs often felt the worst effects of stigmatisation and isolation.

New attitudes about the role of the special education system were among the many changes that came with the 1960s. Cognizant of the broad social changes that came at that time for civil liberties, gender equality, and human rights, the call within educational reform movements was for access to mainstream schooling, equal opportunity, and equal experience for all students. Parents, advocates, and educators rallied around shared goals of equitable opportunity for high quality education and the dismantlement of the special education structure. These changes were not trivial, especially for a teacher workforce that had spent most of its modern (and pre-modern) time considering special education to be a separate concern for teachers with specific training. By the time that the conference delegates were signing off on the Statement in 1994, it was clear that separate educational spaces and curricula were incongruous with contemporaneous conceptions of equality and equity. What remained unclear, however, was how those inclusive ideals might be meaningfully applied to educational reform.

As described in its preface, the purpose of the Salamanca conference was to consider the "fundamental policy shifts required to promote the approach of inclusive education, namely enabling schools to serve all children, particularly those with special educational needs" (UNESCO, 1994, p. iii). The Salamanca Statement was an effort to provide a global answer to the question "what is inclusive education?" at a time when educators were splintered in their efforts to find pragmatic means by which to educate everyone together.

Meeting Allen

My former student Allen was born very far from Salamanca, but about the time that the Salamanca conference wrapped up. From birth to the age of 14 when I met him, Allen's communicative and social difficulties meant that he did not use verbal language to communicate. A lover of cheese crackers and squishy toys, Allen used gestures like pointing and vocalisations to express his preferences. His family was attuned to his way of communicating so that he hardly had to ask twice. His diagnosis of autism spectrum disorder and global intellectual delay meant that he spent most of his early years in specialised programmes, working with behaviour analysts and early childhood educators.

When Allen joined my class, I was working in a classroom for students with autism spectrum disorder (the class size was capped at six students). With a team of four or five educational assistants, we developed and implemented a programme of study for students like Allen—partially verbal and non-verbal autistic students.[3] The students learned the skills that sit at the foundation of pre-kindergarten literacy and numeracy. Like Allen, most of the students in the class were functioning far below what might be expected for someone of a similar chronological age. Reports from diagnosticians and psychologists informed us that, despite Allen's age of 14, his functional capacity was like that of a three-year-olds.

Like every student in my room, Allen required direct support from at least one educational assistant (sometimes two) to avoid the serious consequences of self-injury. The educational assistants and I were trained in providing non-violent responses because, like many of Allen's classmates, Allen was prone to aggression and self-injurious behaviour. Without a way to express non-obvious preferences, Allen often turned to hostility towards others and self-harm to express his anxiety and frustration. We learned to monitor and respond to his emotional distress before it escalated into violence and self-harm, however, violent behaviour was a daily reality. Protective gear was regularly used in the room.

With no curricular expectations (the Ontario curriculum covered content from kindergarten to grade 12) or standardised assessments, part of my task was to create a patchwork programme that matched the individual needs of each student. Our primary mandate was to help the students increase their communication and reduce their anxiety. We did this so that the students could spend as much time meaningfully integrated into the community and within classrooms of age-similar peers. As Allen's teacher, I worked with his educational team (speech language pathologists, behaviour analysts, physiotherapists, nutritionists, parents, vice principal, board learning specialist) to develop programmes that taught the developmentally specific skills he needed (e.g., self-regulation, adaptive skills, self-care, food preparation, communication) within community-applied programming. For example, our meal preparation programme was an opportunity for Allen to learn adaptive community skills such as how to choose healthy snacks, how to safely cross a busy street, how to use money at the store, and how to prepare a simple meal.[4]

Our approach to getting these students to spend as much time as possible with their age-similar peers included teaching them to use pictures to communicate. Allen learned how to communicate his needs and preferences using picture exchange cards and an iPad application called Proloquo2Go. Proloquo2Go is a digital version of picture exchange cards that provides a photograph of the item and a voice-generated description. The app provided new options for the students. For example, Allen had four different types of cheese crackers to choose from! The increased communication did not entirely eliminate Allen's tendency for aggression, but it reduced its frequency and intensity. Accompanied by one or two educational assistants, Allen was able to join a classroom of his age-similar peers for physical education class in the gymnasium, school assemblies for character awards, and science class when it included hands-on tasks.

I tell you about Allen because I want us to keep him in mind as we discuss the four chapters on inclusion. Like many Canadian students, Allen is part of a small but significant subpopulation of students that would have a difficult time in full immersion in neighbourhood classrooms with age-similar peers. Considering the time and resources that we dedicated to helping Allen join his age-similar peers and interact in the community, it might come as a surprise to learn that, for some inclusion advocates, Allen's education in my classroom is not an example of inclusion. In fact, some inclusion advocates would argue that what happened to Allen in my classroom was an unethical contradiction of the fundamental goals of the Salamanca Statement. Allen's situation brings the tensions within the inclusive community to the forefront, but let's leave the perplexing puzzle of Allen's education for a moment.

These four chapters (Klopsch, Kriegbaum, & Sliwka; Boban & Hinz; Köpfer, Veber, & Bollesen; Simon, Muñoz, & Porter), in their own ways, go about the important and difficult task of discussing how inclusive practices work and how they may work better. In the following paragraphs, I will highlight some of my observations, contextualising features, and responses for each of the papers, and then I will follow that with a broader discussion of the landscape of inclusion in Canada and what we can learn from international comparative studies.

Klopsch, Kriegbaum, and Sliwka: "Individual Reference Norm Orientation and Motivation: Perspectives from Germany, Finland, and Canada"

One of the best contributions of the Klopsch, Kriegbaum, and Sliwka chapter is their discussion of the interaction between reference norms and individual attitudes. Klopsch, Kriegbaum, and Sliwka described the history of reference norm orientation (social/criterion-based, mastery-goal [Dweck, 1986], task goals/ego goals) within broader educational frameworks. Their discussion of reference norms is relevant to our discussion of norms because, fundamentally, answering the question of how is a student faring in school requires an answer to the much more complicated question: Faring in school compared to whom? As the authors argued in their chapter, students' attitudes about achievement and ability can have a big impact on their motivation to work hard.

Educators sometimes feel a bit squeamish about how to talk to students about failures. Should teachers not be protecting their students from the sting of defeat? And, when those students bump up against the inevitable limits of their own capacity, what can teachers do to help their students to set helpful goals and keep working? Fortunately, the field of social cognition provides a lot of advice for teachers in these situations.

I want to unpack the statement by Klopsch, Kriegbaum, and Sliwka: "performance-oriented students attribute failure to the lack of their own ability." While this statement is not incorrect, there are some levels of nuance that are important here. According to Dweck (1986), the most important consideration related to failure is not whether the student attributes the failure to lack of ability, but indeed what factors explain the lack of ability. Students who attribute their failure to a deficit of static ability traits (e.g., "I'm not a dancer," "I'm not a math person") tend to have poorer motivational outcomes than students who attribute their failure to lack of effort ("I didn't work hard enough"). One of the factors that affect performance goal orientation is the student's level of confidence in their abilities. Students with performance goal orientation are at risk of harmful learning strategies, such as feelings of helplessness, reduced persistence, and challenge avoidance, especially if they have low confidence in their own abilities. Those students tend to feel helpless to increase their own abilities, so they avoid situations where their lack of ability will be noticeable.

In sum, failure is an important component of trying something new. Educators should not be overly concerned about protecting students from a feeling of failure; instead, the goal should be to counsel students in how to interpret that outcome in healthy ways. In my experience, students need to have clear and uncomplicated conceptions of their levels of ability. It is not a problem, psychologically speaking, to have less ability than others. Lack of ability is a characteristic of being human within a complex social environment. Indeed, failure is a constant companion for anyone who is attempting to do something difficult. As observed by Dweck (1986) and Duckworth et al. (2007), students are at their best when they seek challenge and persist at their chosen tasks. Destigmatising failure is certainly an important goal for inclusive teachers. Whichever reference norm is utilised, students with special education needs need psychologically healthy conceptions of what failure means.

Boban and Hinz: "Human Rights-Based Education—Inclusive and 'Appropriate?' Some Questions after Visits to Toronto and New Brunswick"

Boban and Hinz's chapter demonstrates the possibilities that international comparative analysis brings, including the opportunity to see mundane scenes through new eyes. As a Canadian educator, it was fascinating to have situations and scenes that would be commonplace in nearly every school I have known described by the authors with the enthusiasm and fascination of nature documentarians. Reading their descriptions of Canadian practices as foreign and novel made the prospect of visiting German schools very compelling. I believe that an opportunity for Canadians to travel to the schools in Boban and Hinz's regions to find "I say!" stories would complete this international comparison loop.

As a former teacher of students with complex learning needs (e.g., Allen), I was delighted to read the description of the tasks in the consecutively numbered Tupperware boxes. As was explained to Boban and Hinz, the students demonstrated autonomy by completing tasks (e.g., sorting shapes independently), with little apparent explanation of the purpose or the goals of such a task. To address the authors' apparent befuddlement at these tasks, it is important to note that while the provinces and territories provide curricular expectations for students from kindergarten to grade 12, pre-kindergarten curricular expectations (as well as tasks, exemplars, assessments) need to be developed by the teacher to support those students who are not able to function at the kindergarten level. Indeed, these pre-kindergarten skills might seem strange to an observer who is mostly familiar with the stages of development typical for school-aged children, but tasks like the ones described in the chapter would be quite familiar for someone who develops curricular tasks for students whose developmental levels fall outside of the kindergarten to grade 12 curricula. Of course, I cannot speak to the specific outcomes intended for this task but, for students like Allen, sorting shapes is a precursor to differentiating numbers or letters.

Boban and Hinz describe how students were reminded of land claims over the announcements, a trend of self-aggrandising they call *Canadaism.* I am not a scholar of culture, but I believe Boban and Hinz misinterpreted the inherent tensions between the pressure to be a good Canadian and the pressure to recognise the harm done to Indigenous peoples. Consider the following line: "In keeping with Canada's positive self-image, symbols of the First Nations are also used for this purpose." I can understand their perspective but, from a Canadian point of view, the announcements about Indigenous lands are not an effort to maintain positive national self-image. Instead, those posters and acknowledgements stand in stark contrast to the long-standing narrative of Canada as a pasture of tolerance and acceptance. In fact, as news broke of the 215 bodies found on the grounds of the Kamloops residential school (June, 2021), the first of many subsequent discoveries, a survey found that the majority of Canadians agreed that the discovery of the unmarked burial site made them "question the whole moral foundation that Canada has been based on" (Alhmidi, 2021, para 15). Recent reports of Islamophobic actions (i.e., a man accused of deliberately hitting a Muslim family; Gillis, 2021) and revelations about the treatment of Indigenous people (e.g., sterilisation without informed consent; Zingel, 2019) led to calls to cancel Canada Day, a national holiday celebrating the founding of the Canadian confederation. As explained in this quote by Sabreena Ghaffar-Siddiqui (Quan, 2021, para. 8), professor at Sheridan College, recent events in Canada have challenged long-standing attitudes about Canada:

> Canada Day needs to turn into a day of mourning, not celebration. My idea is not that we should cancel Canada Day, but Canada Day almost needs to be cancelled in the way we celebrate it right now, the way we observe Canada Day as this day of pride and almost chest-thumping—"We're Canadians, we're better than the rest of the world because Americans, they're racists, and Brits, they've gone and colonized the world, but Canadians, we're multicultural and welcoming of immigrants." It's starting to stink. We're starting to see that's all not true.

Through an external perspective, efforts of reconciliation in Canadian schools may seem like they risk descending into the "staging of a chore" (Boban & Hinz), but Canadian responses to residential schools and xenophobia show that these efforts are not simply performative.

Köpfer, Veber, and Bollesen: "Curriculum Design in Inclusive Education—Comparison of Curricular Approaches to Diversity at School in Prince Edward Island (Canada), Finland, and South Tyrol"

What thrills me so much about Köpfer, Veber, and Bollesen's chapter is that their analysis of inclusion documents in three completely different regions provided an opportunity to talk about the intersection of school achievement and individual factors (e.g., language, race, income). One of the big takeaways from this chapter is that inclusion means different things in different places. Their analyses of inclusion documents in Finland and South Tyrol showed that inclusion refers to culture diversity in those regions, not diversity of ability. Finnish schools focused on creating welcoming school spaces for culturally different students. In South Tyrol, efforts for inclusive schools are counterbalanced with efforts to develop schooling that aligns with linguistic-cultural differences (German, Italian, Ladin). As for Prince Edward Island, students attend schools irrespective of language or culture based on a three-tier system of *adapted* (changes to modality of teaching), *modified* (changes to the quantity of curricular outcomes), and *individualised* (significant changes to the programme of study).

The differences between inclusion based on ability and inclusion based on individual factors may seem significant, but unfortunately, even systems that are based on ability tend to be better predicted by those other factors (e.g., language, race, income). Working class and racialised students tend to fare much worse in school than their upper-class peers in terms of reading level, grade failures, drop-out rates, and employment opportunities (Livingstone, 2015). In short, student's success in systems based on achievement tends to be predicted by the student's situation and context. Consider the following description of education in Toronto, Canada's most populous city:

> If you were born into a professional family and finished your schooling around 2004 in Ontario, your chances of completing a university degree were about four times as great as if you were born into an industrial worker's family. If you started secondary school around that time in Toronto, for example, coming from a working-class family, your chances of even getting an offer of admission to university in the past year or two were about half as much as kids from professional families. If you were a Black boy from a working-class family, your chances of getting an offer from a university were about a third of those for kids from white professional families. Less than one-third of those from low-income neighbourhoods even applied to university while over two-thirds of high-income school graduates from secondary income neighbourhoods did so. If you came from

> a low-income neighbourhood, you were more than five times as likely to be in Applied or Basics secondary school programs, and effectively denied access to university, as kids from high-income neighbourhoods.
>
> (Livingstone, 2015, p. 9)

Famously, Germany has one of the most aggressive streaming systems in the world. The fact that Germany maintained the tripartite schooling system after the Second World War, when so many other institutions were reformed, is not well understood. Scholars have suggested that the school system status quo was protected by the politically well-connected, educated elite, the *Bildungsbürgertum*, that benefitted the most from elite education through to the most academically focused type of secondary school, known as gymnasium (Wiborg, 2010). Irrespective of the initial motivation in Germany for streaming students so early in their academic lives, there is significant evidence that the over- and under-representation of student groups in special education (particularly along racial, economic, and social lines)—a phenomenon known as *disproportionality*—perpetuates the economic and employment divide. Simply stated, racialised, poor, and immigrant children are disproportionately represented in less academic streams. Unfortunately, special education, streamed schools, and segregated systems worsen that trend (e.g., Cooc & Kiru, 2018; Morgan et al., 2018)—a phenomenon that has been called a "legalized form of structural segregation and racism" (Blanchett, 2006, p. 25).

While no province or territory separates students as early as the German tripartite system separates German children, Canadian students are separated along achievement levels (a process called *streaming*) within many high schools. Canada may not have equivalent systems to *Hauptschule, Realschule,* and *Gymnasium,* but many students in secondary schools in several Canadian provinces (e.g., Saskatchewan, Ontario, Alberta, and British Columbia) will find themselves in academic streams and applied streams. The practice of streaming has come under fire in Canada. In Ontario (the most populated province in Canada), decades of advocacy from educators and parents have resulted in a commitment from Stephen Lecce, the Ontario Education Minister, to end the practice of streaming in Grade 9 mathematics courses for the fall of 2021; Lecce called streaming "a systemic, racist, discriminatory" practice (Rushowy, 2020, para. 2). While applied courses were designed to offer programming for students with different learning strengths, needs, and preferences, streaming tends to separate students based on class and race instead of educational needs. For example, schools with higher proportions of racialised and low-income families also have higher rates of students in applied math courses. In the Toronto District School Board, only 6% of students from the richest neighbourhoods took most of their classes in the applied stream, whereas one third of those from the lowest income neighbourhoods took most of their courses in the applied stream (People for Education, 2015). There is value in knowing more about how inclusive practices work in other jurisdictions but, here in Canada, streaming exacerbates the achievement gaps in secondary school.

Simon, Muñoz, and Porter: "Advancing Inclusion in Education Systems: Insights from New Brunswick (Canada) and Spain"

In their chapter, Simon, Muñoz, and Porter make a plea for inclusion by arguing that the benchmark for success is that "every person has the opportunity to be educated in regular classrooms in their community schools." As we will discuss later, inclusion models can be a difficult challenge for schools under the best of circumstances. Fortunately, as Simon, Muñoz, and Porter point out, the wording of New Brunswick's inclusive policy (Policy 322) stipulated that every New Brunswick teacher is assured of the support they need to meet this challenge.

I am encouraged that Simon, Muñoz, and Porter emphasised the importance of the assurance of support because the entire enterprise of inclusive practices hinges on appropriate resources. When inclusive educators are not provided with the appropriate resources, they are like carpenters without hammers. Without the tools to do the job, even the most motivated teacher is stymied. Yet educational funding and resource distribution are contingent on political will and economic trends. "The intersection of inclusive education and funding is a cut-throat corner," I tell my students in the teacher education programme here at the University of Lethbridge. I mention this final point because, while resources are vital to the goals of inclusive education, it is rare that Canadian teachers are assured of the support they need.

As mentioned in the opening passages about the Salamanca Statement, since the early days of inclusive education, cost-effectiveness is one of the more attractive elements for governments and school boards. In theory, sending students to their neighbourhood schools should reduce the costs associated with maintaining segregated schools and the costs of transporting those students back and forth from them. For some school districts, moving to an inclusive model of education was an inevitable consequence of funding shortfalls. A principal participant in a recent study on school leadership described for us how funding was a primary motivator for her being asked to include some students who had heretofore been educated in special schools:

> The director sent me out there to save 400,000 dollars in bussing for special needs students to the city. As I say, well, just give me enough staff and I'm good to go. She was good to her word and so that was

> where I, we, needed to develop, change the community and the staff into [an attitude of] "these are our students, they all belong, this is what we're going to do, this is how we do it."
>
> (Gina, principal)

Despite the wording of the World Forum on Education Incheon declaration, which specifies that governments must "ensure that teachers and educators are ... supported within well-resourced, efficient, and effectively governed systems" (World Education Forum, 2015, p. iv), Canadian classroom teachers are often asked to do more, with more students, with fewer resources. During the early months of COVID-19, at a time when students with special education needs required more support to feel safe and connected during the pandemic, the Albertan government ended the employment of education assistants and school psychologists.

Speaking of educational assistants, Simon, Muñoz, and Porter argued that effective inclusive education means that "support for inclusion is not dependent on teachers surrendering their role to an educational assistant or a special education, support or resource teacher." It is important to include educational assistants within a discussion of inclusive education because we rely on them more than ever before. The numbers of educational assistants have increased in nearly every developed nation and they have "become almost exclusively *the way,* rather than *a way,* to support students with disabilities in general education classrooms" (Giangreco, 2013, p. 94). In many educational jurisdictions in Canada, educational assistants are a necessary component of the system. When education assistants are not in school, students with complex learning needs may be asked to stay home. As one mother Nicole Kaler (Quesnel, 2019, para. 18) explained,

> When you start looking at who isn't there then you start to be open to why, and when you start to be open to why then you can fix the issues. I think that's our biggest problem right now: we're calling our schools inclusive or we're trying to call them inclusive but they really aren't.

Despite our reliance on educational assistants, research on educational assistance has shown that they are not as much of a panacea as one might expect. In fact, educational assistants may be barriers to learning and socialising as often as they are beneficial to the processes (Ainscow, 2000). Before 2009, the evidence on educational assistants was uneven, with some studies suggesting that EAs help students quite a bit and other studies highlighting their negative or null academic contributions (for a review, see Webster et al., 2010). That said, any uncertainty about the contribution of EAs was put to rest with the results of the Deployment and Impact of Support Staff project ([DISS], Blatchford et al., 2007;

Blatchford et al., 2012). In contradiction with the commonly held belief that educational assistants contribute to the academic and social development of students with special education needs, the reality is far less optimistic. The robust approach of the DISS study (700 pupil observations, 100 educational assistant observations, 17,800 survey responses, 470 interviews) added credence to its shocking findings: The contribution of EAs to pupils' academic attainment is significantly negative. That finding was so shocking that the research team admitted that they considered the findings "disappointing and counter-intuitive" (Blatchford et al., 2012, p. 20) and reanalysed their results several times. All of this is to say that despite their perennial use in inclusive classrooms, much need to be understood about the training, implementation, and coordination of educational assistants for their contribution to the classroom to be positive.

Final Thoughts

Each of the four chapters in this section discussed very different components of inclusion in Canada but each of them, in their own way, have touched on the same concern with Canadian inclusive education: Inclusive education in Canada is still very much an ideal rather than a reality. The shortcomings of current inclusive practices are apparent whether we are thinking about how teachers evaluate students (Klopsch, Kreigbaum, & Sliwka), how jurisdictions establish curricular outcomes (Köpfer, Veber, & Bollesen), how leadership practice facilitates inclusion (Simon, Muñoz, & Porter), or how inclusive practices are applied in classroom settings (Boban & Hinz). That said, the difficulties translating an ideal to practice are not limited to Canadian schools. Across the world, efforts to develop effective and ethical inclusive practice have "not been smooth sailing" (Florian, 2019, p. 692).

As I mentioned in the opening paragraphs of this chapter, inclusive education is a hotly contested topic, full of controversy and disagreement. As Boban and Hinz highlighted in their chapter that, while New Brunswick has enacted policy for pure inclusion (no alternative school spaces), most Canadian provinces and territories use the differentiated *cascade model* of inclusive education that incorporates "the whole spectrum of integrative, partially integrative, and segregative forms of school organization." Boban and Hinz questioned whether the cascade model could be considered inclusive ("the question arises as to what extent this is still inclusion").

In essence, Boban and Hinz are asking a question at the heart of this issue: *Can special schools and classrooms be components of a broader inclusive programme, or are those spaces anathema to inclusive models?* The appropriate answer is that it depends on whom you ask. There are plenty of examples of Canadian scholars who argue that inclusion requires everyone to be under the same roof, learning the same content, and using the same resources. Katz et al. (2012) defined inclusion as a school where "all students are a part of the life of the classroom ... they learn in interaction with their peers—not separately or parallel, and not solely through adult support" (p. 3). And, pure inclusion is the law of the land in New Brunswick, where they have prohibited "segregated, self-contained programmes or classes for students with learning or behavioural challenges, either in school or in community-based learning opportunities" (Government of New Brunswick, 2013, 6.2.2).

On the other hand, advocates of a cascade model of support argue that, while most students with special education needs are best served within mainstream classes with their non-disabled peers, there is a small population of students who benefit from a continuum of placement options[5] (Imray & Colley, 2017; Kauffman et al., 2020; Warnock, 2005). Which students are part of the small population who require a continuum of supports? Of course, I think about Allen, my former student, whom we met earlier on. According to Imray and Colley (2017), learners like Allen who have profound and multiple learning difficulties are among the worst served by pure inclusion models of learning. Not only does pure inclusion usually not work well for those learners, but Imray and Colley reported that pure inclusion is "positively harmful since it directly reduces the opportunity for learners to learn and wastes extraordinarily precious and expensive learning time" (p. 1). Kauffman et al. (2020) argued that requiring student placement in general education classrooms in *all* cases is an error of extremism that "sent many students away from imperfect special education and into the fickle mercies of general education classrooms supposedly designed to accommodate all children" (p. 83). In their provocative volume, Imray and Colley (2017) argued that pure inclusion is "trotted out as an eternal and inarguable truth, but it is neither" (p. 1).

The potential harm to the most vulnerable students is why any debate about the efficacy and ethics of inclusion must address this question: What would have to change in a typical Canadian high school math class for it to be a meaningful learning environment for someone like him? Indeed, as a non-verbal student with aggressive tendencies who is prone to self-injury, what academic benefits would come from his participation in a pure inclusive model of education? Rather than receiving individualised education plans that support their specific needs and learning goals, students like Allen are at risk of wasting away in the back of classrooms working on colouring pages while the rest of the class learns about pre-algebraic algorithms.

As someone who spent my entire day supporting Allen's very specific developmental needs, I can say that facilitating meaningful learning for Allen, while also teaching the rest of the class the technical skills required for success in Grade 10 math, would be a very challenging task. Advocates of pure inclusion might imagine a future where every teacher is as well trained and as well-resourced as those teachers whose entire job is to support students with complex learning needs (learning resource teachers, special education teachers), but that rosy potential future is certainly not the reality of the present.

What is the current reality of inclusive education? School administrators and teacher training programmes pressure new teachers to accept pure inclusion as the only ethical way to support a student's human rights for inclusion while well-intentioned teachers, who begin their careers with inclusive-positive attitudes, end up leaving the field of education because full inclusion is unattainable with the resources that are provided (Boyle et al., 2012). Despite the case presented by Simon, Muñoz, and Porter that the "fundamental benchmark in New Brunswick has been the defence of human rights" and that those involved in the policy development "share this vision and commitment," there are even inclusion advocates in New Brunswick who do not support pure inclusion. Kim Calder Stegemann and Angèla AuCoin (AuCoin is a collaborator with Porter, based in New Brunswick), explained the tension between pure inclusion and the cascade model from their perspective:

> There are some educators in Canada who staunchly believe that inclusive education means that every child should be educated within the general education classroom, every day, all the time. Our experience, and that of the individual voice presented in this text, leads us to believe that a "one-size-fits-all" approach to education is neither desirable nor appropriate.

The Salamanca Statement may be widely cited by those developing a human-rights-based rationale for pure inclusion, but the Statement also articulated a pragmatic approach that uses a variety of approaches. It is certainly true that the Salamanca Statement argued that the fundamental principal of inclusive schools is that "all children should learn together, wherever possible, regardless of any difficulties or differences they may have" (p. 11), but it also said that special schools or units within inclusive schools "may continue to provide the most suitable education for the relatively small number of children with disabilities who cannot be adequately served in regular classrooms or schools" (p. 12). According to the Salamanca Statement, the assignment of children to special schools or classrooms should "be the exception, to be recommended only in those infrequent cases where it is clearly demonstrated that education in regular classrooms is incapable of meeting a child's educational or social needs" (p. 12). While the Salamanca Statement forwards a vision of education that bends towards pure inclusion, the Statement acknowledges that the needs of the child come before ideology. The most important thing for the education of all students is that the approach is child-centred. A child-centred pedagogy can help to avoid "shattering of hopes that is all too frequently a consequence of poor quality instruction and a 'one size fits all' mentality towards education" (p. 7). In closing, let me clarify that, even as I acknowledge the shortcoming of pure inclusion for students like Allen, I am a passionate advocate of inclusive practices. As we move forward, my hope is that discussions like this one allow us to recognise where our systems underserve vulnerable students so that we can finally achieve the goal of the Salamanca Statement: "that all children should learn together, wherever possible, regardless of any difficulties or differences they may have" (UNESCO, 1994, p. 11).

Notes

1. The fact that the Spanish wine was splendid may not seem relevant to the broader argument, but I included it as one more example of how great thinking sometimes comes along with a libation or two. As you may already know, the connection between alcohol and collaborative thinking has been recognised for millennia. In fact, it was Dr. Theodore Christou (co-editor of this volume) who first told me that the Greek root of symposium is associated with the term *sumpotēs,* which roughly translates to *drinking buddy.*
2. Historians, like Winzer (2007), point out that we should know about the past to understand the present; however, the treatment of many of the people considered *uneducable* was so bleak and inhumane that modern sensibilities may wince to consider it. Unfortunately, education is a field that does not like to look in the rear-view mirror.
3. For many years, I referred to people on the spectrum using person-first language (e.g., "students with autism"), but I have adjusted my language-use to respond to the voices of autistic people who have expressed a preference for identity first language (e.g., "autistic student"). To reflect my continuing efforts to update my language to better respond to their preferences, I will use identity-first and person-first language.
4. We learned about nutrition and hygiene on Tuesdays, planned our meal on Wednesdays, shopped at the neighbourhood grocery store on Thursdays, and prepared a meal on Fridays.
5. Hornby (2015) describes the continuum of placement options as (a) mainstream class with differentiation of work by the class teacher, (b) mainstream class with guidance for the teacher provided by a specialist teacher, (c) mainstream class with support for the pupil from a teaching assistant, (d) mainstream class with some time spent in a resource room, (e) special class within a mainstream school, (f) special class that is part of a special school but is attached to a mainstream school, (g) special school which is on the same campus as a mainstream school, (h) special school on a separate campus, and (i) residential special school on its own campus.

References

Ainscow, M. (2000). The next step for special education: Supporting the development of inclusive practices. *British Journal of Special Education, 27*(2), 76–80.

Ainscow, M., Slee, R., & Best, M. (2019). The Salamanca Statement: 25 years on. *International Journal of Inclusive Education, 7–8(*23*),* 671–676.

Alhmidi, M. (2021, June 8). Majority of Canadians say church to blame for residential school tragedies: Poll. *Global News Canada*. https://globalnews.ca/news/7930326/canadian-residential-schools-church-to-blame-poll/

Armstrong, D. (2017). Wicked problems in special and inclusive education. *Journal of Research in Special Educational Needs, 17*(4), 229–236.

Blanchett, W. J. (2006). Disproportionate representation of African American students in special education: Acknowledging the role of white privilege and racism. *Educational Researcher, 35*(6), 24–28.

Blatchford, P., Bassett, P., Brown, P., Martin, C., Russell, A., & Webster, R. (2007). *Deployment and impact of support staff in schools: report on findings from the second national questionnaire survey of schools, support staff and teachers* (Strand 1, Wave 2, 2006). Department of Research and Skills.

Blatchford, P., Russell, A., & Webster, R. (2012). *Reassessing the impact of teaching assistants*. Routledge.

Boyle, C., Koutsouris, G., Mateu, A. S., & Anderson, J. (2020). The matter of 'evidence' in the inclusive education debate. *Oxford Research Encyclopedia of Education*.

Boyle, C., Topping, K., Jindal-Snape, D., & Norwich, B. (2012). The importance of peer-support for teaching staff when including children with special educational needs. *School Psychology International, 33*(2), 167–184.

Cooc, N., & Kiru, E. W. (2018). Disproportionality in special education: A synthesis of international research and trends. *The Journal of Special Education, 52*(3), 163–173.

Duckworth, A. L., Peterson, C., Matthews, M. D., & Kelly, D. R. (2007). Grit: Perseverance and passion for long-term goals. *Journal of Personality and Social Psychology, 92*(6), 1087–1101.

Dweck, C. S. (1986). Motivational processes affecting learning. *American Psychologist, 41*(10), 1040–1048.

Florian, L. (2019). On the necessary co-existence of special and inclusive education. *International Journal of Inclusive Education, 23*(7–8), 691–704.

Gerber, M. M. (2017). A history of special education. In *Handbook of special education* (pp. 3–15). Routledge.

Giangreco, M. F. (2013). Teacher assistant supports in inclusive schools: Research, practices and alternatives. *Australasian Journal of Special Education, 37*(2), 93–106.

Gillis, W. (2021, June 14). Terrorism charges laid in London Muslim family killing. Decision called "hugely important" symbolic move. *Toronto Star*. https://www.thestar.com/news/canada/2021/06/14/terrorism-charges-laid-in-london-muslim-family-killing.html

Government of New Brunswick. (2013). *Inclusive education*. https://www2.gnb.ca/content/dam/gnb/Departments/ed/pdf/K12/policies-politiques/e/322A.pdf

Hornby, G. (2015). Inclusive special education: Development of a new theory for the education of children with special educational needs and disabilities. *British Journal of Special Education, 42*(3), 234–256.

Imray, P., & Colley, A. (2017). *Inclusion is dead: Long live inclusion*. Routledge.

Katz, J., Porath, M., Bendu, C., & Epp, B. (2012). Diverse voices: Middle years students' insights into life in inclusive classrooms. *Exceptionality Education International*, 22(1), 2–16.

Kauffman, J. M., Anastasiou, D., Badar, J., & Hallenbeck, B. A. (2020). Becoming your own worst enemy: Converging paths. In *Inclusive education: Global issues and controversies* (pp. 73–88). Brill.

Livingstone, D. W. (2015). Class, race, and gender differences in schooling. In D. Clandfield, B. Curtis, G. Galabuzi, A. G. San Vinente, D. W. Livingstone, & H. Smaller (Eds.), *Restacking the deck: Streaming by class, race and gender in Ontario schools.* Our Schools/Our Selves.

Morgan, P. L., Farkas, G., Cook, M., Strassfeld, N. M., Hillemeier, M. M., Pun, W. H., ... Schussler, D. L. (2018). Are Hispanic, Asian, Native American, or language-minority children overrepresented in special education? *Exceptional Children,* 84(3), 261–279.

People for Education. (2015). Streaming students: Excerpt from the 2015 annual report on Ontario's publicly funded schools. People for Education.

Quan, D. (2021, June 11). The case for—and against—cancelling Canada Day. *Toronto Star.* https://www.thestar.com/news/canada/2021/06/11/should-canada-day-be-cancelled-london-attack-kamloops-discovery-stir-debate-over-how-to-mark-july-1.html?rf

Quesnel, E. (2019, May 7). Inclusive education isn't living up to its name, expert says. *CBC The Current.* https://www.cbc.ca/radio/thecurrent/the-current-for-may-7-2019-1.5124875/inclusive-education-isn-t-living-up-to-its-name-expert-says-1.5124891

Rushowy, K. (2020, July 6). Ontario to end streaming in Grade 9 and change other "racist, discriminatory" practices. *Toronto Star.* https://www.thestar.com/politics/provincial/2020/07/06/ontario-to-end-streaming-in-grade-9-and-change-other-racist-discriminatory-practices.html

Slee, R. (2001). Driven to the margins: Disabled students, inclusive schooling and the politics of possibility. *Cambridge Journal of Education, 31*(3), 385–397.

Stegemann, K. C., & AuCoin, A. (2018). *Inclusive education: Stories of success and hope in a Canadian context.* Pearson.

UNESCO. (1994). *The Salamanca Statement and Framework for Action on Special Needs Education.* UNESCO.

United Nations. (2006). United Nations Convention on the Rights of Persons with Disabilities, December 13, 2006, https://www.ohchr.org/en/hrbodies/crpd/pages/conventionrightspersonswithdisabilities.aspx. www.un.org/development/desa/disabilities/convention-on-the-rights-of-personswith-disabilities.html

Warnock, M. (2005). Special educational needs: A new look. In L. Terzi (Ed.), *Special educational needs.* Continuum.

Wiborg, S. (2010). Why is there no comprehensive education in Germany? A historical explanation. *History of Education,* 39(4), 539–556.

Winzer, M. A. (2009). *From integration to inclusion: A history of special education in the 20th century.* Gallaudet University Press.

Winzer, M. A. (2007). *Confronting difference: An excursion through the history of special education.* In The SAGE handbook of special education, edited by L. Florian, 21–33. London: Sage.

World Education Forum. (2015). Incheon declaration. *Education 2030: Towards inclusive and equitable quality education and lifelong learning for all.*

Zingel, A. (2019, April 18). Indigenous women come forward with accounts of forced sterilization, says lawyer. *CBC News.* https://www.cbc.ca/news/canada/north/forced-sterilization-lawsuit-could-expand-1.5102981

19 Conclusion

Inclusion in Canada: An Ongoing Effort

Alexandra Minuk, Kerstin Merz-Atalik, Ian Alexander Matheson, Robert Kruschel, and Theodore Michael Christou

While this chapter concludes the volume *Inclusion in Canada,* the conversations amongst the authors represent a single step in an essential and evolving dialogue. By bringing together scholars from Canada, Germany, and other countries in Europe, we hope to highlight not only inclusive education as an issue of international significance but, more broadly, the importance of collaboration and connection for international comparative education. In the foregoing chapters, the authors have thoughtfully navigated the linguistic, contextual, and geographic barriers before them to inform a more thorough understanding of *Inclusion in Canada.* It is our intention that the lessons learned about inclusive education in this volume are only enhanced through this written exchange, illustrating the value of both the medium and the message.

In the introduction, the editors situated the project in the Canadian context, explaining that the division of educational responsibility amongst the provinces and territories aligns with that of European countries. An anticipated outcome of this work is that readers will be well-positioned to draw parallels and note the differences that characterise the regions. What each individual chapter and accompanying response also manages to achieve, however, is an in-depth look at inclusive education in the chosen contexts, offering readers a chance to travel to distant cities and countries without ever leaving the library. As a collective, the chapters comprising this volume allow us to cast an eye on inclusion from more angles than are typically confined to one text, acquainting readers not only with different places but also diverse populations.

With the knowledge that *inclusive education* is defined differently across Canada, with no two provinces or territories defining the term in exactly the same way (Canadian Centre for Policy Alternatives, 2015), the authors provide us with a picture of what *inclusion* looks like across the country—each with a view of a specific issue from a unique

DOI: 10.4324/9781003204572-23

standpoint. While assigning a single definition to the term *inclusive education* can be problematic as definitions are inevitably affected by context (Forlin et al., 2013), the authors' attention to diversity through the populations studied is well-aligned with Ainscow and colleagues' (2006) conceptualisation of inclusive education, which can be described as belonging to six broad categories: (1) inclusion as concerned with disability and special needs, (2) inclusion as a response to exclusion, (3) inclusion as a response to those who might be at-risk of exclusion, (4) inclusion as a promotion of school for all, (5) inclusion as a promotion of education for all, and (6) inclusion as an approach to both education and society.

Neither Canada nor Europe is immune to the influence of context on the conceptualisation of inclusive education. Central to each chapter, therefore, is a careful consideration of how inclusion is defined in each setting. As Merz-Atalik notes, there exist many different and even competing conceptualisations of inclusion, ultimately affecting its implementation. Though Powell and Merz-Atalik (2019) were referring to Europe when they identified significant differences in the concept, scope, and quality of inclusive education in six countries, nonetheless, "... inclusive practices are everywhere to be found" (p. 323). The chapters from both the Canadian and German contributors share in this sentiment, starting with the ways in which the authors define inclusive education.

How Is *Inclusion in Canada* Defined?

In her chapter, Merz-Atalik guides us through significant moments in the history of inclusive education, including how the term has come to be defined. As Merz-Atalik notes, the publication of UNESCO's (1994) *Salamanca Statement* sparked a global movement for further development of the concept of *mainstreaming*, moving traditionally segregated groups of students out of specialised settings and into regular schools and classrooms. The United Nations *Convention on the Rights of Persons with Disabilities* drew further attention to ideas of *integration* and *inclusion*, spurring the realisation of these goals in countries around the world (2007). Integration and inclusion were further reinforced in the United Nations Committee on the Rights of Persons with Disabilities *General Comment No. 4*, the aim of which was to clarify how inclusive education was to be understood (2016). The different conceptualisations of inclusion are well-represented in the research; however, as noted earlier, the lack of a single, shared definition has led to issues with its implementation.

Definitions of inclusive education vary, but also share common elements (Haug, 2017). In an analysis of their common themes in the international literature, Loreman (2014) identified that they similarly emphasise students' ability to attend their neighbourhood schools, learn in regular classes alongside their same-aged peers, and participate in all aspects of school life. Considering each authors' context and research focus, it is unsurprising that many of them contributed their own definitions of inclusive education. To conclude this volume, we begin to braid some of the common threads that characterise the authors' conceptualisations of *Inclusion in Canada.*

It is difficult, even as a rhetorical exercise, to be *against* inclusion. None of the contexts examined here explicitly promote *exclusive* education. Yet, as Korntheuer points out in this volume, exclusion predominates. While Canada is largely represented as having a progressive outlook towards inclusion, this collection takes some of the lustre out of that image. As a case in point, we note the findings of the *Truth and Reconciliation Commission of Canada* (TRC, 2012), which documented the country's history of genocide through and in the Residential Schools for Indigenous children. Canadians themselves are starting to come to an understanding of this history, which largely runs counter to a popular narrative of Canadian inclusive multiculturalism. The TRC's *94 Calls to Action* (2015), articulate a path forward for Reconciliation with Indigenous peoples, although curricula and policy in schools have been slow to respond, provided they will respond at all.

Inclusion is not an end that will be accomplished, it is a way of living. Inclusion is as vibrant, and as elusive, as democracy. Here, we appeal to John Dewey's *Democracy and Education* (1916/1992):

> The devotion of democracy to education is a familiar fact. The superficial explanation is that a government resting upon popular suffrage cannot be successful unless those who elect and who obey their governors are educated. Since a democratic society repudiates the principle of external authority, it must find a substitute in voluntary disposition and interest; these can be created only by education. But there is a deeper explanation. *A democracy is more than a form of government; it is primarily a mode of associated living, of conjoint communicated experience.* The extension in space of the number of individuals who participate in an interest so that each has to refer his [sic] own action to that of others, and to consider the action of others to give point and direction to his [sic] own, is equivalent to the breaking down of those barriers of class, race, and national territory which kept men [sic] from perceiving the full import of their activity. (p. 87, emphasis ours)

Dewey disassociates democracy as a form of government from democracy in lived experience, defining it as a form of "associated living," which promotes human flourishing *through* inclusion. Exclusion of any form—Dewey explicitly notes class, race, and place of origin, but does not limit his discussion to these—runs counter to the most fundamental elements of democratic living and education.

An Issue of Semantics

Contributors to this volume were quick to point out inconsistencies in how inclusive education is defined not only between countries but also within them. Several of the authors also noted what the term *implies* in their respective contexts, adding another layer to its already complex concept. Merz-Atalik, for example, notes that the words *inclusion* and *inclusive* have come to be synonymous with the structural elements of including students with special needs or those deemed to be at-risk in Germany. This is problematic, she notes, because these terms tell us little about the mechanisms of inclusion and how it is implemented in educational practice. She also distinguishes between inclusion as a *technical problem,* concerned with changes of structures, organisation, and practice, and inclusion as *cultural politics,* whereby it can be seen as interdependent with all relevant aspects of society. Regardless of the definition or description to which one adheres, the culture of inclusive education in individual classrooms, schools, and societies across contexts must continuously adapt to respond to the demands of diversity (Merz-Atälik, in this volume).

Related is Schroeder's discussion of inclusion as a *discourse-bearing category,* which broadly represents individuals with disabilities. Schroeder invites us to consider other *strands of discourse* and *discourse groups* receiving considerably less attention in the literature: vulnerability (at-risk youth), identity (Indigenous peoples), racism (Afro-Canadians), and immigration (refugees). Schroeder captures many of the inequities that characterise the educational experiences of each *discourse group,* highlighting the importance of the language that we use to describe them. We again acknowledge the difficulty in ascribing a single meaning to the term *inclusive education*; however, issues with interpretation and, subsequently, implementation call attention to the need for a common vocabulary with which it can be described, at the very least. Clarifying what is meant by *inclusion* may help shift the dialogue from theory to more practical applications.

A Social Responsibility

One of the most significant documents for inclusive education to date, the *Salamanca Statement* frames inclusive schools with a regular orientation as "the most effective means of combating discriminatory attitudes, creating welcoming communities, building an inclusive society and achieving education for all" (UNESCO, 1994, p. ix). While inclusion can be seen as a social responsibility in any chapter in this volume, it is particularly apparent in the conversations about multiculturalism (Polat) and homeschooling (Jahr & Kruschel). According to Polat, *cohesion* and *belonging* are tied to inclusion, and at a societal level, inclusion can be seen clearly through this lens. In Polat's chapter, inclusion is viewed in terms of acceptance from others—an essential element of belonging in the context of immigration. In discussing the differences between Canada and Germany, Polat points out the importance of developing a school system that responds to the needs of diverse students and especially the immigrant population, drawing in evidence to establish a link between a sense of belonging and student achievement.

In their case study of two homeschooling fathers, Jahr and Kruschel present a nuanced view of inclusion based on Boger's (2015, 2017) trilemmatic model. They pose the question of why inclusive pedagogy should be concerned with educational practice beyond schools, the response to which speaks to a broader society-based anti-discrimination approach. These contributions demonstrate how school inclusion can set the tone for societal inclusion, and vice versa.

A Form of Gentle Teaching

Kress's chapter opens with a statement about the intersection of Indigeneity and disability, noting that the number of individuals with special needs is suspected to be more than double for Indigenous peoples (Statistics Canada, 2017). Focusing on this population, Kress defines inclusion in terms of the psychology of *gentle teaching*. The concept, Kress explains, is not only about the person in need but also the caregivers themselves. Using Freire's (1970) *conscientisation,* Kress explains that aspiring *gentle teachers* can learn to recognise that they have been conditioned to hold on to ableist beliefs and come to understand that the manifestation of a person's disability, often in the form of behaviour, can be seen as a call for support. The job of the *gentle teacher* is then to provide the person in need with unconditional love, safety, and equity, and only then will they feel ready to return the love and fully engage with their classmates.

While this view of inclusion can and should be applied to any place and with any student population, training teachers to understand and apply this approach must be a priority in both the European and Canadian contexts. Boban and Hinz (in this volume) highlight the utility of *gentle teaching* in their discussion of human rights-based education, which can be characterised in Canada by the behaviourist tradition. On a series of school visits, Boban and Hinz describe the opportunity they had to see firsthand the importance of incorporating the sociocultural background of Indigenous peoples in developing school systems. They also note, though, the delicate balance between incorporating students' backgrounds and inadvertently establishing a separate, special pedagogy for Indigenous students who are already severely threatened by such marginalisation (Boban & Hinz, in this volume). It is clear from the authors' focus that the ideas associated with *gentle teaching* are largely missing from current conceptualisations of inclusive education yet represent a necessary element of engagement for many students.

Its Own Curriculum

Inclusive education is typically considered in terms of curriculum access but, in some ways, it can be seen as a form of curriculum itself. This is clear in Köpfer and colleagues' investigation of the Finnish curriculum focused on multiculturality. While the authors identified disability as a distinct focus in Prince Edward Island, in Finland, multiculturality is anchored in the curriculum through linguistically and culturally diverse teaching. The framework also states that students who have a first language other than Finnish or Swedish have the right to learn in that language—an impressive feat that Canada has yet to achieve. De Lugt calls for curricula in Canada to be re-balanced such that it better meets the needs of all students, regardless of their background. While Canada's approach to inclusion is often celebrated in the context of special education, there is considerable work to be done relative to preserving Indigenous and other languages. The authors' observations about the inclusion of diverse student populations, or what Schroeder would refer to as different *discourse groups,* serve as a reminder of what can be gleaned from cross-cultural comparisons.

A Priority for Cross-Cultural Research

In their comparison of curricular approaches in Prince Edward Island, Finland, and South Tyrol, Köpfer, Veber, and Bollesen were confronted with the challenge of understanding how different school systems address diversity. Through their investigation of inclusive education in each country, the authors emphasise how participating in international discourse informed their view of inclusion in education. Though focused on reference norm orientation, in the same three countries, Klopsch, Kriegbaum, and Sliwka use data from different stakeholders in education to understand students' motivation toward academic achievement. The authors emphasise the importance of considering systemic factors and cultural contexts in education which, as noted, is essential in both the interpretation and implementation of inclusive education. These chapters position inclusion as a priority for cross-cultural studies, especially as conceptualisations continue to emerge.

The Process, Not the Product

Throughout the volume, *inclusive education* is framed as an ongoing process rather than a specific set of outcomes. Quoting two contributors to this volume, Boban and Hinz (2003), Herold describes inclusion as a never-ending process of both increased learning and participation for all students. Herold also ties this to ideas of inclusion as a form of social responsibility, explaining that the continuous nature of the process not only results in greater participation in school but also greater participation in society. Jahnukainen et al. also describe inclusion in terms of a process occurring over time, stating that Newfoundland and Labrador, Germany, and Finland can be seen as making similar progress in the realm of inclusive education. Specht also speaks to the historic progress of inclusive education throughout Canada, noting the impact of immigration, the role of regional characteristics such as population density, and the attention that must be paid to human-rights-based approaches before we can meaningfully move forward.

In sharing their insights about the province of New Brunswick, Simon, Munoz, and Porter, for example, break down some of the steps involved in working toward a model of full inclusion, such as how to monitor and sustain the process through providing various supports for teachers, as well as through the flow of continuous feedback. They identify some of the *keys* of inclusive education, such as a legislative, rights-based framework and the commitment of leadership in fostering an inclusive culture. The authors identify a further seven roles that school leaders must adopt to foster inclusion: visionary, partner, coach, conflict-resolver, advocate, interpreter, and organiser. Simon and colleagues' emphasis on school leadership, including through a commitment to teacher professional development, serves as further evidence that inclusive education is a continuous process.

An Ongoing Effort

In their discussion of de-colonisation, Boban and Hinz (in this volume) describe the ongoing fight against oppression as it relates to inclusion in education. They adopt an intersectional approach, explaining the futility of fighting racism without also fighting sexism, ableism, classism, and capitalism. It is only logical, then, that they describe inclusion in terms of the fight for a fair and equitable system of education. Specht similarly comments on the intersection of identities, considering the implications of the inclusion discourse for specific populations. Boban and Hinz identify how, in its current state, the idea of inclusive education is contradictory for Indigenous students; while it should be the norm, it is entrenched in the colonial systems that stole significant pieces of their identity through the shameful requirements of Residential Schools. Considering this tension, Boban and Hinz acknowledge that the fight for inclusive education is ongoing. Sider (in this volume) similarly notes the structural challenges to be overcome in creating inclusive systems of education, both formal (e.g., funding) and informal (e.g., implicit biases that persist through practices like streaming).

Finally, in response to Boban and Hinz, MacCormack addresses a question that characterises the current state of inclusive education in Canada. In MacCormack's words: *Can special schools and classrooms be components of a broader inclusive programme, or are those spaces anathema to inclusive models*? According to MacCormack, the answer depends on who you ask. But one also might be inclined to answer with the admission that *Inclusion in Canada* is an ongoing effort. Much like this volume, the questions surrounding inclusive education represent only one step in what promises to be a lasting conversation.

Future Directions

The contributors to this volume have given us a glimpse of how *inclusion* is approached and defined in different contexts. While we consider these conceptualisations as context-specific, we must also remember the cross-cultural threads that tie them together. Answers to questions about inclusive education will certainly depend on who you ask, but they will also depend on when you ask and where. While we hope that the discussions amongst the scholars here start to answer such questions, we also wish to draw your attention to *how* the questions are addressed. We hope to continue these conversations, representing more regions and research over time. It is also our intention that this project will inspire other national groups of scholars to connect and collaborate, examining their views of a particular subject from a variety of angles, as the authors have here. Issues of international significance warrant international attention, but beginning with this project, we hope to have illuminated all that can be learned from *Inclusion in Canada.*

References

Ainscow, M., Booth. T., & Dyson, A. (2006). *Improving schools, developing inclusion.* Routledge.

Boban, I., & Hinz, A. (Eds.). (2003). *Index für Inklusion – Lernen und Teilhabe in der Schule der Vielfalt entwickeln.* Martin-Luther-Universität Halle-Wittenberg.

Boger, M.-A. (2015). Theorie der trilemmatischen Inklusion. In I. Schnell (Ed.), *Herausforderung Inklusion. Theoriebildung und Praxis* (pp. 51–62). Klinkhardt.

Boger, M.-A. (2017). Theorien der Inklusion – eine Übersicht. *Zeitschrift für Inklusion Online,* 1(12).

Canadian Centre for Policy Alternatives. (2015). *Disability and inclusion in Canada: Policy, procedure and practice.* https://www.policyalternatives.ca/sites/default/files/uploads/publications/National%20Office/2015/07/Disability_and_Inclusion_in_Education.pdf

Dewey, J. (1992) *Democracy and education: An introduction to the philosophy of education.* Macmillan Canada. (Original work published 1916)

Forlin, C. I., Chambers, D. J., Loreman, T., Deppler, J., & Sharma, U. (2013). *Inclusive education for students with disability: A review of the best evidence in relation to theory and practice.* https://www.aracy.org.au/publications-resources/command/download_file/id/246/filename/Inclusive_education_for_students_with_disability_-_A_review_of_the_best_evidence_in_relation_to_theory_and_practice.pdf

Freire, P. (1970). *Pedagogy of the oppressed.* The Continuum Publishing Company.

Haug, P. (2017). Understanding inclusive education: Ideals and reality. *Scandinavian Journal of Disability Research, 19*(3), 206–217.

Loreman, T. (2014). Measuring inclusive education outcomes in Alberta, Canada. *International Journal of Inclusive Education, 18*(5), 459–483.

Powell, J. J.W., & Merz-Atalik, K. (2019). Teaching diverse learners in Europe: Inspiring practices and lessons learned from Germany, Iceland, Lithuania, Luxembourg, Spain and Sweden. In M. Schuelka, C. Johnstone, G.Thomas, & A. J. Artiles (Eds.), *SAGE Handbook of inclusion and diversity in education* (pp. 321–337). Routledge.

Statistics Canada. (2017). *Canadian survey on disability, 2017.* https://www150.statcan.gc.ca/n1/daily-quotidien/181128/dq181128a-eng.htm

Truth and Reconciliation Commission of Canada. (2012). *The final report of the Truth and Reconciliation Commission of Canada.* https://ehprnh2mwo3.exactdn.com/wp-content/uploads/2021/01/Volume_1_History_Part_1_English_Web.pdf.

Truth and Reconciliation Commission of Canada. (2015). *Truth & reconciliation: Calls to action.* https://www.irsss.ca/downloads/trc-calls-to-action.pdf.

UNESCO. (1994). *The Salamanca Statement and Framework for Action on Special Needs Education.*

United Nations Convention on the Rights of Persons with Disabilities. (2007). https://www.un.org/development/desa/disabilities/convention-on-therights-of-persons-with-disabilities.html

United Nations Committee on the Rights of Persons with Disabilities. (2016). *General Comment No. 4 (2016), Article 24: Right to Inclusive Education,* September 2, 2016, CRPD/C/GC/4. https://www.refworld.org/docid/57c977e34.html

Glossary of Terms

Term	*Definition provided or paraphrased*	*Authors*
Ableism	A pervasive and systemic form of discrimination and exclusion impacting those with physical, emotional, cognitive, or sensory disabilities. Similar to racism and sexism, ableism impacts individuals whose positionalities fall outside of what is deemed "normal." Values and beliefs about health, beauty, productivity, and value of life are propagated through social media and societal constructs of normality (Kress, 2017, p. 51).	Kress
Accountability	Synonymous with reliability and security for schools.	Boban & Hinz
Achievement goal-setting theory	Similar to the theory of reference norm orientation, Nicholls (1984) refers to the theoretical relationship between goal orientation and performance comparisons. According to the social norm orientation, performance goals lead to showing others one's own competence, while an ego goal orientation can be compared to the individual reference norm orientation (Dickhäuser & Rheinberg, 2003, p. 48).	Klopsch et al.
Adapted education plans	Involves a change in the curriculum in the sense of adapting the learning content, teaching, or monitoring channels, and does not entail a change to the content of the curriculum.	Köpfer et al.

(Continued)

Term	*Definition provided or paraphrased*	*Authors*
Adultism	Adults see themselves as having the right and the obligation to bring all this, in the form of praise and criticism, to the attention of young people who have to submit to these requirements—unless they have *special educational needs* and appear to be only adaptable to a limited extent (Liebel, 2020; Rempel, 2017).	Boban & Hinz
Afro-Canadians	Includes groups that were brought to North America by force under colonialism, those who fled or immigrated to Canada from the United States, and those who immigrated from the 1960s onwards, especially from the English-speaking Caribbean (e.g., Jamaica, Trinidad and Tobago) or from Africa (e.g., Ghana).	Schroeder
Afrocentricity	A theory that emerged in the early 1980s in the United States within the academic context of African-American studies. In essence, Afrocentricity represents the fact that as human beings, people of African ancestry have the right and responsibility to centre themselves in their own subjective possibilities and potential and through the re-centering process reproduce and refine the best of themselves. The ultimate goal of Afrocentricity is the liberation of African people from the grips of Eurocentrism. The primary and indispensable mechanism to achieve this goal is the fostering of African intellectual agency. (Dragnea & Erling, 2008, p. 14).	Schroeder
Alternative schools	According to the McCreary Centre Society (2008), *alternative schools* encompass programmes that meet the specific needs of students who may not be able to adapt to the requirements of mainstream schools (e.g., timetables, schedules or traditional classrooms).	Schroeder
Appropriateness	Children's actions that can be prioritised over their authentic being.	Boban & Hinz

(Continued)

Term	*Definition provided or paraphrased*	*Authors*
At-risk youth	Vulnerable populations affected by serious individual problems (alcohol or drug use, severe mental illness, homelessness, experiences of abuse and discrimination, early pregnancy, crime; McCreary Centre Society, 2008).	Schroeder
Atikamekw	One of 11 Indigenous nations in Québec.	Herold
Autonomy	Encouraging students with special educational needs to carry out tasks independently.	Boban & Hinz
Behaviourism	The belief that the behaviour and development of young people can be directed in a more or less linear form. This tendency of adultism, with its conception of normalcy, is a necessary prerequisite for *appropriate* performance development and *appropriate* behaviour. Both learners and teachers are under massive pressure—they *play* this difficult *game*, but many of them are also dissatisfied, as becomes evident repeatedly in conversations (Kohn, 2015).	Boban & Hinz
Belonging	Applied particularly where subjective references to collective relationships are made and processes of active establishment and co-creation of belonging are addressed (Geisen, 2017, p. 4).	Polat
Benetton multiculturalism	Neo-liberal interpretation of multiculturalism.	Polat
***Bravery* (Zoongide'ewin)**	Is to face the foe with integrity. In the Anishinawbe language, this word literally means *state of having a fearless heart*. To do what is right even when the consequences are unpleasant (Northern College, 2020).	De Lugt
Breath of Life Theory	Indigenous ontology and ethics merge with western physics and the theory of everything. If "relational worldview[s]. . . are out of balance within the framework of community culture and context, then risks to the child's safety and well-being will increase" (Blackstock, 2011, p. 3).	Kress

(Continued)

Term	*Definition provided or paraphrased*	*Authors*
Broad understanding of inclusion	Based on "the human image of uniqueness, it avoids categorical demarcation from groups and respects the dignity of each individual child and young person" (Wocken, 2015, p. 3).	Herold
Canadism	A working concept created here on an experimental basis. Representatives of the Canadian majority society know exactly which attitudes and actions distinguish *good Canadian citizens* and how the associated values are embodied and made clear in everyday behaviour. Refugees and other immigrants are also taught assertively how to become *new Canadians.* In keeping with Canada's positive self-image, symbols of the Indigenous peoples are also used for this purpose—to be found widely on commercial posters in schools.	Boban & Hinz
Cascade model	Differentiated or selective model of inclusion.	Jahnukainen et al.
Categorisation-resource dilemma	The dilemma of the need for a categorisation of so-called *special educational needs* was based historically on the segregated system in special education institutions and special school types. Continuing categorisation even in a slightly more inclusive system is mainly caused by political implementation strategies in the inclusive education reforms, which does not sufficiently take into account that an inclusive education reform also covers the need for policy and structural changes (for inclusion as a *technical problem*; Slee & Weiner, 2001).	Merz-Atalik
Claimants	The small number of refugees who apply for political asylum within Canada and under the "In-Canada Asylum Program," a process which takes on average at least one year (Garcea, 2017).	Schroeder
Classic immigration society	Immigration as a component of a country's genesis	Polat

(Continued)

Term	*Definition provided or paraphrased*	*Authors*
Classroom assistants	Issues such as *student assistants* moving from school to school and a lack of policy for hiring replacements and using substitutes were highlighted, as well as two previous reviews (Government of NL, 2000; 2007) that recommended the introduction of *instructional assistants.*	Jahnukainen et al.
Colonialism	White Canadians from Europe follow a binary logic that labels behaviour and achievement as *right* or *wrong, appropriate* or *inappropriate,* and *better* or *worse,* and thus constructs and stabilises a "two-group theory" (Hinz, 2004, p. 45). It is criticised in Canada as a form of colonialism since Indigenous peoples do not practice such a mode of thought (Herold, in this volume; Kress, in this volume, 2017; Pearpoint, 2019).	Boban & Hinz
Conscientisation	Brazilian educationist Paulo Freire is responsible for the study of conscientisation, which began with his teaching in Latin America. Here with those most oppressed by the regime, he guided their resistance through awareness or critical consciousness and critical action. These individuals recognized the power of the collective found in both awareness and action. Details of this movement can be found in *Pedagogy of the Oppressed,* one of the foremost and influential writings in today's world of education for teachers.	Kress
Criterion-based reference norm	Comparison of an individual's skills based on an established standard.	Klopsch et al.
Culture or cultural identity	There is a discursive strand in the educational discourse field relating to schools that leads from the Residential Schools to the Aboriginal programmes or *survival schools* to the current commonly used terms *First Nations* and *Indigenous* education. This discourse strand is above all linked to the term *culture,* and it is about the struggle for *cultural identity.*	Schroeder

(Continued)

Term	*Definition provided or paraphrased*	*Authors*
Cultural Perpetuity	Gifts humanity with an understanding that we are whole—when and if we honour our teachings and our ancestors.	Kress
Curricula	The function of curricula to link the school system and its everyday practices with constantly changing social conditions was of particular importance.	Köpfer et al.
Deep diversity	Justifies various validity claims of ethno-cultural groups.	Polat
Direct institutional discrimination	Direct institutional discrimination exists of institutional policies and actions that by intention have a differential impact on members of a group. Often it is created through *positive discrimination* with the intention of providing support in parallel and separated support systems, even if this often has negative consequences and side effects.	Korntheuer
Direct mechanisms of institutional discrimination	Gomolla and Radtke name the location of transition classes at lower secondary schools only as mechanisms of direct institutional discrimination. The application of quotas for foreigners, increased referral to non-selective comprehensive schools, and restrictive decision-making practice regarding the transition to academic tracks in secondary schools are also mentioned.	Korntheuer
Disappearance of childhood	The more intensive and earlier adaptation of children to the behaviours of adults, which finds its expression in language, clothing, posture, and so on. We do not subscribe here to the *medialisation* of childhood that Postman (1987) names as the cause of this process.	Jahr & Kruschel
Discourse	Trans-subjective producers of social reality and socio-cultural patterns of interpretation" (Jäger, 2015, p. 29). As "social stores of knowledge," (Jäger, 2015, p. 26) discourses provide at the same time "guidelines for subject-formation" as well as for the "structuring and shaping of societies" (Jäger, 2015, p. 26). Discourses represent a "reality of their own" (Jäger, 2015, p. 35) because "reality is interpreted according to the discourses by the people possessing knowledge" (Jäger, 2015, p. 36).	Schroeder

(Continued)

Term	*Definition provided or paraphrased*	*Authors*
Documentary method	Based on the difference between communicative knowledge, which corresponds to generalised knowledge (e.g., formal definition of school) and conjunctive knowledge, which refers to implicit knowledge that is documented between the lines due to the way that something is said.	Jahr & Kruschel
Doing belonging	A bilateral process which requires continuous development and active maintenance (Geisen, 2017, p. 7). This is not (always) a self-sufficient process. Hegemonic social discourse on minorities, legal regulations, and practices, and also the issues of recognition and inclusion by others—particularly social groups—are crucial to the success of doing belonging.	Polat
Domination-partnership scale	On the one hand, inclusion is seen to be a normal thing to do, while on the other hand, this is framed in terms that entrench white, Christian, behaviouristic, hierarchical, and colonial systems and practices.	Kress
Dwarf schools	Often remote, small, barrier-free schools for Indigenous students with approximately 15 staff.	Schroeder
Education for Life	Those involved must develop a shared vision of what inclusive education is and how all students can benefit from it, as well as families, teachers, schools, and society as a whole.	Simon et al.
Equality	In this context, it is one of the ideals underlying the education systems in Sweden and Iceland.	Merz-Atalik
Etuaptmumk	Two-eyed seeing	Kress
Feeling at home	In the context of diversity, familiarity and trust are essential to feeling at home.	Polat
Full inclusion	Consistent or total model of inclusion.	Boban & Hinz
Gentle teaching	Unique relational approach to teaching based on building relationships, traced back to working with street children in Brazil (Boban & Hinz, 2019; Kress, 2017).	Boban & Hinz
Grammar of schools	Structures and rules of schools (Tyack & Tobin, 1994).	Merz-Atalik

(Continued)

Term	*Definition provided or paraphrased*	*Authors*
Gymnasium	At secondary level 1 (after the fourth grade of primary school), Germany has a multitrack system comprising *Hauptschule* (lower secondary), *Realschule* (middle school), and *Gymnasium* (upper secondary).	Köpfer et al.
Hauptschule	At secondary level 1 (after the fourth grade of primary school), Germany has a multitrack system comprising *Hauptschule* (lower secondary), *Realschule* (middle school), and *Gymnasium* (upper secondary).	Köpfer et al.
High risk youth	Vulnerable populations who have also lost contact with their family of origin, their base school, and/or the community (McCreary Centre Society, 2008, p. 8).	Schroeder
Holistic model of education	Atikamekw model of education in which the whole person is involved, implying the physical, emotional, mental, and spiritual aspects of life and continues throughout life.	Herold
Honesty (Gwayakwaadiziwin)	In facing a situation is to be brave. Always be honest in word and action. Be honest first with yourself, and you will more easily be able to be honest with others. This word can also mean *righteousness* (Northern College, 2020).	De Lugt
Humility (Dabasendiziwin)	Is to know oneself as a sacred part of Creation. This word can also mean compassion, calmness, meekness, gentility or patience. You are equal to others, but you are not better (Northern College, 2020).	De Lugt
Immigration	In the overarching discourse on immigration in Canada, the terms *integration* and *multiculturalism* are closely linked (Taylor, 1997). Integration is a nation-state coded category because the society into which individuals or social groups are to integrate is the society of a nation state.	Schroeder
Implementation of rights	In this case it refers to the difference of implementing human rights *as a right for inclusive education of each individual or the parents´ right to choose between inclusive and segregative schooling options.*	Merz-Atalik

(Continued)

Term	*Definition provided or paraphrased*	*Authors*
Inclusive cultures	Those that reflect deeply held values and beliefs and relationships. Creating inclusive cultures is about community building and establishing inclusive values.	Merz-Atalik
Inclusive paradise	High expectations leading to frustration when reality is encountered.	Boban & Hinz
Inclusive policies	Structures that are concerned with how the school or education system is run and plans to develop inclusive education. It is about developing the school for all and organising support for diversity.	Merz-Atalik
Inclusive practices	About what is learned and taught and how it is learned and taught. It is about constructing curricula for all and orchestrating learning for everyone.	Merz-Atalik
Indian status	Indian status used to be mainly disadvantageous as First Nations, for example, were not allowed to vote at federal level until 1960 and were not allowed to slaughter and sell livestock until 1951. Meanwhile, however, the status as Indigenous people now also provides advantages, such as certain tax concessions on the reserves.	Herold
Indigenous minorities	Minority groups without a migration background that have been discussed very little in inclusion discourse.	Herold
Indirect institutional discrimination	Policies, norms and routines in institutions, which are neutral in intent, but which have a harmful effect on minority groups. Usually results from the uniform treatment of diverse students.	Korntheuer
Individual Reference norm	Comparison to an individual's previous skills.	Klopsch et al.
Individualised education plans	Contains far more comprehensive changes regarding learning content and therefore requires more far-reaching and extensive planning steps. IEPs are "a process by which educators, support personnel and parents collaborate to ensure that students' needs are addressed in a systematic manner" (DE Prince Edward Island, 2005, p. 5).	Köpfer et al.

(Continued)

Term	*Definition provided or paraphrased*	*Authors*
Inner-city model	Socio-political programme of schools that can also be seen as an example of the behaviourist tradition.	Boban & Hinz
Institutional discrimination	Institutional discrimination refers to the policies or routines in the organizational culture that have a harmful effect on minority groups. These can be intentional (direct) and non-intentional (indirect) (Gomolla &Radtke, 2009).	Korntheuer
Integration	Organisational process by which inclusion can be achieved.	Schroeder
Integration movement	In the early days of integrative schools, the excursions of scientists, educators, and politicians through Europe and the rest of the world to be inspired and irritated by the different ways and understandings of common schooling were an important political argumentation support in the dispute about the establishment of integrative education. This travel trend is sometimes described as a kind of "integration tourism" (Deppe-Wolfinger 1990, p. 18).	Christou et al.
Interactional discrimination	Refers to direct interactions between individuals and groups as well as to social constructions of self and others (Hormel, 2007)	Korntheuer
Itinerants	School board-level specialists typically with graduate degrees—for inclusive education are responsible for supporting schools as they implement an inclusive education framework. They provide continuous and direct support to all schools through school visits, collaboration with teachers and school teams, and provision of in-service and professional development sessions.	Jahnukainen et al.
Knowledge flows	Elements of discourse systems that can be systematised to form an overarching system (Foucault, 1974).	Schroeder

(Continued)

Term	*Definition provided or paraphrased*	*Authors*
Learning from experience	Take advantage of cross-system learning as a whole—both *vertically* and *horizontally*—so policies respond to classroom experience and vice versa, and that innovation in one area becomes a guide or inspiration for innovation in others.	Simon et al.
Learner focus	In the context of the organisation in the school system, *learner focus* refers to selected groups or individuals (with a supposed deficit or difference) or with an intersectional focus (seeing all groups, which are actually disadvantaged or marginalised in education systems) or addressing all learners in their individuality.	Merz-Atalik
Love (Zaagi'idiwin)	To know love is to know peace. Love must be unconditional. When people are weak they need love the most (Northern College, 2020).	
Marginal Poverty	Perspective of social inequality prevalent in many European industrial societies (Paugam, 2008, p. 165). Compared to so-called developing countries, the proportion of "poor" people in these societies is "marginal" and their visibility in public life is rather low (Paugam, 2008, p. 166).	Schroeder
Mastery goal orientation	The idea that striving for mastery leads to students being interested in increasing their competence (Kaplan & Maehr, 2007).	Klopsch et al.
Model of Trilemmatic Inclusion	One of the basic tenets of this meta-theory is that a society-based anti-discrimination approach such as inclusion cannot argue solely on the premise of taken-for-granted normatives (such as compulsory education). For if one sees inclusion solely as a struggle for participation in societal institutions, or "if one fights for the right of children with disabilities to attend mainstream school, one affirms compulsory education with all its normalising consequences" (Boger, 2015, p. 55).	Jahr & Kruschel

(Continued)

Term	*Definition provided or paraphrased*	*Authors*
Modified education plans	Leads to curricular change, which is also noted in the student's file as a modified course.	Köpfer et al.
Motivation	In the context of reference norms, when students have different reference norm orientations, they show different levels of desire to achieve a goal.	Klopsch et al.
Multiculturality	It is increasingly being pointed out that Finnish society is made up of different cultural backgrounds (e.g., the Sami people, an ethnic group that inhabits the north of Scandinavia as an Indigenous people, the Roma minority, Swedes, and immigrants).	Köpfer et al.
Multi-professional	Specialist staff for special education, diagnostics, and counselling.	Schroeder
Narrow understanding of inclusion	Related to special education and focuses on disability.	Herold
National identity	The term *national identity* needs to be re-interpreted for the Canadian context in the respect that the articles on *nationhood* by Will Kymlicka (2015) are beneficial. He understands *nationhood* not as an (ethnic-)national and conservative understanding of national consciousness, but as a society's self-perception as an inclusive community of solidarity.	Polat
Native-controlled school	Founded by a group of First Nations parents in some Canadian cities because they refused to accept the racist attitudes with which their children were confronted in public schools. They also criticised that their language, their cultural heritage, and their perspectives on history and society were completely lacking in the school curriculum (Berg, 1998; Pellerin, 1982). The school mission statement defines its goal as "to enhance the Indian child's self-concept and sense of pride in himself as an Indian person" (Pellerin, 1982, p. 2).	Schroeder

(Continued)

Term	*Definition provided or paraphrased*	*Authors*
Netukulimk	Sustainability.	Kress
Normalism	Educators know exactly what they expect from young people and what goals they set for them—be it in the area of performance or *appropriate behaviour* even including *appropriate clothing* (Link, 1998)	Boban & Hinz
Othering	Criticism that a policy of multiculturalism perpetuates and solidifies that social and economic inequality as based on categories of difference will not be eliminated (Spivak, 1985).	Polat
Performance	One of the basic ideals underlying the education system in Germany.	Merz-Atalik
Performance orientation	Leads students to demonstrate skills and knowledge for others to perceive them without considering their own growth in learning (Dweck & Legget, 1988).	Klopsch et al.
Peruskoulu	Nine-year primary comprehensive school in Finland.	Köpfer et al.
Pimatisiwin	A life in well-being and in self-realisation for all people.	Kress
Programme bilingue	Bilingual programme that covers pre-school to Grade 6 in Atikamekw and French.	Herold
Protection	In the context of immigration, this term most probably refers discursively to the Geneva Convention on Refugees (UN, 1951), which defines fugitives as particularly vulnerable social groups or places them under special protection.	Schroeder
Quasi-adults	The idea that homeschooling can give children experiences that are different to their peers and allow them to enter exchanges on the level of adults	Jahr & Kruschel
Realschule	At secondary level 1 (after the fourth grade of primary school), Germany has a multitrack system comprising *Hauptschule* (lower secondary), *Realschule* (middle school), and *Gymnasium* (upper secondary).	Köpfer et al.

(Continued)

Term	*Definition provided or paraphrased*	*Authors*
Reception centres	For young adults who are no longer required to attend school, access to education and school for refugees is mostly via these centres, which provide language and mathematics courses to ensure the transition to secondary schools or further adult education institutions (Giambrone, 2017).	Schroeder
Receptivity to change	Prerequisite for the success of pluralist social models and processes of inclusion.	Polat
Reference norm orientation	Comparison of performance to others	Klopsch et al.
Re-settled refugees	Granted Canadian citizenship relatively swiftly within the framework of state programmes, in some cases already upon entry, thus enabling unhindered access to education, work, and health care.	Schroeder
Residential schools	Boarding schools for Indigenous children that separated them from their families and robbed them of their culture.	Herold
Respect (Manaaji'idiwin)	To honour all Creation is to have respect. All of Creation should be treated with respect. You must give respect if you wish to be respected (Northern College, 2020).	De Lugt
Response to intervention	Multi-tier approach to identification and support of students with special educational needs.	Jahnukainen et al.
Responsibility for implementation of equality	Equality in education is set: Either as a concept to be claimed by individuals (in contrast to segregation as the regular form), or focusing on the obligations of the system to serve all children or inclusion.	Merz-Atalik
Sakihiwawin	Showing love in your actions (Wilson, 2014),	Kress
SchlaU School	State-approved alternative school for young refugees aged 16 and over in Munich. SchlaU stands for analogous teaching and learning, while the abbreviation also means "smart" in German language (see Schlau School, 2017).	Korntheuer

(Continued)

Term	*Definition provided or paraphrased*	*Authors*
Self-controlled schools	Educational tradition of allowing oppressed or marginalised groups to have their own schools.	Schroeder
Self-Determination Theory	Self-Determination Theory (SDT) is a macro theory related to human motivation, development, and wellness (Ryan & Deci, 2000). In short, the theory proposes three basic and universal psychological needs—autonomy, relatedness or belonging, and competence—essential and vital for optimum human functioning.	De Lugt
Seven Grandfather Teachings	There are numerous versions of the *Seven Grandfather Teachings* and all are considered to be foundational to an Indigenous way of life. The seven sacred teachings are considered to be core ways of interacting with others, and are deemed essential for the survival of communities and the way to live a good life in peace and without conflict. These teachings include: wisdom (beaver), bravery/courage (bear), honesty (Sabe/raven), respect (buffalo), truth (turtle), humility (wolf), and love (eagle).	De Lugt
Special education	Seen as an auxiliary support measure that is organised in accordance with the curriculum. As in the province of New Brunswick (Köpfer, 2013), a support system has been established that defines various individual support measures for students with special educational needs depending on the form of the disability, which also includes the teacher as someone who requires support (Horne et al., 2008).	Köpfer et al.
Special education plans	The central instrument for providing support for students with special educational needs in the classroom.	Köpfer et al.
Social reference norm	Involves a change in the curriculum in the sense of adapting the learning content, teaching, or monitoring channels, and does not entail a change to the content of the curriculum.	Klopsch et al.

(Continued)

Term	*Definition provided or paraphrased*	*Authors*
Systemic ableism	According to Kress (2017, p. 39), *systemic ableism* refers to separate and distinct forms of special educational support and is also accompanied by corresponding *protective ideas*: supposedly, it seems better for everyone if a young person with a clear support need learns *autonomy* on an individual basis rather than being confronted with the conversations with peers who exchange dates, relationships, hip music and concerts, etc. Thus, the question of how their participation in such activities can be facilitated seems not to be given much attention.	Boban & Hinz
Systems-theoretical perspective	Systems observe themselves and other systems in order to respond to environmental demands and balance them with the system's own needs. This relation of systems to each other is expressed in the term *system reference*. In accordance with the theory of system references, societal sub-systems can influence each other. It can be assumed, for example, that the educational system is often strongly influenced by other functional systems, for example, by legal regulations (Merkens, 2006).	Korntheuer
The Medicine Wheel	Though variations exist, many Indigenous nations across Canada use the Medicine Wheel as a fundamental framework for living, learning, being, and thriving. The Medicine Wheel is viewed as a guide to understanding that all things are interconnected and interrelated. The Medicine Wheel is divided into four teachings, four cardinal directions, four winds, etc. (see Figure 1). Although colours, orientation, quadrant titles, and keywords all can vary across nations, the teachings are focused on the idea that we are positioned in a relational way to all things, and through it, we can be guided to follow a good path (Morcom & Freeman, 2018).	De Lugt

(Continued)

Term	*Definition provided or paraphrased*	*Authors*
Truth (Debwewin)	Is to know all of these things. Speak the truth. Do not deceive yourself or others (Northern College, 2020).	De Lugt
Truth and Reconciliation Committees	Official body tasked with revealing wrongdoings by a government.	Boban & Hinz
Universal Design for Learning	Framework to optimise teaching and learning based on science.	Boban & Hinz
Vulnerability	A term from social inequality research used to describe the social risks of falling into poverty and social exclusion (Castel, 2008, p. 142).	Schroeder
Wahkohtowin	This interconnection, relationality or kinship highlights human cries for nurturing, companionship, and acceptance in this search for *pimatisiwin.*	Kress
Wapikoni Mobile Project	Launched in 2004 by the Québec film director Manon Barbeau, it is a mobile studio that brings together young people of the First Nations to create audio-visual and musical works.	Herold
Ways of Being	Indigenous ontologies.	Kress
Wikipetcia Atikamekw Nehiromowin	Official name of the Wikpedia encyclopedia in Atikamekw language. The development of this Wikipedia started 2013 as a school project at Otapi Secondary School in Manawan.	Herold
Wisdom (Nibwaakaawin)	To cherish knowledge is to know Wisdom. Wisdom is given by the Creator to be used for the good of the People. In the Anishinawbe language this word expresses not only *wisdom* but also means *prudence* and *intelligence.* In addition to *wisdom,* this word can also mean *intelligence* and *knowledge* (Northern College, 2020).	De Lugt

Index

Italicized and **bold** pages refer to figures and tables respectively, and page numbers followed by "n" refer to notes.